Mischief in Long Trousers

By
Paul J. Ankorne

Mischief in Long Trousers
First Edition
Published by DreamStar Books, June 2005
ISBN No. 10904166-24-5

Lasyard House
Underhill Street
Bridgnorth
Shropshire
WV16 4BB
Tel: 0870 777 3339
e-mail: info@dreamstarbooks.com

Set in 'Garamond'

Printed and bound in Great Britain by Antony Rowe Ltd

About the Author

Paul J. Ankorne was born in 1936 in London. He became an orphan at the age of 3½ yearsin late 1939, at the outbreak of the Second World War and taken into care for the next 13 years, at Ashford Residential School, ran by the LCC. (London County Council.)

At the age of 13 he won an art scholarship to Wandsworth College of Art in London for 3 years.

On his 16th birthday, he was thrown out of Ashford to make his own way without any assistance and was lucky enough to get a part as Scenery Artist at Lime Grove TV Studios until he was called up by the British Army, just before his 18th birthday. He did 3 years active service with the Rifle Brigade in Kenya and Malaya before being demobbed in Singapore in 1957, the only release allowed that year by Far Eastern Command, to make his own way back to the UK.

Paul decided to make his way overland from Singapore to India, via Malaya, Thailand and Burma, into India, which includes 'Forbidden Journey' in Northern Burma to Assam. (India.) Once there, he took up a number of jobs to earn a crust ending up as a tea planter in Northern Assam for 3 years, before returning to the UK in 1961.

After readjustment, which was painful, he tried a number of different career moves, from Salesman to The Police, and eventually Social Work, until his eventual retirement on the Island of Bute, off the West Coast of Scotland, where he now lives.

Married, (now divorced,) with four adult children all living in Scotland. Paul has designed and built his own home and although now fully retired, enjoys doing art and is undertaking to complete the trilogy, having now completed this, the second book.

How it all begins:

'A Pocket Full of Mischief', was the first part in the trilogy and is available through the publishers DreamStar Books, priced at £8.99

In the first book, told through the eyes of a young child and set in a bombed, war torn Britain in 1939, the story begins when the little boy, only 3 years old, is forcibly taken to the largest orphanage in the land, a place called Ashford. Like most of the 1,000 kids here, Paul's entire family was wiped out overnight, thanks to one Adolf Hitler, during the Second War. Luckily he befriended another 'inmate' and the two became inseparable. The only saving grace of this draconian establishment was a Big Boy Care System, which proved for these two scallywags, a journey together, of hardships, adventure and happiness. Most important of all, of love, forbidden or otherwise, together for one another.

From these early beginnings, springs a love story and friendships of epic proportions, where they explore each other's sexuality, causing havoc with an element of pure devilment, in their adventures of trouble, in their pursuit of happiness. Their adventures, often dangerous, sometimes laughable and occasionally disastrous, make the bond between them even stronger. The exploration of their own brand of sexuality, along with other boys' display of sexual acts is totally honest, often very graphic, very explicit, can sometime be very disturbing and is not for the faint hearted. During their many exploits, they discover a kind of E.S.P. that often makes them closer, than the closest of twin brothers. This brings with it a fair share of joy and sometimes tragedy to both of their souls, guaranteed to tug at the heart strings.

The reader is taken on an emotional roller coaster of experiences, both happy and sad, all within the space of a single chapter. These two rascals, Bobby and Paul, will both have you loving and loathing in equal quantities. The action is often fast and furious, told with simplicity, direct from the heart, with emotion and truth. The reader will be over stimulated at times, with many disturbing thoughts and taboos, which many of us can relate to, and as to what goes on behind closed doors. Especially behind the doors you can't or won't see, in your heart and mind.

Dedicated to Bobby and David Kwan

A special thanks to Christine and Robert McNeilage for all their work and help in the composition of this second book

CONTENTS

CONTENTS Cont ....

Chapter One

Good Riddance

It was a very quiet Christmas, that year end of 1951. I went home to my aunt for a couple of weeks, more to get away from Ashford, and to lick my wounds.Pat came up for the second week, he felt somewhat deserted now that the Turner's had moved over to the States. He was so impressed with the new house, seeing it for the very first time. My aunt was fond of Patrick, who she preferred to call him, and always made him feel very much at home. He had been invited to spend the first week of his holiday with Miss Lowman, so he could be near his girlfriend Maisy, for whom he had a genuine affection.

At night time, once alone in my bedroom, he would ask me all kinds of sexual questions, to do with his relationship with his girl friend Maisy. I did my best to guide him, in his sexual urges, which Pat led me to believe, were very strong in his regards for his girlfriend. Swany, Pat assured me, was doing well, but was looking forward to the two of us returning to school, after our holiday.

I spent long periods on my own, leaving Pat to his own devices, with my aunt, while I took long rides on my bicycle into the countryside. Being the middle of winter didn't dissuade me, as I often preferred my own company. Other times, we would spend time together, reading our own books, often swapping reads with each other. To be truthful, I couldn't wait for the turn of the year, when I could return to Art College, to finish my last three months there, especially knowing all my exams were now over. It would be a solid period of art, with no academic schooling to worry about. Three months of solid artistic pleasure, would, for me, be pure heaven.

With the Christmas holidays now over, I used Ashford as a base only, throwing myself into all my outside interests, with such vigour, I was like an animal possessed.

In early January, 1952 I went back to Wandsworth Art College, attending almost every 'Life Study' class on offer. I built up a portfolio, containing so many nudes, of both sexes, it was almost embarrassing.

One day, in the first days of February, I was standing back admiring my latest artistic effort, of a young woman's body, which I had worked very hard on, when without warning, I collapsed in a bundle on the floor, in front of my easel. I was rushed to the Middlesex Teaching Hospital, the very place of my birth, with a raging high temperature, and in a coma!

It was almost two weeks, before I realised how ill I was, and even where I was. I had vague recollections of being turned onto my side, being injected in my rear end, by ladies in uniform. Apparently, once I first arrived in hospital with such a high temperature, the only other thing that was wrong with me was a highly inflamed sore throat, which according to the doctors, meant I also had tonsillitis. They operated within the hour of my arrival, but the anaesthetic tube, tore the back of my throat, making matters very much worse. For almost four weeks, I was injected every six hours, twenty four hours a day, with penicillin, the new wonder drug of the day. Unknown to me my aunt spent days at my bedside, and was nodding off herself, when I first came out of my coma. She was so pleased to see me, but kept on remarking how much weight I had lost. Several days later, my aunt came to see me again, only this time she was carrying a small package, about the size of a book.

My very first words spoken for more than two weeks, to my aunt, just tripped off my tongue.

"It's Bobby, my brother, isn't it?

"Yes my darling" she said, as I studied her worried brow. I whispered into her ear, "My brother Bobby, is dead isn't he?"

"Yes" my aunt replied "I'm so sorry, my darling, I really am, so sorry," whereby I tried to squeeze her hand, then gently feeling exhausted, I fell asleep again. (My Aunt discovered that I had collapsed at my easel at the same moment Bobby had been killed by a snipers bullet in Korea.)

After four weeks, I had been injected with so much penicillin, my butt resembled a pin cushion. Later on in my life and in my early twenties, a single injection of penicillin almost killed me, as my body was to become violently allergic to this so called wonder drug. As I regained my strength and interest on what was going on about me, I looked at the package, left by my aunt, in my bedside locker. I began to wonder, if it was wise, to open the package but decided, meanwhile to leave it.

At the weekend, in walked my aunt with both Pat and Swany in tow. Swany as usual was beaming from ear to ear, but my aunt quickly prevented him from jumping all over my bed, to hug me to death, as was Swany`s want. I gave him a wry smile, but he had to be content, to sit beside me, holding my hand, in his sweaty palm. I was still too weak to argue or feel embarrassed. My aunt explained she would be taking them both for a treat later, before returning them back to Ashford.

I spent a total of six weeks in hospital, before I was fully recovered, and they, then operated to remove my tonsils. I could be discharged they said, but the hospital doctors insisted on a long period of convalescence. So my aunt took me home to the New Forest. She noticed my package still in my locker, still unopened. It's not that I didn't want to open it. I was afraid it would only serve to confirm what I already knew, about Bob.

Towards the end of the journey, my aunt pulled over in to a lay-by, handing me the package. Inside the package there was a set of motorbike keys, Bob's watch and the compass I had given him for his last birthday. There was also a sealed envelope simply addressed to me, and just marked Paul. I slit open the envelope and read Bob's last words to me. As I read them with difficulty my eyes started to fill up.

"Dear Paul, I've left you my motorbike, but more importantly, I leave you my love, please take great care of yourself. All my love Bob. X X X"

I returned to Ashford at the end of March fully recovered. My aunt explained to me, that Gina the Scoutmaster with whom bobby had lodged, before being called up to do his National Service, had been looking after Bob's motorbike, and he was bringing the bike over to my aunts house for safe keeping, until I was ready for it, whenever that might be, (if ever I thought.) My aunt would ask a mechanic from the local garage, to come up to the house and prepare it for storage in her garage.

By Monday, I was back in Wandsworth for my final week of art. The week went far too quickly, and given a choice, I would like to have stayed on a lot longer. 'All good things must come to an end', I could hear Bob whispering in my head, as he was prone to say, often enough when he was alive. It was good to be back amidst some of my mates in the dorm at Ashford, and Swany had been sleeping in my bed, keeping it warm for me, so he said. He was so good at chess, he had recently become Ashford champion, beating all comers, including staff members, or at least those brave enough to face him. Pat flashed his thickening bush of pubic hair, with great pride, as I thought, Maisy would soon have to fight off his amorous advances, or maybe not, I smiled to myself.

On Sunday morning after breakfast and well before church parade, I was called to Fatty Arbuckle, the headmaster's office. I duly reported to him, wondering what he wanted me for.

"Ah, come in Ankorne, but don't sit down" he said, all official like. He looked up from behind his desk "Do you know what day it is tomorrow?" he asked.

"Monday, Sir" I said as quick as a flash feeling rather smug. Ignoring my flippant attempt at satire, "That's right" said Fatty "but it's also your sixteenth birthday" he assured me.

"That's right" I smiled, thinking he might have a birthday present for me, although I didn't hold my breath in excited anticipation.

"You leave tomorrow," he calmly said, which really knocked the wind out of my sails, and the smile off my face. "Leave Ashford?" I queried not believing what "fatty" had just announced.

"That's right" he said with just a glint of glee in his voice, as I could tell he was enjoying the moment.

"Where will I go from here? "Not my problem" came his snappy reply, the smarmy git.

"But I don't have any money or job and no place to stay" I spluttered feeling very vulnerable.

"That's not my problem either, you're no longer our responsibility" he replied, just a bit too smugly.

I looked at him in complete astonishment, then slowly turned on my heels, as he shouted after me, "First thing Monday" he said.

I wandered around aimlessly for more than an hour, before making my way for one last visit to our secret pool. I sat for hours on my own, looking into the water where so much of my growing up had been spent from infancy to my teen years. After much crying, I realised it was no longer our pool, mine and Bob's, it was now Pat's and Swany's place. I would find no answers here. Where can I hide, and feel safe, I wondered, at least until bedtime. My last bedtime at Ashford, I reminded myself. I decided to skip lunch, I couldn't have eaten anyway, I was too choked up in self pity.

By tea time, my stomach was beginning to ache, through hunger, so I decided it was time to face the music, I now decided to face my closest mates Pat and Swany. What was I afraid of I asked myself?, for years I had been looking forward to shaking this dump from beneath my feet. I had more than enough skills, to find a place to live and get myself a suitable job, I told myself with false confidence.

"Just you wait and see," I shouted out loud, for Fatty Arbuckle's benefit, knowing he was well out of earshot. With a false smile on my face, but a genuine spring in my step, I headed back in time for tea.

While I was taking my last shower, with Pat on one side and Swany on the other, I realised that neither knew yet, of my imminent departure. I decided for the time being at least, to delay telling them, until bed time. I didn't want their tears adding to the waters of the showers.

At bed time, delaying as long as possible before lights out, I called them both over to my bedside. Swany sat on my bed, his usual smiling carefree self, and Pat sat beside him, both totally unaware they would be without my protection and care. The dreaded moment to tell both of them had arrived, So I had better get on with it!

"Well Swany," I started cheerfully enough, as I reached into my locker, and took out Bob's old chess set from its shelf. "This is for you, but you must take great care of it."

I looked at Pat and said with far more seriousness in my voice, "you must take good care of Swany, because tomorrow I leave Ashford, for good."

Pat nodded with understanding, having lost his voice momentarily. Swany burst into a flood of tears, sobbing his wee heart out, so I put my arm around him, in an effort to console him, as well as my self.

"And Pat," I said "you must take Swany to my aunt in the New Forest, as I've arranged for you both to have a good weekend there, providing Swany behaves himself." Swany stopped crying, turning his water works off instantly, like a tap. Now all I have to do is ring my aunt to lay on the weekend visit, to which I had just promised them.

"Swany" I said "you move into my bed tomorrow, okay!" I told him, he nodded his approval, with great gusto.

"Now go to bed" I ordered them both, "I've got a very busy day tomorrow." I lied.

In the morning I timed my departure, to coincide with all the boys heading for breakfast, as I told myself, it was time to make my final move. As I came up to the lodge house, I had a quick word with the gate keeper then, turning to look at Ashford, for the very last time. I walked through the gate, onto Woodthorpe Road, with a brown paper parcel, tucked under my arm, and a bag of mischief sweets in my pocket, which I had forgotten to give to Swany.

I stood outside these impressive Ashford lodge gates for the very last time, with mixed emotions, feeling somehow nervous and very alone. In fact I felt more alone now than at anytime during my entire short life, at the Ashford Orphanage. Perhaps because I was leaving behind me the only world I had ever known, which enhanced my confusion of misunderstanding without fully understanding why.

Standing by myself at the bus stop waiting for a No.117 bus to take me to Hounslow Central with a load of mixed feelings raging around in my body, and numbing my brain, making this new world I was about to face, a very lonely place indeed. The nucleus of my family from my previous Ashford life had all but deserted me or so I felt, which left me with a feeling of utter rejection. I was lost in a fog of misery wallowing in self-pity, with so much uncertainty as to what was to become of my retched soul. Clearly, I was bathing in an attack of self indulgence as the urge to ring my Aunt Joan, now fully retired and living down in the new forest to come up to Ashford for me, and bail me out of my predicament, was very tempting. At least my self pity would be cushioned with comfort in the bosom of my aunt, who was the only person left, that had not deserted me.

The attraction of the good life at the precise moment in time, was very appealing indeed, as I looked at the red phone box across the road, from my bus stop. I was indulging myself in such flights of fantasies, when the Number 117 bus drew up in front of me, demanding my body to step aboard. Having paid my fare, I plonked myself down on an empty seat behind the drivers cab looking out of the window in complete oblivion. I was going through the motions, on automatic pilot, knowing that when I reached Hounslow, I would need to change for yet another bus to take me onto Osterly, my final destination for the day. (I hoped!)

Meanwhile this timely bus had relieved me momentarily for making any alternative decision to cut and run, for cover to my aunt, at least for the time being! I convinced myself that I needed time out to think, time to make a sensible and logical appraisal of my present situation, in how best to fulfil my immediate needs, a constructive plan of action, you might say. To take the easy option by pestering my aunt with all my problems seemed like an act of cowardice, somehow like falling at the first hurdle.

My thoughts were suddenly interrupted by the clippie, a conductress, who's cockney accent cut across my thoughts by ordering me off the bus, which had now reached its terminus. I alighted from the platform of the bus still in a daze, as the cockney clippie shouted at me "ere mate, catch."

The parcel hit me on my chest as I failed to catch the package of my past life, which landed at my feet upon the pavement. I slowly picked up these last vestiges of Ashford and my past life, which was all I owned, after thirteen long years of drudgery. I was sixteen years this very day, the 12 April 1952, but somehow it didn't feel like my birthday. In fact it was my first day of freedom, away from the shackles of the Ashford Regime, but in reality this day felt more like my last day. The only life I had ever known was gone in an instant and with the exception of my Aunt Joan. All my loved ones were all gone, forever I thought.

'Leo' my little black friend, who died in my arms during the London Blitz was first, then Mr. Walton my master and mentor throughout my thirteen years at Ashford was suddenly and very unexpectedly taken and died from a recurring attack of malaria, that his own doctor had failed to diagnose, but most deeply felt, was my brother Bobby, who was killed in Korea, at just eighteen years of age, and whom I worshipped beyond belief. This was the real vacuum of emptiness, I felt every moment of my miserable existence.

On the very threshold of a brave new world that I was about to face, I felt shattered and in despair, when I should really be feeling excitement and anticipation for a bright new future. My one and only true girl friend 'Sylvia' had left Ashford a year before me, and had already been gobbled up by this brand new strange world, and not a word from her since. She left and disappeared into oblivion, the very girl who took my virginity at 12 and gave me my first sexual encounter, an act, in which I hasten to add, I was a most willing participant. The love and affection she showered upon me would excite my loins and memory for many years to come. And last but not least, Patrick my half brother and Swany his beloved friend, whom I thankfully salvaged from the most violent rape, I witnessed in all my time at Ashford. These last two, would have to survive for several more years at Ashford, without my protection, but were now better equipped to do so. Like it or not, I must look forward to a new beginning, and to a new future no matter what life decided to confront me with.

I stood out side the opened gates of 8 Osterly Road House, that had a short but imposing gravel driveway sweeping in a curved crescent shape to a half dozen steps and a very impressive front door. Along the edge of this driveway was a beautifully manicured lawn fronting this well kept mansion house. I loitered outside its portals to feast my eyes and senses on the splendour of the St. Christopher's working boys hostel at No8 Osterly Road noting with awe the magnificent giant cedar tree that occupied most of the front garden of this prestigious address, I was left wondering, if indeed I had reached my correct and proper destination. I spotted a gentleman through the many ground floor windows, observing me from within, probably thinking to himself I was up to no good, as he observed my hesitancy to enter the driveway. The gentleman in question came bounding down the steps towards me, wearing a distinct expression of enquiry upon his countenance.

Should I make a run for it I thought or brazen it out holding my ground.

"Can I help you?" asked Mr Bancroft who was the warden of this lovely building.

"Why yes, I hope so," I answered

"You're from Ashford aren't you?" asked Bancroft

"How did you know that?" I countered, which Bancroft ignored.

"I am looking for somewhere to stay," I asked with spirit and hope.

"You better follow me," Bancroft said politely. So I did, keeping close to his heels I followed Bancroft into the house that was shortly to become my new abode.

Having had my decision more or less made for me, I followed Bancroft into his spacious office, where another gentleman named Mr Kipling was sitting at a very large desk littered with paperwork. This Mr Kipling I hasten to add, had nothing to do with the making of exceptionally good cakes, but was in fact the assistant warden to Mr. Bancroft in this establishment. Both these polite young gentlemen, I guessed, were in their early thirties.

St. Christophers, was a Christian organisation that established and ran a total of four working boys hostels scattered around London. The urgency, so soon after the Second World War, to meet the needs of a large number of homeless working boys, requiring any kind of accommodation after the extensive bombing of London, had now became desperate. This was no bible thumping organisation and helped all working lads regardless to the individual religious belief, whether they be Jewish, Catholics, or Church of England or even if they had no religious leanings whatsoever. Most of the large spacious bedrooms had been cleverly divided into single bed-sits that offer privacy and comfortable accommodation, tastefully furnished.

After Ashford, I was not accustomed to such opulence or total privacy, nor was I used to the idea, of being treated as a unique person in my own right, except by Bobby my dead brother and My Aunt Joan of course. Mr. Kipling a tall handsome figure of a man, who stood a good 6ft in height, assumed rightly that I had not eaten since breakfast (not even breakfast!) I reminded myself, as I was now ready for some food. He sat me down at the head of a long table that could easily accommodate twenty feasting bodies, and told Cookie to feed this ravenous beast. A long streak of a lad called Michael King was hovering in the background supposedly helping the cook with various preparations, in readiness for the main meal served later.

King I was to learn, was between jobs (whatever that meant). The cook, simply known by all as 'cookie', was a middle-aged lady of generous proportions and who obviously enjoyed her food. She had bright twinkling blue eyes and could best be described as a very cheerful buddy, she seemed to get on with everybody. Her motherly skills were instantly apparent, making her a firm favourite with all the working boys that lodged within. Cookie, bustled about the kitchen with ease, which was very much her own private domain, like the floral pinny about her ample waistline. No one knew her real name, as everybody simply called her Cookie, which suited her motherly status and station in life. Her cooking, like her disposition in life, was the finest in the land and her rapport with all the boys was unbelievably good, I rapidly learnt there was no single boy that didn't treat her like their own mother. Turning up my charm to full volume I quickly realised, to keep cookie on side, would be most beneficial for my own selfish well being, and would stand me in good stead for my future comforts. Therefore, determined to ease my feet below her table and making every effort to win her over completely, I set about this task with relish. Meantime, King was quick to inform me, that I would be sharing a bedroom with him, and that he hoped I did not snore. This statement quickly took some of the shine from my face with my instincts telling me not to be overfriendly with this boy King. In any case, previous experience taught me to be mistrustful of building any meaningful relationships, as disappointment was almost certain to follow. Perhaps, I was afraid, having lost Bobby as someone I loved so deeply and whose untimely death had shattered my whole world.

For the time being at least, I was wary in forging any meaningful friendships for, fear of what might happen. The pain I still felt at loosing Bobby was so very real and I suspected, would remain with me for a very long time to come. Perhaps one day, things might be different, but in the meantime this seemed unlikely, as well as remotely impossible. I knew I would be licking my wounds for sometime and therefore to be content in attempting to get my life back on track to some kind of normality. The instinct within me just to survive was a very powerful motive to get my life into order, regardless to what the future might bring.

After filling my belly with some good tucker, I made my way back to the office where Mr Kipling wanted to talk with me. I had plenty of experience of knocking on doors in Ashford I reminded myself, as Mr. Kipling invited me in and politely asked me to take a pew, 'Come into my web said the spider to the fly' was a saying, I recalled from my Ashford days. I made myself comfortable with Kipling putting me at ease. (What a difference compared with the regime of Ashford I felt.) Kipling proceeded gently, to lay out the ground rules of the hostel which I found simplicity itself. This fine establishment seemed more like a hotel than a hostel, and unlike my first impressions of Ashford, I had just found an ideal home to rest my weary head. Kipling went onto explain in a language that left no room for misunderstanding, that my long term stay at St. Christopher`s was dependant on my getting a full-time job of employment and paying my way. After all, it was called a working boys hostel for good reason and purpose. With this fully understood Kipling was kind enough to let me ring my aunt, so I could tell her of my good fortune of finding a great place to live. I also explained to my aunt that I would be seeking employment that befits my artistic talents, first thing tomorrow on Tuesday morning, as my place as a lodger here at St. Christopher's was dependant on it.

My aunt hinted many times while on the phone, that she was anxious to see me again, as soon as possible and perhaps even come down to the New forest to stay for a while. She suggested I might try to get into Lime Grove Television Studios, as she had been informed they were sometimes looking for artists with my particular skills. Bidding my aunt farewell, I told her I would keep her informed, of any progress or lack of it. in the immediate days ahead. With buoyancy in my heart combined with a pronounced spring in my step, I felt my first days of freedom away from Ashford, was now ending on a high note, and I bounced up the stairs, to spend my first night in a new bed.

CHAPTER 2

A hunting we shall go

After a good nights sleep, I awoke early due to the Ashford habit of a mundane routine. Looking at the brown paper parcel, that was still unopened at the end of my bed, I crept out from beneath my bedclothes to investigate.

Carefully and as silently as possible, I opened the package in front of me. Within this created bundle I was delighted to discover the new clothes provided to me by the L.C.C. Among these garments were my very first pair of long trousers (Two pairs), three smart cream shirts, a blue necktie and belt, with four pairs each of socks and underpants. There was also a new pair of black leather shoes in my size that were a good fit. As I was investigating, as well as trying on this gear, Michael King, with whom I shared the bedroom, got out of bed to relieve himself, using the bedroom sink. I could not help but notice, that King, like myself, preferred to sleep naked, or commando style. On returning to his bed he lay on top, flaunting his nudity.

"Bobby whispered in my ear from the past to beware of this strange boy", as I went about my business doing my utmost to behave casually and pretending not to see King, or catch any of his intended glances.

A sharp knock on the door of our bedroom sent King scurrying below his bedclothes as Mr Bancroft came in bearing a mug of hot sweet tea to ensure that I was awake in plenty of time before breakfast. After drinking my tea, I washed in the bedroom sink and brushed my teeth, the luxury of a sink was an important feature in all bedrooms at St Christopher's.

King gave me a somewhat superior expression, tinged with just enough disgust indicating my inferior status as the most junior inmate to St Christopher's, which I chose to ignore! (I knew my place – or at least King got the impression I did.) King receiving no response, promptly turned over with his back to me, pretending he was going back to sleep.

I remember clearly the night before, my very first night, King was lying naked upon his bed reading a pornographic magazine, while furtively studying my every move, I myself got ready for bed. If he was waiting to see how well endowed I was, he must have been disappointed, because I sat on my bed with my back towards him, undressing to the buff, before easing myself below the covers. I have never quite understood a perfect stranger blatantly exposing his full nudity in my face so openly. Ignoring his feeble attempt at snubbing me, I went downstairs for a hearty breakfast.

After breakfast I casually walked along to Osterly underground station taking a train to Shepherds Bush. After several cups of tea, in a café close to Lime grove Television studios, and putting off the inevitable for as long as possible, I decided to make my move. Trying to clear my befuddled brain, I walked past the very imposing entrance several times before picking up enough courage to enter. I was about to boldly go in when I noticed a rather large burly doorman looking somewhat intimidating, and this momentarily put me off my stride.

This doorman was stopping and checking every person who went through the revolving door. I knew I had to choose my entrance very carefully whatever the cost, otherwise I could be shot down in flames before I had any chance of seeing the right person whoever that might be.

I also knew that I would only have one chance to create the right impression with this doorman, and failing to do so, could well see me ejected via the revolving doors at speed, back onto the pavement, like an unwanted street urchin. The timing was critical, I assured myself stalling for yet more time, if I was to get beyond the sitting area of the foyer to the inner hallowed sanctums of importance. Just as I was thinking of going off to find another cup of Rosie lea (tea), in an attempt to calm the tension in my already waterlogged body, a couple of some importance walked nonchalantly through the revolving doors to the interior as if they owned the place.

On impulse and in a fit of madness, putting up a bold front, I quickly followed them in. while the doorman, who obviously knew this couple of high merit, was doing his curtsey and engaging them both in conversation. I slipped in, standing a respectful distance away holding my ground. My presence did not go unnoticed however, as the intimidating doorman with a finger of distaste pointed, to where I should park myself, until he had time to ascertain my business, and justify as to why the likes of me should be in such an important place. As the dignitaries passed muster, the doorman ran ahead of them, to make sure one of the executive elevators was available

On his returning to his desk a snobbish air of disapproval was thrown my way, which did not do much for my composure or self confidence. To reassure him of my credentials, I adopted an air of a man about town, whereby if truth be known, I was less than 48 hours out of short pants. Several times I tried to catch his eye, but he blissfully ignored my silent screams for help. A good hour later, I was still studying the quality of my new shoes when at11am precisely, the company char lady came rolling into the foyer with her trolley gliding silently across the impeccable shining floor. First stop was his nibs, the doorman's counter, where she poured out a large mug of tea and gave him a jam doughnut on a china side plate.

Once settled comfortably in his own easy chair behind the counter, he signalled me to join him. Not to partake of tea I might add, but finally to enquire my business for being there.

"Now sonny Jim" he addressed me, "what do you want?" no preambles here, I noticed quick as a flash, as I bit my tongue in the temptation of correcting him as to my proper monica, and title in life.

"I'm an artist" I found myself blurting out instead.

"Piss artist, more likely" he said, dropping his posh accent in favour of his mother tongue of pure cockney.

"We ain`t got any need for any more artists here, they place is overrun with them already" he replied.

"No, no I'm not an actor kind of artiste, I'm a painter" I pointed out to him.

"Are you now" he queried, "what kind of painter is that then" he replied, taking the piss, being as awkward as possible.

"Well anything really, I'm fresh out of art college," I said softly not really sure why he was willing to discuss the matter anyway.

The phone on his desk rang, so the doorman rudely put up a hand to shut me up, in full flow, while he devoted his attention to the caller on the other end of the phone. As befitting the rank of this caller, who was obviously of some importance, the doorman's Jeckle and Hyde personality changed instantly.

"Yes sir" pause, "yes sir" followed by another pause, then the doorman uttered "well sir, as a matter of fact sir, there's a kid here right now, a kind of artist" replied the doorman. After another pause, the doorman handed me the phone, telling me that a Mr Harper wanted to speak with me.

"Yes sir" I said politely adopting the doorman's new found tone, "how can I help?"

"Have you done any kind of scenery painting?" asked Mr Harper.

"Well I have done some" I replied, but in truth I did not have a clue what the hell he was talking about.

"Right" shouted Harper down the phone at me, "just stay where you are, I'll send someone down to bring you over" with that the phone went abruptly silent.

I handed back the phone to the doorman who obviously heard Harpers request for me to stay put, besides looking somewhat stunned, the doorman's demeanour as well as manner, reverted back to one of politeness and light. Doing his best impression, and a highly polished performance of, Toad of Toad hall, he suggested, "You may like to take a seat, sir!" (I had never been called sir before) and sit myself in an area of comfort, more befitting my new found status. I sat down cradled within a more sumptuous seat, assuming an air of more composure than before and my self confidence returning in abundance. I just wished I knew what Harper meant by 'scenery painting'. Within ten minutes, a lad called Henry not much older than myself, appeared in front of me.

"Are you the new artist?" asked Henry, looking at me from beneath brows full of mistrust and doubt. "

That's right," I answered politely.

"Well" he said "You better tag along with me mate"

I followed Henry through a side door that opened onto a yard that led towards the rear of the studio. I couldn't help but notice that his arse was hanging out of the rear of his rather dirty trousers, while Henry himself turned out to be an incessant chatterbox, hardly stopping to draw an occasional sharp intake of breath, like a deep sea diver gasping for air. Henry was a well known likeable character all over these studio's and in spite of his appearance was well thought of by everybody. It was obviously in my own interest to keep well in with this likeable rogue with his vast knowledge of the place, and his personality was like gold dust to behold. Mr Harper was a man of few words, but then I had gathered as much from our very brief phone conversation

You could say Harper was a man of action, who had very little time for social intercourse, let alone small talk or chit chat, at least until he got to know you well, as I was to find out much later.

"Right" said Harper, "let's see what you are capable of doing."

This was to be a practical interview I gathered, as Harper instructed me to take off my jacket and roll up my shirt sleeves ready for some hands on action.

"You can start by blocking some colours onto this scene" pointing to the large stretched canvas overpowering my eyes before me.

It must have measured at least twenty five feet wide, by all of twelve feet tall. Upon the prepared face of the canvas, was a huge charcoal sketch of a narrow London cobbled street scene, with Tudor style houses that resembled a picture from the Charles Dickens era. The top half of this painted backdrop was being prepared in readiness for some period play or film set, it had already been professionally painted by the gaffer, a Mr Archie Prentice. There were at least twenty or more different coloured paint pots, all mixed ready for use, and were already being applied by the professional artist Mr Prentice, who was to show me the ropes by supervising my practical, hands on interview.

"I'll leave you in the guidance, and expertise of Archie" said Harper as he quickly disappeared like a clap of thunder.

Following Archie's instructions, I got stuck in without further ado and after about an hour or so later, Harper reappeared as if by magic, taking Archie to one side for a private tete a tete, while I continued with my work.

Another hour went by, then Archie showed me where to put all my used paint brushes into a specially prepared vat, or bath, of turpentine.

"Well" said Archie, "you've got the job, providing your prepared to start next Monday at 9am sharp."

"Now you can come along with me to the staff canteen for a bite to eat, but see Mr Harper, before you leave the studio today."

"Lucky for you" said Archie, "we will more than keep you busy when you start next week, but this is what we call a soft week, you can go home after seeing Harper, but just make sure of your prompt arrival next Monday".

After lunch I went to see Harper in his rather posh office where his secretary noted down all my personal details for registration of employment. I was then sent back to Archie who filled me in, regarding my new found trade, he obviously thought I was easy to talk to, and I found him likewise.

Mr Archie Prentice was a middle aged gentleman with a vast artistic talent and experience, gentle in manner, but with a persistency of very high professional standards, not only did I like him, but I knew from instinct, that I would learn a great deal from this master craftsman who was also to be my boss. So this was to be my very first job then, or occupation, and already the vibes I had felt within this environment, were very positive indeed. There was ample room to grow here and stretch my wings, at least until ready to fly solo, that, being some time far away in my future development. With a large brown envelope pressed into my grubby hands by Harper himself, who then bid me good day until the following Monday, I was turned over to Henry, who was appointed to see me safely off the premises. Now, Henry was more enthusiastic about me, as he joked laughing with ease, as we walked out of the gate onto the street.

I was walking on air as I left Henry at the gate, with a spring in my step and happiness in my heart, I danced along the street towards the underground station feeling highly elated and on top of the world. With spirits as high as a kite, I had great difficulty in containing my composure, I was so excited as anyone, landing their first real job of employment, would feel. Not just any job mind you, but as a scenery artist no less!

On my return to St Christophers at 8 Osterly road, I was so proud to hand over my very first weeks rent money, from a ten bob note that had been slipped into my envelope, by Archie. Mr Bancroft was as surprised as myself, as he handed me back my change of two shillings and sixpence. Mr Bancroft, then informed me, that my Aunt was just off the phone, wondering how I had got on with my first day of job hunting, and he suggested I ring her back to give her my good news.

Later that same evening, I did so, whereby she promptly made arrangements to pick me up early the following morning after breakfast.

This was definitely a red letter day for me and one to cherish for many a year to come. When I set out first thing this morning, little did I realise the Gods would favour me with just such a blessing, I was convinced within my own mind that I had finally arrived!

Much later that same evening when I went upstairs to bed, and still in a state of high flux, I walked into my shared bedroom, only to find my roommate, King, as part of his normal behaviour, openly tossing himself off, I was somewhat peeved, but determined not to allow him to spoil what had altogether been such a wonderful day. King was perfectly entitled to wank himself off, I only wished he would use far more discretion as he shot his load onto the palm of his hand, as if it was a normal act. Ignoring his rather arrogant public display of the love he had for this particular body part, I silently got undressed hanging all my clothing up with care, deliberately keeping my underpants on that night, much to Kings displeasure.

Early next morning I had a quick shower, before going down to breakfast, I was in a buoyant mood, knowing my Aunt Joan would soon be picking me up for several days stay at Hindley Cottage in the New Forest.

Chapter Three

The ghost of Bobby, past

As we sped south westerly from London, heading for the New Forest and Burley, I sat in silence beside my aunt Joan, deep in thought. I was remembering my last visit to Hindley, my aunt's new house, it was after spending some six weeks in Hammersmith hospital at deaths door. Hindley was my savoir for recovery, when Bob died in Korea, which was easily the lowest point in my life. Aunt Joan talked away like some clucking hen about to lay an egg, but in truth, I was so preoccupied with my own private thoughts and genuine emotions, I heard very little of her blethering.

Totally absorbed within my selfish protective shell, it wasn't until we drew up on the pebbled driveway in front of Hindley Cottage, my aunt gently reminded me, we had arrived. I apologised to her for my absent minded unsociable behaviour, but she smiled an understanding reply, in recognition of my insular manner.

We unpacked the car, taking everything into the hallway, then I ran upstairs to lay crying on the single bed Bobby had last slept in. An hour or so later, aunt Joan knocked on my bedroom door, bearing a tray of tea. She knew I had been weeping, but said nothing, sitting down beside me on the bed, she poured a cup of tea for each of us.

"I've just rung the garage" she chatted easily, "and one of their mechanics is coming over first thing in the morning to get your bike in roadworthy order."

The B.S.A. motorbike that Bobby had left me, was still under wraps, laid up in my aunts garage, situated below my bedroom window.

"I'm not sure I'm ready for it" I spoke softly to my aunt, "well it would be a real shame not to use it, and I could certainly use the extra space in the garage."

"We'll see", I replied, "but I don't really want to talk about it just now"

"O.K. darling" my aunt replied.

I took the tray back down the stairs and on impulse, I told my aunt I was going to walk into the village and asked if there was anything I could fetch for her?

"No darling thank you, you go ahead and enjoy yourself", she replied.

I strolled along Honey Lane taking in all the signs that early spring surprises us with every year passing. The birds were in full song busily carrying all the nesting material in readiness for their new broods. I felt both guilty and happy at being alive, as I ambled my way in a dreamlike state, wondering what Korea was like, asking myself what kind of country did Bob breathe his last breath in?

I crossed the road to Shutlers garage, not knowing why I did so. Shutler himself came out onto the pavement and stood beside me as I admired his collection of fine vintage cars.

"How are you Paul?" he asked.

"I'm OK thank you" I replied, but without looking him in the face.

"I know someone who will give you a fair price for your BSA 500" he said"

"It's not for sale" I shouted at him, then turned and walked away feeling somewhat peeved.

I returned home to Hindley for a quiet night in, and early to bed. The strangest dream interrupted my sleep pattern, with Bobby doing most of the talking, and as I drifted back into the real world, I found the right nick-name for my bike. I would call my BSA 500, 'The Bishop' a term of everlasting endearment to Bobby. This made me feel comfortable, and gave me the desire to master the beast. I went down to breakfast feeling bright eyed and bushy tailed, a mood to which my aunt responded encouragingly.

Sometime after breakfast, and before mid morning, Robert the 19 year old mechanic arrived on his Matchless motorcycle from the village garage. My aunt knew him well, and ushered him inside for a cup of coffee, before he got to grips with my bike.

"This is Robert, Paul" she introduced me to the mechanic over coffee, he promptly told me his mates always called him Bobby or Bob for short, and he shook my hand rather vigorously. I looked at him with a strange facial expression of surprise, feeling somewhat stunned at this innocent misunderstanding, I snapped at him, calling him Robert, before storming out of the house to take the raps of 'the Bishop'

I was busy taking a duster over the Bishop's paintwork when Robert came out to examine the beast. I moved back into the house leaving Robert to get on with the task in hand, feeling the need to make myself scarce.

Around lunchtime I heard Robert fire up the Bishop for the first time, so I dashed outside with excitement, to see Robert driving down the lane giving the beast its first test drive. Within ten minutes, he was back, parking the machine expertly on the concrete apron in front of the garage. He was invited in for a bite of lunch by my aunt, "that's a lovely machine Paul" he remarked, "if you like I'll give you some lessons on riding her properly."

"That's very good of you Robert" I remarked, "I could certainly use your help in getting to grips with the beast"

" I don't want to prang her!"

"She's a pussycat really" said Robert, "you just have to show her who's master."

On our many bike rides together, I got to know and like Robert, and was very thankful for all his help. I also apologised for shouting at him when we first met, "think nothing of it" he replied, "your aunt explained to me all about your brother Bobby" he paused. "He must have been a very special brother to you Paul"

"He was, and still is" I replied softly.

Robert threw his right leg over the Matchless motorcycle, kicked the engine into a controlled roar, then expertly throttled off down Honey lane leaving me standing in front of my own bike 'The Bishop'.

After a quick tea, I was thinking of taking the Bishop to Christchurch, for a spin on my own, my aunt knowing I was eagerly champing at the bit. On telling her of my intentions she showed no surprise, warning me to be careful and not drive too fast as I was still getting to know my machine. Oh the recklessness of youth! I thought in retrospect, as I assured my aunt, I would be extra careful, so as not to damage my beautiful machine (which was true enough).

The real difficulty was a surface, fraught with potholes, in Honey Lane itself. Having achieved this obstacle course in low gears only, it was a distinct pleasure to turn right, onto a proper tarmacadam road towards Christchurch. There was very little traffic anywhere in 1952 and the call of an open road was heady stuff indeed. With no speed restrictions outside the 30mph zones, the taste for unbridled power to see what the Bishop could do, was impossible to resist. The throb of a 500cc motorcycle between one's inner thighs on opening up the powerful machine's throttle in top gear, was a pleasure to experience like no other. As the inside of my knees firmly hugged either side of the petrol tank, and with both bike and body leaning into the weaving corners of the road ahead, the thrill and sheer exhilaration was better than any sexual high.

My cavalier attitude towards this new found drug, was totally unbridled and dangerous in the extreme, but what a way to die! When the temptation became too reckless, as if I was on some kind of suicide mission, Bobby would whisper in my ear on the passing wind, to slow down and act more sensibly, "easy Paul, take it real easy" he would whisper like some guardian angel sitting on my shoulder. At those daredevil moments I would gently ease back on the throttle with a knowing smile upon my face, remembering clearly Bobby's infectious grin. That summed up Bobby's whole life it was as if Bobby in person was astride the bike just in front of me, giving me a comfortable glow of well being.

Now I was at complete ease with this machine nicknamed the Bishop. I also knew Bobby approved the bike's new name, because he told me so! Perhaps even more important, I was at peace with myself, feeling more control of the Bishop, than I ever had over Bobby when he was alive. The ghost of Bobby was a likeable rogue, but then he always was, despite all the naughty antics in leading me into a life of evil and sinful sexual adventures.

Having parked the Bishop in front of Christchurch's coastline, I stared longingly out to sea, with the thoughts and memories of aunt Joan, who was responsible for bringing both Bobby and myself to this very spot, I also remembered the weekend we joined the 5th Staines Sea scouts together. I hopped over the promenade wall onto the beach below, then lay down on my back looking skyward, like we had done so often at our secret pool, where childhood had been left behind. This nostalgia, I began to realize, going down memory lane was not good for a youth so young, after all I heard Bobby remind me, "life is for living and dying is for the morbid or unfortunate."

A sudden chill ran down my spine which only served to remind me Spring evenings were already wearing thin, time for home to the warmth and comfort, the security blanket of my Aunt Joan, so I fired the bishop back into life and headed back for home.

As the evening drew nigh, I switched on my only headlamp as I turned into Honey Lane and brought my new baby to rest inside the garage, the doors being left open for my anticipated homecoming.

Feeling pleased with myself, I sat down to a plate of sausages and one of my aunt's delicious home made trifles, then after a long soak in the bath, I bade my aunt goodnight, and into my bed of wet dreams I went.

Thursday was a leisurely day for me, putting up some shelving in the garage for much needed storage, then the two of us tidied up the glory hole above the garage, which was long overdue. I cut the lawn, then spent time washing and polishing the Bishop with pride.

Over supper that evening my aunt chose to inform me that both the car and bike, would be going over to Winchester in the morning, as my aunt had made arrangements for me to take a motorcycle test and try to gain my very first driving licence. The thought of me tearing about on such a powerful machine without being road legal, was enough to give my aunt a premature heart attack, as all her life she had been a stickler for law and order. I was easily persuaded to go with the flow, if only to give her peace of mind. Don't worry I was not in remission from some kind of unknown illness, I was only doing my best to give my aunt less problems and worry, to make amends for at least some of my evil past. My aunt also suggested I might like to motorbike over to the 5th Staines Sea Scouts on Saturday, to reacquaint myself with the group, as she felt Gina the Scoutmaster had always been kind to both Bobby and I. Finally she produced a pair of 'L' plates that I was to attach to the front and rear of the Bishop, before I went to bed and in readiness for the morn.

Before going to bed we talked together a great deal, my aunt expressing her joy at me landing such a plumb job with the studio, we also discussed St Christopher's, or the fellowship, a great deal and she was extremely well informed about all of its workings, aims and activities. My aunt was able to tell me that the patron of the organisation was one, 'Princess Marina' whom she had met on more than one occasion, and of whom she spoke very highly. Having filled in many gaps of my ignorance, and feeling more tired by the second, I hugged and kissed my aunt goodnight, so ending yet another memorable day.

The driving test was more of a formality in those early days, if not a bit of a joke. The examiner I was fortunate enough to get was a pushover, and in less than fifteen minutes, and a few common sense questions, I was given a pass certificate to take along to the G.P.O. (General Post Office). My aunt insisted, we do it there and then, feeling there was no escape from her deliberations for proper proceedings, I went along for the ride appeasing her satisfaction for a job well done. The little red card was my first legal document it made me feel very grown up indeed. My aunt heaved her ample bosom with unashamed pride as if I had just received an award winning Oscar, for my outstanding role in acting.

To celebrate my triumphant achievement, she took me first to a beano lunch at some 'high brow' restaurant, then onto a specialist motorcycle outfitter there she bought two pairs of motorcycle gauntlets, one pair to be given to Robert as a thank you for all his help in taming the Bishop. Having got a result so to speak, we drove at a leisurely pace back to Burley, where I was made to hand over my present suitably wrapped, along with my heartfelt thanks and appreciations to Robert. I might add, on receiving them Robert beamed with gratitude, making me feel a right plonker.

Alas, Saturday was soon upon us, having spent most of Friday tinkering and checking the Bishop many times over. It was certainly a smashing bike to look at, gleaming like a new penny freshly minted, with more than enough glamour to instil pride into any owner. My short stay in the presence of my wonderful aunt, who was always there for me, to pick up the pieces, was like a breath of heaven and a spoonful of common sense, forming the catalyst of keeping me sane, at least most of the time. I knew deep down in my innards, I didn't deserve her kindness, having disappointed her on to many occasions to keep count of. I bade her an affectionate farewell, before heading once more onto the open road towards Staines.

On arriving at the bridge over a section of the river Thames, I gingerly negotiated the well worn towpath to the 5th Staines Sea Scouts H.Q., with great care. I heaved the Bishop onto its rear wheel stand as Gina came out from within the scout hut, having heard the distinct engine noise of the Bishop. He hugged and greeted me as if I was his long lost son, I had the distinct impression that he was really pleased to see me once again. I acknowledged his generous welcome, by beaming back at him, telling Gina how pleased I was to see him and the gang. Gina was sensitive enough not to mention Bobby, but I knew instinctively that because Bobby had been his lodger, and had been so well liked by everyone, he would be sorely missed

The boys were busy cooking sausages over an open fire, several came to greet me, one bringing a plateful and a mug of steaming hot tea. We sat down inside the hut, chatting away about scouting matters in a very jovial manner. Later I told Gina my good news about the new job I was about to start at Lime Grove Studios, he seemed very impressed.

"Some of the lads are staying overnight in the hut" he said, "you would be most welcome to stay if you wished," adding he could do with my help in teaching some of the younger recruits who wanted to go sailing this afternoon.

"I would be delighted, but I need to get away first thing Sunday morning, if that's ok?" I asked Gena.

It was great to get out onto the water again, with a gentle hand on the tiller and sails full of wind, it served to remind me how much I missed this fantastic activity. I handled a good half dozen raw recruits, most of whom had never been in a sailing dingy before, with one to one tuition they grasped the basics in helming, and sail handling surprisingly quickly. One or two were naturals, by the end of the afternoon session they were more than ready to go solo.

After some tea Gina asked me how the bike was going and remarked how well she looked.

"You can come home to my place for the night", offered Gina, remembering that Bobby used to lodge with him.

I thanked him for his kind invitation, but declined, telling Gina I preferred, if it was OK by him that I would sooner stay at the hut.

"I understand Paul" he replied, "and I'm sure that most of the gang will be overjoyed and make you very comfortable."

They did just that, but I expected no less, the camaraderie of such a joyful gathering amongst so many of my long standing mates, was just the kind of cheerful medicine I badly needed.

Gina, along with some of the older element, invited me along to a local hostelry where a very pleasant evening, imbibing our merry souls with the odd glass of cider, took place. Gina kept close company with me, as we talked away easily, to all and sundry. It was a memorable night all told, and I was made to feel a vital and integral part of the gang again.

After a hearty breakfast, Arthur Cox, the assistant scout leader, asked if he could cadge a lift to Osterly, as he lived close by in Ealing where his father was the local Lord Mayor. No problem I assured Arthur, so we said our goodbyes to all, before I kick started the Bishop firing it into life with just one stroke.

On arrival at Osterly I pulled up in front of the tube station, to drop Arthur off, when he politely told me it was No 8 Osterly road he was heading for, yes St Christopher's, where I myself was lodging! It was then I discovered Arthur Cox and Rodger Bancroft the warden, were very old mates going back many a year. I parked the bike in front of the main steps and entrance to my new home.

Mr Kipling the assistant warden to Bancroft came down the steps and showed me a more secure, disued outhouse, where I could keep the

Bishop under cover, away from prying eyes, and the elements. I made my way back inside to the communal sitting room, where Bancroft and Arthur Cox were exchanging funny anecdotes with much laughter. Obviously, the two were old buddies.

Just as I was about to make myself comfortable, Mr Kipling signalled me to go with him into the main office. Once securely inside his office, with the door firmly shut, he asked me how I got on with Mike King, the older lad I shared a bedroom with.

I looked at Kipling questioningly, and he was not at all forthcoming, so after a pause I replied, "OK I suppose."

"Well," said Kipling having received my non committal reply, "I've decided to move you into a bedroom of your own."

He could see I was pleased, so he continued, "why don't you move all your gear into No12 just now while its quiet."

With a spring in my stride I did just that, as I felt this was not a prudent moment to enquire after the true meaning or cause behind such a move. After saying cheerio to Arthur and assuring him of my future commitment with the scouts, I had a good shower and went to bed early, as was my want, knowing my first day of honest toil was about to start.

Chapter Four

A new Start

Because of the need to make a slightly earlier start than most of the working lads at St Christopher's, Bancroft who was roistered on early duties this week, tapped on my door softly. I was already awake, the habitual early rises at Ashford, was already carved in stone. Alan Bancroft entered bearing a gift in the form of a mug of hot tea. I looked at my watch, it was a little time after 6.30am, so I knew I had plenty of time in hand before I needed to stir myself proper.

As he sat on the edge of my bed, Bancroft informed me "Cookie has just arrived, and breakfast will be available from 7am onwards, designed specifically for us early birds."

Having washed and shaved, I went down to breakfast surprised to find other lads already seated. Cookie placed before me a plate of bacon and sausages, with a fried egg on a slice of fried bread, and a fresh mug of hot tea. Suitably dressed for the bike, protected by over trousers, waterproof wind smock (anorak), driving into London to Lime Green Studios, I had no problems with traffic. In fact, in my excitement and eagerness to ensure my intent of not being late, I arrived at the side gate of the studio before half eight. I was casually sitting aside my charger, when Henry the handyman/gofer walked up looking somewhat spruced up and rather surprised. A broad grin exploded across his boat race (face) as recognition dawned.

"Great machine Paul," he exclaimed, looking over the bishop with an eye of approval, with a quick glance at his wrist watch to confirm the correct time of day, "your keen aren,'t ya" remarked Henry.

"Just a bit I suppose" I replied watching him unlock the gate.

Henry showed me where it was safe to park the beast before we both headed into what I presumed to be the common room or staff rest room, where he put a kettle of water, over a well used two burner gas hob to make us both a mug of tea. While waiting for the kettle to come to the boil he did a well practised striptease act down to his underpants, then retrieved what looked like a pair of swimming trunks from his locker and without any inhibitions whipped off his underpants before donning the trunks. He was well endowed and wasn't the least bit embarrassed as to who saw his equipment. I learnt Henry used a changing room with three showers in a wet floor area, at the end of every working day, before changing back into his good clothes and going home.

Henry told me, he lived just around the corner from the studio, looking after his mum, who did not fare well. He spoke as if the whole of life was one long lasting joke and had worked for the studios since leaving school at fourteen years of age, more than six years past. I learned much later on from Archie, the foreman in our group of six, that Henry was the breadwinner for both his gran and mother, this had been the case long before he left school. He was extremely well thought of, and very popular all over the different departments throughout the studio. Henry had a number of scams going to subsidise his impoverished lifestyle, but because he was such a likeable rogue, everybody turned a blind eye to his 'Arthur Daley' style enterprises.

Henry was fast approaching his twenty first birthday, but did not look much older than myself at sixteen. Being such an adorable character, I never once heard him speak badly about anyone. He took a real shine to me as the junior of our group of six, but I suspected, he had been asked to take me under his wing so to speak.

As each staff worker came into work, Henry greeted them with a mug of their own particular brand of tea. This was a set routine before anything else happened, and even Mr Harper, the executive, was treated no differently. If you didn't know otherwise, you could easily be misled into thinking that Harper, was Henrys father, as it was obvious to any observer, the relationship between them was rather special. Mr Harper may have been chief of the department, but Archie was most definitely the real boss.

"Right Paul" said Archie, "follow me", so I did.

He introduced me to Terry who was in his early twenties and Harry, who was in his mid thirties. Archie explained to me, "You will be working all week with these gentlemen, there are new scenes to paint, for some forthcoming film shoot."

I found the work absorbing, and couldn't believe how fast the workday disappeared, with this first day being so busy I took a bite of lunch on the hoof, Henry brought it from the canteen and generally looked after us. By the end of my second day, being a Tuesday, I chose to take a shower along with Henry so I could go directly to scouts from work. My scouting gear was in the pannier attached to the bike, so I could change when I got to the scout hut. From that point onwards, Tuesday and Thursday evenings I would make my way to the scouts in Staines which became a regular routine most weeks.

After my first few months it was as if I had been there for years. The team that I worked with, were a great bunch of pros and every last one of them was so accommodating in any shortfalls I may have had, becoming my close mates, and forever teasing me, but in a gentle way. Archie was particularly kind to me and always managed to get the best I was able to give. In many ways he sometimes reminded me of Mr Walton from my Ashford days, although he was nowhere near as strict. I was to learn Archie was a man who always played his cards very close to his chest, he kept his personal life outside the studio very private indeed. I was one of the few people who found him easy to converse with and I even shared some of my own past with him, but would not dream of asking about anything to do with his own personal background, and I believe he appreciated this part of my integrity.

One Thursday evening while I was taking a shower alone, before heading off to my usual scout meeting, Henry entered the shower next to mine, with his usual jovial banter. "Off to scouts again this evening", he asked.

"That's right Henry" I replied, "why? do you want to come along to see what we get up to?"

He followed this question with a long silent if somewhat pregnant pause. "Do you think I could?" he said, "I always wanted to be a scout."

I was tempted to tell him he was a bit old. This revelation was a bolt from the blue and certainly most unexpected on my part. "Well" I said after a short pause, "if you don't think your parents would mind, I don't see why not, I could take you next Tuesday if you wish?"

"Do you mean that Paul, or are you pulling my dick?" he asked with a smile.

"No Henry I wouldn't do that, but if you really want to, I would be delighted to introduce you to the 5th Staines sea scouts, but it would mean you wouldn't get back home till quite late"

"Anyway" I continued, "think it through and we can discuss it tomorrow if your still keen."

This he did and I agreed to take him the following Tuesday.

I was informed by Terry, Archie wanted a word, so I went to see him in his office. "Paul, come in" said Archie "how good are you at graining?"

"Not bad" I replied, "especially with figured oak, and feathered mahogany as my main forte" I said, "but why?"

"I'll tell you later" said Archie, "do me a specimen of oak on this prepared panel here." I looked at the panel in question, which was about four feet by two foot in size. That would only take half an hour or perhaps even less, I fetched my box of tricks and set to work.

Archie disappeared only to reappear twenty minutes later, standing in the doorway watching me put the final touches to the panel now looking every bit a piece of solid oak.

"You were taught well son," said Archie, and he shouted Terry over for a gander. "How much do you think that oak panel weighs?" asked Archie.

"I don't know," said Terry, "but it will take two of us to lift it, why? and where has it got to go?" he asked,

"Nowhere" replied Archie, "at least not for the time being, so you can go back to your work."

Archie turned to me "Terry has one of the best eyes in the trade, and never spotted, it wasn't the real McCoy" he remarked "so I'll set you a challenge and show you what's to be done after the morning break, now scram."

Later that morning, Archie took me with the sample panel, up in the lift to the top floor suite of offices in the main administration block. The big wigs secretary ushered us both into the director's long boardroom, halfway into being redecorated, remodelled and refurbished. This boardroom, at the top of the building, had fantastic views over the skyline towards the City of London. Most of the décor was at an advanced stage, with new ply panels recently installed from skirting to about five feet high on every single wall. "These are the panels to be grained," said Archie. The executive examined the oak sample panel, and it was put up near the real oak doors leading into the room from whence we had come, while I stood by like a spare part.

"Excellent" was all the big wig could say, "how soon can you start Archie?" he asked.

I was told to wait outside in the secretaries office while the finer points regarding the timetable, to what after all was a fair sized job, were discussed.

Over lunch Archie asked me "how long do you think the whole job will take from start to finish?"

"If I'm totally on my own?"

"You will be" interjected Archie.

"Then I think I could do it inside a normal working week" I continued. "One day for the base coat, 2-3 days for all the graining, and a final day for at least one coat of flat varnish."

There was a long silence, then Archie said "ok Paul, if you do it in one full working week, I'll see you get a substantial bonus at the end of the job, "OK?" he asked.

"OK" I replied.

"Right you can start Monday first thing" said Archie, "and you can use Henry for back up"

"Fair enough," I said, "I'll do my very best Archie"

"I know you will" was Archie's reply, "I know you will" he retorted.

Over the mid afternoon tea break. Henry told me his next door neighbour would keep an eye on both his mum and gran for Tuesday night, so if I was still willing he would very much like to come with me Tuesday evening on my trip to Staines.

"No problem" I told Henry, "but we would also need to give thought to the fact that we would not be getting back until late Tuesday night."

At that point Henry was called into Archie's office, so I went back to working with Terry.

After a hectic weekend sailing, canoeing, and some rock climbing I went back to work on Monday full of vigour and ready for the task in the boardroom, set by Archie. Henry was very useful as my assistant in getting all the wall panels prepared and primed with just the right shade of basecoat, which we called country cream. This oil based primer would need all of the overnight hours to go off hard, ready for the first of the graining panels in the morning. The secretary was instructed to keep the heating on low overnight. Henry was meticulous in cleaning up after me, and couldn't do enough to help me in every way possible. The task was made all the more enjoyable, with his bubbly personality and off the cuff witty repartee. It was a great opportunity for me to get to know him well. And his character had many idealistic facets only enhancing his persona as to what kind of person he really was.

On Tuesday, I even surpassed my own expectations by completing a good two thirds of all the room panels, and towards the afternoon, just after the tea break, Archie came up to examine my work thus far. After some time his face broke into a beam, which for Archie was very rare indeed, he told us both to stop work and clean up ready for the morning.

Later when Henry and I were taking a shower in readiness for our evening with the 5th Staines sea scouts, I could tell that he was getting very animated, obviously looking forward of things to come.

"You know," said Henry, "I've never seen Archie take to a member of the team so well, as he has with you."

"Really" I asked "so is that good or what?"

"Blooming good," said Henry as he towelled himself down.

Thankfully it was a fine June evening as the Bishop purred along the open road. Henry was a natural pillion rider with just the right amount of leaning into the winding bends, and was obviously enjoying himself. He was also a big hit with the whole gang and especially with Gina. You could say he was a smash hit, and like myself, no one could believe he was nearing his 21st, birthday. He had his very first short sail in a sailing dingy, which impressed me, especially when I learned later he could hardly swim. I was horrified at first, with the disclosure of this fact, so I told Henry I would give him lessons in his local swimming baths, as it was very important. Henry on the other hand was very apprehensive at such a prospect, replying he had managed to survive so far without needing to swim, so he didn't much see the fucking point, or words to that effect, only a little more colourful.

Meanwhile he didn't want to talk about the subject, so we didn't. Henry promptly changed the subject by suggesting I stay at his place overnight, as it would save me an extra journey first thing Wednesday morning. This casual off the wall suggestion, took me by surprise and

Henry was quick to note my hesitation. "Of course you don't ave to if you don't want to," snapped Henry dropping his haiches, which was normal for a Cockney.

"Its not that I don't want to" I answered, "but I need to ring my folks first to let them know what's happening."

Henry looked at me in silence, not sure if I was real or not.

On the way home I mulled over Henrys suggestion, as I could tell he was not best pleased with my reserve, I drove up to the front of eight Osterly road and parked the bike on the main road in front of the house telling Henry, to give me a few minutes. I went inside and told Mr Bancroft of the situation, which to him made a lot of sense, so I carried on into London, thinking of the grin all over Henrys face, putting him in danger of catching flies as we sped off on the Bishop.

Henry had a twin bedded room already prepared for my arrival, so after a pleasant chat with his mother and gran, then a welcome bite washed down by a cup of tea, we both retired upstairs ready for bed. The graining went well, and I had finished the last panel by Wednesday lunch. Thursday saw all the varnish work completed and by the end of Thursday afternoon, we were all able to stand back and admire the finished workmanship. Archie left instructions that all going well come Friday morning provided the varnish was truly dry, they could have their boardroom back for refurbishing. I used the rest of the day helping Terry with some guilding, with the two of us finished by the end of the working day at five pm. With Thursday evening spent at the scouts taking along Henry, then staying over at his place, it became a set routine most weeks. We became fairly close, but there was always that wariness on my part. Perhaps I was still afraid of our relationship becoming to close, having had several previous experiences of what could happen, and by remembering the loss of all those I have loved before.

I do remember Henry asking me why I called my BSA motorbike 'The Bishop' but declined to tell him the truth by simply replying "it was just a name that took my fancy" which for the time being at least, he accepted. Maybe I was playing my cards to close to my chest, but anyway, Henry respected my privacy without asking any real searching questions as to my previous private life at Ashford and as far as I know, only Archie was aware of some of my background, but even he did not know about my real loss of my brother Bobby. Fortunate for me, Archie was also a very private person, and this made me feel secure in the knowledge that Archie, because of his secretive nature was one of the most discrete men I knew. After several months, I made a deal with Henry that I would continue to give him a lift to scouts, providing he allowed me to teach him to swim, mental blackmail you might say, and you would be right! Surprisingly he agreed, so Wednesday evenings were set aside for a good hour session each week, but Henry made me swear I did not let on to anyone else, especially our work mates, or the deal was off! I still do not know who was mentally blackmailing who!

Within the space of just four sessions he became a very competent swimmer, and our visit to the local baths became a great source of enjoyment for both of us. One of the most interesting parts of my work place was the never ending variation of our workload from scenes, to sign writing, gilding, heraldry, graining etc, etc. I didn't realise just how enjoyable work had become, but then I was working in a team who equally enjoyed their work and took great pride in every task or challenge we undertook. There was never any backbiting among us and even swearing was kept to a minimum with the most blasphemous being Henry, but we all realised it was so much part of his likeable character we agreed it wouldn't be Henry without his colourful turn of language. To be fair I could swear with the best of them, which was more ready acceptable in a youth so young as I, but it was never allowed to get out of bounds.

On visiting my aunt down at Hindley, I was busy telling her about this bundle of energy at work called Henry, when my aunt suggested I bring him over for a long weekend. I was somewhat dubious about the idea at first, and wasn't even sure that Henry would want to come, however, I told my I aunt could ask him, although I was still doubtful that he would get away for a whole weekend. She told me there was only one way to find out and that was to ask!

"Ok" I said to my aunt, "OK" in appeasement, "maybe I will."

So with this in mind one Wednesday evening while we were both larking about at the local swimming baths, I put this suggestion to Henry rather nervously, and to my utter surprise he jumped at the offer.

One Friday afternoon while Archie was handing each of us our pay packet, the gaffer presented us with a conundrum. 'N' signs, a small company who specialised in all kinds of high class lettering work, had approached our gaffer Archie with a bit of a poser. We at the studios often did work for 'N' Signs who on occasions reciprocated by doing some work for us, when we found ourselves somewhat overstretched. The poser was simple enough to understand really, 'N' Signs had been approached by a small company called Britvic, one of the new leading lights in producing small bottles of fruit juices. Britvic were looking for a permanent way of labelling their miniature bottles, without having to re-label the recycled bottles, repeatedly being sterilised for reuse. They were looking to achieve a more permanent cost effective form of labelling. The gaffer having gone into great detail explaining all the pros and cons, was brainstorming the team and requested us to give the matter some considerable thought over the weekend.

"This important matter will be discussed in more detail, come Monday morning," said Archie.

We would all have the weekend to chew the fat, and he made it very clear to each of us, he would make it more than worth our while if this poser could be cracked. While we were having a quick shower in readiness for our spin on the Bishop, down to the New Forest, Henry was throwing all kinds of ideas at me in the response to the gaffers aforementioned plea. In the end I told him to think over his crackpot ideas in silence, as he was rapidly giving me a headache. Except for the odd light shower of rain we arrived at Hindley on the outskirts of Burley in comfortably good time. My aunt as expected made Henry feel very welcomed, and at ease, by taking an instant shine to him, as I knew she would. I found out much later, my aunt thought Henry was a handsome chap and no doubt a big hit with the girls, which he was. After a really good evening meal, laid on especially for Henry, they talked away very comfortably in each others company, this didn't surprise me as I learnt long ago, that Henry was a smooth operator and could be a real charmer without having to put any real effort into his offensive. After a great evening, we went upstairs where I automatically ran a hot bath, forgetting we had both had a shower earlier that same evening. Not wanting to waste the hot water already poured, Henry decided he would love a hot soak, so I let him go first.

Having both slept well in single beds, Henry remarked he had never been in a house before where each bedroom had its own en-suite, and he found this fact amusing, talking to my aunt over a hearty breakfast he told her what a wonderful house she had designed, which was like music to her ears.

After breakfast I took Henry into Christchurch for the day, where I hired a Keelboat and with fair winds we had many hours of great sailing, I worked Henry as my new crew member, very hard indeed!

After an hour or so of tuition on the helm, Henry a natural sailor was shaping up nicely, but the salt air eventually won, making him tired and ready for home. We wasted no time in getting back to Hindley for a substantial evening meal. My aunt reprimanded me for overtiring Henry, as he lay dozing in the chair in front of a warm coal fire. The fatal combination of heat and good food had Henry softly purring, snoring away in contentment. I discussed at length my thoughts, on silk screening possibilities on the Britvic bottles as their new labels. My aunt felt it might well work practically, if it was possible to do at least a dozen bottles or more at one and the same time, and under the silk screen process when bottles went through many washings during the lifespan of their use. The whole thing seamed feasible, but experimentation would be it's only confirmation of either success or failure. My aunt ran a hot bath for Henry and after waking the dozy sod up, he went upstairs alone to submerge himself. After twenty minutes or so, I said goodnight to my aunt and made my way up the wooden hill expecting to find Henry tucked up in bed, but only to find the dozy sod fast asleep still soaking in the bath. I reached down between his legs amid the soapy lukewarm water, then took the telephone like shower head from its resting place and proceeded to turn the jet spray of water at him. He opened his eyes somewhat bemused and surprised, to find himself bombarded in this fashion. Needless to say it had the desired effect as he grinned his way out of the bath. I got in and had a quick shower feeling to lazy to fill the bath up with hot water again. While I was drying myself off Henry went through to the bedroom and promptly fell fast asleep. After having lived only in smoggy London all his days, Henry found country living combined with sea air, too much to handle. I read for a while, before joining Henry in the land of nod.

Early Sunday morning my aunt came up with a heavy tray full of breakfast, including a pot of hot tea, to tell us both she was off to early morning church service and would see us sleepy heads later. It was very apparent that Henry was enjoying himself, as he firstly slipped out of bed to use the loo then still in the buff fully naked joined me at my bedside to enjoy his breakfast, chatting away like a woodpecker hammering into the bark of a new tree trunk. I was most surprised at his lack of total inhibition and the lack of any signs of embarrassment, mostly because he chose to do so with me, someone whom he had only known for about a year. More I suspect to hide my own signs of embarrassment, I started to explain my idea to Henry about screening the Britvic bottles. It was obvious he didn't understand a word, as he didn't know what a silk screen was, so we left it at that and got dressed and went downstairs.

I told Henry "I'm going to take the Hoover around the place."

"Ok" said Henry, "do you think your aunt would mind very much if I cut the grass?"

"She would be delighted" I said and fetched the small roller mower from the garage. I told him to just cut the patch in front of the living room patio windows, because ponies come in to graze the two acre field beyond.

While Henry set to with the grass cutter and with me doing the hoovering my aunt returned from church accompanied by a lady from the village, who had come to pick up some of Aunt Joan's art work for an exhibition, being held in the village hall. My aunt called Henry in for a coffee, when the ladies had discussed the merits of at least a dozen of my Aunt's most recent paintings, and chose some really nice portraits of local characters from the village for the exhibition, Henry made some comment about where my artistic talents came from, pleasing both Aunt Joan and myself.

After coffee I went outside to wash the Bishop in readiness for the journey home later that afternoon. Once the bike was clean and dry, Henry helped me polish all the black paintwork and chrome, until she was shining like a new penny. Over lunch we continued to debate the silk screening idea with Henry doing his utmost to comprehend. Aunt Joan could see that Henry was having difficulty in keeping up, so she suddenly left the table and went up to her famous glory hole. When she returned she was carrying one of my old silk screens, complete with print outs of a Christmas card I had made a good few years ago. After my aunt explained how easy the whole thing worked and that silk screening could be easily achieved on any material, Henry thought it was a fantastic idea especially if it could be done on glass. He began to look at me in a new light realising, that although I was very much the junior of the work team, I was more than capable of making some contributions to the good of our studio department.

Shortly after tea saying our thank you`s and farewells to my aunt, she gave Henry a kiss, much to his surprise, we then set off for London. Stopping briefly at his mother's terraced house for a quick cup of tea, and just long enough to pick up our trunks, we went for a good long swim at the local baths, before returning home for a late supper and then to bed. That evening Henry started to open up, by telling me all kinds of things that I knew nothing about. He had no recollection whatsoever of his father, and in truth didn't remember what he even looked like, as his father deserted him and his mother, before he was a year old. I listened with a sympathetic ear wondering why he decided to tell me so much about himself. He had several experiences with a number of girlfriends, and a recent break up had left him with much dissatisfaction and an unquenchable sex drive. A few male mates he saw from time to time, was his other claim, but in more recent times he had found a more eventful purpose to outside activities, especially since I introduced him to scouting and other out door activities. With so much on his plate I found it difficult to believe he was lonely, because even outside of his work, he had so much going for him. He was a kind natured soul with a very sensitive side that most of the time he kept well hidden. He spoke very highly of my aunt, who in Henry's eyes was really some lady, or "some piece of work" he said with a hint of envy. We talked away easily to each other until I found myself nodding off, but I hasten to add, not from boredom, but just plain tiredness, as it was well past my usual bedtime.

At work the following Monday morning all bright eyed and bushy tailed we both felt ready to take on the world. Once we had a mug of tea in our mitts, the gaffer reiterated over Fridays conundrum. Several ideas were put forward, including the idea that Coke-a-Cola used, by making the letters of Britvic, in glass, at the time of bottle manufacture. At this time in the early Fifties this was fraught with all kinds of problems including legal liability.

The suggestion that perhaps some kind of steam proof label that could resist washing was being bandied about, when Henry chirped up "me and Paul have come up with the ideal solution."

"Cheeky chappy", I thought as the gaffer looked at me especially. "How about silk screen printing" I proffered, with everyone looking blank, except the gaffer himself and the recently indoctrinated Henry.

"Right you lot off to work, but not you two" said Archie, "you can come in to my office."

We kicked the idea about, with a lot of input from both of us and I could see the gleam in the gaffer's eye, as he thought it might be a goer. He pointed to a small crate of Britvic bottles sitting in the corner of his office, "take those and show me what you can come up with by lunchtime" he said.

Henry and myself set to work and by lunchtime we had a prototype model silk screen ready to go. I cut the pro-forma stencil exactly to size and shape of Britvic`s existing labels that were evident on the bottles we had from Archies office. After lunch, mixing up poster paint to the right colour and consistency we did a first run on twelve bottles at one time, but using clean glass on the opposite side from the existing labels.

Several days later having perfected the base to prevent roll or movement and with just the right tension in the silk screen, and using fresh sterile label less bottles, a craftsman from 'N' Sign and a representative from Britvic came over to inspect our efforts. The Britvic executive was very impressed, especially as we were able to demonstrate the silk screen print was fully intact after many hot soapy water washes. 'N' Signs were sure they could make a silk screen large enough, to do up to 100 bottles at one time.

After much experimentation the idea was deemed to be a success. However, Archie would only agree to the use of this method with a commission to be paid to the studio at the rate of one farthing per bottle. This was eventually agreed by all parties. Archie then called me in, I took Henry with me, much to the gaffers disdain. "How about ten pounds as a bonus for coming up with such a brilliant idea" he said.

I looked Archie dead in the eye and with sheer bravado said, "that'll be ten pounds apiece then", pointing to the two of us, while Henry stood with his mouth open catching flies.

Archie at first just looked stunned as if I had just punched him right between the eyes. The seconds began to seem like an eternity, when suddenly he broke into one of his rare grins then simply said, "alright Paul, your worth it, the pair of you are," he added as an afterthought.

Then for the first time in my working life he put his arm around my shoulder and said, "I made a good move the day I took you on son" he said.

"So did I by coming to see you before I went anywhere else" I replied softly.

I left his office taking Henry, who was still standing gasping like a spare part, with a mouthful of flies. Henry promptly ran off to the toilet, in urgent need of a dump!

Chapter Five

One Year Later

It was very early April, and thankfully April fools day had passed with only a little embarrassment, as still being green about the lugs and not yet fully in tune with the way of the world and in particular certain working practices, I was taken for an April fool Charlie! Just before lunchtime I was called into the toilets, where before I realised what was afoot, the four likely lads as I will refer to them, namely Henry, Terry, Harry and Archie, stripped me bollock naked. A pot of green axle grease was plastered liberally all over my body including in all of my nether regions, and I was then left wrestling and writhing on the shower room floor by myself, while they all went back to work laughing their heads off! I was taking a shower when Henry who had been instructed by the gaffer. Came in with some kind of solvent in a bucket. He made me stand still, away from the shower head, then as casual as you like, Henry got hold of my dick and lifting it out of the way, proceeded to wipe me down with wads of engineering waste fibre, dipping it frequently into the cleaning solution. By this time I was well and truly past any form of embarrassment or caring!

I just stood there thankful for all the help Henry gave me. He paid particular attention to my bits, to ensure no real damage was done, not so much from the grease but from the industrial cleaning fluid which, if left on the skin to long, could result in a rather nasty rash. Ignoring my partial erection, the moment this vital area of my body had been cleaned, he pushed me under the shower telling me to use plenty of soap, which I did. On proceeding to do the back of my body from the neck down to my ankles, he seemed to be enjoying my humiliation. Henry then left me to it, to soap and rinse myself down. An hour or so after this somewhat silly practise or prank, and what some might call a right of passage, I came out of the shower to thunderous applause, looking as if I had been sand blasted. Later that same day, Terry told me I had got off lightly, as they were thinking of using paint, as was their usual custom, only the gaffer persuaded them not to, "so we went for grease instead" said Terry.

Within a fortnight on the 12th of April 1953 on my seventeenth birthday, a celebration party at the local hostelry had been carefully arranged in secret. At the end of the working day, I was instructed by the gaffer to follow him to have a look at my next job for the following morning. Like a lamb to the slaughter. And in spite if the very recent April fools prank, in my complete naivety, or was it blind trust, I went along in complete ignorance, following behind the gaffer, even when he took me into the snug bar, the penny didn't drop! I might add at this point, I wasn't even aware that anybody knew the date of my birth, and I myself had momentarily forgotten the significance, not remembering exactly what day it was anyway.

"Sit yourself down there young Paul, I'll be with you directly" said Archie.

Meanwhile the gaffer had slipped out to get the rest of the motley crew of reprobates, but still the penny didn't fit the slot! Less than ten minutes later the whole gang appeared including Mr Harper, who as a rule we only saw once a week, if we were lucky. The look in my face as they all sang a hearty chorus of 'Happy Birthday' must have been priceless, as they all roared with laughter, fit to burst. A really hot meal; of roast beef, roast potatoes and buttered cabbage followed by apple crumble with custard, which I declined and was then rapidly followed by glass after glass of cider.

A few hours later and before I got completely rat arsed, the gang dispersed, all except Henry who had been instructed to take special care of me, by the gaffer. As it was obvious I was no longer capable of looking after my self, Henry took me back to the staffroom at work, sat me down and undressed me to the buff. Then undressing himself he stood me under a cold shower in a brave attempt to sober me up. He took great care to dry me off properly, then wrapped me in a dry towel and sat me down in the staff room easy chair. After sorting out a pair of sleeping bags he put me in one, while he made some black strong coffee. He got into the bag along side mine and I soon fell off to sleep, not capable of holding onto my senses any longer.

The rattle of china over the sink area woke me up, as I looked at my watch all bleary eyed. 8am, I murmured as Henry put a plate of grilled sausages down on the floor beside me. "How did I get here?" I asked Henry who had an unusual twinkle in his eye, or was I still drunk? "I'm sorry about this Paul, but I could hardly take you home the state you were in" he said.

After a short pause I said, "That bad was I?"

"You bet," said Henry with a knowing smile upon his face as he obviously knew a great deal more than I did. It was pointless on my part to enquire any further, besides I was still feeling somewhat delicate and that's putting it mildly.

"Did you undress me Henry?" I asked noticing I was naked.

"And showered you in cold water" answered Henry, "not that it did you much good mind you."

"Do you realise I blame you lot of bastards for getting me drunk, that has never happened before in my life" I replied.

"I hope you enjoyed it," said Henry, "that bash cost a pretty penny," he added. "You promised to take me to the scouts tonight" said Henry.

"Is that right" I answered vaguely, not really knowing what day it was, or not caring very much either. "We'll see," I said, not feeling up to much, which was the first time I felt like that in many a year.

When Archie came into work he told Henry and myself to scarper as the rest of the crew would manage the little workload until the end of the week. "See you both sharply on Monday first thing," said Archie, so we both cleared out, before Archie changed his mind.

"Just a moment you two", the gaffer shouted after us, and then he put a ten pound note in each of our hands. "That's for the silk screen job" he said, "so don't spend it all at once."

With a spring in our steps we headed off to Henrys gaff, where he promptly put his ten pounds into the hands of his mother. This gesture knocked me for six, and made me realise how good Henry was to his parents. It made me determined to share my own money with him, I felt it was the least I could do, as I was aware that our weekly pay would not be lifted until Monday. After a swim, which really sobered me up, I suggested to Henry he might like to come home with me before heading to the scouts later that same evening. He checked with his mum first who was having one of her better days and told Henry to go off and enjoy himself. After collecting the Bishop we set off for Osterley. At this point in time I still hadn't told Henry I lived in a working boy's hostel, and felt it might not be a bad idea to let him find out for himself, the better to gauge his true reactions I thought.

This time I drove up the drive, parking the bike to one side of the impressive front door entrance. "Don't worry," I said to Henry, "I only lodge here, but I think you will like the place."

Both Mr Bancroft and Kipling came out into the hallway to meet us, as we both climbed up the front door steps.

"Shouldn't you be at work?" asked Bancroft, as we both went into his office.

"It's OK" I replied, "We have been given a few days off".

"Lucky buggers" said Kipling.

"Oh Paul, a parcel arrived for you yesterday, from your aunt I presume" said Bancroft with a smile lighting up his face knowing it was my birthday.

We went up to my room where I opened my aunt's parcel to reveal a shiny black leather motorcycle jacket, my emotions ran high as I thought of the wonderful birthday I had enjoyed. Now a leather jacket I could wear! My badge, to commemorate my new found driving skills, I tried it on and it made me feel like a pilot receiving his wings with great pride!

"Wow! That looks good!" Henry said.

"It feels good" I replied "but I'll take it off for now and let's get back downstairs."

Bancroft and Kipling were still standing at the bottom of the stairs when we came down, and still on a high, I decided to introduce Henry properly. "This is one of my workmates, called Henry" I told them, in turn they both shook his hand keenly.

"Are you the lad that's joined the 5th Staines?" asked Alan Bancroft.

"That's right," said Henry with enthusiasm.

"I've heard very good reports about you both from Gina" said Alan.

"Oh before I forget" I said to Bancroft, "can you take my rent from this tenner, for this week and give Henry the fiver I owe him?"

"OK" said Alan, "you had better go down see Cookie to see what she can rustle you up for lunch, I'll join you in a short while" said Bancroft, "and I'll bring your change with me".

"You don't owe me any money," said Henry.

"Yes I do I'm sharing my tenner with you, that's the least I can do."

He opened his mouth to say more, but I put my hand over his gob, so he stayed gob smacked. He got on great with Cookie, but then so does everyone. We got stuck into some real home made soup and lashings of home made bread and butter. This was followed by cake and tea, as we both ate more than our fill.

Bancroft handed Henry a fiver, giving the rest of the change to me.

"Do you need a bed for the night?" Bancroft enquired from Henry, which took him off guard.

"I do, do, don't know" stuttered Henry, "do I?" asked Henry to no one in particular, but looking at me for guidance.

"Its up to you" I said, "if you think your mother can manage without you?" I said casually to Henry.

"Can we let you know later if he needs one?" I asked Bancroft.

"That's OK" he said, "but if you do find you are in need, I can put up a camp bed for Henry in your room" said Bancroft.

"That's dandy" I said, "we'll be sure to let you know if need be."

We both headed off to the sitting room, getting the place to ourselves as all the lodgers were still to come home from work.

"What is this place?" asked Henry, as if he needed assurance.

"It's a working boys hostel for those like my self who don't have any real parents" I answered,

"Oh!" exclaimed Henry at such a revelation, "but, but, what about your Aunt down in the New Forest?" he asked.

"Exactly" I replied "there's no work down there, at least not in my field of expertise, otherwise I would not have to work with you bunch of plonkers!"

He smiled more to himself, having gleaned even yet more information about me that he didn't know before. "You're a bit of a dark horse" observed Henry, "I didn't realize about this side of your life".

"There's no shame in being an orphan" I barked, then casually walked out of the room, in fear of breaking down completely, feeling just a little to vulnerable. I went to check the bike over for want of something better to do, and to help keep my mind occupied.

About an hour later, Henry came out to find me, with a mug of tea, which he handed to me, like some kind of peace offering.

After a suitable pause Henry picked up a duster and joined me in polishing up the wheels. "I'm sorry if you thought I was prying Paul, but I really didn't mean to."

"That's OK Henry, I can sometimes be over sensitive for my own good, then overreact in an attempt to hide my real feelings."

"I think you're a smashing kid and I know my own life is all the richer for knowing you and I don't mean money either!" said Henry quickly.

"I know you don't understand Henry, but I have very good reasons for not wanting too close a relationship, and its not got anything to do with you personally."

"Pleased to hear it" said Henry, looking rather perplexed.

"Just trust me Henry, I think you're a great lad also, and I like you very much, but lets take our friendship one step at a time OK?"

He looked at me long and hard not really understanding, but readily agreed anyway. "Shall we shoot off to Staines early, as I want to show you something at the town hall" I said. Now, Henry really was intrigued, so naturally he was anxious to set off. A quick word with Bancroft and once again we were on the Bishop and the open road.

We were soon parked outside Staines Town Hall, as Henry followed my eyes up to the Coat of Arms set above the huge arch top doorway. What do you think of the Coat of Arms, I asked Henry who studied it at some length then looked at me enquiringly. "One of my earlier works" I told Henry with some pride.

Henry gazed again above the doorway then looked me in the eye, saying, "Your pulling my dick again aren't you?"

"I wish you wouldn't use that expression, even though it doesn't mean anything remotely what it sounds like!" I retorted quickly.

"Its just a saying Paul, you don't need to be so touchy and get your knickers in a twist, real mates say it to each other all the time."

"I know," I said, going slightly red, for making such an issue out of it. After all I'd heard Henry say it often enough to our workmates who just smiled in reply, telling Henry to "Fuck Off! and pull your own dick!" But I haven't known Henry as long as the rest of our workmates and would feel very uncomfortable telling him to do likewise. The lanky bastard was standing by smiling raptures at my expense, before I realised he was just teasing.

"Did you really do that he asked?"

"Yes I did" I told him, it was my final piece for my Heraldry exam at Art College.

I could see Henry was really impressed but before he had chance to reply, I jumped astride my bike and drove off towards the bridge and down the towpath to the Scout hut. I sat down on the river bank gazing out towards the river, remembering this was one of Bobby's old haunts. Henry came up to me slapping me on the back, a little short of breath from running to catch up with me, as Gina came along on his own Triumph motorbike, earlier than usual. He gave us both a wave, as we ambled towards him while he was unlocking the door to the den.

"Why are you two earlier than usual?" asked Gina.

We explained our extra two days holiday to him.

"You will be available for the trip to Maidenhead then?"

"We plan to take the Gig upstream and sail her back on the return leg, providing we get a good wind" explained Gina.

"Camping overnight if you both fancy coming on the trip" he added, looking at the two of us.

"That sounds fantastic," said Henry to Gina.

"Have you done much rowing "I asked Henry, whose enthusiastic mouth I suspected, far out weighed his ability in the rowing stakes.

"Not a lot" confessed Henry, "but I'm a fast learner."

"This will be no picnic," I pointed out to him, "and it can also be dangerous in some stretches of the river, Thames which has claimed a good few lives."

"Its just as well I'm a good swimmer then," said Henry.

Cheeky bastard I thought but realised this was said more for Gina's ears than my own, but I will give Henry full marks for his keenness.

"Well" said Gina, "both of you would be most welcome as long as your prepared to make an early start, because rowing upstream to Maidenhead against a strong current is not only hard work but is also a long tiring day. Perhaps I could put you up overnight, or you could doss down here in the den?" said Gina.

"Down here in the den will be just fine" I told Gina, "at least it will save making a double run into London and back" I added with Henry shaking his head in agreement.

Later that evening Henry put a lot of effort over the obstacle course set up behind the hut, although at one point he fell off the rope bridge almost doing a real mischief to himself, which he played down for the benefit of the others. He assured me he was perfectly alright as he walked away with a slight but definite limp. We both went inside where I gave him and the others a map reading challenge, mainly for the benefit of some of the younger element who was about to sit their pathfinders badges.

Henry did his best to keep up but was obviously struggling a little. Long after the gang had all gone home, he could be found sitting in front of the fire place while I made a cuppa.

"What was Gina saying to you?" I asked Henry, "just before he went home."

Henry looked up with some bewilderment then replied, "he offered me a massage for my leg" said Henry speaking softly.

"So?" I looked at Henry with some consternation on my face, "So?" I repeated, "why didn't you take him up on his offer?"

"I don't know," replied Henry with uncertainty in his voice.

After a long deafening silence, I looked Henry square in the eye asking him "Do you think Gina is a Nonce?"

Henry went very red, very red indeed, and although he made no reply to my question, I could see he was most uncomfortable and was even sweating a little.

"Let me just say one thing Henry, I have known Gina since before I was twelve years old. For your info Gina was a Spitfire pilot during the Second World War, and their isn't anyone I would trust more in any kind of emergency! For fuck sake Henry he's given me a massage many a time before now, and he's a fucking natural! Does that make me a nonce also?"

Henry looked up at me fighting hard to stem the flow of tears that were on the very brink of pouring from the windows to his soul. He could see I was angry, nay I was furious as I put on my jacket, stormed out and kicked the Bishop into life.

Half an hour later, I returned with fish and chips safely tucked up into the bodice of my new leather jacket my aunt's birthday present and handed Henry his food, which he accepted in silence. I noted that Henry was lying down on what looked like a made up blanket bed for two. Without saying a word I moved into an easy chair and still sitting in silence got stuck into my fish and chips while still hot.

After washing and tidying away, I took my own sleeping bag from the cupboard, undressed and climbed into bed, to read a book.

"I hear you give a mean massage according to Gina," said Henry.

"That's right I do, but I'm not giving you one," I told Henry, who was stripping ready for bed.

He came across to me absolutely starkers, "why not?"

"You're not on!" I replied, looking at Henry in such a way, that he knew without question that he stood no chance whatsoever.

He looked at me awkwardly before lying on top of his blankets in a sullen state.

After a while I closed my book, got out of my pit and put the light out. I could see Henry in the light of the dying embers from the fire still lying on top of his made up blanket bed naked. I turned over with my back to him and without further ado went to sleep.

Early next morning, Henry woke me up to a hot mug of sweet tea, and I note he was now fully clothed. As he moved away I also noticed his limp was more pronounced. "How's the leg?" I asked him.

"A little better" he lied bravely.

"You're a lousy liar Henry, and if it's as bad as it looks, maybe you should stay behind, and have at least one day of rest."

The jovial Henry I knew disappeared, as he burst into tears, saying how sorry he was for thinking badly of Gina, and as he meant no real harm, and that he had no cause for evil suspicion either.

I got out of my pit and quickly put on my underpants, before going over to him. "I'm sorry Henry maybe I've overreacted again, let's have a look at this leg of yours?"

Henry slipped of his trousers, and was just about to take off his trunks, but I told him to keep them on. Both the back of his thighs showed a fair bit of bruising.

"OK Henry, you better lay face down with your legs apart, while I fetch some ointment from the first aid cupboard in the galley." (Kitchen)

Having found something suitable for the job I went back to find Henry had removed his trunks after all. I hesitated, but Henry interjected, "I removed my trunks because I didn't want to get any ointment on them" he said.

I kneeled down between his legs without saying a word, pummelling and flexing the muscles that so badly needed attention. Finishing of with more fluid and gentle strokes for a total of half hour or so, I slapped his bum telling him to roll over. He rolled over onto his back as I went to fetch a towel to cover his exposed mid drift, and gave the front of his legs a good workout as well. Having finished, I went to wash my hands and make us both some toast and a fresh mug of tea.

Meanwhile Henry had tidied everything away and seemed to be moving about more freely. "That was just great, thanks a lot Paul, I badly needed that."

"Even if you don't deserve it!" I told him. "Believe me, by the end of the day you will be feeling very sore and perhaps you should skip this trip up river today."

"Not on your Nelly", spat Henry in reply.

"OK Henry as you feel so strongly about this trip, perhaps you should find out the hard way for yourself!"

Steve, one of the senior scouts, along with Arthur Cox the assistant Scoutmaster came through the door followed by Gina, Brian and another group of three lads all rearing to get all the gear together in readiness for the big adventure up river. This was all before nine a clock in the morning and we were all bubbling with enthusiasm and anticipation.

"Right" said Gina to four of us, "let's get the gig from the boathouse and into the water, ready for loading!"

This beautiful craft was Gina's pride and joy and belonged to Gina personally and it was always treated with such reverence. Arthur Cox was put in charge of all provisions and sundry items of equipment to supervise the ferrying from hut to boat. I helped Gina in the boat, ensuring all gear was properly stowed and maintain the boat trim for balance and ease of handling, with well practised knowledge and previous experience from past events, everything was stowed ship shape and ready to take on the crew. A quick head count revealed a total of ten all told. Gina selected two crews of four each for rowing, with two spare. As Henry was an unknown quantity, he became one of the spares, but was warned he would still get his fair share of work to do. The crew of four would handle a pair of rowing blades each, and after half an hour or so would then be relieved by the second crew in waiting, sharing the same seat. This pattern of working was well established, as most of us were well experienced with this method.

The Gig was a skiff like craft with a very light wetted surface area below the waterline. An easily propelled craft normally, but with all this extra gear aboard, it required much more determined effort. Remembering we were also going upstream against a fair to strong current.

After three hours we had made good progress, so we pulled over to the river bank for some lunch. The two youngest were sent to find wood and build a fire, while we sorted out the rations to feed us all. The distance by river from our scout hut base to the upper reaches just beyond Maidenhead was approximately some nine miles. According to Gina we had already exceeded more than half way, with a good five nautical miles below our hull. Henry was given a tryout at rowing for the first half hour after lunch. Even Henry admitted it was much tougher than he thought, and couldn't quite understand why the rest of us made it look so much easier. He was eventually relieved and every one of us including Henry, breathed a long sigh of utter relief. The Gig however made better progress than all expected, and by four thirty pm, we were pulling into the bank to moor alongside a pleasant and very familiar meadow.

It was a warm sunny afternoon with a splashing of sunshine making us all sweat profusely. Four lads along with Arthur Cox were responsible for erecting a total of six tents one of which was the mess tent. Two lads were sent off to dig a latrine, with the appropriate shelter. Gina and I went foraging for wood aplenty to build a fire in readiness for the evening. Henry was asked to clean the Gig inside and out, so he got stripped to his trunks and got stuck in. When the campsite was laid out with expertise, someone suggested a swim in the camps favourite pool before the evening meal, might be in order for a job well done. It was a splendid late afternoon as we all cavorted about skinny dipping, just as God intended. Henry having finished his task satisfactorily, threw off his trunks to the wind then joined in the frolics and fun. Arthur Cox often designated himself as chief cook on these occasions, and very thankful we were, for his culinary masterly of campsite cuisine. It was Gina who spotted Henry who was limping once again, and who also suggested that he gets me to give him a total massage at bedtime. This rather put me on the spot, not easily being able to refuse. Henry did make some amends to the previous evening's slander of Gina, by telling

Gina, that if I wasn't able to give him a body rub, perhaps he could call on Gina's services.

We all sat around the camp fire joking and singing till late, as one by one we felt the need to turn in for the night. Once inside our tent we prepared for bed in our usual fashion, when Henry asked me if I would give him a massage. In spite of the late hour and my tiredness I agreed, if somewhat reluctantly. I sprawled astride his back manipulating his shoulders, spine and lower back, then parting his legs wide, I set to work on all his leg muscles from his groins down his thighs and lower calf's to his ankles and then the very soles of his feet, remembering Bobby's expertise in this field. I lay down beside him to take a breather when Henry rolled over onto his back. His front received the same treatment giving my all. We lay there together naked side by side, cooling off after so much exertion. I warned Henry to keep his muscles warm, so he climbed back into his sleeping bag chatting away while I was still waiting to bring my body temperature down. He purred with joy having just received his very first full massage and soon drifted off to sleep.

Sunday morning broke into a fine sunny day, so I went off for a quick solo swim. On returning I stopped to talk to Arthur, who was expertly coaxing the previous night's fire back into life. A billy can of water soon came to a rapid boil as he made plenty of tea. I took a can to Henry on impulse only to discover I had walked in on him while he was busy masturbating himself off, so with tactful discretion I left his tea just inside the doorway and beat a hasty retreat. I went back to the fire to warm myself up by pouring myself a another cup of tea.

Later that morning as we started to fold up the tent in readiness for the return trip, Henry made several attempts to talk to me about the 'incident'. Later I told Henry "It's me that's embarrassed for walking in on you without thinking. You have nothing to be ashamed of, as we all wank ourselves off when the need dictates, so why should you be the exception to the rule?" I asked.

He smiled at the grasp of my understanding, thanking me for taking it so well.

"If you had been brought up in an orphanage with 500 boys and just as many girls, you would understand my liberal attitude, I've seen it all before" I told him.

Henry looked at me with surprise plastered all over his boat race, (face,) which in itself was a rare sight to behold. When he did find his voice Henry spluttered over this sudden font of knowledge I had just imparted to him.

"I knew you were an orphan I just didn't think" as he cut short his sentence.

"Where else would orphans be expected to live?" I answered.

Henry remained silent.

Once we got underway going with the current, a fair wind came up from the South, so we set sails to both short masts and the river quickly meandered under our bow, swiftly leaving a good wake astern. The return passage took less than three hours down river, as we were all lulled into a sense of enchantment at the tranquillity and wonder of Mother Nature. It was truly a memorable sail, idealistic in every respect that left it's mark on all of us. Once everything was stowed away in it's proper place, we said our thankful farewells to Gina and the rest of the gang, then we both climbed aboard the bishop for London, I spent that night at Henrys gaff and he was delighted that all was well with his parents. Henry spent many a week, talking longingly about that weekend, as it had obviously left a lasting impression on a Cockney's heart and soul. Somehow both Henry and myself had entered a kind of meeting of the minds. This was not done by intentions or by design on either of our part. This meaningful relationship we both enjoyed between us was a sensitive experience, with some restraints imposed by me, due mainly I felt, because of my own personal background at Ashford. With Henry on the other hand, what you saw is what you got with undiluted honesty.

Chapter Six

"All good things come to an end," Bobby whispered

Several weeks after the river trip to Maidenhead, memories still lingered on. Both Henry and myself were getting ready for Tuesday scouts, when Archie came into the shower room looking very glum indeed and stood in the doorway. "What's wrong Archie?" shouted Henry across the steam filled room, "not got a home to go to? `As the old woman thrown you out then?" he joked in his usual jovial fashion.

"Turn off the showers" Archie shouted at the top of his voice, rinsing the smile off Henries boat race.

The sudden silence, without the sound of running water, filled this empty sounding cavity with impending doom! The gaffer stood in the doorway with a look that made him seem unbelievably old and dejected. In just a matter of seconds, the atmosphere within the room had changed dramatically, to one of strong sombre undertones. Archie looked up, doing his utmost to fight back a tear clearly visible in his eye, the two of us just stood there, stark naked, water dripping from our bodies like raindrops falling into freshly made puddles.

Looking at Henry solemnly he blurted out "your mother has just passed on" and unable to hold back the floodgates any longer, he burst into tears. I stood stunned, then looked at Henry, it was like watching a film in slow motion as he collapsed in a pile upon the hard tiled floor. I quickly picked up his limp body as Archie came forward towards us with an open bath towel. Between the two of us we carried Henry to the staff room, desperately trying to bring him round from his faint.

Archie went for another towel and between us dried Henry as best we could. Archie lit the gas fire while I struggled to put trousers onto Henry's damp shivering body. In desperation and in an attempt to revive him, I smacked Henry's face several times, to bring him back into the real world. He slowly opened his eyes, looking at me in disbelief, doing his utmost to keep from crying. I dried Henry's upper torso before slipping a shirt and then a pullover over his head.

"Stand up a second Henry" I ordered.

This he did still in a trance like state, I then tucked his shirt tail ends into the waistband of his trousers and buttoned him up. He stared into space obviously suffering from shock. Archie asked, "Will I put the kettle on to make him a mug of tea.

"Very sweet" I said as I continued to finish dressing Henry.

"Don't you think you should get dressed yourself?" Archie asked, pointing at my naked body I had momentarily forgotten I was still naked. "Here" he added handing me a mug "see if he will drink some hot sweet tea."

I wrapped Henry's two hands around the body of the mug, but he just let it rest on the chair arm making no attempt to drink.

Archie lit up a cigarette and without thinking he proffered me one, I accepted willingly, and lit it from the same match, I drew hard on the tip inhaling the false comfort it gave me. Again I tried Henry's mug to his lips, thankfully he took a sip, followed by another, before taking hold of the mug in both hands. As an afterthought, I asked Archie how Henry's gran was handling all of this trauma.

"The neighbours are looking after her but she is in a bad way gone into her shell like" he whispered.

Henry just sat there looking into space, this seemed to concern Archie more than it did me.

"Henry" I said loudly, "come on mate get a grip!!"

"I'm not dead yet" said Henry softly, with a calm air of acceptance, or was he putting on a brave face for our benefit? I wondered. Bending down to extinguish the gas fire

Archie said to the two of us, "come on out side, let's get him into my car, I'll run you both home."

Suddenly Henry raised his voice loudly and looking at Archie pronounced very firmly "no you won't, Paul will walk me home, won't you Paul?" he turned looking at me in such a pathetic state.

"You've got it," I confirmed as I lifted Henry to his feet and put my arms about him.

"OK" Archie said, "I'll walk you both down the street, and Paul" he whispered in my ear.

"Whatever happens you stay with him no matter what!" I nodded as we all walked towards Henry's two up two down terraced home.

We got Henry into the sitting room and at once put the fire on for some heat, there was a distinct chill about the place.

"Archie you go home as I'm ok and besides, Paul will take good care of me, won't you Paul?" Henry pleaded seeking confirmation, as he looked at me with begging eyes.

"I certainly will" I replied giving Henry an affectionate hug for reassurance. "He'll be just fine," I added giving Archie a knowing wink.

"OK I'll stop by in the morning to see the lie of the land, take care of him" Archie said, and once again gave me a pat on the shoulder.

"I'll see you to the door Archie" I said with a false lightness in my voice.

"Watch him very carefully or he'll go to pieces long before morning" Archie warned in a hushed voice.

"I'll watch him you can be sure of that" I whispered in reply as Archie disappeared from view.

As I came back into the room Henry looked up like the lost soul he was "Is it cold in here, or is it just me? He asked.

Thinking this will be the shock I asked "Do you want me to turn up the fire to full?"

Henry's reply was a muted "No I just want my bed."

"Come on then mate," I said, "let's get you tucked up into your bed."

We helped each other up the narrow stairs funny I thought, I never realised how narrow the stairs were until now when the two of us have to go up them together.

Sitting on the edge of his bed wondering what he was doing there, he repeatedly went back into a trance like state. I stood there watching him, but he made no attempt to move or undress himself. I undid his shoe laces, removed his shoe's and socks, but he continued to just sit there in a world of his own withdrawn from reality and full of shock.

"Can you manage to undress yourself and get into bed, while I go down and make us another mug of tea?" I asked softly.

Henry responded by nodding his head, so I dashed downstairs and made tea and jam sandwiches, as jam was all he had!

I went back up bearing a tray to find Henry still sitting on the side of his bed, just as I had left him, I put the tray down on my own bed then went over to Henry and gently pushed him onto his back so I could slip down the trousers over legs and ankles, leaving his top on. I stood him up for a few moments supporting him in my arms while I folded back the bed clothes. I then helped him into bed, sitting him up with a pillow wedged between the wooden headboard and his back.

"You won't leave me will you Paul?" He suddenly pleaded, gripping the sleeve of my new leather jacket in a vice like grip.

"I didn't know we were married?" I jibed, his blank expression made it quite clear my attempt at humour was meaningless as he was on another planet at present. I handed him a jam butty and a mug of hot sweet tea.

Henry put the sandwich down on his bed but started to drink the tea, which was some kind of progress I thought. Having finished his tea he put the empty mug down beside the untouched sandwich. "Don't you want your sandwich?" I asked him.

"You won't leave me?" Henry blurted out again looking for further reassurance.

"I will if you don't eat your sandwich" I joked.

At that Henry broke down completely, sobbing uncontrollably. I took him into my arms and assured him "I am only jesting and have no intentions of deserting you."

Henry continued to sob with no signs of abatement as I held him close to my chest I decided it would be more beneficial just to let him cry, and let it all out so to speak. We sat on the bed with Henry clinging on to me for dear life. I don't know how long for, but each time I made the slightest attempt to stand up or move he gripped me even tighter.

"Listen Henry" I said to him during one of his sobbing lulls, "I want to get ready for bed my self, but I need to tidy everything away downstairs first, will you be alright for a few moments while I'm downstairs?"

At this point Henry sobbed "Ok, but please don't be long Paul."

"I'll be as quick as I can" I assured him, as he reluctantly released me.

When I returned upstairs I undressed to get onto my own bed, having turned the light off first, only to discover Henry was already in my bed! I hesitated but as he was now silent, I thought what the heck, so climbed in beside him. Henry snuggled tightly into my back for warmth and mental comfort, putting his arm around my chest and holding me close into his own body. Within minutes he fell soundly off to sleep but without releasing his tight grip on my chest. I eventually fell over to sleep myself until early morning when I awoke desperately needing a piss, I released Henry's grip, breaking his sleep pattern and in a sleepy voice he asked me "where are you going?"

Putting on my underpants I said gently "I won't be long," and dashed off downstairs, returning with two mugs of very hot tea.

We sat alongside each other drinking tea together in silence. "I wonder how my gran is" he remarked suddenly, staring blankly at the opposite wall.

"Once we have drunk our tea we'll get dressed and while I make us some breakfast you can pop in next door to find out" I replied looking at my wristwatch.

"Yes perhaps I should," he said but without any conviction in his voice "I mustn't be late for work" Henry said, looking at the time again."

"I don't think Archie is expecting you in today," I said casually.

"No I must go to work!" he insisted.

"You know best," I muttered, not wanting to upset him, "as long as you go and see your gran first" I emphasized.

With that Henry jumped out of bed and got dressed. Having finished my tea I joined him. As we reached the bottom of the stairs together, he went out the front door, I turned and went into the kitchen to see what I could rustle up for a bite to eat. Ten minutes later he rejoined me for breakfast, which consisted of a few slices of toast and a mug of tea. He ignored the toast but started to drink his tea, I eyed him sideways to gauge his mood and reactions.

"How's your gran?" I asked Henry.

"She's fine, come on Paul, let's go round the café before working time" he said standing up to leave, as if in a hurry.

I managed to catch up with him just outside the front door as he lengthened his stride with a burst of speed. I followed him down the neighbourhood street in silence, not knowing what to say to him. We then sat down in a typical fifty's style café, locally known as the 'greasy spoon'.

"So your gran is ok?" I enquired.

"I said so didn't I?" barked Henry in a rather disgruntled manner.

He ordered a number twelve from the menu, which was the full English breakfast, so I did likewise. Halfway through our breakfast, which I was really beginning to enjoy, Henry slammed a florin coin onto the table top, got up and said "come on Paul I mustn't be late for work."

I looked at Henry in utter astonishment, he was still lingering close by waiting for me to obey his barked order. "Sit down you selfish bastard! At least let me finish my breakfast first," I yelled at him.

He sat down instantly, looking at me his face full of hurt as if I had just slapped him hard. We both remained silent as I continued to finish off my meal, but I could see he was on the verge of loosing it. He was determined to go into work, almost afraid of being left alone to face what was left of his shattered life. It was more than that, as I was to learn later from Archie who knew him like a father knows his own son. That same week Henry's gran died of a broken heart, having lost her daughter.

The following week was one of my worst ever, as Henry clung to me like a baby feeding at a mothers breast. The weeks ticked by, and with Henry having a lot of support from workmates, he slowly picked up the pieces of his changed life, forming them into some semblance of the steady life he once had. I thought by and large he handled this terrible chapter of his life remarkably well, but the real depth of mental scaring he kept hidden from all his workmates, including myself.

Once Henry had made some very difficult adjustments to his life, he returned to scouting and other outdoor activities with a vengeance, the hunger for company being very strong. For several months we became inseparable, and slowly, very slowly, I was able to wean him off his dependency on my constant attention. Our friendship grew stronger, as did our total trust in each other, sharing the secrets of our innermost thoughts. Archie on more than one occasion told me I wouldn't always be around to pick up the pieces, I often wondered what he meant by this remark. Or did Archie know something that I was yet to become aware of?

For a good four months we spent two nights a week and almost every weekend at the scouts, in each other's company. More and more on Tuesday and Thursday nights Henry would sleep on a camp bed in my room at St Christopher's. He just hated to go back to an empty house even though it was his own home. We spent most of our weekends camping climbing sailing or swimming. One weekend I even persuaded him to go Pot Holing along with me, Arthur Cox,and some of the gang. It wasn't his bag as he said and found it very scary. Between us we amassed enough camping and climbing gear, all that camping in a self-sufficient manner required including a new lightweight tent with all the paraphernalia. I even invited Henry down to St Christopher's gala day, an annual event where all four working boy's hostels got together to share this rather special occasion. It just so happened that this year it was the turn of Osterley house to organise the event and an extra large marquee was set up on the spacious front lawn in readiness for the big day. Weeks before this event, I was pressed into service by Alan Bancroft to produce an artistic piece of work to present to our patron Princess Marina. It was decided by that an oil painted portrait of the Princess resplendent in all her royal regalia, would be a most suitable offering. I worked like an artist possessed, until I was anywhere near satisfied with the results. With only days to spare for the portrait to dry properly, it was left in Bancroft's charge under wraps ready for the presentation. It was one of those calendar events that the media always attended, so I prayed my efforts were deemed good enough, to fit such an auspicious occasion.

The big day arrived with everyone over excited, making it a far bigger deal than was necessary. Thankfully it was held on a Saturday, so come early evening Henry was easily persuaded to escape with me for an overnight camp upstream from the scout hut. We spent most of the Sunday sailing by arrangement with Gina, before we returned to Henry's gaff, we also had a good swim that evening before bedtime. I took Henry down to the New Forrest several weekends later for a more tranquil weekend, where my aunt as always, spoilt us rotten, and where we could completely unwind from the burdens of working life. We often shared a hot bath together, frolicking around like a pair of five year olds, with no sexual connotations or inhibitions between us. There had been very few occasions in my life so far, where this kind of utter trust and mutual understanding was so rare, and to which I felt comfortable with. I counted myself very lucky indeed, as I never dreamed that after loosing my brother Bobby, would I ever experience the like ever again. Unlike the ESP, that I shared with bobby, and along with the intimacy I could never share with anyone else, the relationship I shared with Henry never the less was rather special. Henry became very protective towards me, as many of our workmates were quick to point out. Needless to say, the one failing he shared with my Bobby was that Henry was a randy bastard especially with girls usually much younger than himself. His idea of a one night stand must have lasted all of one hour, and the girls were lucky to get him or so he thought! He had spent all his life dominated by a woman, either his mother or his gran, and although he was very fond of the whole female species, and some might say excessively so, he was determined to play the loose bachelor game for all it was worth!

In a long intimate conversation I remember Henry telling me he had no desire whatsoever to get hitched and I knew he meant every word. Perhaps being an only child, smothered by two females all his life so far, the selfish streak in all of us was more predominant in him, a condition due to his upbringing perhaps? With afterthought I suppose we were a right pair of Cockney sparrows, and as any true Londoner in the fifty's would tell you , no one ever in this era at least referred to his dick as his cock, which had an entirely different meaning. As Archie once told me in confidence, Henry had been a very changed lad these past months, and in spite of all the tragedy in his life he is altogether a more rounded and more sensitive soul, with a great deal more understanding towards others. I could tell Archie was extremely fond of Henry, and he always spoke very highly of him, except on the rare occasions when he would lose his head and give Henry a right bollocking if he deserved it, but there were occasions when we all came in for some of Archie's thunder. I liked Archie's down to earth philosophy in life, which made it easy for all of us to know exactly where we stood with him. He was an honest hard working man, a very rare commodity in today's society. I suppose the main difference between Henry and myself, was Henry thought he was Gods gift to woman, where I was more of a mans man. Not surprisingly I suppose, when you stop to consider that Henry was brought up in a female dominated household whereby all my life so far, I had been very much dominated by an all male experience.

One day there was an incident at work, when Henry passed some remark by which I took particular offence, I ended up in a fit of rage giving Henry a bloody good slap. He ran out of the workshop, very upset and I wouldn't talk to him for days. Terry, unfortunately made a snide remark about a lovers tiff between Henry and myself, and as I flew into yet another rage which by good fortune Terry saw coming, he disappeared like greased lightning, and made a point of staying out of my way for the rest of the week. He had to eat a large slice of humble pie, and make amends towards me, I learned later it was due to the threat of being sacked by the gaffer. I always was to sensitive for my own good, but I was young, with a lot to learn about life. Henry skipped scouts that Tuesday night, so I adopted an attitude of not caring less, as I was determined to teach him a lesson. Taking a shower on my own, thinking that Henry was unable to face me, he promptly proved me wrong by slipping into the shower room and before I realised it, he was standing under the shower next to me. There was an awkward silence between us and not being able to contain himself any longer, he stepped up towards me asking for forgiveness, then threw both his arms around me. Feeling very embarrassed I pushed him off me, fully aware that should anyone happen to look in, seeing us both naked and in a wet embrace, both our reputations would quickly disappear, like the soapy water down the drain in the middle of the shower room floor. His embrace along with the apology were both genuine, and there was I, showing signs of rejection to the one person I was closest to. "I'm sorry to" I told him with real feeling as I fought hard to keep the waterworks from getting the better of me. "Come on mate, let's head off on the Bishop to Staines" I uttered.

Their was no mistaking the pure delight on Henry's dial with a grin across his boat race that easily went from ear to ear. Once we were dressed I gave him one hell of a hug, not caring who saw us, now that we were fully clothed. Like real friends should be able to do we yelled with exhilaration as we sped off on the Bishop, without a care in the world the wind through our hair also contorting our silly mugs out of shape. I didn't need any persuading by Henry to go back to his place after scouts. The real love and friendship we had for each other couldn't be stronger, especially now that Henry understood my sensitivity, and the tendency to overreact, on my part.

My second year at Lime grove was even happier than the first, if that was possible, but I began to get an impending feeling that some thing was bound to upset the balance of this heavenly bliss. I started to get a kind of E.S.P. a feeling that used to disturb my equilibrium when Bobby was on the scene. It wasn't possible he could reach out from the grave, could he? I thought, especially as he was buried in Korea, where he fell fatally wounded. Even I was sceptical enough, not to believe in ghosts, or was I? "All good things must come to an end" as bobby repeatedly mentioned.

This nagging line from some forgotten poet was interfering with my head, and was almost persistent enough to make me scream. I convinced myself with a little help from Henry, that I was just being silly, so eventually I tucked it away, out of sight, in the far recesses and shadows of my feeble brain.

Things more or less returned to some kind of normality, as Henry and I discussed the forthcoming Christmas of 1953. That same week in late November, Mr Bancroft St Christopher's warden, handed me a letter. Not just any letter mind you, this brown envelope looked mighty official. Income tax I thought, shoving it into my rear pocket, promptly putting it out of my mind, at least until later. Late this Monday night after a shower in readiness for bed, I took myself upstairs into the privacy of my own single bedroom, which over my long stay at St Christopher's in Osterley road, the walls, I had festooned with colour pictures of some of the most famous rock faces and mountain scenery from around the world. Having undressed to the buff as was my want, I was hanging up my trousers on a hanger, when this ugly brown envelope I had forgotten about, fell to the floor. I got into bed with every intention of reading a good mountaineering book (what else?), but decided to read my mail first, you never know I told myself, maybe it's a tax rebate which I surely deserve! I opened it and looked at the official letter within, reading it several times over, trying to grasp it's full meaning. It was an order, as far as I could make out, to report to some Army recruitment office in Acton, London, to report for my NATIONAL SERVICE. I sat staring at this notification refusing to believe, "I WAS BEING CALLED UP FOR NATIONAL SERVICE"! The thought of doing two years of regimental square bashing, did not make for happy bedtime reading! "Bloody cheeky bastards!" I swore out loud, how dare they have the nerve to call on me, and disturb my only real chance of happiness. Wasn't thirteen years of hell at Ashford residential home enough? More than enough to give to my Queen and Country!

In my irrational state, and with highly charged emotions coursing through my veins, I was at this precise moment ready to KILL! I charged down the stairs to confront Bancroft the nearest official I could lay my hands on. I barged into his office, throwing open the door, ready to do anyone in my path a mischief. Bancroft looked up from his writing, and with the only light in the room coming from the desk lamp, I must have been a very unusual sight indeed, as in my haste, I had forgotten my nudity and my dick was swinging about with the gyrations of my body movement. Bancroft, burst into a spontaneous burst of laughter, and pointed at me in an attempt to make me realise just how ridiculous I looked from his side of the desk!

Ignoring his bait I threw the letter onto the desk at him, he casually picked it up, at the same time asking me politely to take a pew. Having taken the sting from my tail I began to feel a right prize prick! As Bancroft quietly perused the letter in front of him, I sat there feeling more and more of a jerk with each second that passed. "Tell you what Paul, you go upstairs and get into bed, I'll come up directly to you and explain exactly what this means".

Feeling a right Pratt, I casually walked across the office floor to the opened doorway, with all the sophistication and an air of nonchalance that an alley cat could muster, before scooting up the stairs in disgrace. Bancroft kept his word, by spelling out all my options.

"You could become a conscientious objector," he said with tongue in cheek. "You could leave the Country and go abroad, or you might even fail the medical," he observed, encouragingly.

"What if I get myself a criminal record?" I suggested to Bancroft.

"No! No! that would make you even more qualified than you are right now!" he replied in a serious tone.

Was he pulling my ding dong and taking the piss? I thought. "Just leave it until next Monday, go by and have a word with them at Acton" said Bancroft "after all there's no point in worrying yourself until you have all the facts" he added without conviction.

I spent most of the night tossing and turning, thinking up the most fantastic excuses and reasons to stop me from going into the army. With having spent so much of my life in a repressive regime, thirteen years all told, to get my freedom on being thrown out of Ashford on my sixteenth birthday, and now face another military discipline, it gave me good cause to feel very depressed! More than a year had gone by since I walked through the Ashford gates with so much uncertainty ahead of me. Unbelievably, I had achieved all my aims by finding a place to live, and one where I was very contented. I had also landed the job of my dreams, and having come through the Second World War as an orphaned child, I was happy, no, that's not quite true, I was very happy, in fact I was ecstatic! My friendship with Henry and the excellent relationships with all of my other work mates gave great definition and purpose to my life. The thought all of this could end suddenly and come to an abrupt end, filled me with horror and foreboding.

This last night of turmoil filled me with negative vibes, and I seriously thought over many alternatives to avoid any possibility of going into the armed services.The very thought of being forced into another dictatorship, like the one at Ashford was abhorrent, especially as I felt my country had raped me once already! It robbed me of my childhood and had taken so much from me already! Now 'They' wanted once again to remove me from my new found family, to do with me as they wished, under the guise of serving my Queen and Country.

"Well, you're not on!" I shouted as I woke up suddenly in a sweat. "Life is so unfair" I concluded.

Chapter Seven

"Your Queen and country needs you" (as the poster said)

What a load of crap, I thought, as I kicked the Bishop into life then roared into work that morning full of nervous anticipation.

"What's wrong with you Paul, You have a face like a smacked bum?" Henry asked on seeing me at the gate.

"I'm in no mood for your banter," I told him and he unlocked the gates without another word.

Henry knew from experience that this was not a good time to ask any probing questions. Far better for me to tell him in my own good time and given just a little space, he knew I would. Our closeness and friendship was built on well founded principals, but he knew there were times when I still needed my own space, along with my own thoughts. He busied himself with his early morning routine; I fought my emotions and desperately tried to keep my composure as he filled the kettle with water; I pretended to watch him with interest, trying to occupy my mind. I thought of how I would miss this lovable jerk. Several times while we sat drinking our first cup of the day, Henry gave me the odd look anticipating an answer.

"I'm staying at your place tonight" I heard myself saying without thinking.

"You've got it" he replied with an inquisitive look still on his face.

Just then Archie came in to the room so I turned to Henry muttering "I'll tell you tonight OK?"

He replied "OK Paul" with an even more puzzled look written all over his face. Henry turned to hand Archie his tea and I glanced at the gaffer in a manner that he new instinctively meant I needed to see him on a personal basis. I was ushered into the office for a chin wag, and produced the offensive letter, a copy of a specimen Archie had seen many times, he showed no real surprise as I handed it to him to read.

Having seen this form of letter and understanding the contents of the official jargon better than I could, he knew exactly how I felt and putting on a concerned face, he just looked at me with caring eyes, but speechless never the less. Archie had himself been in the Armed services, and in fact, was one of the few among his mates, who returned unscathed from active service in the recently ended Second World War. He also knew about my background at Ashford and therefore had a good idea of what I must be feeling regarding institutions. He had seen me blossom in the workplace and was more than satisfied with all my work. He was especially pleased at the growing relationship I had formed with Henry. On eventually finding his voice his first question was, "have you said anything to Henry yet about the letter?"

"Not yet, but I'm planning to break it to him tonight after work" I uttered.

"Well be very gentle with him when you do, as I'm concerned it could trigger off" he paused, "lets just say a reaction, he's vulnerable at present" he added.

"Why? It's me that's got the fucking call up papers!" I blurted.

Archie looked at me in surprise and after a short pause and with a softer tone in his voice answered "I don't think you realise just how much that lad loves you."

Altering the tone of my voice in response I softly asked "I thought I was supposed to be the lad here?"

"Only in age son, only in age" he repeated.

"I think you had better go along to Acton this morning" Archie responded, with a sympathetic expression all over his face. "Would you like me to come with you"? He offered.

I thought for several minutes before giving him an answer, "no thanks Archie I think I would sooner go alone."

As Archie looked at me with genuine concern in his eyes he uttered, "let me know how you got on when you return."

I answered "If I return."

I left the studio and made my way to Acton, as I entered the recruiting office apprehensively a Corporal looking up from behind his desk politely asked, "Yes Sir can I help you?"

Without opening my mouth in reply I handed him the letter, he glanced at it and in a distinct change of voice barked "Right Sonny Jim take a seat over there" and pointed in the direction I should take.

My name is Paul I thought, but his change of attitude along with the new tone of voice, made discretion a better option than valour so I decided to keep my mouth shut. As I sat down the corporal left the office taking my letter with him to some inner sanctum. After a few minutes he returned with the recruiting sergeant, who came over to speak with me before asking me to follow him into his office. Once inside the office he looked at my name on the letter head again, and asked me to certify the correct pronunciation of my surname Ankorne. "Right, Paul isn't it?" I only nodded in reply.

"Ah yes" he suddenly seemed to remember something said to him on the phone earlier that morning, "You work for a good friend of mine at Lime Grove Studios, Archie, don't you?"

It wasn't a question it was more of a confirmation. It transpired that Archie knew this sergeant well, as they had served together during the recent war. "From what Archie tells me, you should be ideal fodder for the army, Paul," he added.

Already, I was beginning to dislike this sergeant, sitting at the other side of the desk that conveniently separated us both. "Fodder" I reminded myself, is what they feed horses, whereby this jerk was trying to bullshit me. Perhaps he could read the disapproval written on my face, because he immediately changed tack completely, enquiring, "Tell me Paul, have you ever thought of going abroad to make something of yourself?"

"Only recently sergeant" I replied, not disclosing the option of doing a runner from this lot!

"Well Paul, if you sign on for an extra twelve months, I can guarantee you'll go abroad."

I looked at him convinced he was pulling my dick, but curiosity got the better of me and I enquired, "Really, and how does that work exactly?"

Now he had my full attention, the sergeant went on to paint a glorious picture of army life. He explained things in great length and ended by concluding that no idiot in their right mind would do two years of square bashing, and all the bullshit that goes with it, when, if prepared to sign on for an extra years stint, they could be sunbathing on an exotic beach in the tropical sun. The sergeant certainly made it sound very attractive and being a professional con artist the seduction of my soul was now a fact!

Within fifteen minutes of being in his office he had suckered me into signing on for three years active service instead of two, and as a bonus I would be assigned to a crack regiment called the Rifle Brigade, or Green Jackets as they were also known. Plus, and this was a big plus the sergeant emphasized I wouldn't need to report to the R.B.'s depot at Winchester until early May of next year 1954, just after my eighteenth birthday! Now that I had signed up, selling my soul for the Queens shilling, I was enslaved for three years instead of two. "Come along with me now Paul," said the seductive sergeant "and let the doctor have a quick look at you while you are here."

I suddenly found myself in a large room, sitting with about a dozen blokes stark bullock naked, their clothes folded neatly in front of them upon the floor. Another sergeant took over enabling the first recruiting sergeant to return to his office and no doubt, give some other poor unsuspecting sucker the same bullshit he fed to me. I was instructed to strip off to the buff, aware the others were just as much strangers to me as I was to them. We sat about for half an hour during which another four victims were added to our merry throng. A spotty young delinquent entered fresh out of medical college, was wearing a stethoscope like a badge of honour around his neck, he also had National Health Service glasses covering his face in a vain effort to hide the spots. We were ordered to line up in Indian file fashion, and pass before this spotty faced gitt, who was not only as nervous as myself, but was just out of short trousers as long as I was. Maybe this was some form of preliminary medical I thought, and a second full one would be given on arrival at Winchester, so I had my doubts, as to this git's qualifications.

In no time at all I was standing in front of pimple face, who then unceremoniously grabbed a hold of my balls and told me to cough, I had no sooner done so, than he shouted next, allowing me to return to my bundle of clothes and get dressed. "Is that it then"? I whispered to the guy with a big dick, who was next to me, as he had also started to get dressed.

"That's it" he replied. Fucking hell I thought, a medical lasting all of five seconds. No wonder the army is full of fucking criminals, misfits and reprobates!

"Listen up," shouted the drill sergeant, "you will all be notified when and where to report to in due course and anyone failing to do so will be court marshalled and shot."

Well I thought, at least this sergeant had a sense of humour! I didn't waste any time in reporting back to Archie, who after much debate assured me I was doing the right thing and was prepared to bet I would enjoy myself after basic training, which for me would be a piece of cake he added, making me think, did I look that robotic?

After a rather long chat with Archie, I felt completely different compared to less than twenty four hours before, don't misunderstand me I still wasn't keen on going in or being called up for National Service in the first place but at least this way I'd be getting away from playing toy soldiers with all the spit and polish in some Godforsaken barracks here in England. The chance to travel was the real carrot for me, and looking back with hindsight it proved to be correct, however I digress. Henry took me for tea that night, as I still wondered why I had invited myself to stay overnight at his gaff.

I could tell he was itching to know what was going on, and I was just as keen to tell him, but I realized I had to pick the right moment carefully and to break my dramatic news to him gently. I took him into the snug bar they had used for throwing my seventeenth birthday surprise, hoping after one or two drinks, I could pick my moment. I got him a pint of his favourite Pale Ale, while I stuck to cider, but just the one mind you, remembering what happened the last time I had entered this place! I could hardly forget ending up smashed out of my head, could I?

Henry was smiling across the table at me full of anticipation, so I told him everything about the farce of that so called medical, which soon had him in stitches. He was putting on a very brave front; I thought when suddenly he got very serious himself by leaning across the table and lowering his voice to an audible whisper said, "I need your advice, but I'll tell you once we get home."

"Is it a girl?" I enquired.

"No nothing like that" he replied.

"Have you got VD then?" I joked, as he went bright red and clamped up completely.

As we left the pub I could see he was troubled, but I was still none the wiser as to why. Henry went through to the kitchen to make us both a mug of tea, so I followed with the idea of coaxing him into spilling the beans.

"Its not VD, I'm sure of that, but there is something wrong with one of my balls" he told me eventually.

I looked at him astonished by his frankness, but he then went into the bathroom and started to run a bath, he returned and while waiting for the bath to fill we continued to drink our tea.

"Will you come into the bathroom when I give you a shout," he asked in an earnest tone of voice.

"Yes, I suppose so, as long as you don't expect me to give you a wank or something," I said in jest.

He looked at me and smiled, knowing I was only pulling his plonker, then said, "It's nothing like that, but you will see for yourself when I call you through."

I wondered what this piece of drama was going to result in and I must admit I was now intrigued, as well as nervous. If this plonker is pulling my dick I'll kill him I thought as I drew on my cigarette waiting to be summoned.

"OK Paul," he shouted.

"Just a moment," I shouted back wanting to finish my fag and trying to play it cool.

I knocked on the door and pushed it wide open half expecting a bucket of water to come cascading down on my head, but no, all was as it should be with Henry lying full length in the bath. "Look at my dick" he said.

To me it just looked normal, normal for Henry that is, as he was blessed with a far bigger one than average. "What am I supposed to be looking for?" I asked.

"Can't you see it?" he replied.

"I can fucking see it but see what?" I asked getting impatient.

Henry lifted up his penis and laid the floppy appendage on his stomach, now I could see what he was going on about, as one of his balls was swollen almost to the size of a small apple, and the other the size of a plumb or of normal size in his case!

"Fucking Hell Henry when did you do that"? I swore.

"I didn't that's the point, it just appeared" he replied.

"When did you first notice it I asked?"

"I'm not sure but maybe a couple of months ago," he answered.

"What? Why the hell did you leave it so long?" I shouted.

"Well I didn't want to talk about my dick, you don't do you?" he asked.

"Why the hell not? It's never prevented you from bragging about the size of it before," I said rather unfairly.

At this point Henry was about to break into tears as my unjustified and cutting remarks were well out of order. "I'm sorry mate I didn't mean that snide remark, why don't you finish your bath and I'll take a better look when you get upstairs."

"OK, thanks Paul" he said in a soft voice.

I went back into the sitting room for another smoke as I needed to collect my thoughts and compose myself. After a while Henry came out of the bathroom with a knotted towel around his waist and headed upstairs, a few moments later he shouted "I'm ready Paul."

So I then made my way up and found him lying on the bed stretched out on top of the towel. I sat down beside him and looked at him as he stared back full of apprehension. "Is it sore to the touch?" I asked.

"Not really, but it does feel funny" came the reply.

What kind of an answer is that supposed to be I thought to myself, but instead of sharing my thoughts with him I just enquired "Do you mind if I touch it?"

"Help yourself" he said, so I did just that and lifting his dick out of the way and placing it on his lower abdomen I cupped my hand very gently enclosing the swollen testes in my palm.

"Does that hurt at all?" I asked as I squeezed him gently.

"No" he replied , so I squeezed the enlarged testicle with a little more pressure and found it to be a little harder to the touch with little or no sponginess than the normal sized one.

"Well" I said covering him up a little hastily, as I noticed his dick starting to get aroused, "if that was me I would be down the doctors post haste like yesterday". I lay back on my own bed trying my best not to stare at the full blown erection he was starting to get, albeit out of sight below the folds of the towel. "As long as it doesn't interfere with your reproductive juices," I muttered, not wanting Henry to see I was becoming somewhat embarrassed.

"Well I think it's already beginning to" came the reply, with a lot of doubt in his voice.

"Are you telling me you can get a hard on and can't come or what?" I asked him.

"I think so" came the nervous reply.

"Do you mind if I ask you a really personal question which you don't have to answer if you don't want to?" I added.

"Well you can't get more personal than you have already" he retorted.

"No, I suppose not really" I added, no longer sure of the ground I was on, "fire away Paul I trust your judgement anyway," he murmured obviously tossing himself off under the towel slowly but perceptively, "go for it be a devil, while I show you how little I come."

Somewhat shocked I blurted out "How long since your last wank?"

"That's easy" he replied clearly manhandling his dick below the shelter of the towel, "about two months ago I think but I can't be absolutely certain."

"Was the quantity or spurt, quite normal?" I asked as casually as I could, feeling my face becoming redder all the time.

"No not really, it was less than half of what I normally shoot, that's why I'm beginning to get worried," he confessed.

"If I came less than normal I would be very worried, you are one hell of a prat! Like it or not I'm taking you to see a doctor first thing in the morning and won't take no for an answer" I told him with real venom in my voice.

"Come over here quickly Paul" he replied, on removing the towel from the area in question, and with his last stroke he started to come but the strength of his spurt was, let's just say pathetic. He pumped away in a vain attempt to increase the quantity and did his utmost to produce as much fluid as possible. I looked at the dribble all his efforts had produced, it was clear that Henry was bitterly disappointed; he began to cry at the same time as his dick started to deflate.

"Come on mate get into bed, it might not be as bad as it looks," I lied in an effort to console him as he wiped the dribble away. First thing in the morning I left a note for the gaffer after we unlocked the gates and opened the studio doors.

I ordered Henry onto the pillion of the Bishop and ran him up to Hammersmith Hospital. He was admitted on the spot and I stayed with him until they took him to theatre, where his enlarged testicle was removed in less than an hour, as I waited for him back in a ward. The sister told me that everything went well under the local anaesthetic and although feeling a little sore he might even be allowed home the same day, as there was a rush on beds due to a road traffic accident nearby.

The stitches would be removed in about a week, and things should return to normal, the doctor explained to Henry that the lack of fluid production and ejaculation strength was due to the enlarged and defective testes, which if left any longer, would certainly have affected the normal one.

Henry was told that both his sexual appetite and ability to produce a normal rate of sperm should not be effected, and having one testes was far more common than he would have thought, as nearly all professional jockeys have one removed for practical reasons when horse riding, and there was nothing wrong with their sex drive he concluded in a matter of fact way. Anyway in a short time Henry was just fine and ended up more than satisfied with the performance and capabilities of his own private sex toy!

Henry started to become excited at the thought of Christmas fast approaching and was overjoyed at the personal invitation he received from my aunt, to join us for the Christmas holiday down in the New Forest.

The odd night that I stayed at his house, or he joined me at St Christopher's, he talked about nothing else except my aunts invitation down to Hindley.

The average Londoner neither loved nor loathed the countryside, it was unimportant to them either way, fortunately for me Henry loved it.

Being in the country opened up a lot of new and exiting things for him to do, in these early days you were lucky to get three or four days holiday over the Christmas break, for Henry it would have been a travesty in the extreme, to have been on his own at this particular Christmas. There was no doubt in my Aunt Joan's mind that this would not be allowed to happen, as besides thinking Henry was the bees knees, she felt he would be good company for me during my last Christmas in England for a while.

I purchased a new pair of swimming trunks for Henry as one of his presents, the old ones having seen better days and were a bit to revealing, though not enough to bother Henry they gave me a lot of undue embarrassment!

Aunt Joan got him a smashing sweater and as usual we each received an enjoyable book from her, my book was 'Midshipman Easy' a cracking read it was too. I also remember the way Henry, very much in love with his latest acquisition, pranced about in his new 'Cozzy', till I finally got a bit pissed off with his shenanigans and told him so. The new costume meant a lot to him, his old trunks had been acquired by dubious means, and needless to say they soon disappeared never to be seen again.

Despite the clock ticking down to my impending permanent departure around my eighteenth birthday, for the time being at least, we were determined to enjoy what little time we still had left together.

It was the middle of winter, a season I have always loved, but the heat in my bedroom was uncomfortably warm throughout the year.

My aunt, enjoyed what I always thought to be too warm a temperature, but then Aunt Joan just loved it, as she was getting on in years and felt the cold more than most. At nightly bath time, Henry often enjoyed an excessively long soak, whereas I preferred to take a quick shower. After bathing

I lay on top of my bed reading for some time; meanwhile Henry would prance about outrageously displaying his nudity, trying to wind me up and sometimes succeeding. On one occasion I remember him waving his dick in my face, demanding me to check the new scar to see how it was healing after his recent operation. This rather trusting frankness we obviously had between us, was a little overpowering sometimes. Once he was waving his pride and joy in my face, so close I could easily have taken offence had I chosen to, "For fuck's sake Henry go to your bed and behave yourself" I reprimanded.

"Only if you give me a full body massage," he chirped back at me.

"You must be joking," I sniggered, "with you flaunting your dick about like a tart on heat; anyway I'm reading so you're not on!"

After a while Henry shouted across to me, interrupting me for the umpteenth time, "Can I give you a massage then?"

I looked over the top of my book, "no way, do you think I would let you loose all over my body? The randy mood your in and besides you have little or no expertise in giving a massage, I wouldn't let you astride my body anyway" I told him.

Clearly in the huff at my remarks he turned onto his side, exposing his naked arse to me. After a while I was beginning to feel a little to warm under the covers, so I turned off my bedside lamp and spread myself on top of the bed covers to cool down. The room was pleasantly dark but still warm, "is it OK to open the window to cool the room down a little" Henry asked.

"OK but just a little as a frost is predicted for later in the night" I replied, getting off his bed he opened the window slightly, then came and sat beside me on my bed.

I was taken by surprise at this move, but he was so casual about it he left me speechless, then he interrupted my uncomfortable silence with an equally casual remark "you don't trust me as much as I trust you Paul, do you?"

"Of course I do" I replied quickly to cover any doubt I felt.

"Then why won't you let me give you a massage, after all I let you give me one," he muttered.

I didn't know what to say so I just kept quiet, after a while a sulking Henry could tell he was not getting a reply to this question, so he stormed over to his own bed in a quiet rage. I could hear him huffing and puffing in the dim glow, turning one way first then the other, giving vent to his real feelings and trying to tell me something. Suddenly I said to him, more to appease than anything else, "maybe tomorrow Henry, alright!"

"No it fucking well ain't, don't bother trying to cover your arse," he replied in a loud voice.

"OK, I won't" I replied climbing under the bedcovers, the atmosphere in the room was a lot cooler now, in more way's than one!

I soon fell asleep, and this disagreement was the only blight over the hols, I think we both had some regrets over it. The last two days before we headed back to London were great, but there was still an undertone of begrudging acceptance, I felt more on Henry's part than my own. On our arrival back in London, Henry just assumed I would stay over at his place before going to work in the morning, not wanting to upset the uneasy peace between us, I went along with his assumption. On arrival at Henry's house it was freezing so he promptly lit the coal fire, we then went for a swim, leaving the place to heat up. Henry came up with this suggestion because he was dying to show off the new trunks that I had given him for Christmas, so off we went for a swim and a heat. As he moved about the pond waxing and waning, the staff at the baths soon spotted the trunks, observations, which had the proud Henry purring with delight. He put on a good show for his audience by prancing around the pool side showing of, loving every minute of his performance. He was a lovable character, especially when in one of his jovial moods, his humour is infectious I thought. On leaving the baths we went for a jar at the local hostelry before going to bed. Having had a great swim there was no need for a bath tonight, so we returned home and went upstairs to our beds.

Lying on top of our beds, naked as the day we were born and both in a joyous mood, a high spirited Henry asked "you know what Paul? I want to give you a massage, I promise to behave myself."

Throwing caution to the wind I said, "OK, but only if I give you one in return."

He bounded towards me "sure can! Turn over" he demanded, this I did willingly enough. As he straddled my lower back I told him "take it slow and be gentle, massage is not supposed to be a form of punishment."

He started doing my shoulders being just a little heavy handed at first, and then he knelt between my legs, becoming gentler as he moved down my body in a methodical manner. "Turn over" he ordered as he smacked my bum, I complied and on doing so he proceeded to work from my chest down the full length of my body. When finished, he casually climbed off my bed and went over to his own, lying down on it without speaking a word.

"That was good as you were using just the right pressure, with more practise you will become even more adept" I told him.

"Who taught you?" he asked. I went over to him, ignoring his question momentarily as I straddled his back; I then started pummelling the shoulder muscles with practised know-how, paying attention to the base of his neck. "Bobby my brother" I told him as I started working on his spine.

He remarked "you don't talk about him much, do you?"

With my full weight I sat on his bum in an effort to shut him up, "open your legs as wide as you can" I ordered as I moved my hands down between them, manipulating the base of his spine. I continued to his inner thighs before working on his calf muscles, then right down to his ankles. Lightly smacking his bum I asked him to turn over, he took his time and slowly I began to realise why, it was obvious he was beginning to show sings of semi erection. "You said you were going to behave yourself!" I spat.

"I will, I am" he stuttered, not opening his eyes in order to avoid looking at me directly.

"I'm going to turn off the light," I said, not wanting to embarrass him any longer.

"Good idea" came the reply.

"OK, behave" I warned him as I climbed back over his legs and started to reach up to massage his upper torso, "just make sure you keep control of yourself." Not receiving any answer, I continued to massage him, without making my actions too obvious and kept as wide a berth from his genitalia as possible. I concentrated on the front of his upper thighs with care, and perhaps too much gentleness.

Henry encouraged me with a soft purring voice, saying "I'm really enjoying this."

I thought this meant the relaxing effect it was having on him. I could sense more than feel he was enjoying himself, just a little too much perhaps, then I felt his thighs go rigid either side of my knees as the spurt of his spunk hit me! Once his body stopped convulsing I sat there on my haunches, between his legs, in total disbelief. I felt my own body parts to check the spread of his come, Henry remained deathly still, but I could remain silent no more! In a rage I shouted at him "You fucking dirty bastard - you've come all over me"!

Not a murmur came from him as he lay there not moving and holding his breath. I got down off the bed and turned on the light to inspect my body more closely, finding my nether regions plastered in his goo. Meanwhile Henry just lay there terrified of what he thought I was going to do to him. I looked at him in disgust while he did his best to avoid eye contact with me. "You fucking pervert, I'll never give you a massage again, you dirty bastard!" I screamed at him. He winced as though I had just landed a brutal punch to his body; he started to twitch uncomfortably as I walked over towards him.

I then noticed the mess of spunk plastering him in the same way I was plastered, suddenly finding the whole image rather funny, I said laughing "there's fuck all wrong with your reproductive organs now, even though you've only got one ball." It was Henry's turn to look startled, not believing his own ears, and slowly very slowly a smile returned to his face.

He then issued a verbal statement "it just happened, I didn't mean it, I'm very sorry, is there anything I can do? I've not had a wank for over a month and it just exploded out of control" he muttered.

"Go fetch the towel and you can clean me off" I demanded, so without another word he ran downstairs and fetched a towel, handing it to me on his return. "It's your fucking spunk, so you can clean it up" I said handing back the towel, this he did with great care remaining silent the whole time. We then returned to our beds and lay on top of them each of us with our own thoughts, and in total silence.

My mind returned to the nostalgia of Ashford, and the hive of sexual activities I remembered getting up to, I then wondered why I was so dramatically offensive towards Henry. After all he had given his assurance that it was not deliberate, he had not 'pulled himself off,' and he stated it had been a long time between wanks. I looked over at him out of curiosity, as he lay on top of his bed, now in a placid and very calm state.

I then realised that up until now, Henry had been studying me in the same manner and a perceptive smile crept over his face, thankful perhaps at me not loosing the rag with him completely. His facial expression then turned to one of a questionable look, "what is it now?" I asked.

He looked at me examining my facial expression in search of comfort and forgiveness, then not sure of his ground, asked "why did you take it so well?"

In order to see him better I turned onto my side, instinctively he did the same, we looked each other in the face before I finally spoke to him. "Look perhaps you couldn't help yourself, although I'm not sure about that, but there's no point crying over spilt milk or in your case splashed spunk!"

Henry found this quip rather funny and a broader smile began to slide across his boat race, "don't worry Henry, I intend to get my own back, you see if I don't" I added, wiping the grin off his face instantly.

After a good five minutes Henry plucked up even more courage and asked "do you ever wank yourself off, cos I've never seen you do it?"

I looked long and hard at him and simply replied "what do you think?"

"I don't really know because I've never seen you," he answered.

After a pause I really caught him off guard by asking him "why, do you want to wank me off and check me out for yourself?"

At this point Henry went very red, very red indeed, and became absolutely speechless; in fact he did not know where to hide his look of total embarrassment. To add to his embarrassment even more, I looked at him with a deadpan expression on my face, and asked, "you can suck me off if you prefer?"

Another pregnant pause followed, then suddenly finding his voice Henry erupted in the most blasphemous manner "Jesus Christ! You're taking the fucking piss, you're pulling my dick, you fucking bastard".

Still wearing my straight laced face I wound him up a bit more by answering "come on over Henry and help yourself!" At that remark, he got out of bed and going over to put out the light replied "Very funny, you truly set me up, you bastard," then he turned the light off. I knew then that somehow someday, I would get Henry back and teach him a lesson when he least expected it, this thought was in my mind as I drifted off to sleep.

Once back at work, we soon picked up the threads of our usual routine, I for one was determined to enjoy every moment of the freedom I had left. Most weekends we went camping and hill walking in the Lake District, where I introduced Henry to some good and difficult rock climbs. Other weekends we would dash off to my aunts, where she would spoil us rotten, that always was a good thing for our evil souls. I noticed with pride the progress Henry made, giving me a great deal of personal satisfaction; it was more than good for stroking my ego. We went swimming more often during the working week, as well as attending the scouts regularly together; to most observers we became more and more inseparable.

At work one day Terry remarked to me that Henry worshiped the very ground I walked on, I looked at him very strangely, causing him to add an assurance of how sincerely he meant the remark. His healthy respect for my quick temper, a sample of which he had received on one previous occasion, was duly noted as I carried on with the job in hand. This was a special panel for the powers that be in the office tower, another addition to the marbling panels I had done before. Towards the end of March and with less than three weeks to my eighteenth birthday, I was staying overnight at Henry's 'doss house', having had a particularly strenuous evening at the scouts.

On telling Henry he might have to give me a long massage to loosen up my lower back and thigh, he was very keen to have a go having had more practice on other victims, and had been bragging to me how good he had become at massaging. "OK save the mouth because after a long soak in the tub I'll give you a chance to prove your worth" I told him, as I headed for my bath. While having a soak in the bath I thought this is payback time, after my bath I dried myself off, and with evilness in my heart I went through the hall turning all the lights off before climbing up the stairs to join Henry in the bedroom. I noticed a towel spread out in readiness on top of my bed, so I turned off the light and sprawled face down on the towel.

"Don't you want the lights on Paul?" he asked.

"No your alright, I trust your hands" I replied, as he climbed onto my back and started to work his magic on my shoulders, before moving down to my spine and buttocks. He had certainly improved I thought as I started to become drowsy, he then moved his body between my spread-eagled legs. Moving his hands slowly and massaging my gluteus maximas (bum), he expertly softened up the largest pair of muscles in the human body.

"Leave the inner thighs till I turn over, just concentrate on my calves first" I told him, so he then spent a good five minutes on each calf muscle until he was satisfied. He smacked my bum as a signal for me to turn over onto my back, on doing so I moved my legs close together forcing Henry to straddle my body, so that he could work on my chest muscles. As he moved over my body I could feel his placid dick making contact with my stomach area, so I asked him to move himself and I then opened my legs to let him kneel between them.

At this stage I was still placid myself as Henry worked on my hips and outer thighs, sitting back on his haunches Henry now started to work my inner thighs in tandem, with the flat and outside edges of his hands.

"Gentle and slower" I whispered to him, using Henry's obliging hands to help my arousal, I closed my eyes stimulating the arousal in my groins. "Slower, and use lighter strokes going just a bit deeper" I told him as the arousal became stronger, his efforts were working well enough as my sex toy had sprung into a full blown erection by now. With Henry completely unaware of my intentions I kept my right hand in readiness across my chest. He started to work with the palms of his hands, using full length strokes around my now sensitive groin area and down the length of my inner thighs, right down to the area behind my knees.

I could feel the sap rising within me ready to explode as I muttered "that's great, just a few more strokes," he unknowingly obliged as I took hold of my shaft and pointed it in the direction of his body hovering just above me.

I let go full blast and kept going until I knew I had emptied myself completely, spurting all over his nether regions, and thinking revenge is sweet at the same time! Henry sat back on his haunches utterly dumbfounded in a state of shock at my actions. He sat there for several moments, long after I had emptied myself he was still in total disbelief, and speechless.

A short while later and almost in a whisper he said "I hope you enjoyed yourself," then climbed down off the bed and went over to put the light on. Still inspecting himself he came back over to me, still in a bit of a stupor, but noting that as well as having a bit of an erection left, my body was totally free of spunk. He pondered on this fact mentally as he looked again at his spattered body, noting there were very few parts of his midriff, uncovered by some of my sticky white goo!

Looking him in the eye I said "I told you I would get you back when you were not expecting it, didn't I? So now it's your turn to feel offended."

Looking at me, he said in a soft voice "I deserved that, didn't I?"

Breaking into a smile, I said nothing as I got off my bed and started to wipe him down as best I could with a towel. It was amazing where the stuff had got to, I held his dick in my left hand, lifting it out of the way to clean between his legs and the one and only ball. He never said a word until well after I had finished handing over the towel to him. "Now you know, I too can wank my self off when needs must" I told him.

"You certainly can," he muttered as he went back to his bed.

"By the way Henry, you give a mean massage" I added.

"Thanks Paul, in future the only massage you'll get from me will be with the lights on", was the reply, and he meant it!

On my eighteenth birthday, which happened to coincide with Easter that year, Henry did something that I shall never forget. With me not having a liking for ordinary sweets but knowing of my fondness for dark or plain chocolate, Henry bought me the most expensive, highly decorated Swiss Easter egg he could find, made of dark chocolate and full of black liquors. It must have cost him several weeks' wages and without thinking of the cost, I was so moved by his gesture, I broke down completely. He knew me better than I had ever given him credit for as on the twelfth night of April, on my eighteenth birthday, he give me the egg just as I was about to get into bed. He also gave me a birthday card, but it was impossible to read the writing on it, due to the tears unashamedly cascading over my face. It was a very emotional moment in my life, and a gesture totally unexpected from 'jovial Henry' as I had taken to calling him. I was full of emotions and crying, when he calmly climbed into my bed and put his arms around me, without any sexual connotations whatsoever.

It seemed the most natural gesture on his part as he comforted me and said, "You're just a big softie really aren't you?"

Bringing my emotions under control and drying my eyes, I insisted we share the chocolates between us, after a little persuasion he agreed to do so. Henry hugged my bare torso as I started to regain full control of my emotions; I told him how much I was going to miss him. When I started to elaborate on how I would loose my freedom in a few weeks time by serving three years in the army, we both started to sob uncontrollably, each trying to out perform the other. A right pair of dipsticks we would have looked, to any fly stuck on the wall, watching our performance. On regaining our composure we started to demolish the Easter egg, until having had more than our fill and almost on the brink of feeling sick, we felt very sorry for ourselves.

In a very soft voice and picking his words with great care Henry said "You know Paul, you have had the most profound effect on my life, I will never forget you, but you needn't worry about me when you are gone." In a stronger voice he added "although I will miss you deeply, I now have a lot more to live for, thanks to you."

"You do not know how pleased I am to hear these words" I replied, and with both of us now becoming less emotional, we fell asleep. Come the morning he was still snuggled tightly into my back.

A few weeks later the dreaded letter of notification arrived on my door, I had to report to Winchester Barracks, no later than the seventh day of May 1954!

"There" firm in my hand, in writing, was the confirmation that my last days of freedom were now numbered. With less than a week to go, I decided to leave my job before the end of the week at Lime Grove Studio, giving me time to spend a long weekend with my aunt at Hindley. I hate emotional goodbyes maybe because I am oversensitive, I don't know, but I can assure you the very brief goodbyes to all my workmates and especially Henry, were more for my own benefit than anyone else's.

A peaceful weekend at Hindley lost in the timelessness of my soul, soon passed and I found myself driving towards the gates of Winchester Barracks on my beloved Bishop.

So here endeth another chapter of my life, I wonder what the next chapter of my new life will bring?

Chapter Eight

We're in the Army now. (Status Quo)

As the Bishop slowly approached the barrier at Winchester barracks a squaddy, armed with a lethal looking weapon, stepped out barring my way. I brought the Bishop to a halt just in front of him and he asked the purpose of my visit, satisfied I had a right to be there, he then lifted the barrier letting me through. Once the B.S.A. motorcycle was clear of the barrier he closed it immediately, and then gave me instructions where I could park the Bishop, pointing towards an open fronted shed opposite the guardhouse. This long structure contained a number of cycle racks, and had a large open space for motorised vehicles; this was where I was told to park the Bishop.

Having obeyed my first order, I returned to the soldier on guard duty, for instructions on what to do next. He pointed to a set of large barrack buildings at the other end of what I thought was a yard and said, "cross the parade square and go the extreme left hand building named Mons block."

The vision in front of me was not dissimilar to the residential blocks and playground of Ashford Orphanage, and that was a vision, which still haunted the darker regions of my soul! Before moving off I stood for a moment, and watched a group of men playing soldiers on the parade ground, with a rude little man wearing a peaked cap barking orders at them.

I then started to proceed across this vast openness of a parade ground, making a beeline for Mons block, as I had been instructed by the guard. I was less than halfway across the parade ground, when two of the toy soldiers broke rank from the others, and marching at the double came beside me ordering me to stand perfectly still. The very rude man, who had been making a lot of noise and barking nasty remarks, turned out to be the drill sergeant major and he marched smartly over to stand in front of me impeding my progress. He then barked an order at the lads either side of me, who doubled away to rejoin their band of merry men. The sergeant major wore an immaculate uniform, tailor made to fit in all the right places. A military style peaked hat fitted perfectly, but the peak itself covered most of the top half of his face in such a manner he was forced to tilt his head backwards to see. This revealed a pair of evil slit eyes, like a big cat has when on the prowl at night. The curve of this peak was tight across the bridge of his nose, exposing only a large pair of nostrils that looked ready to spit fire at you. Standing rigid with a yardstick (or pace stick) smartly tucked beneath his right armpit, he surveyed the pile of shit in front of him, I, who had dared to invade his private parade ground. In his eyes this act would have been a court marshal offence. Stepping slowly around my body, he surveyed me with a distasteful scowl. He looked at me as if needing to scrape something messy from the sole of his boots, so highly polished he could see his face in them. He paced slowly around me and after several very unpleasant moments, I became aware of the bastard standing close behind me, and just inches away from my left lughole barked "Am I hurting you laddie?"

I replied "No Sir" as a cold shiver ran down my spine.

"Well I bloody well should be as I'm standing on your hair" he paused for breath and added "Get your hair cut."

I whispered "Yes Sir."

"Now get off my parade ground at the double you miserable little turd!"

I made good my escape and reached the barrack room door without further embarrassment. One of the lads had been standing in the doorway of Mons block, observing this event taking place, and he was obviously highly amused at being a witness to my antics on the parade ground. He then introduced himself as Chris, one half of a set of twins. Chris was a touch taller than myself with Scandinavian fair hair and striking blue eyes, a lean framed body, and was what the girls would call a smasher. His brother was inside guarding the two beds they had commandeered for themselves so when I went to stow my gear Chas Walker the other twin was lying prone on top of the second bed out from the left hand corner of the room. I put my gear down at the third bed next to his and had to make several double takes with my eyes, as I could not tell the difference between the person lying on the bed, and his identical twin I had met at the door. The barrack dormitory, which held about forty beds, started to fill up slowly, this was another reminder of my days at Ashford I thought. I was becoming acquainted with my new surroundings, and noticed men were arriving at regular intervals, adding to the number of new recruits all meeting each other for the first time. After a while in walked, or I should say marched, a platoon sergeant and two corporals. We were told to leave our personal belongings on our respective beds, get outside, formed into a group and marched over to the quartermaster's stores. We were kitted out with a mountain of gear, more equipment than I ever thought I would need or use, including bedding and items of clothing to numerous to mention.

Our new platoon was nothing short of a 'Mob', and were the biggest bunch of misfits the Army had ever seen fit to recruit. This was an undisputable fact and our platoon sergeant a sergeant Jones, was eager to point out to us the truth in his statement. Sergeant Jones who had served in the Welsh Guards, bore no resemblance and was no relation to Corporal Jones of dad's army fame, this fact was made clear to me by a corporal White. Corporal White was assigned to our platoon, and the more we got to know him, the more most of us realised he was just a bit of a wanker.

After the first months training the 'Mob' had progressed in the eyes of sergeant Jones, into becoming 'his rabble'. I was reliably informed this was some kind of backhanded compliment from the sergeant, but failed to see anything complimentary, about any remarks he ever made to anyone!

Our training was altered ten weeks into basic training. The Green Jackets were separated into two sister regiments, one the K.R.R.C. (Kings Royal Rifle Corps), and the other simply known as the R.B's (The Rifle Brigade).

Only riflemen scoring the highest number of bull's eyes on the rifle range, were eligible for this regiment, and they were filtered off into the R.B's at this time. My forte was to be in sharp shooting, and I turned out to be one of three marksmen within our platoon. The barrack room had lost more than half of it's occupants by this stage, but fortunately for me my closest friends the Walker twins, also remained with me in the Rifle Brigade regiment. Outside of the regiment we were known by other members of the British Army as the 'Treble B's' (Black Button Bastards) we were and still are the only regiment in the army to wear black buttons on the standard regulation khaki tunic issued to all British army units.

I suspect there were other reasons the treble B's enjoyed their title, as they fought hard to maintain it, on numerous occasions.

The change in composition of our barrack room members was not for the good, as most members of the original group were quick to notice.

Those observant enough to notice the changes between the original 'mob' and the present lot were, to put it mildly, not best pleased in the slightest.

I spent my first forty eight hour pass with Aunt Joan down in the new forest, and on returning from it, my mates and I were soon to find out we had now been joined by a group of rather shady characters.

They had formed into a rather nasty group at the other end of the room, led by wanker called Hawkins. He had gathered around himself some of the worst criminals in the British Army. His actions lead me to think of Ashford once again and the school bully system that exists in all establishments, when people are placed together in large groups.

Hawkins was typical of most school bullies, when surrounded by a number of misguided jokers; he survived by using their ignorance to protect himself. Hawkins real talents were at best mediocre or almost non existent, but he had gathered a following, who for all the wrong reasons sucked up to this arrogant swine in some kind of false idol worship.

His power was only activated by the hero worship of his followers, alone he was a pathetic specimen, more to be pitied then admired. The hard core or nucleus of this unbelievable gang were all misfits, one jerk named Brown was just an arse licker, Hunter a sexual predator, and a guy called Joyce an ex farm worker was nothing but a sheep shagger. Thankfully there were others who could be looked up to and respected, they included some great characters, and this group easily made up the majority.

Out of many in the platoon these are just a few outstanding characters, who helped to relieve the drudgery, and make army life more interesting. Joe Treacle , a lovable 'Del Boy' type of character, always wheeling and dealing in dodgy contraband, that somehow managed to stick to his mitts. The Smith brothers (Dave and Mick,) who perfected doing absolutely nothing into an art, making it another wonder of the world! They were a pair of harmless lazy bastards who would do absolutely nothing, they could not even create a ripple in still waters, never mind a wave. Saunders was the practical joker in the platoon, his life was just one big joke, and he never took anything seriously.

As the ten weeks of training seemed to be rapidly coming to an end, I was reminded of Ashford by the regime I had entered into, the difference being at Ashford we wore short trousers, here in the army we were wearing long ones. 'Mischief in long trousers' you might say!

In the army almost everyone cultivated a small circle of muckers or close mates, this could be of great importance when under fire in the field, as your very life could depend on this kind of mutual trust. Having shot at Bisley for the Queens Hundred, in competition against all comers, I became the platoon's number one bren gunner and one of the three top marksmen in B company R.B's.

The Walker twins were to become part of my bren gun team in the field. Due to their striking similarity they had been nicknamed 'Quack and Quack' by now, and for some unaccountable reason they had named me 'Andy', a name which rapidly stuck to me and became widely used by all. Quack, Quack and myself done a M.T. course (Motor Transport), where we all learned to drive, the twins excelling in this particular area of training. Between them when given the order they could drive any vehicle, from Jeeps, to sixteen ton Scammels and other combat vehicles. They both saw driving as a cushy option, although in reality, it could be anything but easy. They always seemed to be enjoying themselves and could never be separated. It was almost impossible to tell them apart, and believe me many have tried, but Quack, Quack had their own way of dealing with those who tried. Often one would claim to be the other making it impossible to tell who was who, the corporal or sergeant would often give up out of frustration.

Plan 'B' was an alternative by detailing someone else to the task, or plan 'C' would be implemented by detailing then both to the same duty, this was a failure on the part of the officer, as Quack and Quack only wanted to be working together in the first place!

One of the many illegal scams on the camp was obtaining live ammunition for personal use, which with care, was easier than the powers that be ever realized and several of us did so. Ammo was a great bargaining currency for even more contraband or illicit goods, and when required could be used to open many a door, that should have remained firmly closed. I even heard it was used to obtain and pay for prostitutes, because unlike credit cards of today, it was untraceable.

Within every barrack room there was the 'Lawyer', an idiot who thought he alone could interpret every army regulation in the book, he often helped to fight the very system which created the rules and regulations. There was a guy we named 'The Evening Echo', he was in fact the biggest gossip in the platoon, who spent all of his time passing on information. He was an ideal person to spread news, but sadly one lacking the talent, to separate fact from fiction. Unofficially of course we had the services of Shirley and Betty, who for as little as one round of ammunition would perform sexual favours, acts which could be useful in a totally male environment full of hormones and testosterone. Their services could be useful and called upon if need be, they could also be classed as local tarts in one sense, but in truth they were only homosexuals or gays enjoying themselves.

There were also some great characters, like 'Harry the Hamster', one of the best dog handlers who could track anything. We had Nobby Clark and Smithy, the best mechanics you could ever wish for in a breakdown situation, or vehicle repair job.

There was some form of compensation to be had, in this enforced slave camp, and most of it was a lot closer to hand than you might think. Unfortunately there were a few who not only thought they could buck the system, but when all else failed went A.W.O.L. (absent without leave), which could sometimes be one way of getting out of the army. This would certainly result in a court martial followed by a dishonourable discharge, but not without spending a long time in the military prison, a sentence which rather defeated the object of the exercise.

When the ten weeks basic training was over Aunt Joan made a point of attending my passing out parade, making it a very proud moment in my life, but at the same time adding to my embarrassment and discomfort. This was followed by a pass for one weeks leave, a short respite from army life, before an intensive six weeks basic jungle training course. I had already informed my aunt I would spend my last weekend in her company, at her home in the New Forest.

I left the barracks in high spirits, firing up the Bishop, and headed for the open road once more. I drove towards my previous workplace at Lime Grove Studios. The Bishop was entering the works yard as Henry rushed out to meet me, having heard the sound of the 500cc B.S.A, long before he could see it coming. You would think we were long lost brothers, the way we greeted each other, his welcome was so overcoming. He was even more chuffed when I told him I would be able to spend a few days with him at his gaff, on asking, he had no difficulty in getting time off from work, as Archie gave it to him willingly and with pay no less!

It was wonderful to see all my old mates again; they all remarked how much I had grown physically, and complimented me regarding my appearance. In an unashamed display of over excitement Henry was all over me like a rash, "he missed you a hell of a lot" said Archie, as I became embarrassed by Henry's behaviour. When felt I could no longer stand his excessive exuberance any more, I was forced to tell him to cool it, which, thankfully he did.

Henry then went on to tell me he was still scouting, and now participated in every activity going. We talked long and hard and I needed to come up for air on several occasions, but Henry was still the same old Henry, and like a rash was highly infectious. We went swimming at the local baths once more, I enjoyed myself enormously, making me realise just how much I had missed this activity. We went to the local hostelry for a jar or two, ending our great reunion with a wonderful evening catching up on lost time. We rang Gina my old scoutmaster and Alan Bancroft from St Christopher's, making arrangements for a get together, as we were all anxious to get up to date with each other on gossip.

After a hectic first day with Henry, it was just like old times, as we spread out on our respective beds after bathing.

Without warning he came over to my bed and sat beside me, "you're a lot bigger with a lot more muscles" he said examining my naked body closely.

"That's all that army training" I replied.

Then he gently pushed my dick to one side saying "even your dick's got bigger."

"That's even more army training" I replied and he just smiled to himself at my humour.

I then got up and went downstairs in need of a quick pee, but coming back up the stairs, I could see Henry on top of his bed openly tossing himself off!

"I see your sexual appetite has returned to normal, in spite of only having one ball,."

He looked up at me as he ejaculated a massive amount of come all over his own body, more than happy with the recovery of his manhood, if that amount was anything to go by! He said nothing as he got up and went downstairs to clean himself off, as I was tired I just got into my own bed, it had been a long day.

Henry returned putting off the light as he entered the room, he then climbed into my bed beside me, "what's wrong with your own bed then?" I asked him.

"Nothing I just wanted to be near you for a while" he replied.

"OK, but no hanky panky" I said and he just laughed out loud.

We got up at our leisure and went for lunch with Mr Bancroft and Mr Kipling from St Christopher's, we talked a great deal over lunch and Alan Bancroft remarked it was just like old times. Then, making our excuses we left soon after lunch, as we were keen to reach open spaces and get down to Staines early. I left Henry in the town looking around the shops, making arrangements to meet him at five o clock, in my favourite tea room.

Once alone I went down to the river bank to pay homage to Bobby, I lay on my side at the river enjoying the peace and tranquillity that this spot always gave to me, it was of one of our favourite places. There was very little activity on the river at this time of day, just an occasional rower, and someone fishing on the far riverbank. I then lay back to soak up the warm sun on my face, closing my eyes day dreaming the time away, thinking of all the wonderful memories I had of this place over the years. Begrudgingly time soon passed, I stirred my limbs back into life with a considerable effort, and went back into town to meet Henry. I met him on reaching the tearoom and we ordered our teas, I then proceeded to stuff my face in the usual manner, just as I had done so many times before in this very tearoom.

The high intake of cholesterol was a small price to pay for all the pleasure I received from eating the wrong things, in any case I thought was indestructible, as one does at such a tender age. The temporary change was a very pleasant alternative from army food, so I ate with relish enjoying every mouthful. Henry watched my every gesture, "stop watching me so intensely, as if you're in love with me," I muttered with a mouthful of cake.

He just laughed rather nervously and softly replied, "maybe I am," then looked away quickly.

"Shut up you tart" I jested, "stop acting like a slut trying to sell your body," I teased.

He went even redder at this last remark and having finished his tea, got up and went outside to wait near the Bishop.

On joining him he still looked upset, so I said "I'm only winding you up and teasing you stupid, you fall for it every time," this remark brought a smile to his face once more.

On arriving at the scout hut Gina and the gang were most welcoming, and they were all really pleased to see me once more. I was allowed to take out a firefly dinghy on my own, while Henry got involved in a more physical game with the rest of the gang, it was a newer game called 'Murder Ball'.

I had a fantastic few hours on my own, which after being constantly banged up twenty four, seven, with forty other men in a hut, was just what I needed to help me unwind once more. I had become used to my own company over the years and actually preferred being on my own, most of the time. I had put the dinghy away and stowed all the gear, it was now long after everyone had left to go home, Henry remained alone in the den busy cooking our supper. He had already made up a double bed on the bare floor near the unlit fire; it was to warm for a fire at this time of year, and the heat in the hut was more than comfortable anyway.

We ate a good supper before preparing for bed, and acting on an impulse, Henry suggested we should go for a swim before the late summer sun went down. I wasn't so keen, especially after having just eaten a meal, but, as the currents could be tricky at times I said I would keep an eye on him. He then handed me a towel to hold while he stripped off, "where's your new trunks?" I asked, as he stripped to the buff.

"Back at home "he managed to say, as he ran to the river, plunging into the water without hesitation.

Thankfully he stayed close to the river bank, and after about ten minutes or so he came out shivering.

It must have been colder than he was prepared to admit, as his dick was obviously suffering badly, having now shrunk to less than half its normal size! "You're a looney" I said to him, as I wrapped the big towel around his shivering body I told him, "you get off inside, and I'll bring in the rest of your gear in behind you."

Once inside he really did start to shiver, so I went for my Alpine sleeping bag, to get him inside it quickly for some heat. Henry's hands were shaking so bad he could hardly hold the towel to dry himself off.

"Here, give it to me, you dipstick, I'll finish you off." I rubbed Henry's body vigorously until colour started to tint his skin with a healthy glow. "Now get into my sleeping bag to warm your body." (Which he did.)

Within the hour, he was glowing from the warmth generated by pure eider duck down, and begging to be released, Henry didn't know how the draw cord worked. "Just stay where you are" I ordered, "You can't get into any more mischief there."

"Please Paul" he begged, "If you don't let me out soon I'll wank off all over the inside of your bag" he threatened.

"If you do that Henry, I'll kill you," I replied. "No one has ever been allowed to use that bag, until now."

"Please let me out Paul, I'll be good, I promise I will" pleaded Henry.

"O.K."I said and released the special draw cord from the mummy shaped mountaineering bag and Henry slipped out. He was now so warm he just lay down on top of the double blanket bed upon the bare floorboards. I asked the now fully recovered Henry "do you fancy a final mug of tea before bed-time?"

"I'll make it," said Henry jumping up still naked, then he went over to the galley and brewed up. Meanwhile, I got undressed and lay down on top of my own bag, waiting for Henry to return.

My own sleeping bag was far too warm at this time of year unless you were on top of a mountain, so I peeled back half the blanket bed, putting it down on my side to lie on, giving me more padding.

While we were drinking our tea, Henry suddenly said to me "can I give you a massage Paul?"

"No thanks you're alright Henry I don't really need one, anyway the army keeps you pretty fit" I replied.

"Of course" said Henry, "maybe you could give me one later instead? That game of murder ball is very intense," he added.

"You've got a fucking cheek Henry I remember the last time I gave you one, you ended up spunking all over me!"

"I won't do it again," promised Henry, "honest Paul, I won't."

"OK Henry you don't need to beg, we'll see, meanwhile just finish your tea." I thought Henry had satisfied himself enough last night, and I should be safe enough, for tonight at least.

"What part of your body needs attention?" I asked him.

"Well if it's not too much to ask, could you give me the full works?" he said hopefully.

"OK, but this time the light stays on" I replied.

He got up and snibbed the door before closing the curtains, then lay down spread-eagled on the bed ready for me to start. I finished the last of my tea before I knelt down between his legs to start working on him; I worked on his shoulders first, and then worked methodically down the entire length of his body. I intended doing the front of his body next, so I slapped his bum hard, harder than normal making him wince.

"What the fucking hell did you do that for?" he exclaimed as I stood to one side, examining the red imprint of my hand starting to appear on the right cheek of his arse.

"Do you remember saying I had a face like a slapped bum? Well I just wanted to see what a slapped bum would look like" I said with a laugh.

"That fucking hurt me," he added.

"I'm sorry I was just playing, and didn't mean to hurt you or anything," I said, realising my mistake in hitting him so hard.

"That's OK, I'm fine now, but be careful in future," he pleaded, closing his legs ready for me to sit astride his body.

I climbed over him and kneeling astride his torso, I worked my magic into the front of his shoulders and upper arms. Then moving down to his chest waist and hips, "open your legs" I asked, to enable me to start on the inside of his thighs. I then deliberately caressed his groin area, just out of pure devilment on my part, wondering if I would get any response.

Henry opened his eyes and looking at me intensely said "your trying to get me a fucking hard on aren't you? You bastard!"

"Am I, would I do that?" I asked, moving my hands down towards his knees.

It was already too late for Henry to escape the inevitable, his dick was growing like a beanstalk, but it was still under control for the moment.

"That's not fair, I try to control myself, and you take the piss you prick teaser," he growled at me, turning over in an effort to cover up his stiffy.

Feeling somewhat sorry for him because of my deliberations, I got up and turned off the light, Henry had already got below the covers so I climbed into the bed myself. "I'm sorry I teased you Henry, I didn't mean any harm really, I was just trying to wind you up," I said meaningfully.

"Well you fucking succeeded then," he said.

We lay there in silence until, with a bit more feeling than usual, he muttered, "it's alright Paul, you know I ain't 'alf missed you, you know."

I said "me too," and started to become aware of him playing with himself below the covers once again.

"You randy bastard Henry give it a rest, you wanked yourself off last night, give it a break before it falls off!" I said angrily.

To my amazement he then replied "I can't help it, I've been as randy as hell ever since I've had that op to remove my dud bullock, it's made me even more randy than before."

Suddenly he got out of bed and turned on the light, going back to his bed it was plain to see he was already in an erect state, lying back on the bed and forcing his stiffy against his stomach he asked me, "do you think my one ball has got bigger, or what?"

I looked down at the single goolie, thinking it was a good size but not too big, and said to him "It looks OK to me but it's difficult to tell while you have a hard on anyway."

Henry looked down at his dick and said, "can you see how hard it is now; I'm not touching it as it's full of spunk and ready to come?" After a few moments he started to bring himself off to a full climax, controlling his ejaculation with great care, remembering events in the past I thought.

Now I noticed his one and only ball was returning to a more normal size, having discharged its load. "Its fine, just normal" I said, noting he was now busy feeling it for himself.

He then laid back and exclaimed "that was just fantastic," and started to wipe himself off with a towel, still enjoying a self inflicted high.

I lay there myself thinking how Henry was quite a performer, and the lack of privacy had no effect or inhibitions on him what so ever.

I then started to think about my own misspent youth, in particular my first girl friend Silvia, who went down on me all those years ago. In my mind I started to create an image of Silvia St John giving me a blow job and taking everything I had, until instinctively and without having to check, I knew my arousal was complete. I returned to reality and suddenly became conscious of the light being on, "turn off the light please" I said.

"Sure Paul" he replied on starting to make a move, but then noticed why I wanted the light off. Easing the covers back revealing all he exclaimed, "Well you randy bastard, you are normal after all!"

"What did you expect; do you think I came from Mars or something?"

"Right" said Henry, "start wanking yourself off."

"Blunt little runt aren't you? Not now maybe later" I said.

"Do it now or I'll do it for you" he replied, moving his hand towards me in a threatening manner.

"Alright, alright, but move back from me and give me some space" I muttered, as he moved back and waited for me to start masturbating.

I started to stimulate myself with both hands, touching below my testicles and my groin area, already my over hard erection was throbbing like mad, and I knew I required very little stimulus. On the very brink I took my hands away, allowing my dick to do its own dance for a few moments. With my balls pulsating like mad and not being able to hold back any longer, I lay back until the second before lift off. I gently took hold of my shaft ensuring it remained vertical, and with just one long stroke I erupted, the first spurt leaving the end of my dick like a bullet out the barrel of a gun.

Henry laughed out loud, and several more strokes later, my discharge was over, I could only lay back and enjoy a soaring high, and boy was I on a high. Henry then started to wipe me off with his towel, taking great care as he did so, "you came one hell of a lot, far more than me "he said.

Ignoring his comment, I pronounced to Henry, "I hope you're satisfied now that you've seen me toss myself off."

There was an unscheduled silence as he continued to wipe me dry, and in an effort to calm the tension between us I said, "I needed that badly."

Henry suddenly leaned over with his face close to me and said, "Do you think I'm a pervert Paul?"

In a flash I replied "don't be stupid, you can be a right dipstick at times, but I do wonder why you need an audience to wank yourself off."

"I fucking well don't, I've never done it in front of anyone else, nor would I" he said with real venom in his voice.

"I'm sorry, that was unfair, I didn't mean to suggest you're perverse!" I replied quickly.

Then he told me "I only do it in front of you because I feel safe in your company, I trust you," adding "Completely" to verify this trust.

"I know you do Henry, I really am sorry if I offended you, but it came out all wrong. I trust you as well, but I prefer my sex life in private or at least in the dark" I said.

Having sorted ourselves out we then pulled up the bed clothes, and instinctively turned to face each other in a sign of trust.

After a short period Henry asked, "have you ever had a blow job Paul?"

Don't miss the wall in asking frank questions I thought, but answered, "Funny I had just been thinking about my old girlfriend Silvia giving me one when you spotted my hard on, and put me through that performance. She gave me the best blow job ever, and it's still fresh in my mind, why?"

"Well I've had quite a few girls, but none of them would ever give me a suck off" he said, "I've often wondered why" he added, in a vague tone of voice.

"Come off it Henry with a dick the size of yours a girl would choke on it, let alone find it comfortable stuck in her gob!" I said, "besides, it's far too big for anyone to chew on."

"Is that the real reason?" Henry asked, finding the size of his dick becoming a problem for the first time in his life.

"I'm afraid it is I wouldn't want anything the size of your dick stuck in my mouth, choking me to death, thank you."

This image made Henry burst into spontaneous laughter, "I think I can see what you mean" he said gleefully, and after that we both dozed off into a peaceful sleep.

After a nice cooked breakfast on Wednesday morning we went sailing in the little firefly dinghy, finding plenty of wind, enabling us to race across the Thames on a plane. With both sails full of wind; the jib was out to port and the mainsail out to starboard, with the bow just lifting out of the water. We sat in the stern with the centreboard up, enjoying every moment of such a thrilling experience. This method of sailing is exhilarating and full of excitement, it filled us both with an adrenalin rush, and we just grinned at each other like a couple of Cheshire cats.

Coming off the plane I changed our tack as the wind increased, I decided then, to reef in the mainsail a bit. I rounded the bow into the wind to take in at least one reef on the mainsail, then told Henry "you take the helm, I'll reef the sail."

Still on a bit of a high Henry said, "no, you keep hold of the helm, and I'll reef the sail."

Knowing he was competent enough to carry out this function, I said "OK but take great care not to upset the trim or balance by prancing about, because we are quite a long way from shore."

Starting to move away from me, across to the other side of the dinghy, he tripped on the centreboard casing. In desperation for something to hold on to, he grabbed the boom for support, we lurched over quickly and as the dinghy started to capsize I shouted "don't hang onto the boom with your full weight!"

The dinghy was now very low in the water on the port side, I leaned to starboard in desperation trying to stabilise the craft, managing to bring her onto an even keel, just as water started coming over the gunnel. "Let go of the boom you twerp," I shouted in anger, with Henry responding to my command, and falling into the water at the same time!

He took a ducking, but was still hanging on in desperation. My mind immediately conjured an image of Bobby falling overboard on this very stretch of river, and knowing it was in the very same dinghy, made me react to the situation with even more urgency.

"Swim around to the stern and climb over the transom, but don't let go whatever happens" I told him. The slipstream in the river was now taking the boat crabwise, side on across the rip tide, as I fought to regain control.

He followed my instructions to the letter, and I was able to pull him bodily over the transom and back into the boat, "just stay on the floor," I ordered. Starting to take in the mainsail I completed the reef, in a longer time than anticipated.

"Hold on Henry" I said, on taking in the mainsheet and starting to fill the sail with wind, ignoring the small jib, which I just left flapping loose in the wind. The firefly responded instantly, and now fully under control, I sailed her back to the slipway. On reaching the slipway, I had little difficulty in lifting the dagger board, gently bringing the dinghy to rest on the slope.

"Are you alright?" I asked.

"Bit wet, but otherwise never better" he beamed.

"Not too cold" I asked.

"No I'm fine" came the reply.

"Well you go inside and get dried off while I sort out the dinghy" I added.

"OK" was the reply as he sploshed off heading for the den.

We made ourselves some grub and after several mugs of tea, decided to change into clean gear, and head for town to replenish our stocks of food. We bought food before going to the cinema, on leaving we had fish and chips, eating them on the bridge while watching the river traffic below.

After having a very full day we turned in early, but chatted long into the small hours of Thursday morning, before dropping off to our respective dreams. After a good ham and egg breakfast, with lashings of tea and toast, we both felt ready to face our last day together.

It was a very warm sunny day, so we took to the road giving the Bishop a well earned spin. "I've never been to Runnymede or Windsor" Henry said in a wistful voice.

"OK, let's go then" I replied.

The trusted Bishop was kicked into life, and with a roar we sped off on our merry way. You must remember that in the fifties crash helmets were not compulsory, with goggles on your eyes and the wind rushing over face and through unkempt hair, it gave a kind of freedom that has long since gone with the passing of time and new regulations. Being in the army, my hair was cut short to the style of a then fashionable crew cut, but the rush of wind in my hair was still very enjoyable. We were a pair of fresh faced youths enjoying whatever life had to offer, and had carefree attitudes matching our young minds, with no real pressures to speak of, the pace of life was very different from today. In those days without Hi Tech gadgets; we never became bored, but grateful for being alive after the war, had a wonderful time at every opportunity. After a fantastic time in Windsor we returned to the scout den, I said goodbye to Henry, telling him I wanted to spend the weekend with my aunt in the New Forest. With the knowledge Arthur Cox would see Henry home, I waved goodbye to all the gang come early evening.

Once more I headed for the open road, enjoying the drive down into the New Forest. To meet my aunt again, would be the perfect end to a perfect day. I was more than happy to have a leisurely slow weekend, doing odds and sods for Aunt Joan, whom I had grown to love very dearly.

On leaving the New Forest, for the drive back to Winchester Army Depot, I heard Bobby's voice echo in my ear, "All good things come to an end"

Chapter Nine

More bloody training

The squaddy on guard duty at the gate waved me straight through, recognising my motorcycle, as I approached the check point. The six day break, I was returning from, was just what I had needed. The last few days with my aunt, surrounded by love and lots of peace, cleaned and refreshed my soul. I was ready for anything. However early next morning this serenity was rudely shattered when both the platoon corporals came into the barrack room with their usual morning wake up call. Starting at my end of the room, each corporal taking one row of beds apiece went down both sides of the dorm. These two barnpots performed their morning chorus with great gusto in our dormitory full of soldiers sleeping peacefully. In tandem they screamed filthy abuse at all the sleeping beauties. "Hands off cocks on socks you bastards," they yelled at the top of their voice range. "You Saunders, stop wanking yourself off and leave your dick alone you animal," the corporal would shout. Not exactly the ideal way to start the day, the two corporals would then reverse their walk along each chosen row, pulling away the bed covers from off our bodies leaving us exposed and vulnerable, especially when most of us were in various stages of sexual arousal, that even the bromide in our tea, was unable to prevent. This was also a time when the very dregs of our platoon namely Hawkins - Joyce - or Hunter would lay in wait for any unsuspecting bleary eyed lad, ready to sexually molest or harass their likely victim. Unfortunately for me, I was already a target of this particular bunch of reprobates but so far I had managed to fend them off, on more than one occasion.

During the previous ten week basic training period I had retaliated against these bastards, which resulted in physical violence on my part, to protect myself from Hawkins' little bunch of henchmen. Needless to say, I knew they were waiting, just biding their time, using each other for back up, looking for an opportunity to deal with me in what ever way possible. If faced with a one to one confrontation I had no real worries, because as individuals they had no backbone and their teeth were not sharp enough to deal with me.

On our first full day of return, the entire platoon was issued a full range of jungle greens for war ops, to come. To be honest, this was the part of training; I was most looking forward to. I felt I was better equipped for this six week training period, having done extensive outdoor activities with the scouts. Twenty mile route marches carrying a heavy rucksack, before bivouacking for the night under primitive conditions, was my idea of fun, I found I was in my element. Needless to say, most of my mates within the platoon thought I required certifying to the nearest funny farm. Wading through deep flowing rivers in spate, carrying a bren gun above my head to keep it dry, or planning a sortie in darkness to reach a given six figure map reference point, was for me, great fun. The Walker brothers, Quack, Quack, entering into the spirit of excitement and the unknown dangers of the devised exercises on offer, shared my sense of fun and adventure. We also shared the bedevilment of taking the mickey out of Hawkins and his gang of henchmen, who thought the whole affair was nothing short of torture.

These first three weeks living under temporary man made shelters, surviving in wild places, and always on the move regardless to what the elements threw at us, was for me heaven. It was like being on permanent holiday, especially as Quack and Quack (Chris and Chas) decided to bunk up with me. These two jokers were great to be with, adding to the ambience, never treating anything too seriously. The more I got to know the twins, the more I realized the very special relationship they enjoyed with each other. Being devoted to each other, they fed off each others needs in harmony. God forbid, anyone, and I mean anyone, attempting to interfere or get between either of them. They were reliant on no one except each other of course, and the lure of the attraction for me was their independence as a single entity. Thinking the same thoughts, speaking the same words together verbatim, they always acted together, took a shower or a dump and even cleaned their teeth as one. They were not only twins in every physical detail, naked, dressed or otherwise, but were as close as I've ever seen, they might well have been clones - it was impossible to tell them apart. I perhaps knew them more intimately than anyone else, but I never could tell, which one was which. Their heightened sense of pure mischief made for many hilarious moments, I found myself envious of their unquestionable trust and faith they shared in each other and they were always great fun to be around. For me this six weeks training could go on for ever as far as I was concerned, I was enjoying myself so much, it was like being on one big holiday, and we even got paid for it. No one was more enthusiastic when it came to obstacle courses, long hard route marches - rock climbs- parachute jumps or anything else the army wanted to put my way. To think, in civy street this kind of adventure, especially as well organized as ours, would cost a pretty penny. Perhaps this was what that recruitment sergeant back at Acton meant by "ideal fodder material" I thought. As long as there was no spit and polish, and you could throw away the bullshit the British army thrived on, such as endless kit inspections and uniformed parades or marches, I was in my element, happy as a sand boy playing in shit. I positively ate up with gusto any challenge in the field.

The platoon usually spent all of five days during the so called working week, in the field, most squaddies saw this as horrendous conditions, with a return to barracks as a form of respite at the weekend. It was these weekends I could well do without, given a choice, I would have willingly stayed in the field all of the time. (No wonder most thought I was destined for the nearest looney bin.) Half way through the six weeks of intensive jungle warfare training course, we were all given a thirty six hours leave pass, which I spent just down the road at Hindley, with my aunt. The second and final three week stint in the field was even more exciting than the first. (Is that possible? I hear you ask.) Learning the art of laying a successful ambush, setting booby traps, clearing dangerous tracks and erecting a shelter for the night in the most unlikeliest of places, to me, was absorbing and interesting. After all I was learning skills to ensure my future survival. We had a variety of weapons training, mortars, hand grenades, 3.5 rocket launchers and an assortment of automatic and semi-automatic small arms, along with a variety of some stealth commando training specifically designed to kill the enemy in complete silence, appealing to the blood lust, latent in most of us. This bloodlust was always simmering just below the surface. Especially in those who harboured mischief towards myself or any of my real friends.

During the final week of this training we made an overnight camp on the edge of some thick woodland, at an old disused farm steading. I parked the bren gun carrier near these outbuildings beside the two three ton R-L Bedford trucks driven by the twins, Quack, Quack (Chris and Chas) Naturally under Army regulations in the field we were compelled to stay with our respective vehicles and keep our armed weapons with us at all times. The rest of the platoon was as usual roughing it out, somewhere in the nearby woods, but an empty small stone barn building close by was taken over by a bunch of plebs; half a dozen reprobates led by Hawkins no less. These jokers were looking for a more comfortable billet for the night, although none of them should have been there anyway.

This same night Hawkins along with his bunch of henchmen decided to overplay his false sense of bravado, by ignoring field orders and breaking platoon ranks in commandeering this outbuilding for his own use and comfort. Sometime after midnight and long after most of us were dead to the world, save for the two sentries posted on guard duty some distance away on the periphery of our encampment, my sleep was suddenly broken. I was awakened by one of the twins in an agitated and forlorn state. It transpired that Hawkins group had grabbed the other twin from his lorry, having taken him back to their barn as a hostage. (This was not part of any Army exercise.) Don't ask me which of the twins was taken, because to this day, I still don't know. With stealth afoot and bad intentions in our hearts we set out to investigate. Regardless of the fact we were deserting our respective posts, (a court martial offence) we proceeded with our weapons in hand to find the hostage. We could hear clearly some kind of disturbance, albeit with much hushing, going on within the building. Silently we entered; I lead with my bren gun at the ready. The only light was the candle light concentrated at the far end of this stone building, it was abundantly clear what was going on, we had both walked into the start of a gang rape! The captured twin had been stripped naked and was forcibly being held down by most of Hawkins henchmen. The shadows cast by the small half a dozen or so candles, were creating eerie ghost like puppet figures on the ceiling of the roof overhead. Hawkins had taken his trousers off, revealing his hard erect state; he was in the very act of attempting to force entry into his unwilling victim, who naturally would not keep still for him. Being so absorbed with their evil intentions they were unaware of our presence. This excited state of play, with much noise of encouragement from all those participating, made our intervention that much easier. When only less than two paces from my target, Hawkins, I aimed the end of my Bren gun barrel at Hawkins rectum. I lunged forward and with one final push, I felt, indeed I knew, the gun barrel had entered his anus, as he let out one almighty scream of agony at this penetration of his arse. With no sense of logic in my behaviour I told Hawkins his mouth was about to taste his arsehole, as I cocked my weapon ready for automatic fire. Two things happened instantaneously, his erection deflated like a burst balloon as a rush of urine left the end of his dick in uncontrollable shock soaking his victim and himself. The enforcers of his little gang backed off completely, by now they were covered with the automatic weapon held in the arms of the twin who came in with me. By this time, I had Hawkins face down on the earthen floor of the barn, the tip of my bren gun barrel still firmly stuck up his arse. He was now crying and shaking from the utter shock, his body turned white. He was begging for mercy whimpering like a child. Meanwhile, the victim in all of this wiped himself with Hawkins trousers to get rid of the traces of urine on his body, then calmly dressed himself, before joining his beloved twin. I suggested that one of Hawkins henchmen go for the Company Commander to arrest and lock up their brave hero, lying on the floor in such a pathetic state. Needless to say no one took up the offer to leave. I told Hawkins to get up, as without ceremony, I vigorously retrieved the end of the gun barrel from his anus.

He raised himself slowly to his full height, his back still towards me, I ordered him to turn around and face me. When he was facing me fully I struck him with the butt of my weapon, across his right cheek, which burst open on impact. With blood spurting out both ends, he now had even more reason for another bout of sobbing, as he fell in a heap at my feet. The twins and I made an uneasy retreat, returning to our respective vehicles.

The next morning we checked the barn, and although there was evidence of the previous night's occupation the cupboard was now bare. I spent most of the day looking over my shoulder, expecting the Provo Police to arrest me and take me off to the glass house, to await court martial. It never happened, but I do know that Hawkins was carted off to hospital with serious injuries to his posterior and face; at least that's what I was told. I never saw Hawkins again before we went on our ten days embarkation leave. The next time I saw Hawkins, he was sporting a two inch scar across the right cheek of his face. I never saw the state of his arse and that suited me just fine. At first, I lived in dread of someone telling the sergeant about my illegal use of a fire arm in the field. However, I soon realised these events would not be easily explained away by any of the perpetrators to the authorities. When I did meet up with Hawkins's henchmen, I made it very clear to each and every one of them, that should they come near any of us again I would kill them. (I think they believed me.) In any case, neither the twins nor I were troubled ever again.

The rape of Swany came back to haunt me for several nights. As was our code, the bulk of the platoon instinctively closed ranks, but the sergeant was more than aware that something bad had taken place on that final night of jungle training. The sergeant also knew of the bad blood existing between Hawkins and myself and suspected I was deeply involved, somewhere along the way. He must have heard some whisper, because he questioned me closely about firearms offences, with a mere wisp on how serious the illegal use of weapons in the field was. "Would I be so stupid?" I asked, but knew he wasn't totally convinced, thankfully I never heard any more about the matter. Naturally, except for Quack and Quack, the rest of the platoon now knew I was stark raving mad, where as before they only suspected it. Under the circumstances, I didn't find my actions too difficult to live with, and given time, the whole matter would be forgotten. (I hoped.)

When we arrived back at base, all our equipment (and any evidence) was safely handed in. We became rather animated at the thought of the ten days embarkation leave due to us, before the whole battalion was shipped off abroad. The rumour all over the base relayed by the one and only 'Bertie Echo' our platoon gossip, was we were all off to Korea.

"Where my brother Bobby fell and died," I remembered, speaking to myself. Oh well I thought "What will be will be." In truth, I wasn't exactly over the moon about this prospect, but was resigned to the fact, that my future fate lay in the lap of the Gods. There was nothing I could do about it anyway. On a windy but bright sunny day, I kicked life into the Bishop and was off, once more heading towards London to meet up with Henry.

Hindley Cottage – Burley, New Forest – Newly Built

Henry, Climbing -
Final Rock Pitch

Henry, Abseiling without the
safety of a top rope

The author, checking out a new tent

Window Buttress - Lakes - Crack & Chimney - Lakes

Chapter Ten

A few more climbs

On arriving in London I met up with Henry, who had arranged time off work with Archie and was all geared up, raring to go. My tent and the rest of our gear, had already been carefully packed by an anxious Henry, who was eagerly awaiting my arrival. As usual his exuberance was rather overpowering in the excitement of our reunion. He was all over me before I had parked the bike, but the final insult was when he first hugged me then unashamedly kissed me full on the lips, which he had never done before. As my embarrassment was now complete it made me go red, very red indeed, especially since this display was in full public view outside his house, causing my credibility in the immediate neighbourhood to take a nose dive. I was completely shattered he'd left me totally speechless, as this was Henry's birthplace where everyone knew him. In great haste with Henry on the back of the fully laden bike, I got out of the district like a scalded cat.

On the road heading for the Peak district, to climb Pillar Rock, this image stayed with me for many miles. Once on the open road and with the first few hours tucked up behind us, I began to relax and even enjoy the hugging character on the pillion behind me. We pulled off the road, into a well known café forecourt, where we both dismounted for a break and bite to eat. I had every intention of giving Henry a bit of a rocket for his display of public affection, but when I saw how happy he was my irritation just melted away. I spent some time studying the small climbing guide of Pillar rock, loaned to Henry by Arthur Cox, and I marked out a good camping site nearby for our intended climb the following day. As usual Henry was bubbling away like an excited schoolboy and it was sometimes necessary to remind myself of the fact that Henry was actually twenty – two years old even though he looked much younger, almost as young as myself I thought. We made excellent time, and by the last rays of the setting sun we erected the tent not far from a nearby stream, with the foot of the climb of Pillar rock only a short distance away on the other side of the river. The sunset held the promise of a fine day tomorrow as I took myself off for a stroll and a look about, while Henry busied himself lighting the primus stove to make a quick and simple supper. Having eaten our fill, we settled into our sleeping bags with a final mug of hot sweet tea, then Henry left the tent for a quick leak. On climbing back into his sleeping bag, I noticed some very pronounced claw marks on either side of his hips, below the waist. I didn't mention this to him, but Henry noted I had seen them! He talked away pleasantly until I told him we should both get an early night, as the climb tomorrow would be hard going, then we both fell asleep fairly quickly.

Along with the weather the climbing was superb, we climbed together easily in complete harmony, with very few problems. I made a point of leading the more difficult pitches, which Henry was only too pleased to let me do, as he was not yet ready to climb beyond his new found ability. I preferred this code of conduct between us, which seemed natural, but I noted his abilities had vastly improved since I had last seen him in climbing action. It turned out Arthur Cox had taken Henry under his wing raising not only his climbing ability to a very good standard but also his confidence. Having negotiated the vital crux we reached the top of the Pillar and both sat down to admire the fantastic views, with ample time in hand, before making our decent. I told Henry how much I admired his present climbing skills and in particular all the safety aspects of the excellent belays that he employed. Henry positively glowed with satisfaction and was obviously enjoying himself. After a good rest, having satisfied our thirst and egos alike, we descended with great care, both aware this was not the time to take chances, to be careless, or slapdash in our endeavours.

In under an hour we were safely back onto the lower slopes leading to the stream we would have to re-cross, in order to get to our tent, clearly visible and not far away on the other side. In less than half an hour, we were both sitting at the waters edge, with boots off, cooling our feet, before crossing back over the stream, which was less than eighteen inches deep but full of slippery boulders. I set off ahead, carrying the bulk of our gear, with Henry just a few yards behind me. I scrambled up the far bank on the other side and pressed onwards in bare feet towards our tent, now less than fifty yards away. I heard Henry cry out "shit" making me look over my shoulder to see him sitting on his bum in the middle of the river, up to his waist in swirling water.

I burst into spontaneous laughter, then quickly dropped my rucksack and ran back to help him. "Are you all right?" I shouted over the noise of the fast babbling water.

"I'm fine," he said bravely.

I helped him to his feet and got him across to the river bank, then I went ahead once more to uplift my gear and moved it into the tent. I quickly found a towel to dry him off and discovered that he was now limping, I then vacated the tent to give him more room to move about as he quickly stripped off.

It now transpired he was hurt more than he was prepared at first to admit. After brewing up some tea I handed him a mug full, but by this time he was beginning to look rather pale about the gills.

"Why don't you get into your sleeping bag?" I suggested.

"I might just do that" he replied taking another big slurp of his tea. "I don't feel too good" he said softly.

I got into the tent beside him to take a closer look. "What's wrong?" I asked anxiously.

"My hips feel really sore" he replied calmly.

"Roll over and let me examine you closer" I suggested.

Without hesitation he rolled over onto his side with some difficulty and turned his bum towards me, making it easier to see the gash on the lower portion of his rump.

"On to your front" I instructed, and as he moved into a face down position, I gently prodded various parts of his anatomy looking for further damage. Both hips had taken a bashing and the gash on the lower part of his buttock looked particularly nasty, although I suspected it was not bleeding a lot, due to the very cold temperature of the water. This cold water had acted like a local anaesthetic.

Reaching into the side pocket of my Bergen I pulled out a first aid kit. "You might have to lie on your front for a while," I hinted as I cleaned his wound with some medical alcohol, making him wince, as the sting took its bite. I put a small but adequate sterile field dressing over the wound on his rump. "Get back into your bag and rest face downwards to keep warm," I told him.

When Henry dozed off I let him sleep for a good hour or so, as soon as he awakened I gave him some tea, which helped the colour return to his cheeks. "How are you feeling now?" I asked him.

"Better, but both my hips still feel sore" he remarked.

"I've got some muscle liniment in my sack, I'll give your hips a good massage with the stuff later," that prospect fairly made him smile. "It's only your hips mind you," I said, knowing what a sex pot he was.

"That will be just fine," he said smiling.

"I don't think you have broken anything. Otherwise you would not have been able to stand or walk," I assured him. "Do you want another mug of tea before I take the dishes down to the river to wash them?" I asked.

"I wouldn't mind" he replied, enjoying the pampering he was receiving.

After washing all the dishes and putting them away ready for immediate use, I turned to Henry and remarked "look how the clouds are gathering, we could possibly get rain later this evening."

Henry seemed to lose some of his sparkle. Quite worried I said, "OK. Get yourself on top of your sleeping bag face down, and let me have a good look at you, but take your time."

This he duly did with a little difficulty, feeling much stiffer than he had a few hours ago. Gently I started to rub in the liniment to his hips and thighs, noticing the large scratches on his rump, as they were very conspicuous. Seizing the opportunity I asked him "how did you get the large claw marks on each side of your arse?"

Henry declined to answer, mumbling "I'll tell you later," so I didn't persist in giving him the third degree.

"Open your legs wide," I instructed, then kneeling between them I asked, "Can you raise yourself up a little on your knees and all fours?"

This he did without hesitation as I brought my knees together under his body. "If you get tired or sore, just sit back onto my knees," I told him.

"OK" he replied. I then spent a good twenty minutes applying deep heat massage to both hips and buttocks, before finishing off on his thighs.

"OK Henry, I'll move out of the way now, but see if you can lie on your back."

Gingerly he moved over onto his back, lowering himself down onto his sleeping bag. "I think perhaps you should get back into your sleeping bag to keep warm," I said, noticing he was already wearing a partial erection.

He got into his already warm sleeping bag with a sigh of relief. "Are you comfortable enough?" I enquired.

"Yes thanks Paul" he sighed again.

"Resist lying on either of your hips for the time being and I suspect you'll be very stiff by morning and will probably need more rest, but we'll wait and see," I said.

He reached over and gave my arm an affectionate squeeze, "Thanks a lot Paul" he said.

"That's OK." I said, "It could have been much worse. Now close your eyes and try to sleep, you badly need your rest."

After he had closed his eyes, I leaned over and gave him a brief kiss on his forehead. His eyes remained closed, but a perceptible smile fleetingly crossed his face, in acknowledgement. Once he was sound asleep, I crept outside to relieve myself; I had a last good look about before settling down into my own sleeping bag for the night. I decided to put an empty Tizer bottle between us, on the ground sheet, in case Henry needed a piss during the night. I doused the light and turned over to sleep and was dreaming about the climb on Pillar rock we had done earlier that same day, when Henry shook me awake.

"Yes Henry" I mumbled, sleepily.

"I'm bursting for a piss," said Henry

"There's an empty bottle next to your bag," I murmured.

"Give us a hand," he said, as I turned over to see what I could do he was already kneeling down, facing towards me.

"It won't go in the neck of the bottle," he complained.

I looked at his dick, which I could now see was far too big to enter into the narrow neck of the empty Tizer bottle. "Hold on Henry" I said, scrambling out of my bag. "Try this for size" I said handing him the largest of our Billy cans, which I knew held two pints of liquid.

"Be careful not to splash any," I said as he emptied himself with great relief. "Fucking heck, you've almost filled the pot up," I remarked as I took it from him with care. I left the tent still naked, careful not to spill the contents.

Once I got away to a respectful distance I emptied it. By the time I got back to the tent Henry was fast asleep again. In the early hours of the morning I awoke to the sound of a shower of rain noisily pelting the canvas roof of our tent. I just loved the sound of rain, especially under the canvas of a good stout tent. The smugness, the feeling of comfort and wellbeing, always warmed the cockles of my very contented heart. Suddenly, I became aware of a kind of a rubbing noise against some material next to me, surely not, I thought. "Henry" I said softly.

Many moments later he answered, "yes Paul, I didn't know you were awake."

"What are you doing?" I asked suspiciously.

"Nothing" he quickly replied.

"You fucking liar" I said reaching down into his bag knowing just what I'd find. "You're supposed to be recuperating, not pulling your dick off." I retorted, drawing my hand away quickly.

"I can't help it, I woke up with a massive great hard on and it wouldn't go away," he said rather sheepishly.

"Another thing Henry how did you get those claw marks?" I asked, shining my torch on him.

With a wry smile on his face he replied "my girlfriend Carol gave them to me."

I was a little surprised because Henry hadn't mentioned any girlfriend till now, although I was more than aware he was very fond of the female species. "Bit of an animal is she?" I found myself saying.

"No - well yes" Henry stuttered, "kind of" he added.

"Does she like rough sex?" I asked.

"Sometimes," he said "sometimes" he murmured repeating himself.

"Okay Henry what happened exactly?" I asked, "or maybe you can't talk about it" I added.

"She likes me to sit over her face bridging her chest to wank me off," Henry started to explain.

"Go on" I said encouragingly, now very intrigued indeed.

"She licks the end of my knob," he said hesitantly.

"Did you put it into her mouth?" I asked.

"I tried to persuade her, you know Paul, but she said no, it was too thick for comfort."

"So what happened next?" I asked.

"I tried to but she wouldn't let me" he replied. There was several seconds of silence before Henry added. "Well, I did it when she wasn't really expecting it."

I thought for several moments then asked, "did you put it in?"

"All of it, I didn't mean any harm by it," he replied sheepishly. "That's when she clawed me to make me take it out, but I refused to until after I had come to my very last drop" he admitted.

A long silence followed, "you bastard, you fucking animal" I exploded, losing my rag completely. "You utter arsehole," I yelled.

Now followed several long seconds of silence you could cut with a knife, "Did she go the Police?" I enquired.

There was a pause, "No," he whispered, "but she did dump me!"

"Surprise, surprise" I shouted "It's a wonder she didn't bite your dick off! Believe me Henry, you got off very light, very light indeed," I emphasized.

After a long and very uncomfortable silence, I went on to tell Henry about the recent attempted rape of one of the twins in my regiment. Leaving the torch on, down between us on the ground sheet, I watched Henry's face go into all kinds of contortions. Realization of what he had done was dawning on him and he burst into an uncontrollable fit of sobbing. When I couldn't bear to look at him any longer, I turned off the torch.

While he continued to sob loudly, I got dressed and started to leave the tent. "What are you doing?" Henry asked through his sobs.

"I don't know" I spat at him, covering him with spittle. I had seen this kind of sexual behaviour at Ashford throughout my childhood. "Henry, I need some fresh air," I barked.

"What time will you be back?"

"When I fucking well get back," I yelled in anger.

Making my way up to the Bishop, parked on the road, I fired her up and switched on the headlamp before speeding away in disgust. Was I overreacting? I asked myself, as the cool night air rushed by my body. I must have driven for about an hour before finally pulling off the road.

I slowly back tracked events in my mind and several cigarettes later, I told myself it was none of my fucking business anyway! Perhaps I would have been better off not knowing, after all most of us have some dreaded secret we don't want anyone else to know about, I know I have plenty, I reasoned with myself.

I decided to go back from whence I'd come and fired the Bishop into life, then made my way back to camp, at a much slower pace. When I returned and looked through the door of the tent, Henry was busy trying to get himself dressed. "What do you think you are doing?" I demanded of him, as he looked up at me through very red swollen eyes. I thought he looked awful with a face like a slapped bum.

"I was afraid you were going to leave me here on my own" said Henry softly lowering his face.

It was obvious he couldn't look me in the eye, not yet anyway. "Get back into bed" I said in a more normal tone of voice, having regained control of my temper.

I picked up several large Billy cans, to fetch some water to boil. Down at the river bank in the first of the early morning daylight I looked at my watch - 6.30 am it read. As I returned to the tent, I looked up at the cloudy sky overhead and just knew we were in for a wet day ahead. I set up some water on the stove ready for making tea, then on impulse decided to play my harmonica, while lying down on my bag. At that moment in time the only tune in my head was Shenandoah, which I played over and over again. I was thinking of Bobby, expressing my feelings through the music. Tears rolled down my face unashamedly, the memories this tune provoked only added to my suffering. I felt alone, totally lost in space and time, cocooned, not even aware of the presence of Henry. He was under the same canvas just feet away, also suffering with his own private thoughts, but at present I just couldn't care less.

The hot water on the stove then boiled over, spitting its hot globules onto the hot metal of the fire head, bringing me back to the present with a sudden rush of reality. I made some tea, handing a mug to Henry without a word.

Later I went about cooking breakfast, starting with some really thick porridge, followed by sausages, baked beans, fried eggs and tomatoes. We finished off our feast with lots of toast covered in butter and marmalade. Mid morning long after breakfast and with just as much concern as I could muster, I decided to give Henry a bed bath, followed by more liniment and massage. I was feeling a little guilty at having given him such a verbal beating, I suppose, but he took all this attention without as much as a single word uttered between us. I left him to get more rest and went down to the river to punish myself with a cold dip.

Now feeling much better, I returned to the tent and tidied up a bit, then settled down to study the climbers guide book brought along for the climb of Pillar rock. Several times that morning Henry tried in vain to make verbal contact. By lunch time I plucked up enough courage to talk to him at length. The relief on his face was dramatic. His hips he assured me were now only a little stiff, so if I wanted us to move on, he was more than willing. I told him about the bad bruising I had noticed during his last massage and I thought today at least, should be treated as an extended rest period, hopeful of a full recovery by the morrow. Later I told him how sorry I was for blowing my top and the cause of this harrowing incident was never ever again open for discussion. Henry was just as anxious as I was to remove this bad taste. I also told him how privileged I felt for such a confidence he had imparted and how on reflection, somehow I felt I had abused the implicit trust between us, by over reacting. After all I told him, I was no angel, I had done far worse things in my life, things that I couldn't bring myself to tell anybody about. I don't know if he believed me, but there was hope that in these crumbs of comfort, our friendship stood some chance of recovery. He looked at me kindly, about to cry with sheer relief. As I hugged him for reassurance, the face of the Henry I once knew slowly reappeared. This incident was never mentioned again.

Next day we headed off to the Lake District, to climb Raven's Crag and one particularly tricky climb called Amen Corner. This short climb was tremendously exposed, it was eventually hard won, but the many attempts added excitement to the satisfaction of surmounting the crux. Any bad feeling we may have had between us, had now been well and truly buried. Henry's bum had healed, leaving only a healthy looking scar to show for it. His hips had fully recovered and we were both able to laugh about that, with some fond memories. The stupid things we have done, falling back on the ignorance of youth to take the blame, making the learning curve of life never ending and seeking redemption for our misguided souls upon this earth of ours. This earth is supposed to be shared by all, but only for a short time. No wonder Henry found it difficult to understand me. There were times I didn't understand myself.

The weather then took a turn for the worse, so after just five days out, we decided to make a run for the New Forrest to visit my aunt, where we knew we would receive more T.L.C. than either of us deserved.

As usual my aunt spoilt us rotten, knowing my days were numbered, so to speak. Like any mother with her brood, she was determined to make my last days in the country count. I gave my aunt my army uniform as it had been bundled up tight in one of the Bishop's saddle bags all this time, it also badly needed of some of my aunts T.L.C.- with a hot iron. Henry had obviously forgiven me completely and without being blatant, his minute signs of affection towards me were sometimes very touching, without being suggestive or sexual in any way, Henry also spent a lot of his time helping my aunt in all sorts of ways. She enjoyed having him about so much he was easily persuaded to change his plans and stay on, at least until my departure. The bike would then be carefully prepared, for a long lay up in her garage once more and my aunt would put Henry on a train bound for London, after I disappeared.

With only a few days left before once again surrendering up my freedom, we did our best to be pleasant to one another in the most amicable way. On my last night but one, I was taking a shower and running a hot bath for Henry, when he asked "is it OK for me to use the bath at the same time?"

"Of course" I replied, "come in and help yourself."

Henry was stretched out in the bath while I was at the other end, enjoying my shower. Henry was in a very playful mood, throwing a wet soapy flannel at my body, trying hard to provoke a positive reaction. I unhooked the showerhead from its bracket and directed the full pressure head onto his face, then every time he put up his hands to protect himself I redirected the pressure to other parts of his body. He decided at that point to admit defeat and got out of the bath.

Henry having vacated the bath, I turned off the shower and lay down to relax in the hot bath water. I studied Henry's body from behind as he was drying himself off. The recent scar was clear to see but looked healthy enough. The claw marks either side of his buttocks were fading fast.

"Henry" I said, as he turned around he had a massive hard on at my eye level, I forgot what I was going to ask him.

"I can't help it" Henry said, "it's been at least a fortnight since I had a wank and I need to empty my sexual frustrations away OK."

I said "OK" getting out of the bath with haste. "Make sure you clean up behind you, once you get rid of your waste."

He quickly stepped back into the bath, soaping himself up, before I even had time to towel myself off properly he ejaculated his cum into the bath. "Sorry Paul" he said "I just couldn't wait any longer. I suppose if you gotta go – you gotta go!" He got back out and pulled the plug, as I went through to the warm bedroom and climbed upon my own bed and lay down.

Having finished his chores Henry came through also to lie on his bed, but still with an erection, which was in no hurry to obey mental orders to go soft. "Gee man," uttered Henry "I was desperate," then suddenly shut up deciding not to finish his sentence. "Remember Paul" Henry started, then stopped.

"Yes" I interjected. "What?"

"You said one day you would tell me about the Bishop," said Henry with hesitancy in his voice. "I mean, why call a bike the Bishop?" he asked.

"OK," I don't suppose it will do any real harm anyway." I eventually agreed. I looked across at Henry who was busy checking he still had one ball to play with; I left my own bed to sit beside him.

He looked up in interest as I said to him "can you pull your foreskin back as far as it goes?"

He looked enquiringly into my face, but started to peel back his skin all the way. "Will it stay back on its own?" I asked Henry.

"I think so, it usually does" he replied.

"Right, take your hand away and leave it to stand on guard duty alone" this he did.

"Now Henry, take a good long look at your dick and you tell me what it reminds you of, what it most resembles" I added.

I went back to my own bed meanwhile, waiting to hear what sort of an answer he would come up with. After a good ten minutes and with his dick now refusing to stand upright alone any longer, Henry turned on his side to face me looking very bewildered, but finally said "No, I give up."

"Have you ever played chess?" I asked him.

"No" he said. "But I've often watched Terry at work play the game" he added.

"Think long and hard Henry, what chess piece do you think your dick most looks like?"

The clouds from his brain cleared slowly to reveal pure blue sky with a sudden smile of recognition upon Henry's face. "The Bishop" cried Henry with glee, having worked out the clue to this crossword puzzle.

So I found myself telling him all about my beloved Bobby, who always referred to his own dick as the bishop after the very same chess piece. How Bobby like Henry was a sex maniac who also never stopped playing with it in all kinds of experimentation. I told Henry about our secret pool and our joint sexual exploration while growing up through our childhood together over thirteen long years at Ashford. I reminisced about Bobby's many girlfriends (too many to count) and how he always got his wicked way with them.

I poured out my soul to Henry, holding nothing back. It seemed a long time since I had climbed under my bedclothes, getting ready to go to sleep. "So you see Henry," I said "The only real difference between you both is Bobby was circumcised. You could say I named the BSA motorbike The Bishop to make sure I never forgot Bobby or his bishop." Then I remained silent.

Many minutes later, Henry climbed into my bed, lay down beside me and after a while said "What a wonderful story," then more softly he whispered into my ear "what a wonderful story" he put his arm across my chest and fell asleep.

Later I eased myself from my own bed, leaving Henry there and escaped into Henry's bed to sleep. (This was the very bed that Bobby slept in I remembered.) We had a great breakfast, for some unknown reason I was in an extra buoyant mood, which rather unsettled both my aunt and Henry, who between them never missed a thing.

"What do you plan to do darling on your last full day? My aunt asked softly, looking at me to gauge my response.

"Well I thought Henry and I could take a slow leisurely run down the coast, as it looks as if the weather has taken a turn for the better."

"That sounds like a wonderful idea Paul darling, because I have so much to catch up on here," she said. "What time do you have to be back at Winchester barracks tomorrow?" my aunt looked at me searchingly.

"You know what time," I replied softly, "ten a.m." I added.

We stayed long enough for a final coffee, then I fired up the Bishop and with Henry hanging on closer than normal, we bumped our way down Honey lane. Before we hit the tarmac, I stopped the Bishop put her into neutral and looked over my shoulder at Henry, while the engine purred nicely in tick over.

"Do you fancy driving for a while?" I asked Henry.

"Why?" asked Henry suspiciously "you've never let anyone drive the Bishop," he pronounced, looking very puzzled indeed.

"I know" I said "but if you don't want to drive her, I'll understand" I said to him.

"I would love a shot," Henry said, realizing my offer was genuine and he now looked very excited.

"OK" I said "but be very gentle as she is a beautiful lady and must be treated with great tenderness, love and respect.

We changed positions with Henry in the driving seat, he then proceeded to amaze me, with his total control and the dexterity of his silky smooth gear changes. Not once did he default, it was as if he was at one with the machine, it left me completely gob smacked. Without any prompting from me he glided to a smooth halt on the coastline road, putting the Bishop into neutral gear and after I dismounted he managed to easily pull her up onto the stand by himself.

"Where did you learn to drive?" I asked.

"I didn't" replied Henry, "but I've watched every move you make handling the Bishop over the last couple of years," he said with pride.

He was delighted with his newly discovered talent, beaming from ear to ear, just like a Cheshire cat. We sat on the nearby bench together, looking across at the sea view. Every now and then, I stole a glance at Henry; I was in awe of his outstanding performance with the Bishop.

"Do you fancy a run down to Brighton?" I asked Henry.

He looked at me as if he was in love or star struck or something, and asked if he could drive. "I don't see why not" I replied.

Henry fired up the Bishop in a state of high elation, once again in full control, as if he had been riding the bike all his life.

The journey to Brighton was thrilling and very enjoyable. We had a great lunch, and then headed for home, stopping several times on the way, just for the sheer pleasure.

"She's a real smasher" exclaimed Henry. "No wonder you love her so much" he remarked.

"Yes, she's been very good to me" I replied.

On our return Henry insisted on giving the old girl a loving wash and spent another good hour with the polish, until gleaming in black and chrome, she could have just come straight from the showroom. I took myself off for a wander down through the village on my own, leaving Henry busy cleaning the Bishop.

At bedtime taking advantage of the en-suite bathroom to myself for once, I had a shower and was laying on top of my bed when Henry came up. "You alright?" he asked.

"Just fine, but I want a word with you when you have finished in the bathroom, and are ready for bed" I told him.

While Henry was in the bathroom I wrapped a towel around my waist and bolted downstairs for a quick word with Aunt Joan in private. "I've decided to give Henry the Bishop," I said, as my aunt raised her hand to stop me in mid sentence.

"I know dear, and think it's a wonderful idea," she said, taking me aback.

"How did you know what I was going to suggest?" I asked in amazement.

"You forget Paul darling, I've known you most of your life, I just knew you would do such a thing" she added looking at me in a tender way.

On finding it still hard to say anything I heard her continue to explain "Henry will need to get a full licence before he can take the bike away, but I can help him with that" she said with conviction in her voice. She then pulled me towards her with tenderness, as if holding a child to her breast, then hugged me and kissed me making me totally dumfounded. "Now off you go" she said, turning and heading for the kitchen on some pretence or other, as the tears started to flow from her eyes.

I looked at her with longing as my own eyes started to fill, then very slowly I climbed the stairs, removing the towel from my waist and used it to wipe the tears from my eyes.

On reaching my room I dropped the towel on the floor as I climbed into bed, oblivious to Henry watching my every move, as he lay in his own bed. I must have looked such a pathetic sight, as Henry continued to study me, still without saying a word. Several moments later he climbed onto my bed silently, he wrapped both his arms about my body.

"Can you turn the light out?" I asked Henry in little more than a whisper.

He did so in absolute silence and then returned to his previous position, waiting for me to say something. "I'm leaving the Bishop to you Henry" I said in a soft voice.

"Don't be silly" replied Henry, once he had found his power of speech. "You'll come back from abroad just fine" he started to say.

"No Henry, you misunderstand me, of course I'll come back, although I'm not sure when." I explained. "What I mean is, I want you to have the Bishop, she's now yours," I said softly.

A good few moments went by then Henry asked "but why Paul, why?"

"Because I can't bear the thought of the Bishop being locked up for such a long time, she needs freedom, the feeling of the wind licking her body work and the throbbing of her engine on the open road. She must be free, but most of all she must be used and looked after with tenderness and great care."

Now it was Henry's turn to be gobsmacked. Henry became very emotional and throwing his arms around me he started to kiss me on the face.

"Stop that you tart, or I'll change my mind," I shouted, bringing instant sanity to his over exuberant antics. "Now go to your own bed and leave me alone" I said with conviction, "I want to be with my own thoughts and alone in my own bed."

Henry without a word slipped out of my bed and into his own. Sometime much later, I fell asleep and dreamt about the first time Bobby gave me a ride on his bike. The very first time in fact when he roared into Ashford school playground to take me to the scouts in Staines. Every detail, every gesture, every expression on Bobby's face it was all so clear I could touch him, all I had to do was reach out.

The Bishop would continue to be in caring, loving hands, I assured myself because somehow I knew the Bishop would always belong to

Bobby. In this world we mere mortals would only ever be its custodians I thought returning to consciousness and back to the land of the living. It was time to return to army life, and I set off for Winchester barracks early next morning. The time had come to race into a new world of reality, whatever that might bring. "I must be brave, or at least look as if I am," I said to myself, as I went once more through the main gates of Winchester barracks only this time on foot. Not knowing how long it might be, before I saw my Aunt Joan, Henry or the Bishop again.

Chapter Eleven

Preparations

On my return to Winchester Barracks I went to bed that first night in the certain knowledge, that I was now firmly locked in the tentacles of the military. We would shortly embark as a Battalion by sea to Korea. (Perhaps I too would fall as a fatal casualty, in this very same country which took my beloved brother Bobby.) I was to dream of Bobby that first night back in barracks. In any case, I concluded we were stuck with each other, the army and I, for at least the next three years.

After a hard ten weeks basic training and with further six weeks highly specialised jungle training below my belt, it was time for a reality check. The Walker twins Chris and Chas were in a very joyful mood, greeting me with exuberant hugs and kisses, almost as if I was their own kin. We soon learned there were just five days to get the entire Battalion fully mobilised, before boarding a troopship ready for the off, one might say a logistical nightmare. This imminent embarkation bound for foreign climes, (Korea still being the favourite on the short list) would mean a very hectic five days of preparation, to enable the thousands of tons of cargo to be assembled in readiness for shipping. The twins and I were involved on the transport side, constantly ferrying load after load, to the port from Winchester H.Q. The mood throughout the regiment was buoyant, with a great deal of excitement percolating like delicious strong black coffee amongst all the ranks, overflowing with anticipation at the unknown adventures which lay ahead.

Along with the excitement there was also an undercurrent of controlled fear, a kind of unspoken language, knowing many of us would be forced to kill or be killed, in the performance of our so called duty to Queen and country. There was also an unspoken awareness, that some of us may never return. Besides being a distinct possibility, it was also a fact of life, I told myself - as I needed to look no further than my brother Bobby for evidence of this reality.

These last few days before boarding our troopship for the Far East were hanging very heavily. We knew we had yet to find out for ourselves the realities of jungle warfare and what we might face in the field of battle. The survival equipment and all kinds of weaponry to be employed in the field were extensive. Every soldier was issued with his own private large kit bag, along with an assortment of jungle greens and other clothing. Once our individual kit bags were expertly and tightly packed, most of us discovered it weighed more than our own body weight. My own, clocked in over eleven stones, compared with my own body weight of just over ten stones. Every kit bag was then stencilled with the Battalion flash insignia and our individual rank and army number thus: RFN 23.202513.on the outer stout canvas casing with bright paint. This along with an abundance of other gear was then transported to the dockside for loading. The twins and I spent the five days driving to and from the port of departure. We drove a fleet of army trucks, combat vehicles and ancillary vehicles, all needed in the field of operations on arrival at our destination. (Which at this moment was still speculative?)

I myself drove a number of bren gun carriers, Land Rovers and a particularly new issue of a combat vehicle known as the Austin Champ. This was a unique vehicle at this time and innocently looked very much like any other jeep, except this all terrain vehicle was fitted with a lifting snorkel exhaust system, allowing it to breath and travel partially submerged below the normal river level. It also had five gears forward as well as five gears reverse – enabling it to travel just as fast in reverse, as it would going forward, besides this it had the usual four wheel drive traction. The Champ had a Rolls Royce designed engine, made under licence by Austin Motors Ltd. The Champs were very fast and very exciting to drive over rough terrain and off road conditions. At the end of this five day preparatory period there was a definite full stop within the Battalion as all its equipment was now safely aboard ship.

We were now sailing towards the unknown, on the point of no return. Now with the hectic five days comfortably behind us, we felt a huge relief as with open seas behind us, at long last the regiment was heading for the Bay of Biscay towards the Suez Canal and the Far East. During this first week at sea, our ship took a battering in heavy seas. The ship was heavily laden, right up to the plimsoll line, which I suspected made this crate (which was once an old ocean liner) sluggish in answering to her helm. In the first two days alone, we saw the decks awash with the heavy Atlantic rollers sweeping her decks from stem to stern. Many men had great difficulty in keeping their food down, spending most of their time retching the contents of their stomachs over the side rails.

After the first full week at sea we entered a warmer climate, with more settled seaways and improving conditions. I was one of the more fortunate minorities who had found his sea legs within forty eight hours of being on board. I found myself revelling in the bracing sea air, even more so once we entered a warmer climate. Night times were the worst for me, with the cramped sleeping conditions, all packed like sardines with so many body odours adding to the stench. However, now that we were in sub-tropical waters, I took to sleeping on deck like so many others including the twins. Where, I could slumber undisturbed, beneath a starry sky, with sea air flowing sweetly all around me. Overdosing on this salty air had only one disadvantage for me, I found I was always ravenous and constantly looking for the extra food required to sustain my growing, demanding, youthful body. We were now faced with an exercise regime, designed to bring us all up to ideal fighting fitness, ready for combat. We also spent a great deal of time practicing our sharp shooting talents, aiming at moving balloon targets which had been let out on a long line over the stern. Then we had an assortment of deck games to keep up morale, designed to preoccupy as much of our body's physical energy and short circuit our sexual frustration. Bromide in our tea had little or no effect on our healthy fighting physiques; we were awash with hormones, testosterone fuelling our sexual appetites, alas, with no females in sight! Once we were well clear of Suez the captain of this tub, made a profound statement over the ship's tannoy system, he had just received new orders. The Battalion was now to change course, for East Africa or Kenya to be precise, we were to fight African Mau-Mau tribesmen. So instead of going to Korea, we were now heading for a more enjoyable climate in one of the most exciting countries on the east coast of Africa. I was more than thankful and pleasantly surprised, to be going to this beautiful country of dramatic mountainous landscape, this was for me almost the fulfilment of one of my many boyhood dreams. (Anyway it had to be better than Korea, where Bobby breathed his last.)

This surprising announcement was followed by a series of compulsory lectures or talks, each one specifically designed to indoctrinate us into a new form of positive thinking and attitudes towards the new found enemy. The dominant and easily the largest in population, of any single tribe, were the Kikuyu, who were also at the heart of the Mau-Mau themselves. In our ignorance we were told that the Mau-Mau was nothing short of a bunch of marauding butchers, indiscriminately killing their fellow countrymen. In reality, we later found when confronted by the Mau-Mau they were expert in the execution of mind games and in fact quite sophisticated. Their main beef was against their white master's wealth and power. They were ruthless in this undertaking, wanting rid of their old colonial ties once and for all. They were determined to seize power by whatever means possible, overthrowing their own government. The main tool of persuasion was mass terror used against their own tribe. The unfortunate backlash that resulted was because most of the Kikuyu, who were loyal to the British throne, were more than content to work for the wealthy land owning white settlers.

The home guard established at most of the African village settlements were a hundred percent Kikuyu but were being butchered by their own tribesmen in the Mau-Mau. This was the conflict then, which had escalated out of all reasonable control; it was causing so much hardship and heartache amongst the tribesmen.

The lectures ended aboard our tub of a ship, as we slowly ploughed our way north along the east coast of Africa. Now that we had all been informed of our impending future, we could at least dream a little, still using rose coloured vision, before reality kicked us in the teeth.

If truth be told, I was far more interested in my own selfish thoughts, because I was very much looking forward to getting my first sighting of Mount Kenya. This dramatic Alpine like mountain offered a far more challenging prospect, than chasing a bunch of lunatics calling themselves the Mau-Mau. (What a joker, or even a traitor, I hear you say!)

My love of mountains had its own kind of madness, which only another mountaineer would understand. The climbing techniques involved with these two mountains were totally different, but I digress. Mount Kenya was a truly magnificent twin peaked, snow capped beauty of 17,058 feet in height, one of the mountains I had only ever dreamed about, but was longing to climb. It was an impressive sight, far more important than Africa's highest mountain Mount Kilimanjaro at 19,340 feet, which to me was little more than a giant round topped mound. Mount Kenya soared up majestically from the African plains to join the piercing cumulous clouds, which hung around its neck like an ermine stole.

Aboard ship the weather turned even warmer as we ploughed our watery furrows ever northwards with Mozambique, on the port side of the East African coastline, leaving the large island of Madagascar on the starboard. The enjoyment of sleeping on deck became increasingly popular as more and more bodies appeared nightly the further north we headed.

In the early evening of the following day we passed close by to Dares Salaam, the main port of Tanganyika being off our port beam. Now we had only some 200 nautical miles to go, before reaching Mombassa the main port for Kenya, our ultimate destination by sea.

In the early hours of the following morning, while most aboard were still fast asleep, we tied up in the port of Mombassa.

Over the next few days, unloading the Battalions equipment was a reversal of the performance of loading in the U.K. four weeks previously. This massive disembarkation was a huge logistical undertaking and although of a laborious nature, it went smoothly and was completed in less time than the original embarkation had taken in England. Our long convoy wound its way up country, along the high ridges of the rift valley, slowly towards the equator. The red dust from unmade dirt roads covered everything; like red ash with a fine chocolate coating, on a lush dessert pudding. The countryside was wild, with vast expanses of sparsely covered plains. It was unbelievably beautiful and herds of wild antelopes were visible for miles. Dotted along the way were small groups of African village huts, with grass or reed covered roofs, usually surrounded by woven spiky branches of manmade fences, protecting the inhabitants from prowling wild animals come nightfall. The African children both sexes and all ages, were scantily clothed, they rushed to cheer our convoy on its way, beaming from ear to ear, in awe of seeing such a long line of military vehicles. We could easily see any on-coming traffic from miles away, because of the clouds of red dust on the horizon long before we reached any vehicle ahead of us.

After a long drive of many hundreds of dusty miles, we pulled into our base camp at Nanyuki, it was the most impressive sight imaginable. The Royal Engineers who built this tented city had done us proud; every basic service necessary for our survival had been expertly installed. The M.T. (motor transport) section, where the twins were eagerly waiting to greet me, was very impressive and set up in a most orderly fashion. Each heavy duty canvas tent could easily sleep four bodies in sheer comfort. The tent had four foot side walls which were internally reinforced with bamboo lattice work fencing. There were proper iron beds complete with mattresses and blankets, each bed had its own Mosquito net and the luxury of a small wooden bedside locker. The twins and I were alone in this tent, whereas the other six tents in this M.T. section were all fully occupied, with four bodies to a tent. The twins had specially reserved a bed for me, making me feel very privileged indeed, their jovial banter was like music to my ears.

This was to be our new home for God knows how long, and now I felt we had finally arrived. I for one was very pleased to be in Kenya-East Africa, but best of all I could see the majestic twin peaks of Mount Kenya's snow capped tops from the doorway of my new found home. What more could anyone ask for I thought!

With some good tucker inside my belly and after a quick shower to cleanse my body of the red dust, I went to bed that night content and full of hope.

**Mates having a laugh outside
Motor Transport Office, (M.T.) Kenya**

The bane of my life – M.T. Sergeant, with myself

**Mate & self, on top of my lorry, after swim.
Buffalo Springs, Kenya.**

**Buffalo Springs – A shoulder hug from film star Victor Mature.
Spot the twins, kneeling in front of me.**

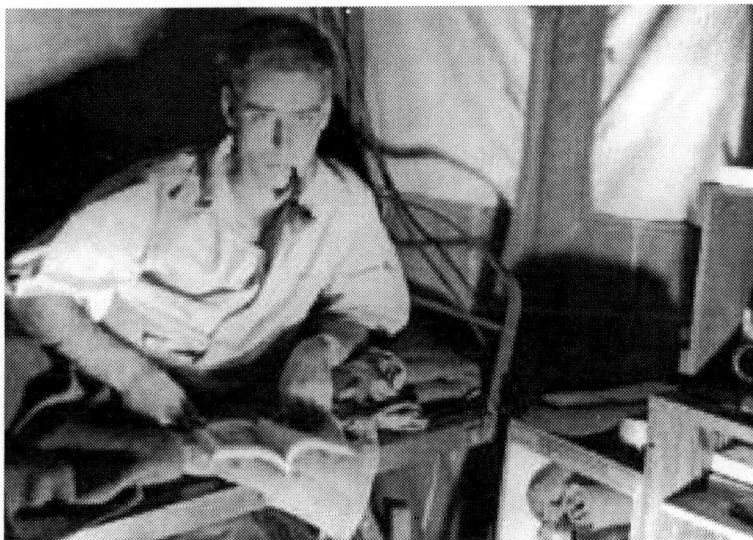

The author, under canvas in Kenya, 1954-5, sharing a tent with The Twins (Quack & Quack) M.T. Section

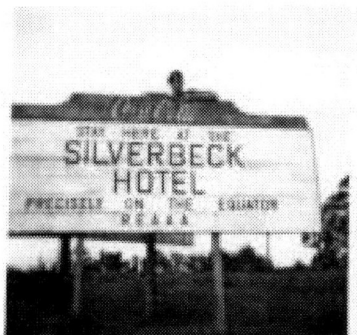

You could sit at each end of a table, either side of the Equator

The view of Mount Kenya from the door of our tent, above Shipton's Peak

Top-Hut at over 10,000 feet, from where we lived and operated from, to find stolen beef, to supply back to the Army

Twin Peaks – with 'Shipton Peak' in the foreground, to right

Shipton's Peak – Our first rock climb

**The Lewis Glacier, a fantastic climb of both peaks,
(Batain & Nelson,) with the Lewis Glacier to the
right, where we camped the night**

The author, on the edge of the Lewis Glacier, 16,000 feet.
Leading the final rock climb pitch on Shipton's Peak (Left)

Chapter Twelve

Twins Batain and Nelion

The bright morning burst of sunlight flooded through the open doorway of our new tent home, this was to become a regular feature of our environment.

Ignoring my misbehaving early morning erection, I would spring out of bed and meet the glorious vista that God had created. The grand panoramic view was on such a splendid scale, I could feast my eyes upon this wonderful scene set out before me. The twin jagged peaks of Mount Kenya piercing the soft fluffy clouds around its ermine neck, rising high into the sparkling deep blue sky above. The dark green vegetation nestling below the gathering early morning cotton wool clouds, helped dramatically to underline the purity of the snow encrusted peaks that penetrated the azure blue heavens overhead. This was the stuff that dreams were made of - well my dreams anyway! I was becoming obsessive, spending hours day -dreaming about the dozens of possible new climbing exploits appearing before my very eyes. (Could this be a court martial offence?) However the reality of the daily tasks we were allocated harshly focused our minds, serving to remind all of us, that this was not a picnic or holiday, on which we could indulge our fantasies, but a more serious business of fighting the Mau-Mau terrorist within our midst. We were constantly reminded about these gangs of marauding thugs, with regular daily reports of their attacks on nearby outlying village encampments, when raids of death and destruction were very apparent.

After a substantial field breakfast, the entire section assembled in readiness for the daily routine orders, mostly transport allocation duties required by Battalion H.Q. Three volunteers were required to enhance troop entertainment and perform a month's mobile cinema tour in the field. This was in order to build up morale, by relieving some of the discomfort found in the wet jungle conditions that most of the brigade had men living under, in some of the more remote areas. The twins and I decided to put our names forward for this one month duty tour, as it became clear that sooner or later we would be nominated, each month three different drivers were ordered to take their turn on this essential duty.

The three ton Bedford R.L. truck had been especially equipped with a generator, collapsible screen and film projector, fulfilling the task it was designed for. After a few hours of instruction on how to operate the projector and with personal gear and weapons aboard, the three of us set off on the first leg of a tour covering several hundred miles. We travelled between different divisions or platoons, all encamped in a large area spread out across the forests of North West Kenya. Regardless of what ever time of day we arrived at each destination, the three of us got into a routine of unloading and setting up a makeshift theatre, in readiness for the evening film performance. The jungle drums between these far outreaching villages were always busy, ensuring that all indigenous Africans within the locality would make their way to us, enabling them to enjoy our source of white mans magic. This also created its own security problem, which had to be solved, it was a simple matter for Mau-Mau terrorists to slip in and out as individuals, in normal village life. (The Mau-Mau did not wear any kind of uniform and in most cases looked just like any native from the village.)

This was the army's Achilles heel as it were, becoming more and more dependant on the head man of each and every village. We used the local knowledge with squads of African soldiers attached to their own village as a home guard, serving to protect their countrymen. We learned very quickly, to protect our backs at all times, when dealing with so called normal African life. Most of the twenty four hours in each and every day, our weapons were always cocked ready for immediate action and never left our sides, even when in bed asleep. At bedtime, one out of the three was always on guard duty in the truck, while the other two slept. Two did four hour shifts on a rota basis, from 10pm to 2am then 2am to 6am each night, meaning we each got a full nights sleep every third night. We trusted each other implicitly not to doze off or sleep, when on guard duty during the nights on tour. None of us would dare abuse the trust we had in each other; all knowing our very lives depended on it. We also knew from personal experience, how some men on guard had been caught napping while on duty, with consequences that were very dire indeed. In some cases it had resulted in serious injury and even death. In practice, while on tour we always slept fully clothed, with weapons fully loaded and the safety catch on, ready for any immediate action. The cleaning and care one devoted to one's own personal firearm, was far more important than the love of your own dick.

Although the bren gun becomes a trusted weapon that you learn to love very deeply, I can tell you from prolonged experience, it's impossible to make amorous love to one in bed.

The one month tour soon sped by and once again we found ourselves back at M.T. headquarters, in our own tented house and even more important, in our own beds, enjoying a full nights sleep. On our return, we were given two days off with no duties to speak of, except to recuperate and attend to our own personal bodily functions and getting our clothes laundered in readiness for the next stint of duties. From time to time we were all made to play our part in night ambushes, which always meant depravation of sleep for at least one all-nighter. For some reason, best known to the powers that be, the R.E.M.E. were busy building a dirt track, suitable for a truck to use, up the west slopes of Mount Kenya. From an engineering point of view, this was quite an undertaking, starting at a small village base camp called Naro Moru, not far from where we were based at Nanyuki, situated at an altitude of about 6,500 feet above sea level. The idea was to push this 'met track' as it was called, as high as possible up the western flank of Mount Kenya. On several occasions when I escorted an engineering army officer, we travelled in my Austin Champ to the top of this track. He went up to give advice and measure the progress his men were making, as well as solve any building problems they were experiencing. This task presented many hardships in its undertaking, but the whole operation came to an abrupt halt once they cleared the tree line and ran into what was known as elephant grassland.

This area immediately above the jungle belt of tree growth proved impossible to build foundations on, due to the swampy nature and bogy terrain covering this part of the mountain, it continued for several thousand feet before reaching the rocky scree below the snow line, at about 11,000 feet. It was at this time herds of prime beef cattle suddenly started disappearing from surrounding white settlers farms, situated in a nearby small mountain range called the white highlands of the Aberdares, named after a mountain range in Wales back in the United Kingdom. This went on for several weeks, before the army realized why this valuable source of food was made such a target by the Mau-Mau. Under the cover of darkness, the cattle were being rustled and driven up to the snow line on Mount Kenya via the Met track, which we had kindly provided, only to be slaughtered and then buried in any of the many glaciers on Mount Kenya. This provided the Mau-Mau with a prime beef food supply, stored in a natural deep frozen condition, which they could call upon in times of hardship or famine. This clever ruse used by The Mau-Mau was only discovered by accident, when very early one morning one of our spotter plane pilots, sighted about a dozen cows or more, high up on the west slopes of Mount Kenya.

The Army was already overstretched in trying to provide around the clock cover with guard duty to a number of farms along with other commitments and so many other routine but equally important duties. Because of this predicament we in the M.T. section, were given a very unexpected visit by our commander and colonel of the battalion, Colonel Boden.

Much to my surprise I was called up before him and then grilled extensively as to my climbing ability, particularly on snow and ice. I wasn't asked but informed, the engineers were busy building a wooden cabin at 10,000 feet to accommodate and sleep up to ten people, within days it would soon be ready for occupation. This was followed by a visit from Sub Lieutenant Ronald Smythe, one of the most junior of the officers, with no mountaineering experience whatsoever, but never less he was put in charge of operation 'Top Hut'. This very young gentleman was fresh out of Sandhurst, and had just newly arrived on attachment to our regiment in Kenya. He could hardly walk the length of himself let alone climb anything.

Such was the wisdom of so called Top Brass, attaching no importance to his lack of actual experience, indeed they felt experience was unnecessary to equip this badly spotted faced youth, for the task in hand! 'Sir', as we politely referred to Ronald Smythe junior, was a tall gangly youth of about 22 years old and although well over six feet tall, he had a bad kink in his back, giving him a permanent stoop. With an eagle beak like nose, sandy coloured wavy hair and a badly marked skin to match. He spoke with a full size plum in his cakehole, and used a post Etonian accent.

According to his Mummy and Daddy, he had been sent to Kenya, under some kind of sufferance, and for him the warm climate of Kenya was most uncomfortable. This twit born with a silver spoon stuck firmly in his gob, had feminine tendencies that made him a soft target for any macho red blooded male (usually officers) to poke fun at, where as the common rank and file just took the piss. He was an unfortunate misguided youngster, who was best kept out of sight, and accordingly given no real responsibility. Perhaps this was the reason he was now put in charge of the Top Hut operation, which was certainly away from the mainstream of normal operational duties performed by the majority of army units, fighting the Mau Mau in Kenya. This twit proposed he set up camp within the M.T. unit, with one of our wireless operators on call to do most of his bidding. Also in attendance was his batman, a known poof with feminine mannerisms that easily surpassed his masters affected ways, but who was more than able to fulfil all of his master's desires.

Once safely installed in a quickly erected tent next to our own, a further four football louts were sent over from 'B' company to make up our merry band or gang of eight climbing hooligans. All the volunteers I hasten to add were not of my choosing. The twins and myself, along with four football fans and one radio operator called Fred from 'C' company, made up this party or motley crew, of eight in total. In truth, I was the only none volunteer amongst us, because I had been ordered to head this unusual expedition, that would move into Top Hut as our working base camp. It was rightly assumed I would be more than willing to perform any army orders or duty above the snowline, for a period of up to three months, because of my love of all things alpine. This was solely for the benefit of supplying back to the army, any fresh beef that we could find in food dumps buried within glaciers by the Mau-Mau.

This was our main objective then, but not the only objective, as I had definite ideas of my own to fulfil. The equipment and especially food would be taken up the Met track and then higher by mules. A special native tracker who owned a dozen of his own mules and also had a good local knowledge of the west slopes of Mount Kenya to the snow line was employed. This man would be responsible for bringing our meat finds on the frequent return journeys, back down the mountain with a military escort, to the army H.Q. as well as provide us with provisions to sustain body and soul. When we discovered the slaughtered meat in the glaciers it would be taken to the Met track by mule and reloaded into army trucks to supplement the regimental food stocks. Usually most of the meat was in fact found on the edges of the glaciers, the periphery of the snowline surrounding Mount Kenya was the better part of fifty miles in total circumference around the mountain on all sides.

For the first four weeks or so, we had little real mountaineering equipment and the ropes provided by the army were heavy and difficult to use. I drew a sketch of an ice axe that the engineers made to the best specification they could muster. I was the only person who had real climbing boots, they were my own but the standard jungle boot with commando soles were really quite good especially on rock. Although our equipment was basic our attitudes and enthusiasm more than made up for our achievements.

At that time in the early fifties to my knowledge the top twins of Batain and Nelion had only been successfully climbed by the two previous expeditions. I also knew that Sir Eric Shipton had more than left his mark on Mount Kenya and a very impressive rock pinnacle known as Shipton peak, was one of the most difficult individual climbs amongst many of the sub peaks this mountain had to offer, with some technical pure rock climbs to tempt us. One of the most amazing climbing exploits, reported to be successful on the twin peaks already mentioned, was achieved by Italian prisoners of war who escaped especially for the sole purpose of climbing the twin peak summits of Mount Kenya.

This daring adventure, [only the second successful attempt] was carried out by a small number of prisoners who made all their own equipment for the purist delight and of their love for climbing, a true alpine mountain worthy of challenge. A remarkable and most outstanding achievement that truly belongs in the golden age of mountaineering annuls. The football mad fanatics of our little climbing fraternity spent a great deal of their leisure time kicking a football about well above 10,000 feet. This certainly kept them very fit, as well as truly acclimatized to the thin atmosphere. Eric a football nut, was the same age as myself and besides his love of football (he was an ardent Arsenal supporter) also had a fondness for rock climbing and he was one of the best free rock climbers I had the pleasure to meet. For the duration of our stay we got together to climb on a regular basis, getting to know each others style and rock climbing skills. There were times when I found it necessary to reprimand him for his lack of care to safety but I couldn't help admire his daring skills always pushing himself to the outer limits of his abilities.

One morning we decided to attempt Shipton Peak together and so with much encouragement from the rest of the gang, we set about this climb with relish and pure devilment. Both fighting fit and rearing to go we topped out this climb in less than four and a half hours. After we abseiled off to the glacier below, we decided that maybe a climb of both the highest peaks, might be worth considering with careful planning and preparations. It would certainly mean a long climb with at least one night spent high up near the tops. We studied the glacier that could lead us to the gap or saddle between the twin peaks at their base. At the time I couldn't for the life of me remember which peak Batain or Nelion was the highest although it was only a difference of several feet in height between them. "Does it really matter?" asked Eric "We'll just knock them both off anyway." He said this in such a cavalier fashion as if cracking the final clue in a crossword puzzle, but I quickly realized he was deadly serious.

As a group we debated the pros and cons, as well as the ideal route we felt happiest with and a good estimate on a time scale to complete the entire climb. You have to remember that all previous expeditions would start from well below the Met track and tree line then spend many a day acclimatizing en route to the snow line carrying all their own provisions on their backs. We had the real advantage because we were living and working above 10,000 feet from Top Hut, where we had all our gear and provisions already assembled. The twins Quack and Quack volunteered to carry our gear up the gap overnight, then return to the hut for the night only to climb back up the following day, measuring our progress and ultimately help us in our return with all our equipment, successful or otherwise, thus conserving our energy for the actual climbing of both twin peaks.

So after a more than usual leisurely weekend, we set out on the Monday morning, in a group of four on two separate ropes of two. By mid afternoon we had reached a small plateau or gently angled snow slope saddle where we set up a suitable bivouac tent. The twins set off to go back down to Top Hut at speed, with more than enough time to spare to make the hut before dark. Eric and I snuggled into each other after a substantial tupper (tea /supper) giving each other our shared bodily warmth and doing our best to sleep. Well before four am I awoke desperate for a pee so I made my way out to relieve myself.

On returning to the flimsy tent I started to boil a Billy can of water over the paraffin pressure stove. Eric watched me from the comfort of our makeshift bed and it became clear to me then that Eric was most definitely not a morning person. I made some porridge and this was followed by hot mugs of tea and slabs of date bars for high energy. Once we had filled our stomachs satisfactorily, we put on our warmest clothes and prepared our empty rucksacks, with just enough gear for a full days climbing ahead of us. Just before six am we left the camp and I started cutting a series of ice steps, traversing to our far right well below the base of the peak called Batain.

By 8am we had already climbed to the snow arête or shoulder ridge that led directly to the base of our first rock face climb. Eric led off easily with a good steady natural rhythm until the rope length was exhausted. After putting on a good secure belay I climbed up to then lead through the next pitch, to a small but adequate rock shelf for the end of our second stance. The climbing so far, although steep and very exposed was only moderately difficult, presenting no real problems. At this point, Eric chose to relieve himself of a rather full bladder. So I lit up a couple of cigarettes, giving one to Eric, who puffed away with contentment. After this short break we continued upwards, with no real hardships. At about 10.30 am we were within 100 feet from the top of this first peak, and it was my turn to lead off the next pitch. All went well for about 60 feet, when a small protruding ledge, barred my way. At almost 17000 feet I didn't feel much like doing a mantle shelf move so worked out a small intricate traverse to take me around but above this shelf. Now feeling a little more secure, I put on an extra strong belay shouting to Eric below, to come on up to join me when ready. Eric had been watching my antics with interest and with the security of a top rope in place above him he set off like an express train in a hurry to leave the platform. He made very good time to the ledge that I was safely perched on and with just a little hesitation, decided to attack this shelf with a direct frontal assault swinging his body in one movement easily over the top, executing the perfect mantelshelf technique coming to rest within inches of my booted feet. "Well done Eric, you made that move look a doddle," I said as he stood up grinning like the preverbial Cheshire cat.

With only 40 foot to the top, he quickly decided to press on and continued climbing as easy as if he was climbing a ladder at the side of a building. In moments he was sitting astride atop of Batain the highest of both peaks with his legs dangling in space over the face as if ready to spread a picnic lunch across his knees.

"Climbing" I called up as I quickly joined Eric remembering very little of the rock face in my excitement to reach the top and join him. Looking almost due south from our topmost perch we both thought we could see Kilamanjaro more than 200 miles away. As I sat down beside him I removed my signet ring from my left hand and with my empty cigarette packet I wrapped the ring in silver foil before putting it back in the packet then stowing it carefully below a small cairn of stones away from the wind.

I was happy that my ring, given to me by my brother Bobby, would now rest peacefully up high, for safe keeping with the Gods in this magical mountain kingdom. Eric started to prepare the two ropes in readiness for an old fashion rappel (abseil), while I spent some quality time out with Bobby and my own thoughts, in this silent space where everything was pure and free of any kind of human pollution. The decent was performed with ease abseil after abseil at speed, as the twins Quack and Quack shouted up to us with encouragement from their stance below, our final abseil on the safety of hard ice that gave us both a short respite. I reached the twins first just seconds ahead of Eric as Quack and Quack informed us they had already prepared lunch for us which we should both eat, before tackling peak number two Nelion. While we were both enjoying rich turtle soup from self heating tins (popular army rations), the twins told us about a rather nasty crevasse that had suddenly opened up overnight, barring part of our return route to our base at Top Hut. Quack and Quack would be more than happy to stay around until we had accomplished our second ascent of the peak Nelion.

With this in mind and the realization that we had already entered into early spring, which meant with every passing day as the weather steadily warmed up these mountain tops, it would become increasingly more dangerous as the warm air thawed making the snow and ice caps ever more treacherous. Nelion proved just as easy a climb as Batain and on reflection, perhaps just a bit too easy at times, luring us into a false sense of security. However without any real problems after living on the edge, by 4 pm on Tuesday afternoon of that final week in March 1955, we slowly made our way back to Top Hut feeling very contented but also very tired by 8.30 pm that same evening on our return. An early night after lack of sleep perched high in the gap between Batain and Nelian was most welcomed. Both Eric and I overslept sleeping soundly for more than 10 hours apiece, but feeling somewhat refreshed, we left our sleeping pits to welcome yet another beautiful sunny day.

For almost three months we had been extensively excavating glaciers as a group, searching for beef stockpiles and returning this stolen booty back into the catering sections of the regiment. The raids by the Mau-Mau on the white highlands of the Aberdare mountains, had all but stopped, as the Mau-Mau realized that they were now providing fresh meat back to their adversaries – the British Army. Sadly our tasks were over and we all returned to our separate units going our separate ways, although Mount Kenya was now firmly in complete control by the Rifle Brigade which only seemed proper at this time. No civilians were allowed near the mountain, let alone climb on it and the exploits of our climbing adventures and in particular the climbing of the twin summit peaks to the top soon became common knowledge as well as written about.

We never saw our Sub Lt Smythe again, although come to think of it, we never saw him once during the whole three months we were based at Top Hut on Mount Kenya. I don't think any of us really noticed, or missed him. With the privilege – nay honour of Mount Kenya climbing adventures all but a memory my thanks to God who is over all power in charge of military thinking served only to whet my appetite and thoughts of ever more yearnings. A return to more mundane military duties did not sit comfortably within the spirit for yet more unusual adventures.

The daily duties and routines within the M.T. section had lost its appeal for me. Within this frame of mind I decided to seek out a certain Major Hargreaves, with a view in mind of seeking something a little different and more worthwhile and exciting to do. The second night of our return with Chris and Chas the twins we talked long into the night scheming our plots of future action. One of the twins heard there was a paratroops course in the offing and extra money attached to our basic army pay for successful applicants. After breakfast and at morning parade we three asked permission to have an audience with the one and only Major Hargreaves who was in charge of 'B' Company to whom we were all attached. As our three requests were one and the same in nature, it was deemed more expedient for the Major to see us all as one package, killing three birds at once, so to speak.

Major Hargreaves was a big dark haired bear of a man, as well as being one of our most senior officers in the Riffle Brigade. He was a lawyer in civilian life, easy to talk to, but not a push over. "Well boys" he started, looking at all three of us rather questionably. "By what privilege am I honoured with your presence here, today?"

I looked at him wondering if he was pulling my dick, or just being jovial towards us, for some unknown reason. "I hear there is a parachute jumping course up for grabs," I mentioned tentatively, looking at Hargreaves facial expression trying to gauge a flicker of hope.

Hargraves looked through us to some spot in space beyond our realm, with a dead pan expression as if playing poker for high stakes. The seconds ticked by in a bemused silent confrontation, when Hargreaves returned from his dream like ponderance, before looking up at us with a grin full of mischief written across his broad face. "I'm afraid you're all too late for this course, which was filled last night," he said.

"But there is another one in six weeks time I might put you down for, providing you're up to full fitness" he said, with just a hint of another but more impish grin on his face.

"That would be fantastic," I said with all three of us nodding approval, like the rocking heads of three dogs, in the rear window of a car.

"OK, I'll put you all on patrol duty for the next five weeks which will ensure you get up to a very high state of fitness before the para course."

As we left I was quick to notice, that none of us was smiling with the distinct feeling between us, that we had just walked head long into a rather slick confidence trick. "Well" I said "it will make a change from driving all the time."

The following silence only served to prove, that none of us was at all convinced by my profound statement, as we were soon to find out.

Chapter Thirteen

Come into my web, said the black widow spider

After a very restless night, I could tell from the furtive glances passing between us, that we were all wondering just what we had let ourselves in for. On parade that very same morning, the M.T. sergeant called the three of us over and we were ordered to wait outside his tented office. After dishing out routine orders to the rest of the M.T. pool drivers, he then turned his undivided attention on us, and carefully aimed a verbal blast from both his twelve bore barrels. After insulting all our pedigrees, we were instructed to get our equipment together for ten a.m., when transport would despatch we three mugs to an active platoon about to go on a prolonged patrol up country, somewhere north of Nivasha. The M.T. sergeant sarcastically warned us to only take what we were prepared to carry on our backs, as shanks pony would be our only method of transport.

As the first of the seasonal periods of rain clouds gathered on the horizon, I looked up in search of the twin peaks of Mount Kenya rapidly disappearing below these ominous clouds of pending doom. All three of us looked into each other's eyes, which mirrored the darkness overhead. The day light rapidly turned into a late evening twilight, with the sound of eeriness becoming so noticeable, as the silence increased until it became almost deafening, with an absence of birdsong and no sounds uttering from the wildlife in the undergrowth around us. A dark swarming cloud of locust came into sight with a buzzing noise, just like electricity cables humming, as the darkness overhead deepened, turning to blackness with hundreds of thousands of three inch locust descending on the ground at our feet. The vegetation was alive, with these beasties completely covering and devouring everything, from grassland to the trees. As far as the eyesight could stretch, this column of locust a good five miles wide and at least fifty miles long, ate everything in sight. They stripped every blade of grass and every single leaf, with their sheer numbers a good four inches deep, now covering the bare soil. This living carpet of locust was pinkish in colour moving about like thousands of fresh caught large size shrimps. The natives in turn, came out of their village huts in hordes, gathering up this bountiful harvest sent from heaven by the Gods. It had been many along year since nature had provided them with so much food rich in protein. The daylight returned just as suddenly as the darkness befell us less than two hours ago, the buzzing column headed westerly towards the upper slopes of Mount Kenya, full daylight flooded the devastated landscape. The aftermath and debris, strewn over this five mile wide corridor for hundreds of miles long, was like a new scar of waste land laid across the countryside for many a week to come. This phenomenon of nature fattened the bellies of many thousands of natives, not forgetting the Mau- Mau, who left their bolt holes to enjoy participating in this free feast of such abundance. The lure of so much food, also increased our capture rate of many Mau-Mau, who were tempted to break ranks and fill up their skeleton like starved bodies. This surge of easy captures, gave added momentum to the army units in active pursuit of these animal thugs, called the Mau-Mau.

At this stage of the Kenya emergency we found that many Mau-Mau who had previously spent years hiding in dense cover, like hungry hunted animals, were only too willing to surrender to the army in exchange for a prison camp life that offered shelter and food on a regular basis. Some had simply had enough of prolonged jungle warfare, running out of physical steam as their reason for fighting the cause became even more blurred. This was a contest they realized they could not possibly win. Anyway, our trio of three musketeers was whisked off to a platoon designated for a lengthy jungle patrol, we now found our selves among new faces.

Facing the inevitable the three of us put smiles upon our mugs with the twins Quack and Quack chatting away to the strange men who we were also being transported with, to some unknown destination many miles away from the shores of Lake Naivasha. Rather like ourselves they also felt they had been tricked into making up the numbers for this ill fated patrol.

My bren gun was taken off me and replaced by a pump action shotgun, while the twins were armed with a pair of F.N. rifles, a new weapon that certain sections of the regiment were guinea pigged to try out. This Belgian made F.N. rifle looked like a finely engineered piece of kit, until it was soon discovered, when in use, some of these experimental weapons had a nasty habit of exploding and spitting the barrel into the face of the user. After just several weeks, these weapons were withdrawn from use and replaced by short arm automatic sterling machine guns and the old faithful sten guns. Mind you, even the sten guns could be dangerous in the wrong hands, as they were likely to cock and fire themselves off automatically, for example, when jumping from the back of a truck. The jerking shock caused by the user jumping down to the ground, when carrying this weapon, was often all it took to set the firing mechanism in motion. We certainly knew of at least one soldier who shot holes into his foot when landing from such a vehicle. The sten gun therefore, had to be treated with the utmost respect.

On arrival at our destination, some power crazed corporal attempted to divide our ranks, by making sure that all those inexperienced in jungle patrol service, were mixed together with the trigger happy patrol veterans. This was not a pleasant event, as both twins were to be separated by this dickhead of a corporal, who was still positively delirious with the new found power on gaining his second stripe. The twins and I jointly refused to budge, even the threat of a court martial while under active service conditions, had no effect on us what so ever. Now feeling very frustrated with us at such outrageous disobedience, he resorted to call on even more powerful persuasion by bringing in the platoon sergeant. The even more determined Sgt Mick Whatson, took the three of us aside and gave us a dressing down, at one point he even threatened to shoot the three of us. I blatantly challenged this sick nasty piece of goods, by cocking my pump action shotgun and rapidly wiping the snarl from his face. I told him to calmly go ahead if he felt he would get away with it - or words to that effect only just a little more colourful. It was apparent that I had suddenly become extremely unpopular, at least in the eyes of this particular sergeant.

With the moment of crisis now fully abated, the sergeant in his begrudging wisdom, decided he personally would take all three of us with him in his patrol team of ten. Not exactly a good start I thought as we set off, but at least the three of us were all still together. The whispering voice of Bobby persisted in annoying my egotistical sanity, by bugging my brains with unreasonable questions lurking in the shadows of my skull. "Who do you think you are?" and telling me over and over again how stupid my behaviour was becoming. "Get your act together" I would hear Bobby chide me, and "stop being a complete dip-stick" he would mock.

For the first tour or more, I was doing anything but concentrating on the job in hand, but eventually I settled down to a more tolerable state of thinking. Come nightfall the sergeant ordered the three of us to construct our makeshift night shelter together, as he sarcastically inferred he didn't want us to contaminate the cream of his patrol. By the end of the first week our Sarawak tracker informed us we were hard on the heels of a large moving gang of Mau-Mau, possibly at least fifteen strong in number. The order was given for no smoking, using soap for washing or shaving, or even lighting wood fires for cooking, as all of these acts were now strictly forbidden. Guards were posted at night time to ensure our camp was secured and remove any element of surprise attack. We shared guard duties equally, which meant we also shared a certain amount of sleep deprivation, which was no real hardship.

By the end of the third week, while still supposedly tracking this gang of Mau-Mau, much to everyone's relief, a radio message ordering us back to base camp at Naivasha, was received by our wireless operator. I personally enjoyed the silence to be found, when living under the most primitive conditions imaginable and would have willingly endured it longer, but for this radio message. We changed onto a more direct compass course that would take us back to base within three long hard marching days, the moral of our patrol moved up several gears, now knowing we were all homeward bound.

On this return journey we came across a cold and long abandoned Mau-Mau campsite, where we decided to take a short breather. The tracker with his Semee sword like bush knife, started to poke around a pile of disused rags or old clothing. Without warning he yelled and ran away as if being pursued by some savage wild animal as a small dark spider that looked harmless enough, ran out of this heap of rags. This, I was reliably informed was no less than the dreaded 'Black Widow Spider', looking anything but dangerous or deadly. With this amusing incident behind us we continued to put as much distance between us and the old campsite as possible. I did give some fleeting thoughts as to what

I might have done with the spider, if I had been brave enough to have caught and safely contained that little monster. The sergeant's was just one of the two names my mind conjured up, when this voice on my head told me not to be such a plonker. I smiled at the thought of Bobby's presence always there to tease and advise me, as I went on my merry way. These thoughts and malicious feelings towards some of my fellow men soon passed as I took another malaria tablet.

The smile that lit up my face caused one of the twins to ask, "What were you thinking about?"

"Don't ask" I replied, "You don't want to know believe me!"

After one final long day, we arrived back at base feeling tired, but satisfied that our self imposed hardships were now over. We spent a long time in the showers that evening, scrubbing each other down until the colour of our dirty soiled skin was restored to a more lobster like hue. It was great to turn to the comfort of a proper bed, which gave our bruised and battered fatigued bodies a chance to sleep soundly.

Early next morning soon after breakfast we were offered the chance of a few days holiday camping well away from Mau-Mau territory, to a more remote oasis called 'Buffalo Springs'. Naturally we three musketeers gleefully accepted the kind sergeant's suggestion, much to his displeasure as he was hoping we would want to escape by returning back to our beloved M.T. base forthwith. We on the other hand felt strongly that we deserved a pleasant interlude if only to restore our faith in the milk of human kindness.

On arrival at this remote part of an interior beauty spot, so different from the mountainous regions of the Kenya that we had become accustomed to, we established our camp to a very comfortable standard far removed from our recent jungle experiences. We were carried to this wonderful setting by one of our own, no less, called Jimmy from our M.T. section and who was made available for our camping holiday party, for the duration of our stay at Buffalo Springs. This azure blue crystal source of natural water in the middle of nowhere was very inviting for skinny dipping frolics or just killing time sun bathing, soaking up the vibes from this unexpected oasis.

On our second day swimming 'au naturale' we were invaded by an American film crew whose main film stars were Victor Mature and Janet Leigh. Buffalo Springs had been chosen as just one of the locations in a small film shoot and was supposedly a crucial part of the film being made. Victor Mature himself was a powerfully built Tarzan type but unbelievably friendly towards us layabout Tommies. We were easily persuaded to pose for photographs with him, while Janet Leigh did several film shoots swimming in these crystal cool waters, away from the heat of the East African sun.

This leisurely spell alas, was soon over, and once again we found ourselves speeding back to our M.T. base. It was like returning home to such familiar surroundings it made one appreciate even more, after lengthy periods away on detachment among strangers and sometimes hostile morons. Within days we quickly resettled, back into a well known comfortable routine, that held no real surprises or threats. In less than a week of our return to the fold, the M.T. section sergeant swung by our tent late one evening. "Well you three cowboys, I have been hearing some alarming reports from a fellow sergeant and friend of mine, Sgt Mick Whatson."

The unearthly silence that followed this revelation was deathly. Quack Quack and my good self looked at each other, with court martial alarm bells reverberating around the inside of all our heads. Not bearing the silence any longer I spluttered my reply "Well sarg what would you have done in our place?"

After a pregnant pause the sergeant broke into a rye smile answering, "That's exactly what I said to Mick Whatson. Anyway," he continued "You three skivers are off for a week on the next parachute course starting Monday, and at least I'll get some bloody peace!" he added for good measure.

With this statement, he about turned and left. Naturally, we three were delighted with such news, patting ourselves on the backs, congratulating ourselves most heartily. The weekend passed quickly and soon after breakfast Major Hargreaves appeared in person, in readiness to accompany a party of twelve to Squares farm, for a one-week parachute training course. We bumped up the track leading onto Squares farm, or cattle ranch, as farmer Squares preferred to call his extensive spread.

Squares was a long term white settler, from the coal mining valleys of Wales. Having started some forty years ago, when he first came to Kenya to make his fortune, the results of his massive success was clear to see.

He owned and ran one of the biggest prime beef farms in the Aberdare Mountains and was quick to tell us that on his arrival forty years ago, this entire mountain range was completely uninhabited. In fact, his labour force was built up over many years, recruited by the hundred from many miles away from this one hundred thousand acre spread. His prime beef herd, including Aberdeen Angus, numbered in thousands of head. He was one of the few white farmers in the area and had been so successful he piloted his own light aircraft. It was in fact Squares own light aircraft homemade dirt runway that we would be operating from.

He was a proud man who was justifiably pleased with the measure of his ultimate success. The army kept and operated a number of small light aircraft of their own from Squares farm, which were mainly used as spotter aircraft, that various regiments in Kenya could call up for reconnoitre purposes.

Our first day was spent on learning how to fall correctly, without breaking our necks, along with instructions on all the kit paraphernalia to do with the chutes themselves. We were all warned to wear an extra pair of underpants, "ha, ha" at least for our first real jump.

After our first virgin jump we were all feeling pleased with ourselves, if any of us wore a brown lining to the inside of our long trousers, we certainly didn't let on. Over the course of this one week, we all performed a total of ten jumps apiece and were awarded our wings. More importantly, it meant an extra few shillings a week attached to our basic pay. To retain this monetary incentive throughout our army career, we would be required to do a minimum of eight jumps a year. [What a great skive.]

As usual, when one is having a fantastic time, it always passes by at the speed of light and once again we found ourselves back at base camp. On Monday I was ordered to service an Austin Champ vehicle, in readiness to take three officers to Nairobi to play for the regiment at a cricket match. Inter regimental sports competitions were always taken very seriously in the army, but the thought of escorting these brown nose snobs was not particularly appealing, so with some resentment in my heart, as their driver, we set off for Nairobi someone hundred and sixty miles away on dirt roads. All went swimmingly well, until half way along the very dangerous escarpment shelf top, I was run off the road over a sheer cliff top by a civilian blue-green Renault car. We met in a thick cloud of chocolate dust, as he was attempting to overtake an army lorry travelling in the same direction as himself. The escarpment dirt track was narrow at the best of times, with continuous skull and crossbones signs, signalling the dangers and spelling "poli-poli" which meant slow-slow in Swahili. This idiot was as surprised as myself, when we met head on in this thick cloud of dust, with this joker taking all my section of the road.

In a vain attempt on his part to avoid the inevitable collision, he attempted to swerve back in behind the army truck he was trying to overtake. His breaking swerve, trying to duck behind the lorry, swung the rear end off side of his car, in the direct path of my Austin Champ vehicle. I was already hard up against the rock face of the escarpment road, when his back end hit me. The Champ spun out of control, veered across the road and over the edge of escarpment, plunging downwards towards the Rift valley floor many hundreds of feet below. I desperately held on to the steering wheel, as the three officers were thrown clear from the topless Champ. I kept with the Champ as it took off [without wings] towards the valley floor below. Meanwhile the army truck driver, who heard and witnessed the crash, stopped and took the number plate of the Renault civilian car. As luck would have it, my Austin Champ now came to rest in the fork of a tree trunk growing out of the rock face of the escarpment. The Champ's engine was still ticking over, despite the fact it was upside down and some sixty feet below the road. Needless to say, the owner of the Renault car never stopped. As far as I could tell, at this time I had no injuries, not even a scratch. An immediate rescue was affected by the boys from the army truck, under the supervision of my three officers, who had received no more than a few bruises apiece.

Once I was rescued and back on the road, all seemed well, until I attempted to stand on my own two feet. I went down in a heap like a bundle of loose drapes with a collapsed lung and nine broken ribs. [Spontaneous pneumor thorax.] Now breathing on one lung and with my broken ribs feeling very sore indeed, I was unceremoniously spread out on the floorboards of the R L Bedford truck, which then rushed me off to Nanyuki field hospital. [So much for the cricket match, which I didn't really want to attend anyway.] I was strapped up around my upper torso and chest, then made to lie on my uninjured side, after x-rays my collapsed lung was re inflated.

After about five days rest and now feeling much better I got talking to a young soldier from another regiment, lying prone in the bed opposite. After a while I asked what he was in for, apart from a cage over his nether regions under the bed covers, he looked perfectly healthy. His face suddenly turned dark crimson at my enquiry, as well as becoming very non-committal, he was obviously very embarrassed by his medical affliction. I wandered over to his bed, as my curiosity now got the better of me, "What's the problem?" I asked.

He sheepishly looked up still wearing a red face and without uttering a word, proceeded to lift up the bed clothes to make his point. He had been just been circumcised that morning and his swollen monster was standing bolt upright, looking inflamed and very sorry for its self.

Remembering back to my early Ashford days and Bobby's bishop, I did not have the heart to ask any further questions, which I don't believe this victim would have answered any way. After several evening visits from the twins it was deemed I had recovered sufficiently enough to return to base. Needless to say I exploited my fragility for all it was worth but in truth I felt great and lucky to be alive.

Chapter Fourteen

Baboon Alert & Kilimanjaro

Mainly due to my recent accident, the M.T. sergeant took pity on me, by giving me light duties for a fortnight. (Or was he just getting me out of his hair?) Anyway, I was promoted or demoted, depending on which angle you looked at it from, being made the personal driver to the Battalion's highest officer in command, a Colonel Boden. (Only for two weeks I hasten to add.) Col. Boden's own personal driver had been given two weeks leave, to attend to his very sick wife back in Blighty. This meant I would be working away from my own base and sleeping constantly in different beds, as well as making myself available twenty four hours a day, for the sole purpose and for the commander's exclusive use. (The personal dogsbody, you might say at the Colonel's beck and call, sometimes with only a few minutes notice.)

Col Boden was a short five foot nine inches squirt of a man, of medium build, with never a smile worn on his plain countenance. He had a well groomed moustache, below his insignificant button type nose, with a mean tight lipped face above it. Boden was always so well dressed, as if ready for immediate inspection of guard duty outside Buckingham palace. His constant companion on field trips, to every one of his out reaching posts and all the different parts of the regiment, was his private batman. This character called John, worshiped his lord and master (Boden) who could do no wrong. John was never allowed to mix, or converse with anybody within the regiment including me, or perhaps especially me. John always sat in the back of my Austin Champ along with his lord and master's baggage and other paraphernalia.

H.Q. had received some kind of emergency radio message, from an isolated platoon on the top of the Aberdare Mountains requesting urgent assistance. The radio message conveyed that the platoon, based on a small dome shaped hill top, was apparently being threatened by a substantial group of baboons. On receiving this unbelievable S.O.S.

Boden as head honcho, was determined to track down the radio operator responsible for this practical joke. On arrival at the scene on the top of this dome shaped hill, surrounded by observation posts on all sides, it became very obvious that something was afoot. The hill top looked down onto extensive jungle vegetation, completely surrounding the base camp, rather like or similar to the bald crown pate of a human head, but on a very much grander scale. There were sporadic bursts of machine gun fire from all six outposts aimed at the greenery below. The platoon commander had already radio phoned ahead, for one of our spotter planes to parachute drop in more ammunition supplies. Thankfully, we arrived just before this vital drop was made and could plainly see for ourselves the importance of the occasion. It was estimated that the hundreds of full grown baboons surrounding our hilltop station, outnumbered the platoon, by at least twenty to one. The threat and intentions of these vicious wild animals, that were far more powerful than any man, became clear by the hour, as they gathered in hoards threatening to invade the camp from all quarters.

This scenario, though unbelievable, was in fact real enough and very frightening to behold. The invasion had started at first light and lasted many hours into the morning. The cause of this rather sudden and strange behaviour, which had never been seen before on such a scale, now resulted in all kinds of speculative theories being put forward. Including the theory, that Mau-Mau were responsible for driving the baboons in our direction. One suggestion put forward had the Mau-Mau, who were by this time desperately short of food, wanting the army to kill the baboons for them. In doing so we would unintentionally provide them with vital rations, ready for the taking. What ever the reason, we were now faced with a dilemma, being attacked and overrun by the savage frightened beasts or having to shoot the baboons in order to protect our troops.

This carnage however horrific it was, had to be carried out in order to ensure our very own survival. I personally had witnessed just how vicious these animals could be, when out on patrol once, I saw a group of only half a dozen baboons descend from the roof canopy and without warning ambush one of our own full grown Alsatian tracker dogs. They tore this poor dog to pieces within seconds, leaving not a trace. (At this time in the fifties there were no animal rights activists to be seen – thank God, if there had been we would have probably shot them instead.)

As big as this frightening baboon incident appears, it pales into insignificance when compared with the Lasa village massacre that happened during the height of the Mau-Mau emergency, where every living thing, humans and animals alike, were slaughtered overnight with horrific and terrifying results. All led by its leader Jomo Kenyata who many years later became president of Kenya and sometimes referred to as the Grandfather of Kenya or East Africa. Such is the unbelievable fickleness of human nature.

Weeks after returning to my beloved M.T. base, I was called before our 'B' Company Commander Major Hargreaves, who requested I enlighten him about Kilamanjaro and precisely to what extent I had any dealings in bringing it into fruition. It transpired that a request by a certain Major D. Stroud, working exclusively for the Outward Bound Trust, had been made to our Commander in Chief Col Boden. As a result of this, I was to be put on temporary loan to the Outward Bound Trust of Great Britain. Outward Bound were attempting to set up the very first climbing adventure school in Tanganyka on Kilamanjaro and were looking for able instructors to compliment the start of this new venture. I was as surprised as Hargreaves on this subject, as well as being delighted at one and the same time. It seems to have stemmed from an article I wrote for The National Geographic magazine, although published, I had yet to see a copy of it, anyway, I was informed the Outward Bound could have me for at least a month.

When I had packed suitable equipment, transport would take me to an old disused mission school building, situated at a place called Loi-Toki-Tok well over the borders into Tanganyka. This remote school building at an altitude of over seven thousand feet, was high on the slopes of Kilamanjaro, it also had good access trails leading high into the upper reaches of the mountain. Major Stroud himself collected me in his Land Rover, he was a very jovial character, with a tall but lean frame and rugged good looks. He conversed easily and as I was to learn in time, was a very experienced all round mountaineer. He had worked for the Outward Bound Trust for some considerable time, since leaving the army with the rank of Major having served in North India. (This deeply interested me.) This likable fellow had brought out another two expert rock climbing instructors from the U.K. He was hoping my expertise, particularly on snow and ice, would compliment this happy band of misfits and adventurers. I was honoured, just to have been head hunted for the task at hand, and endeavoured to do my utmost to fulfil his faith in my abilities.

Around the old school building, which was the only semi permanent structure on this site, many tents of various sizes were pitched. The larger ones were to house the mixed race pupils under instruction, while the smaller ones were for instructors only. From this camp site a clear and very impressive view of most of Kilamanjaro sprang up out of this landscape and looked very powerful indeed. Kibo the highest point could sometimes be clearly seen depending on cloud cover. A small but difficult obstacle course was laid out for the sole purpose of knocking us into peak physical condition and was used extensively by all. A clear watering hole nearby was suitable for swimming, and some rocky crags about sixty feet high, were available for teaching rock climbing, abseiling and rope handling skills. This was the set up then, with a sprinkling of only a few white pupils easily out numbered by black Africans, all chosen for this very first course founded by the Outward Bound Trust.

At this period in history in the mid fifties Sir Eric Shipton was also working for Outward Bound, running a mountaineering school at Eskdale somewhere in the English Peak districts (reminding me of the climb of Shiptons Peak on Mount Kenya.)

The first five days of a two week basic course of Outward Bound enabled us to get reasonably fit, in preparation for the bigger climb, a combined assault on Kilamonjaro, with a total climbing party of some twenty one strong. This comprised of six pupils for every one instructor, without including Major Stroud the principal. Many small but intricate new rock climbing routes were established on our nearby rocky outcrop of crags. The pupils themselves were champing at the bit, itching to get to grips with their very first assent of Kilamanjaro.

There was a well established hut at about sixteen thousand feet, offering a good jumping off point for the ultimate summit of Kibo itself. The march or hill walking trek up to this hut, could easily be achieved comfortably within a three day period, or even two days if you were in a hurry. There was also a large cave approximately half way between base at Loi-Toki-Tok and top hut offering overnight accommodation en route. In reality any competent hill walker could certainly manage up to sixteen thousand feet, with only the altitude to really contend with. For an Outward Bound training adventure course this was ideal, bearing in mind that the raw recruits had little or no climbing experience. Needless to say, the sense of pure achievement it gave our pupils by climbing the highest mountain in the whole of Africa, was certainly more than worthwhile. The real climbing of this majestic mountain started on the final three thousand feet, above over sixteen thousand feet, to the summit of this snow capped mountain.

Leading away from the rounded top of Kilamanjaro, in a south westerly direction or in the general direction towards Arusha, was a lower but more demanding climb on a small cluster of craggy peaks called Mawenzie. This could be reached by a continuous saddle ridge, some seven miles away from Kibo. I digress, away from the main Kilamanjaro expedition walk, which was accomplished without any real problems, the party en-masse made steady progress towards the snowline and the comfort of the rather generous hut at our disposal.

There were occasions, when some of the pupils suffered from altitude sickness and this was usually because they didn't pay heed to the advice they were given, taking it slow but steady between twelve and sixteen thousand feet. Having suffered myself on one occasion from this same aliment, I could sympathise with the conditions this sickness inflicted, leaving one very weak with a constant sense of nausea. However, one learns rapidly from one's own unpleasant experience.

Over the next three months with a steady influx and flow of new recruits every three weeks, I found my altitude climbing improved tremendously. There was a particular place on Kilamanjaro called Gilmans point, several hundred feet below Kibo the highest peak. This landmark was highlighted with a silver cross, from the top hut at sixteen thousand feet, it presented a difficult snow and ice climb.

On one of my many climbs to the main summit of Kibo, when leading my usual team of recruits to the top, I found on returning back to the safety of top hut, I still had many hours to spare before the end of the day. Anyway, feeling very fit, with ample energy still to burn off, I decided in a moment of madness, to climb solo to Gilmans point.

(Named after a past climber called Gilman who had been laid to rest below the silver cross.)

I spent a very pleasant sunny afternoon climbing these difficult ice pitches for almost three thousand feet to the marked cross. Several hours later, on my return to top hut, I was met by Major Stroud who unbeknown to me, had studied my climb through binoculars. He proudly told me I had just shaved almost one and a half hours off the existing record from the hut to Gilmans point, a record which I knew nothing of. Needless to say, I was very surprised to learn of such a record and certainly slept soundly that night feeling that I had truly extended myself and my alpine abilities, (this knowledge I kept very much to myself.) This solitary achievement put a purposeful spring in my step, while I consciously did my utmost to control an egotistical state of euphoria. As the youngest instructor on loan from the army to the Outward Bound school, I certainly felt highly privileged, with my recent achievement doing no harm to street credibility! Towards the end of three months on this venture, I knew my motor was running on empty, the army had already made several requests for my recall to the Battalion and we now found ourselves rapidly running out of excuses. Even the threat of listing me as A.W.O.L. (Absent without leave) did little to persuade my speedy return to the ranks, I was still enjoying myself far too much and was simply in my element. Major Stroud was far more concerned about my delinquent attitude of mind, when one bright and very early morning two monkeys, (red capped military police) turned up long before I had the chance to rise up out of a rather warm sleeping bag.

This affront to my serenity, shockingly brought my present wonderful life style, to a very abrupt halt! Needless to say, I wasn't exactly chuffed at this rather rude interruption. After no discussion what so ever, they packed up my personal gear into my rucksack and with some very quick goodbyes to my fellow instructor comrades I departed. I certainly felt under arrest and was forcibly sat in the back of the M.P. (military police) Land Rover, rather against my will, I was taken back over the very long drive to G.H.Q., and without handcuffs I hasten to add.

During the long dusty journey back across the border of Tanganyika into Kenya, the voice of Bobby percolated my cerebral wave lengths on the slip stream of a balmy breeze, created by the speed of the Land Rover. As my escorts talked away to each other, I noted I was not invited to participate in their rather juvenile small talk. I had done nothing wrong, or at least I certainly felt that way, and wondered why they were treating me very much like a captured prisoner. My self imposed silence continued as Bobby reached out from the grave, many thousands of miles away, to rebuke and chastise me. It was late afternoon, well before teatime and I was now feeling hunger pangs from the lack of food, when we at last reached my now estranged M.T. base camp. I was met by Major Hargreaves no less! Having safely dumped me at the Major's feet, the two red monkeys, completing their regimental duty, departed in haste. "Did you think we would be mean enough to leave you?" stated the Major with an expressive wide grin across his face.

"No sir" I replied. "No such luck" I added as an afterthought.

"Well" said Hargreaves "I think we will be able to keep you very busy, as the Battalion is off to Malaya in just over a week" he stated.

I looked at him with some surprise at this sudden revelation, he then told me to "get ready for tea time."

I was feeling rather famished and was only too willing to obey. As I made my way over to my old tent the twins, Chris and Chas, greeted me with such a show of excited exuberance along with unashamedly physical affection. The warmth of their welcome left me embarrassed, it felt great to be alive and not on some kind of military charge. The relief and comfort of having back my two mates, was immediate, making me instantly realize how much I missed these two lovable scallywags, with whom I had shared so much. I was naturally very sorry to have been pulled so abruptly from the wonderful luring arms of Mount Kilamanjaro, but I was thankful for having had such a thrilling experience.

The thrill of my Outward Bound adventures would have to last for some considerable time to come, as I fought the feeling of anticlimax, which threatened to overpower me. The Battalion had been in Kenya on operational duties, for exactly one year and one hundred and ninety nine days, from the tenth of November 1954 until twenty-seventh of May 1956. (Almost nineteen months.) With this realization of the facts, it became obvious that I still owed the army at least another full twelve months, which would continue in Malaya, where the Battalion was now being sent, to complete their three year tour of active duties. Two years had already gone from the day I walked through the gates at Winchester to start my training.

Now having one year left to complete my contractual agreement, of three years with the colours, providing I survived the next twelve months, with luck I would once again become free from the military shackles of pure regimentation. In the final days of departure from this amazing country I looked up longingly at the beautiful vista called Mount Kenya, with enduring love in my heart and feeling all the richer, for the exploits I was more than fortunate enough to have experienced upon her virgin snow capped peaks.

"Mountaineer"

1. When armoured rock through thinning cloud
   and filtered light stirs climber,
   his inner vision may feel proud,
   - but only if God's kinder.
   The sun is high, the ice so hard,
   assent grows ever steeper,
   he ventures up, while life retards,
   God's time becomes the keeper.

2. A dream unfolds, as crest is reached,
   ice axe strikes the final blows.
   My long awaited harvest reaped,
   spirit of the mountain knows.
   A breath at height, a rest in need,
   in haste I must retreat;
   Fear that I've trodden new born seed,
   a virgin at my feet.

3. An icy wind, form's strong defence,
   now trespass is forbidden,
   down into a dangerous silence,
   cloak of anger, peak is hidden!
   Through raving blizzard-storm I fumble,
   by accident my tent is found,
   avalanche nearby doth grumble,
   Lord my saviour, holdeth ground.

4. Then all is quiet, and joy returns,
   O windy battle, fought and won.
   Mine is the joy of "mighty heaven"
   now yonder mountain is my son!

The Lone Camper

Above me the canvas, peaks a roof in the sky,
with wide open eyes, in my tent I doth lie.
The warmth of my bag, like a trustworthy friend,
high on the mountain, my life may depend.
The harsh rule's of nature, a healthy respect,
for the life that one chooses, not always select.
Wild open country – the eagle the rook,
a wonder behold, like an unwritten book,
while camping close by, a melodious brook.
I tramp across highlands, the flowers in bloom,
the colours, the vistas, and birds sing in tune.
Branches of trees, like tendrils of God,
babbling of rivers, the untrodden sod.
Young game aplaying, the parents at rest,
perched high on the rockface, the hawk builds its nest,
Clicks from my camera, shoots game on the by,
the long day's been full, and dusk is on nigh.
Snuggled down deep, contented I sigh,
all about me in darkness, in peace I do lie.

As I sit by my fire, gain warmth from the flame,
sipping hot beverage, surrounded by game.
Dwelling my life spent, so little, I've led,
passage of time quickens ......so off to bed.
With knowledge so shortly, to town I'll concern,
the bustle from traffic, and crowds take their turn.
Now back to the office, to work I'll retain,
laborious routines, all over again,
the call of the wild, doth strongly remain.

Chapter Fifteen

Lookout Malaya "The black button bastards are coming"

The battalion arrived in Singapore on the second stage of a three year tour of active service overseas. The talk and rumours doing the rounds at this time, were of how very different the jungle warfare in Malaya would be, compared to what we all had experienced fighting Mau-Mau in Kenya. We were assured the C.C.T.s or Chinese Communist Terrorist was a very different animal and a far harder nut to crack. For one thing they were far more astute and expert in so many more ways at fighting back, it would be no picnic in bringing them back into a more civilised society. The Chinese internal population, who made up a significant part of Malayan life, were far more sophisticated than their Malay brothers and were already in control of the financial and business side of life, as well as the cultural directions within the whole of the Malay peninsular. Outside the Malay capital of Kuala Lumpur and other large townships, the C.C.T.'s effective reign of terror and control in most of the countryside, was very real indeed. The British Army casualty list was evidence, if not proof of this fact, in this part of the Far East. Once the Battalion had fully disembarked and when completely mobilised in Singapore, we started the long drive up country.

We were to have several day and nights stay in a large established camp at a place called Johore Bahru, which was but a short driving distance north. We then drove across the causeway that linked the small island of Singapore to the mainland of Malaya. Johore Bahru at this time was very much the established base of the Black Watch, the famous or infamous Scottish regiment that had been in Malaya for some considerable time, they had a reputation envied by many regiments within the British army. A very tough bunch, they were feared by many and well known for holding their ground. The Rifle Brigade known endearingly as the 'black button bastards', because they were the only regiment within the whole of the British army, who wore black buttons on their standard khaki tunics. Equally, they took pride in their own envious reputation so naturally, every man found himself duty bound to uphold the honour of his regiment, making a clash between them inevitable. The wisdom or judgement, by the so called powers that be, when they decided to put these two regiments together for any length of time, was questionable; they should have known it would have the makings of a very explosive mixture.

With much reorganising of the Battalion's resources, the Rifle Brigade was destined to stay, for the better part of a week at Johore Bahru barracks and share the Black Watch facilities. The facilities available were, a fully fledged NAFFI with canteen, shop and a proper cinema. We in the Rifle Brigade had not seen such luxuries since leaving England. We were delighted with the comforts on offer, but unfortunately for us, the Black Watch did not share our enthusiasm when it came to sharing their creature comforts. For some known, as well as unknown reason, there certainly was a great deal of animosity and bad feeling between the two regiments. You must remember the treble Bs (black button bastards) recruited mainly from poor areas of hardship in London, over 80% in fact, but in fairness we had more than our fair share of criminals and thugs in our midst. For some reason this composition of ne'er-do-wells, were felt to make a good fighting force in the field of fire. There was no real argument against this supposition but it did mean our reputation as a fighting force often had to pay a high price. Our main claim to fear and fame was the recognition, as being the best crack rifle shooters in the entire British army. This reputation was defended rigorously every year at the annual world famous shooting competition at Bisley.

It started with a kiss - The Rifle Brigade were doing their utmost in trying to see and more importantly listen to the films sound track, as most of the Battalion were intent on enjoying a highly rated film in the cinema, which backed onto the main cafeteria/bar of the NAFFI. Meanwhile the Black Watch were doing their utmost to be deliberately rowdy, on the other side of the flimsy partition both facilities shared. Several N.C.O.s from our regiment went through to ask politely if the lads in the Black Watch would attempt to abate their over excessive noise, to a few decibels below a roar. The request was made on more than one occasion, but it only had the opposite effect. The Black Watch only redoubled their noisy efforts, by increasing their chants to an unbelievably louder crescendo. The Rifle Brigade objected very strongly to this over active taunt and decided en masse to do something drastic, in retaliation to appease the Black Watch's outrageous response to what we considered to be a reasonable request.

As a group we vacated the cinema, with fury in our hearts, determined to rectify the situation. With no further grounds for negotiation, we set upon the Black Watch and their sacred facilities, to prove once and for all time, exactly what we thought of our Scottish brothers. Very few escaped injury, as we systematically smashed up their most prized facilities. The devastation was unbelievable, several hours later many hundreds of us, ended up in the cooler overnight.

The whole Battalion was paraded next morning in disgrace, Col Boden ranted and bellowed, but only until he lost his voice, then he could rant no more. The Rifle Brigade was now responsible to bear the total cost of repairs; most of it was to be deducted from every single man's weekly pay packet for months to come. We in turn felt we had done ourselves proud, in spite of, or perhaps because of, the black cloud of disgrace hanging over the Rifle Brigade's soiled reputation.

Within the next thirty six hours the very last vestiges of any sign of the Rifle Brigade transit stopover, [save for the debris and damage left behind] was removed in haste from the Black Watch base at Johore Bahru. As our regiment moved ever northwards up the long miss-shaped arm of the Malayan peninsular, 'B' company including my beloved M.T. section, were made to move just about as far north that you could get, to a place called Kuala Kuba Bahru not far from the borders of Siam, or as it is known today Thailand.

After all the recent excitement of Johore Baru and with the exploits of Kilamanjaro still fresh in my memory, I was personally up for something or other, rather than have the relative comfort and safety in the usual mundane routine life of an M.T. section employee. The twins and I discussed this readiness to seek more action, if only for a period of a few months long, by talking late into the late evening hours, debating our options away from the routine of driving. The twins Quack and Quack were even more ready to seek out a little more excitement, outside of their driving skills, than I was. Although I was keen enough, you might say I was to some extent still catching my breath from my last adventures in Tanganyika. Accordingly, we opted to rejoin a platoon on operational duties and jungle patrol, as there were always more willing volunteers to replace us and do driving duties.

When we were detached to a platoon some hundred miles or so to the south of us, at Kuala Kuba Bahru, we entered into the spirit of this band of gun happy cut throats, who already had a number of kills to their name. We quickly learned that the jungles of Malaya were truly tropical rain forests in their composition, movement through this evergreen hell, made for extremely slow progress. This was real jungle compared to Kenya, in the past we had been accustomed to the semi bush covered slopes on Mount Kenya, unlike Borneo and the island of Sarawak. Because of the sheer hardship of living and operating under such difficult conditions, the patrols were geared to a three week stint maximum, followed by a week off, which believe me one needed, if only to recover in readiness for the next patrol. Progress in any direction was usually measured in hundreds of metres covered per day, due to the density of heavy undergrowth, one of the C.C.T.s favoured targets were the rubber plantations and their workers.

These estates all over Malaya were by nature cut deep into the jungle and usually well away from native villages, this added to the problems and difficulties reaching them entailed. Rubber plantations were a favourite location for ambushes, often sprung by both sides on each other. Unlike our African enemy in Kenya the Mau-Mau, the C.C.T.s were better armed and often shot back.

While on patrol, the lighting of any kind of fire, on our side at least, was forbidden. The constantly wet and always damp humid conditions did not lend to fire lighting anyway. We became a target from the thick roof canopy, being ambush victims from above, as often as we did from the ground. Most of our highly trained trackers came from the island of Sarawak, similar to the Gurkas from Nepal, they were a fearless bunch, superb at the highly skilled craft of tracking. The concentration and extra care always required while on patrol required as much effort on our behalf, as did the almost impossible terrain we were expected to exist in. A typical hard day's patrol, often lasted as long as ten hours, before we made rudimentary shelter for the night. It usually involved stripping naked at the end, in order to detach the hoards of leeches invading every part of our body. This was a time for real mates to get intimate and personal with each other, by using a lit cigarette end to burn these blood sucking worms from each others body. Only a mate could effectively reach the vital more intimate parts of ones body – which you as an individual could not hope to reach. Sea salt and bicarbonate of soda were also effective in persuading these blighters to relinquish their blood sucking grip willingly. Somehow leeches could find their way into invading your body, regardless of how many openings in ones clothing was sealed off. It was on such an occasion I discovered how one twin could without dispute be identified from the other. – For all the good it might have helped in identity anyway.

While burning off leeches from more delicate parts of his anatomy, I instructed a twin to lift his penis clear from his testicles, as I could see a somewhat bloated leech that had obviously sucked its fill on the underside of my mate's dick. Telling him to hold very still while using the lit end of my cigarette, I was about to burn this little monster when the twin in question quickly knocked my hand away. "That's a birthmark," he yelled as I was about to burn his dick with a cigarette.

I gently rubbed the mark carefully that looked every bit like a leech, only to find my mate's explanation was true. "Does your brother have the same birth mark?" I asked at this unexpected revelation.

"Why don't you ask him?" was my friend's non committal answer.

I discovered later that only one of the twins had such a mark in such a place, but I concluded this was hardly the ideal way to prove identification between one and the other. Anyway, once clothed they still wouldn't admit to who was who and even when naked they wouldn't tell you anything, apart from their respective names of Chas and Chris. (Quack and Quack.)

The loss of part of our basic pay for many a week was no real hardship, mainly because there was no where in these jungles we could spend it, even if we wanted to. The daily crossing of many small and sometimes very fast flowing rivers was also par for the course. We frequently came across venomous snakes and other unwelcome varieties of very large insect life, unfortunately they all went with the territory that we were forced to pursue our enemy in. On rare occasions we would get close enough to our sworn enemy, to fire at and sometimes even kill them. This part was not particularly enjoyable and I knew of no soldier that enjoyed this part of the job - although there is always the exception to the rule. These periods of three week stints always seemed much longer than they actually were, mainly I suppose because of the intensity of the duration of twenty four seven.

The week off following the completion of every patrol, brought extreme relief, from both the physical and psychological pressures endured from such living. At the end of two such patrols we were sent to the island of Penang, on our much needed first ever one week Malayan holiday, to fulfil the pleasures that civilian life could offer. We were all looking forward to having a break, especially as we had heard the flesh pots of Penang were more than well equipped, to satisfy even the most demanding cravings of our sexual appetites. After all, until this time our sexual urges were dealt with by private masturbation, under impossible conditions and that often meant discretion went out of the window. The twins were OK because they found a way to satisfy each other out of pure necessity. The words, 'when needs must with the devil driving' came easily to mind.

The island of Penang off the west coast of mainland Malaya is an idyllic tropical island, it was popular and well established in the mid to late fifties. Georgetown, its capital, had more than enough to offer the typical Tommy, with good beaches, shops, sea and it even had legalized prostitution, all very carefully vetted by the army. These lovelies were mainly a mixture of velvet skin beauties from Hong Kong, Singapore and Indonesia, who were more than expert enough to satisfy and fully quench even the most demanding of sexual fantasies, with the added knowledge that they were V.D. free. Artistically they were able to fulfil any appetite, in a most professional way.

In these early days the beer was cheap, and spirits a plenty were available to while away long leisurely evenings, with exotic dancing as part of the entertainment. The long balmy sunny days were spent relaxing on the beach, in an era when getting a sun tan was very much in vogue. Swimming in the warm tropical sea, day dreaming to our hearts content, just wearing out the daylight hours in readiness for yet another evenings entertainment, of eating, drinking and sometimes being very merry. One evening the three of us decided it was time to surrender up our manhood to this wonderful place of sexual demands. The twins however refused even in this pleasurable form of sexual exercise, to be separated. It was eventually agreed one particular lady of the night would pleasure them both, together and at a discount, to her it was just a job lot. On the other hand, as an individual I had to pay full whack and I hasten to add, it was well worth every Singapore dollar of anybody's money. The tenderness and sensual feelings expressed physically, by this Madonna of mercy, would be impossible to put into words. Unfortunately it only helped to underline the intricate and varied pleasure of pure sexual delight, which most of us were experiencing for the very first time in our lives. It is at wonderful interludes in our life, such as this, that one gains an insight into the real meaning of sex. The explosive joy of both sexual love and even pure lust, of almost animalistic pleasure in one so young, is understood the world over. Those who preach the reproductive organs are purely for reproduction, either lives on a different planet to ours, or are married to such Christian ideals they may well live in another world. They truly don't know what they are missing from such a vital part of the human nature, regardless on how they choose to dress up their own self imposed doctrine.

On a particularly fine afternoon one of the twins suggested we could swim over to the mainland, less than nine miles away. Although it was definitely not my idea, the lure of warm seas and the challenge of a rather reckless adventure, which had no real point to make, was appealing. A boatman was easily persuaded to accompany us for a small handful of dollars, in case any need or emergency should arise. The three of us were all competent swimmers and felt such a swim was more than within our capabilities. Some of the mates with whom we had shared our last patrols, enthusiastically encouraged this folly, mainly just to make pocket money on the side with a few bets. Their bets were made with other squadies that did not know us, giving favourable odds on our side. The swim went well, especially for the first three quarters of way over to the mainland. The last few miles or so proved difficult, as by then our very tired bodies began to lack the effort needed to carry on. We chided and swore at each other, in order to egg each other on to the finish, after almost five hours of being in the water we eventually struggled out of the water on all fours, crawling onto the foreshore wondering why we were afflicted with such madness. The native boatman looked at us in amazement, knowing that the three of us must surely be affected with some rare tropical disease, called madness. We climbed into his boat and sprawled out like drunken men. (We were all sober, honest)] We were in a state of collapse, but grateful that we didn't have to inflict upon ourselves, the dubious pleasure of rowing back to Penang Island.

On our return we were all given a heavy dressing down by my old friends 'the monkeys' (the red capped military police) who threatened to run us in, as they felt a spell in their special cages might serve to sober us up. After we all solemnly promised to remain on our best behaviour, we were given a recorded reprimand. Dressed only in our swimming costumes and just before we departed, these dickheads informed us they could tell we were from the Rifle Brigade, because no other lunatics existed in Malaya, outside of that regiment. This insult and slur on our impeccably unstained character, cut us deep and hurt more than any action taken against us, would have done.

With only two days left to live it up so to speak, we decided to overdose on one last visit to the sexual house of pleasure. Being just a little short of the readies, we were successful in getting a discount as a job lot of three. Our appetites knew no bounds, my only fear as an individual was that I may not be able to perform, in an open forum with the twins looking on. I needn't have worried as the twins opted to go first, which soon had my sexual juices running in abundance. The insatiable thirst of my beloved friends, the twins, astounded my imagination, I was gobsmacked at their inventiveness for pure sexual delinquency. Alas all good things must come to an end, as Bobby whispered in my ear "I hope you're satisfied now, you sex maniac"

I looked up in surprise as if I might see his infectious grin all over his face, before realizing where I was. The twins both jointly asked me if I was OK as I got dressed, still grinning to myself. I slept well that night with Bobby coming and going, interrupting my dreams and the thoughts of pure mischief we both got up to in times long past. I was still licking my lips with the thoughts of forbidden far eastern delights as we passed back through the gates of reality, entering the real world of the M.T. section where we felt we had returned to our just and rightful place.

Chapter Sixteen

"An ambush too far"

Having recharged our batteries, and with the memories and feelings still teasing our minds with the forbidden fruit of carnal knowledge, now having quenched our sexual appetites, within the lustful regions of many youthful loins of recent sexual plunder, a definite anticlimax descended upon us after such delicious participative action. So much so, that to return to the relative safety and mundane routine of our station in life seemed almost sinful by comparison. When the M.T. sergeant asked for volunteers for an overnight ambush to take place nearby I immediately put my name forward in a rash moment of enthusiastic madness. Looking at my best buddies the twins, I quickly felt as well as realized I was somewhat isolated, it became abundantly clear the twins and I were not quacking the same tune on this venture. Oh well I thought, I was only on my own for one night and comforted myself that after the night ambush, I would be sleeping soundly, as my mates the twins would be toiling in the heat of the sun all of the following day.

Being the only bren gunner in our party of eight, we set off for a clearing on the other side of a nearby rubber plantation, to set up the ambush in a chosen location. We would first have to cut through the forest of rubber trees, they offered limited cover, but made observation of any movement within our sights easier to detect. Because of the sparse overhead cover offered by the rubber plantation, our merry band of eight felt it would be wise to widen the spacing between us considerably stretching the patrol of eight, to cover a distance of about one hundred feet long in Indian file fashion, with me bringing up a rear guard action and doing my best to keep a stealthy distance from the men spread out ahead of me. Two of our eight individuals were placed far out on both right and left wings, to avoid any element of surprise, any sudden attackers en route to our proposed ambush might make. Intelligence we had received indicated the intended insurgents would not break cover until well after midnight, but it was imperative we did not blow our cover, until well after we were in our ambush positions.

Thinking of the long night ahead and my recent sexual enjoyment in Panang still invigorating my mind and in all honesty, with such meanderings going on within, my brain was not on the job at hand. Without warning and to my utter surprise, I suddenly found myself spread eagled flat out on the ground, with my bren gun digging viciously into my rib cage. I saw the last of the daylight flash onto the silver blade of the panga (bush knife) as it passed my limited vision en route, somewhere near the top of my head and towards my outstretched arms as I felt the dead weight of my passenger on top of me. In an instant or maybe a micro second, I realized I was under attack, as the adrenaline rush and primeval fury kicked into the automatic intensive jungle training that instinctively took over.

With one immense huge surge of physical power that only sheer fear can suddenly summon up, I quickly found myself standing with one foot on top of my attacker. The automatic fire of a full magazine of twenty rounds of three-o-three ammunition unloaded in a flash or a second or two, from the barrel end of my bren gun, as I felt the drill like motion go through his chest into the earth below his body. I did not realise at this time during my defensive reaction that the now dead victim's panga had passed through part of my left forearm. The blood gushing out from my open wound, (which didn't hurt at the time) was now squirting all over my victim's front, as well as on the ground about this bloody scene. I was pulled off my victim's body by several members of my own patrol, whose identity at this time were faceless. A tourniquet was quickly applied to my upper left arm, to stem the rapid flow of my blood loss. I knew somehow or felt, I was being carried to a clearing not too far away and the sound of helicopter rotors could be clearly heard before I fainted. It is in emergencies such as this that one realises the value of rigorous army training and the dependency on such good mates. Their immediate positive action and speed of their duty was certainly most appreciated.

In the hospital at Kuala Lumpur where I had been taken I was quickly stitched up as only about two inches of the tip end of the panga's blade had sliced through part of my forearm. The scar, which I still carry to this day almost fifty years later, was hyper sensitive to touch for many years to come. It could have been many, many times worst but within a week, I was back with my mates in the beloved arms of my M.T. section. I would be unable to put any real stress on my left arm for some time, but being a young blooded healthy youth, it would heal quickly and in a relatively short period of time. I was very pleased to discover it was only my left arm and not my artistic or writing right hand that was very temporary out of action. Needless to say I did not compound the disclosure to anyone, of my stupidity at the time, for the lack of concentration on the operational ambush in question.

With this in mind I felt to some extent that I had let my muckers down, as they were forced to abandon the said ambush, because of my selfish neglect. The twins also felt deeply somehow neglectful because as they themselves put it, "they wasn't on the patrol to the ambush, to protect and watch over me." The attention they smothered me with was both touching and embarrassing at one and the same time. Their overtly show of concern and affection towards me only served to remind me of Bobby, which at the time I found very disturbing. The severe reprimands I personally experienced within my head, were dished out on a regular basis over several days, with Bobby's persistent whisperings hurting far deeper than anything the army might have done, had they known. At least from the army I got sympathy and no reprimand for which I was grateful.

This unfortunate affair occurring just six months short of my final demob date, did change the army's attitude towards me and they felt I had more than my fair share of risky adventures. Under the instructions of 'B' company Commander Major Hargreaves, I was detailed to become the M.T. clerk for my troubles. The thought that I was now trapped and pushing paper about did not make me the happiest sand boy in the platoon. Certainly not to be able to drive on a regular basis I was now dramatically curtailed and kept well away from anything remotely classified as active or considered as remotely dangerous. The army had reached an impasse where I was concerned and felt very strongly the need to clip my adventurous wings. My pleas and even offers of volunteering for anything remotely with risk attached fell on stony ground and were sometimes bluntly ignored. This shackling of any impulsive action on my part, that may have tempted the flow of my adrenaline juices, was for me a hardship like a caged bird and given enough time I was very slowly able to come to terms with.

Meanwhile I became like a bear with a very sore head, very sore indeed. (Or so I was told.) It was about this time, that I received a written and very exciting invitation from the London Himalayan Expedition Foundation, which I found extremely flattering, which immediately put my life on a high. The expedition in question would be assembling in North East India, at Darjeeling in March 1958. The pleasure of my company should I choose to join them, would be most welcomed, the letter read. There was no question of choice on my part. My wildest dreams imaginable had now been answered as my spirits lifted higher than any Himalayan peak, my soul soared above the clouds in a state of high voltage elation. I quickly did my mental arithmetic as I realized I should be getting demobbed in May 1957, which gave me a full ten months before the following March 1958. "What could I do that was worth while to fill this ten month gap?" I asked myself. I would need to give this some very serious consideration and at least I had a full six months left before deciding what best I could do with this time.

Meanwhile I wrote a very lengthy letter home to my aunt, explaining all about my wonderful news of this fantastic opportunity. Once my euphoric state eventually abated somewhat and I was more capable of looking at the whole of the picture in a realistic and objective light, I slowly began to realise as well and formulate a rather outlandish plan of action, the possibilities of realising yet another one of my scatterbrain dreams might just be possible, I'm sure it was. The germ of an idea began to spring roots in the back of my highly excited brain matter. First however, I would need to lay my hands on certain large scale maps that would cover an overland journey from Singapore to India. They would enable me to sharpen up my idea of plan, as well as look carefully at the feasibility study of such a rich notion.

I knew from this point forwards there would be much correspondence involved and many other obstacles to overcome. Meanwhile I would have to temper any impulse I might have to blurt out my secret thoughts through official channels to the army, before I was truly ready to formulate exactly my intended plan of action. The army on my past hair raising experiences, were not yet ready for yet another one of my mad adventures and I harboured doubts they might never be ready for what I would eventually propose!!

I despatched letters urgently to Blacks of Greenock, for despatch of certain mountaineering equipment, another to the ordnance survey map making people to enlist their help with maps and finally a third to the Himalayan Foundation accepting their generous invitation to join their expedition in March 1958 to meet them in Darjeeling India. Patience was never one of my strong points as I waited with bated breath in answer to all of my correspondence. For once I easily accepted my new role as M.T. clerk which was not only a vital and responsible job of work, but enabled me to keep on top of all my new essential correspondence. I also wrote to Picture Post, a prominent popular magazine, offering my service as a travelling journalist for this particular trek I had in mind and was more than delighted when they accepted my offer, which would help pay some of my expenses hopefully on route. However I would save every penny of my army pay towards this exciting venture that was emerging clearly day by day in my confused but very excited state of mind. When I was not actively busy with my job as M.T. clerk, (the only clerk you understand.) I could often be seen dreaming the hours away in a state of heavenly bliss, especially as the jigsaw parts of my puzzle slowly began to take shape into a more defined picture.

My mates and especially the twins with whom I shared intimate sleeping accommodation, began to think that more than my injured arm had been seriously affected, as I received more and more strange gazes from my brothers in arms as time increasingly went by.

With only three months left before my divorce from the army, I felt the need for speed, as I knew only too well the cumbersome slowness of the army wheels of bureaucracy would need ample time to consider my proposal. At this vital point in my plans, I suddenly realized I did not own a British passport and would be going nowhere without one. This important document had been over looked in my present euphoric state. A hurried letter was despatched to my aunt for my birth certificate, which was quickly written stressing the urgency of my plight.

An audience with the Company Commander, Major Hargreaves was requested, as the importance of going through official channels was imperative, if I was to make any real headway. Besides, I was banking on enlisting the Major's support with whom I felt had some inkling and understanding of my overactive fertile mind towards my everlasting yearning for adventure, no matter how far fetched it seemed. I had to wait several days for my special if some what unusual request to see him, as the Commander was spending several days away from camp. I knew I would have to tell all and come clean with all my plans, to stand any chance of winning him over on side. (My side.)

Having already received my maps and most of my climbing gear from Blacks of Greenock, along with letters from The Himalayan Foundation and the Picture Post, all of which opened many an inquisitive eye among the M.T. section. I at least felt I now had sufficient ammunition to put my case.

Several days later, over breakfast one morning, Major Hargreaves put in his usual appearance, enquiring about our grub, when he caught my eye and ordered me before him at ten am that very same morning. Understanding with afore knowledge that he had been a barrister in civvy street, I knew I would only get one crack, at presenting my case. The time duly arrived and precisely at ten hundred hours, I was marched into his office before him. Feeling more like a criminal on a charge, than a plea of mitigation, and with the M.T. sergeant who escorted me in with no intentions of missing any of the following proceedings, I felt a right plonker and extremely inhibited with this unwanted audience of me. Taking a bold initiative, and getting my brains into gear, required a super human effort on my part. Feeling I was giving the Major the courtesy of my best laid plans, I took the bull by the horns and hidden courage in my now parched mouth and started to unfold my plans. I told him of my full intentions, firstly of getting permission to get released (demobbed) in Singapore, then hitch hiking up through the length of Malaya, Siam and then across Burma up through the Hurkong valley and over the 13,000 foot high Paunsau Pass to Nampong the first village in Assam India. Then make my way up to North East India to Darjeeling, to join the Himalayan Expedition.

I gave Hargreaves everything I had and the credit for not interrupting me once, while I illustrated with my maps and letters the trek, I was proposing. A very long silence followed, while Hargreaves looked long and hard at the sergeant first, who wore an incredulous expression of disbelief on his face, before turning his somewhat puzzled gaze in my direction. After what seemed like an eternity, Hargreaves, who spoke firstly to the dumbfounded sergeant, who was still standing aloof gobsmacked, "What do you think sergeant?" Asked the Major.

A nervous cough ensued, expressed by the sergeant, before breaking wind, "I think he should be locked up sir" said the sergeant in a matter of fact voice, then shut up thinking he had already said far too much.

"I thought you might," said the Major slowly breaking into a knowing smile. That really said it all.

"Do you realise fully the implications of your proposals Ankorne?" Asked Hargreaves.

"Yes sir," I replied. "I have given this whole matter very serious consideration," I emphasized.

"I do believe you have," he said. Then changing the subject, stalling for time, "and how is your wounded arm?" He enquired politely.

"Fully healed with total feeling and movement" I assured him, just as politely.

A pause followed "OK Ankorne, leave it with me, I certainly need some time to consider your request" said Hargreaves rather bluntly.

"March out" barked the sergeant and once we were no longer in earshot of the Major's office, the sergeant turned towards me saying "I always thought you were touched, but now I know you're stark staring bonkers" he spat.

"Yes serg" I replied politely before quickly escaping from anymore of his verbal abuse.

It was hard to gauge how this interview went, but I felt I shouldn't hold my breath. Well, I thought, now the cat really is out of the bag, and if the sergeant had anything to do with it the jungle drums would be very busy indeed. I just had to wait for the men in white coats to take me away, I smiled to myself. I wasn't too worried about the twins, as they more or less already knew of my scatterbrain scheme and secretly at least in the confines of our own tent were both very supportive, but made no offer I could refuse to join me, in my crackpot venture. Perhaps it wasn't quite their cup of tea I surmised. If members of my own section thought I had escaped from the nearest looney bin what might they think of me at G.H.Q. where the powers that be are far removed from the realities and thoughts to any dreams of the average recruit serving far away, without any comforts of home from home, that these morons took for granted. The permutations and variations of these so called wise men's way of thinking, well I shudder to contemplate, but my mind was already boggling in daring to think such thoughts, might favour towards me.

A disappointing gloom descended as the weeks on the passage of time dropped off the pages from my weekly calendar, with still no reply to my request. These were worrying times for me as I received my full birth certificate in readiness to apply for my very first passport, but still not a word from the big wigs at G.H.Q. My frustrations were mounting and building slowly as the snail like pace of the red tape the army were famous for, ground slowly onwards, with less than a month of count down days to my official release date nearing, regardless to where this would take place. The local rags, both in Singapore and Kuala Lumpur were running my story, of my intended journey overland to India. I didn't need to guess, or look very far, to know where my intentions had sprung a serious leak, although my one and only main concern was the fact of pre-empting the Top Brass decision, especially if they thought I myself was responsible for the source of the leak. This, I was to learn much later on, stimulated the kind of response, that turned into my favour.

Within a week of the press printing my proposed adventure, I was called up before Major Hargreaves who without any emotion, informed me that the army was in full agreement in releasing me in Singapore on sixteenth of May 1957 with certain provisos of course. The simplicity and ease that Major Hargreaves made this official statement to me, more than knocked the wind from all my sails and with the suspicious mind and dubious faith I held in regard to these faceless wonders, now put me on tenterhooks waiting for some evil catch to deflate my over active egotistical state of high euphoria and expectations. It just couldn't be that simple, I told myself in fear of over doing completely on utter disbelief. My attempts at casually accepting my ultimate wishes by acting like Mr Cool himself, was impossible to maintain indefinitely. With the healing qualities of time itself, I came to slowly convince myself that all was in order and in fact my wildest wishes were truly about to come within the realms of reality.

One week before my due release date for demob in Singapore I received a strange letter of request from a lad called David Kwan which after due careful consideration, I agreed, I would meet once I arrived in Singapore, after my official release. It was a sad and deeply moving experience to have to say so many goodbyes to all my mates in the M.T. section, especially having lived so closely with all of these guys and having spent so much time within this section. The twins were detailed to escort me south to Johore Baru in readiness for my ultimate day of release back into civilian life and freedom from the powers who would relinquish all the regimental controls the army held over my life, these past three years.

I HATE GOODBYES

Chapter Seventeen

Transition

At precisely five am on this red letter morning having packed all my personal equipment into the back of an enclosed Land Rover, we set off from Kuala Baru our M.T. base, for the very last time heading for the south. With all my gear in the back, the three of us sat up front easily, in silence at first as I had much to chew over. My trusted bren gun was no longer at my side, and only the twins carried their personal weapons, for the long arduous journey. The mixed feelings of emotions swimming about my physical being were hard to describe, let alone put into words, as I sat alongside the twins up front. The scenes that flashed by our windows, as the Land Rover hurried along the early morning deserted roads, noisily winding its way with only the effort of the engine sound conversing with us all. Chas or was it Chris? Who sat closely by my side within touching proximity, gave me the occasional side ways glance-without actually communicating his thoughts into words. The sudden realization, that I would soon be seeing these two rascals for the very last time at the end of this all day journey south, began to affect my emotional state. I looked casually at the other twin, who was driving with a face of concentration on the road ahead, I felt humbled for knowing these two fantastic mates, with whom I had shared so much of my personal and sometimes intimate life. It goes without saying, I was going to miss this pair more than words can express.

I was wondering within my own thoughts, if they would miss me just as much, when the twin next to me suddenly put his arm about my shoulders as if reading my personal thoughts. I looked at him with understanding, bravely attempting a smile, which he instantly returned with genuine affection clearly visible within his deep blue eyes. I could feel my emotions beginning to well up inside me, so before I reduced myself into a blubbering wreck, I asked if we could stop, as I was in urgent need of a piss. The twin driving signalled a quick thumbs up sign, then quickly pulled off the road coming to rest. He then got out, cocking his sterling apache light machine gun, before giving us the all clear to stand against the nearside of the vehicle in readiness. The twin nearest me decided to join me, as we urinated in tandem with complete inhibition. I started to make light of the situation by pissing in as high an arc as I could manage and the twin joined me in doing even better by out performing my efforts. Having relieved ourselves the twin who had been standing guard then quickly came round to join us, gaining at least some protection shielded by the side of the Land River. My escort south were taking no chances, as sudden attacks on any military vehicle was a common occurrence. After he too had relieved himself, we set off once again to continue our journey.

After three hours or so at about eight thirty, we pulled into one of our other platoons base camp for breakfast at Kuala Koto Bahru. By this time we were conversing and joking with each other as we set off on the long road south again. Having passed through Kuala Koto Bahru we knew we still had some three hundred miles to go, to reach Johore Bahru in the extreme south before nightfall. The road soon opened up onto a major artery at the same time, more and more heavy traffic coming from the south heading against us, increased in numbers.

Most of this traffic was civilian heavily laden commercial Lorries with the odd military vehicle as well. The twins started to discuss my forthcoming plans, once I had been released from the army. We debated the pros and cons on the best road routes to head north to the Thailand (Siam) border and for the best possibilities of hitch hiking or cadging lifts along the way.

We made good speed at a steady fifty five miles an hour and pulled into Johore Barhu H.Q. just before five pm, feeling tired but more than satisfied to arrive safely, after almost ten hours none stop driving. Land Rovers are not the most comfortable of vehicles and we were all suffering from back ache and sore bums. After a really good hot meal and a refreshing shower we all decided an early night was in order, especially as I knew the twins had to make the same monotonous journey when returning tomorrow.

We bedded down in a spare tent that was kept for 'unwanted' visitors. I say unwanted because members of the Rifle Brigade were not exactly welcomed after our disgraceful performance with the Black Watch, who still held a long standing grudge against the whole of our regiment.

The twins set about giving each other a massage before bed, while I stripped off ready for my own bed, having first checked over all the gear packed in my new rucksack. Once they had finished pampering each other they came over to me and unashamedly started to pummel my body between them. Without any embarrassment on my part they gave me a wonderful relaxing work over my entire body and by the time they had finished with me I was more than ready to enjoy one of my best nights sleep ever.

After a good eight hours sleep and just before five am, the twins prepared for the off, making their return trip back up north. Each of them in turn came over to me hugging and kissing me, saying prolonged goodbyes, then just as suddenly, they were gone and I knew I would never see both of them ever again.

I hate goodbyes, especially long ones.

After a hearty breakfast (my very last as a soldier) I was taken by a staff sergeant across the causeway into Singapore at G.H.Q. on this sixteenth day of May 1957.

Without any further delay and even less red tape than I expected I was made to sign a number of forms, given my army back pay which amounted to almost three hundred pounds and politely but very firmly shown the door. Why did I get this distinct feeling that I was being given the bum's rush? The overwhelming feeling that they were even more pleased to get rid of me than I them came over me as I walked into the township towards dockland where I had arranged to meet David Kwan. With the weight of my new rucksack comfortably adjusted to my back shape, already like a trusted friend, with my full length ice axe being used as a walking stick, I strode along at a comfortable gait.

**Self – Centre, standing,
David – Right,
With two of his brothers
and young sister**

**Brother – Ex Naval –
David Kwan,
who taught me so much**

**Brother – Doctor Chong,
Penang, Malaya**

**World Peace Pagoda –
Rangoon, Burma**

Army discharge papers, containing my release

General Headquarters
FAR EAST Land Forces
c/o GPO SINGAPORE

Tele 2801 Ext 183

FE 418CP PA1 (668)

18 Feb 57

HQ MALAYA Command (4)
- - - - - - - - - -

        Subject:- Local Release
                  23202513 Rfn AHKORNE P. - 1 RB

        Reference: CRMC 1710/86/71/A4 dated 8 Feb 57 ... 'A'
                GRO 37 of 1953 .... 'B'
                GRO 399 of 1956 .... 'C'
                QR 1955 para 473 .... 'D'

1.   Authority is given for Rfn AHKORNE to be released in MALAYA for the purpose of travelling to UK under private arrangements.

2.   Reference para 4 of GRO 399 of 1956. It is unlikely that any refund of travelling expenses will be admissible. However, if desired application may be made to PS3 at this GHQ in the normal way.

3.   UK Holding Unit will be notified in accordance with the final sub para of para 2(b) of GRO 399 of 1956.

                          (Sgd)   XXXXXXXXX

                              Major General
                 Major General IC Administration
                     FAR EAST Land Forces

Copy to:- GHQ FARELF
             Q(Mov)
             PS3
             Fd Records

Part Two

Forbidden Journey

Chapter Eighteen

The meeting of two minds

I was walking along the dockside, which was bristling with Malay and British warships, feeling very conspicuous, as my eyes darted about looking for David Kwan. David was visiting some of his old shipmates, he was in the habit of doing this since leaving the Navy only a few days ago.

I was passing nearby when I heard a shout of "Ahoy there!" as someone aboard hailed me. I looked up in surprise, as David ran down the gang plank in haste to meet me. The grin that covered his face in sheer delight as he came bounding towards me, with exuberance and a very light step, certainly made a very favourable first impression. He shook my hand vigorously, and then clapped me on my shoulder as if he was meeting a loving relative, taking me completely by surprise, leaving me somewhat dumbfounded and speechless. This was the first meeting that was so animated by David it really took my breath away and gave David a distinct advantage over me.

David Kwan Yung Thian to give him his full title, was simply called David, by all his shipmates and relatives, appeared very young indeed, perhaps too young, I momentarily thought to myself at first glance. David was just a tadge shorter than me at five feet nine and half inches tall and looked rather thin. (As if in need of a good meal.) With an unblemished skin and a positive expression of mischief, worn openly on his boat race that was lit up by a pair of inviting eyes set into almond shaped sockets beneath jet black unruly kempt hair hanging with attitude loosely about his clean shaven very fresh face. The first impressions although favourable, was one of a livewire like over enthusiastic, bundle of troublesome joy. His apparent openness came easy, if somewhat disarming for our first meeting. I felt he may have been just a little contrived in his efforts to create a good impression on our first sight of each other, which left me with certain guarded doubts somewhere deep in the recesses at the back of my suspicious mind. Perhaps, when getting to know each other better, this early impression might mellow between us.

After we introduced ourselves, David suggested we both retire to a nearby dockside café, to talk together over a glass of ice cold coffee. David had just reached twenty one years of age this very month of May and had served in the Malay Navy. Starting as a raw recruit at sixteen years of age and having completed some five years in total, he had recently been discharged and was itching for a more adventurous way of life.

Although of Chinese origin, David also held a British passport, a document that he was very proud of. He had served most of his time in the Malay/British Navy as a medic and according to most of his mates that I had the pleasure of meeting later, he was the best manipulator of bones and massage expert in the business. David's cooking skills were also very good, and he had been a strong member of the Singapore Sea Scouts for most of his life. In fact, since leaving the navy officially less than a week ago, he was camping temporarily in the scout hut, which was like a second home to him. It was not far away, also on the dockside, and offered me a place I could also lay my head should I want to do so.

On the face of all this information, we obviously had so much in common, so why was I hesitant in thinking of having slight doubts about letting David join me? Was it his abundance of unbelievable, almost desperate need to make friends and to team up with me at our very first meeting? I don't really know, nor could I put my finger on exactly what it was that made me just a little uneasy about this meeting of two like minds, which on the face of it seemed to have so much in common, it just appeared to be too good to be true somehow. Perhaps it was my past life experiences, that were obviously tinged with a fair dollop of mistrust, ringing false alarm bells of disappointments.

David with his own instincts and intuition began to spread the treacle of human kindness just a little thinner. Showing me more realistic intentions of his genuine endeavours towards the planning of such an arduous trek, he showed me all of his privately owned possessions, which included a lightweight tent, sleeping bag, and rucksack, with a whole range of camping/hiking gear, that composed to make a realistic approach towards his intentions for the undertaking of such an overland journey or trek.

I decided at short notice to at least spend several days with David, the better we should get to know each other, and expressed delight at accepting his kind invitation to stay with him at the scout hut. The memories of both Bobby and Henry having spent so may wonderful times at the 5th Staines Sea Scout hut came flooding back which only added comfort to my acceptance of David's kind invitation. So for the time being at least, we used the scout hut as a base to formulate future plans, with the strong possibilities that David and I would team up together.

After spending an uncomfortable night pestered by mosquitoes without a net, we decided to go to a local bazaar to do some shopping for bits and pieces and I, in particular for a pair of mosquito nets for each of us. But no such ready made nets were to be found. We met many of David's friends for lunch, Chinese style, who all spoke their best English for my benefit. We had a very fruitful day, ending with the hand washing of clothes to keep ourselves up to date and in trim. David never ever wore underwear, which reminded me of my many years at Ashford. He preferred to wear loose fitting shorts and singlet, which seem to be very much the vogue of fashion worn by most of his mates and Malayan youth today. The Chinese, I was to learn very quickly, expressed their feelings openly and without the slightest trace of our form of inhibitions, this David explained was the sole reserve of the British, with their stiff upper lip, which the Chinese and other Asiatic natives found most amusing.

In the enclave of their friends and relatives, nudity was of no consequence, especially when bathing or within the confines of their own home and I found this took some time to accept, due to my sheltered and somewhat prudish upbringing. Physical touching of affection towards one's friends, regardless to their sex was easily accepted as normal and bi-sexual relationships abounded as a kind of normality among many Asian nationalities, which was strange and very different for me, coming from a so called strict or straight laced society that frowned on such practices. The freedom of sexual expression between friends (male as well as female) was perfectly normal in David's society, who could not understand this cultural difference between us.

At first I did not accept these foreign ways, which were a cultural shock to my delicate way of thinking. David understood and resisted any physical contact with me, which I appreciated very much. This led me to trust David and get to like his many qualities, which eased any qualms I may have originally harboured.

I began to feel more and more trust towards him, as we became firm friends. I knew now that David's thoughts towards this trek that festered in my brain were shared equally by both of us just as fervently as they had once alone been part of my own ethos and fertile imagination. As we became friendlier towards each other, any doubts I once held disappeared completely, and my confidence in David's abilities grew daily, leaving me comfortable in his company. I grew to realise that although inexperienced in some areas, never the less he had much to offer.

David was only one month my junior in age, although his exceptionally youthful appearance was deceptive, he was far more experienced than I, in the ways of native traditions, especially Chinese culture throughout Asia, and could teach me a great deal. Having both failed to buy any mosquito nets in the local bazaar market, David was able to get one of his many relatives to make one that fitted the shape of the tent we intended to use on our travels.

Before leaving Singapore on the first of many legs of our journey, we tested this double net by sleeping inside it, while at our scout hut base. We were both fully satisfied with the very effective results, being able to sleep soundly without any further pestering from these very annoying insects. We got down to making up an itinerary of dividing up our equipment between us, taking only items that with careful consideration we both felt essential, including a few items of luxury. We both fully agreed on our exact plan of action, whereby we would hitch hike when ever possible, and would hike or walk when this became unfeasible. For protection purposes and vital safety of each other, we would always stay together, no matter what. We both realized that crossing the length of Malaya would be relatively easy, especially with the contacts that David had throughout Malaya as well as the vast extensive amount of distant relatives, he intended visiting along the way. We poured over our maps together planning a very full itinerary of travel to explore extensively, without any need of urgency or speed of progress. These were days of high excitement, never sure what we would encounter along the way or when, giving us both highly charged anticipation, with untold excitement of what was yet to come, expected or otherwise. We sorted out our personal finances between us, and although David was less well off than myself, it was both our aim to manage and survive, on the minimum required to keep body and soul together. Control of our joint spending with care, became our watchword, as neither of us knew how long our trek would take, or how far we would be forced to stretch our finance, this was always of great concern to both of us.

Having obtained my passport with the essential visas our vital official documentation was now complete. David and I jointly agreed to share all revenues that we were able to make from any written articles or photographs we had published, as part of our adventure forthwith. Thus we both entered into the spirit of this great adventure, prepared to share with each other every part of our lives as one.

David's sense of humour and general joviality of taking life by the scruff of the neck was refreshing, in many ways he was the perfect companion. His negotiating skill in dealing with the local inhabitants of this fabulous country, by always managing to strike up a bargain, sometimes left me breathless and in shear awe of his hidden depths. It would be fair to say that David's knowledge and understanding of both cultures would prove to be invaluable, I was reassured that accepting him to join me on this trek would be extremely beneficial to both of us. All of his scouting friends that I got to know quite well, were interested in every detail of our plans, and went out of their way to help us in any way they could.

Tonight would be our final night in Singapore and we both spent time writing letters to our loved ones, as well as checking all our documents, before we left Singapore to head north in the morning. Our friends, mostly David's, gave us a feast to remember, with ample lubrication of the local brew to wash it all down with ease. Once alone, with prolonged goodbyes over, we prepared for bed lying side by side on top of our sleeping bags, in an attempt to cool down from the oppressive heat of the late evening. I was attired in a pair of army issue underpants, and David lay beside me in complete nudity as was his custom. I studied David's body, which lacked any real definition and was very slender in build. His skin was clear of any spots and save for his pubic hair, the rest of his body was hairless. He noticed with amusement my study of his anatomy, but showed absolutely no embarrassment or inhibition towards my interest in his physique. We talked together closely, within inches of each others naked torsos, as if it was the most natural of surroundings, enjoying each others company and both feeling completely at ease with each others presence.

"What do you think?" asked David pointing to his own body.

Taken off guard by the directness of his innocent question, I jokingly made some comment that "I had seen more meat on a butcher's pencil."

David looked puzzled, not grasping the understanding or irony of my comment, but held up his limp penis, asking what exactly was wrong with the size of his manhood. He misunderstood my jest completely, and an Englishman's sense of humour. I assured him there was nothing wrong with his manhood which he was now studying with some consternation. "You're just perfect," I told David, who smiled easily at his own appendage, satisfied that I was not belittling him in any way (no pun intended,) as David was easily well enough endowed.

He broke into one of his winning smiles, satisfied that I meant no disrespect towards him. He then straddled my torso before telling me to first turn face down. Not wanting to upset him any further, I obeyed his request as he sat on my rump astride me. I waited, wondering what exactly David had in mind, as he cracked the knuckles on both hands, which I had seen him do several times before.

"Do you want to keep your shorts on?" asked David. "Before I start on you," he added.

"Yes" I replied softly, as he reached down and took both my shoulders in the palms of his hands, then pulling them backwards, with just the right amount of pressure.

He quickly and expertly worked his magic hands between my shoulder blades, in towards my upper neck muscles. I felt his nudity as he climbed higher onto my back and worked the upper torso like I have never experienced before. The soothing and total relaxation of my upper body, all the way down to my lower back, was so hypnotic that I was now relaxed in a euphoric state of meditation. The movement of his hands, always knowing exactly when to apply just the right amount of pressure, was totally professional. David knew every pressure point in the body, many of which I knew nothing about or of their existence.

"Right" said David "Lift up your rump" which I did without question, as he removed my underwear without a word. He gently moved slowly, down the length of my body towards my feet. Ordering me to turn over, he started with the soles of my feet, applying the highly developed technique of Chinese foot massage, then perceptively moved up each leg in turn, until he came to my inner thighs and groin areas. I closed my eyes, as I absorbed his subtle touch, marvelling at such expertise in one so young. After finishing my upper torso and near completion, it felt as if my body was floating. I realized then, that although I had received a full body massage many times before, this was something else, I knew I had never before experienced anything like this ultra highly sensitive massage in my entire life.

David, having finished, returned to the top of his own sleeping bag, then leaning across, calmly placed his hand on top of my chest asking "How do you feel now?"

"Absolutely fantastic" I answered softly with a long contented sigh. "You really give one hell of a massage" I continued "and I've never experienced anything near so special in my life" I added, as I lay motionless, in total peace, not feeling the least bit vulnerable or exposed.

"Wait until you really need one" replied David, "believe me you will be thankful I came along!"

I couldn't argue with that fact I thought, as I drifted gently in and out of consciousness.

"You know," said David, "your in pretty good physical shape" he remarked, as he continued to look me over with innocent casual interest.

I continued to enjoy what I can only describe as a profound religious experience, as I felt at peace in both body and mind to my inner core, and beyond. I apologised to David for not offering to return his favour, because I knew my amateur attempt to do so would not be worthy, compared with his masterly skills.

"That's OK Paul" he replied," I am not in need of one anyway, and I really did it as an exercise to see how much trust you placed in me as a person, a friend and as a long term companion."

With David imparting this little wisdom of knowledge, I felt sufficiently cooled down to climb into my sleeping bag, minus my underwear, now feeling no need to wear such a garment. Having done so, I leaned over to David and gave him an affectionate hug, to prove not only to him, but also myself that I trusted him implicitly, although we had known each other just over ten days, I felt I had known him for a considerable time longer. We said our goodnights to each other, as David in turn climbed into his bag to quickly go off to sleep first. I lay awake a little while longer, studying the serenity on his face of peace, and wondering what other hidden talents he possessed in one so young. The feeling of utter contentment washed over me, as I too gently but quickly, passed into the land of boyhood dreams. For tomorrow is a new day and into the unknown, as we leave Singapore to seek our fortune amongst the lands of mystery and unforgettable experiences, to find and search for new challenges to satisfy our youthful stirrings for ever more adventure.

Chapter Nineteen

Our big day and K.L. Interlude.

We awoke early; it was just after 6 a.m. and to my surprise David was already preparing our breakfast, as he brought me an early morning cup of coffee. Like David, I too am very much an early bird, and can say we both equally enjoyed early mornings, which I felt was a bonus in helping us to relate pleasantly with each other. While I was drinking my early morning cuppa, I checked the abundance of mail I intended to dispatch to various parts of the world, including one to a certain couple Mr and Mrs Dobbs in Kuala Lumpur who were friends of my Aunt Joan in Hampshire back in the U.K. It was now that David asked if I could help him in writing a letter to a relative who was a doctor, and also lived on the island of Penang, which we both intended to visit on our travels northwards.

David was very animated with excitement, now that we were both due to start our first day on our long journey of discovery. Although we had known each other for less than two weeks, it felt good to both of us that at long last we were underway. David's spoken tongue of the English language was excellent, but his written mastery had a fair way to go. However, language wise, he spoke four different languages (English, Malay and two Chinese dialects,) which put my tongue of foreign speech to shame, and made David a very talented young man indeed.

Before 8am and now fully packed up, both carrying heavy Bergen rucksacks, we said farewell to the 9th Dolphins Sea Scout's hut and many of David's mates had turned out on this beautiful sunny Saturday morning to see us off. We both cheerfully hiked our way through the busy suburbs of Singapore knowing only too well that we were unlikely to get a lift, until well after we had cleared the causeway, that linked Singapore to the mainland of Malaya. David, who was always up front in all his dealings, had carefully prepared a cardboard sign clearly marked Kuala Lumpur, which was the direction to where we were heading.

Although the Malay emergency was coming to an end, we both fully understood that we would need to rely on the kindness of civilians, because it was strictly forbidden for military personnel to give any civilian a lift, which both David and myself had recently become. We chatted away to each other freely, as we carried our loads on our backs, side by side. At this relative early hour the traffic heading north was still light, as we both paced ourselves, striding across this famous causeway, from one side towards the first of many border posts, manned by military armed guards. At this point, we both showed our British passports, and one particular soldier expressed a great interest in my full length ice axe, that I was using as a walking stick. He obviously viewed it as some kind of weapon, although the head of the ice axe was covered with a protective stout Rexene hood. At this time in Malay's history, it was strictly forbidden to carry any form of gun, and even large bush knives were treated with great suspicion, although most of the natives carried them, especially up country away from towns, well into the interior.

Having satisfied himself of my intended proper use of purpose, we were both waved through the barrier onto Malayan soil. We walked for several hundred yards on, then settled ourselves down, sitting on top of our rucksacks, facing the traffic northbound waiting for our first lift. Many cars as well as military vehicles ignored us, but after only twenty minutes or so a ramshackle heavily laden lorry pulled over, just ahead of us. Within moments, David was conversing with the driver in pure Malay, he gave us a lift to the outskirts of Johore Bahru several miles up the road. David talked away easily with the driver, who had his rather beautiful teenage daughter with him, before turning his attention onto this lovely girl who was even more interested in what ever David had to say. While in her presence, David casually filled his recently purchased smoking pipe with pride, as if to make some kind of masculine gesture, which obviously impressed this damsel of untold beauty, with his adult manhood, and as a man of the world. The father on the other hand, was not impressed, telling David to extinguish his pipe, because of the nature of the cargo he was carrying behind us. The closeness of the four of us sitting cosily up front, with David and the girl almost sitting on top of each others laps, didn't worry David, but the father was obviously not too comfortable with these two young things, in such close proximity to each other.

As we alighted down from the high step of the lorry, it was plain to see that David was already in a high state of arousal, which remained with him for some considerable time. This aspect of David's physiology was new to me, but I seemed to be the only one that showed any sign of embarrassment. On the theory, that least said, soonest mended, I did my utmost to ignore David's prominent display of his manhood that poked up beneath his lightweight shorts.

Several lifts later and at least a hundred miles further north, we both felt the need for something to eat and rest. We realized that we would not make Kuala Lumpur on this first day, so set about finding a safe camping site to pitch our tent, far enough away from the main road. We set about making a comfortable camp, nearby to a fast running stream, and once established, decided to have a dip before cooking our first evening meal under canvas. There was still ample heat in the late afternoon, as we both stripped off to go skinny dipping in our new found stream. We discovered once submerged in deep water, there was an abundance of fish that looked almost like brown trout. Standing upstream of David, who was openly urinating a few yards from me, I tried my hand at tickling these trout like fish. Within a matter of minutes, I was successful, throwing several fine specimens onto the grass bank, with David now happily dispatching them quickly, in readiness for our supper.

We both ate well that night, with these fish on a bed of wild rice and wild herbs picked by David closely to hand. This was followed by some fresh fruit that we had with us, and washed down by Saki beer that I was introduced to, by David for the first time. Having sated our appetites and thirst, we studied the map to measure our progress for our first day. We knew we were about two hundred miles or so short of Kuala Lumpur. Now feeling full, with contented burps expelled by both of us, we settled down atop our sleeping bags, talking the evening away with excited ease. We both realized this had been a fairly easy day, but as our very first, we were feeling somewhat tired and starting the first page of my log-diary, I quickly fell asleep below our trusted mosquito net.

Next morning we started early, again in anticipation, wondering what this new second day would bring. By 9am we were back on the road, getting a lift almost immediately in a privately owned pick-up truck which was going all the way to Kuala Lumpur. The driver was a Malay of about thirty years of age who also spoke very good English, he invited both of us to take breakfast with him, as we pulled off the road into a typical Malay roadside eating house. I continued to be amazed, at the kindness and hospitality that these people showed us, but David more akin to these people's ways, took it all in his stride, almost for granted you might say. While in conversation with our host, David asked him about the caves that David had once visited, which our host knew about, and said he would be passing close by. He wondered if we would like to camp near to them, but David for some reason suddenly changed his mind, and asked if we could be dropped in Buhta Pahat, as David suddenly realized he urgently needed to see someone who lived there. I could see the driver for some reason was disappointed, but said nothing, until after the driver had dropped us off. "What's wrong?" I asked David.

"Did you notice the gun strapped below his baggy trousers, just above his ankle?" he replied.

"No, I can't say I did, but then, I was sitting further away from him than you."

David managed to find us a small room at the M.C.A. (Malay Chinese Association) and one of the tenants insisted we use his bed for the night. (A real bed.) As we lay along side each other stripped to the skin, the night proved very long and sticky, with heavy rain noisily rattling upon the tin roof above our heads. (The start of the monsoons.) I don't think either of us slept very well, in spite of all the comfort offered to us.

The following day started well, with the warm sun this early hour, drying the ground before our very eyes. We found the first fifteen miles very hard, as we were wearing hard walking shoes on a rocky surface. By midday with the sun's searing heat, we were beginning to wilt very quickly indeed, as the parched knot in our throats tightened, screaming out for liquid refreshment. On reaching a tiny village shop we rested, the owner came out to greet us and had been reading all about us in the local Chinese newspaper. He gave us iced glasses of coffee to quench our thirst, refusing to take any payment. We continued, feeling a lot better, but not expecting to get much further than a small hamlet called Mour, which was a good twenty miles away. Girding our loins for a long hike, suddenly a Mr Lee pulled up alongside of us, and spoke in Chinese to David. Our luck changed instantly, as Mr Lee was very persistent, showering us with hospitality and giving us a lift in his car to Malacca, where he treated us to yet more refreshments. Feeling very thankful, he then took us on to Port Dickson that had plentiful water, so we all took a cool shower, after which we headed for Sarrombau, where Mr Lee very generously treated us to a great meal.

With our stomachs full to bursting, Mr Lee dropped us off in the outskirts of Kuala Lumpur, to show us one of his many properties. Mr Lee was most insistent that we sleep at his father's house, where because of the lateness of the hour we thankfully accepted, but on the strict understanding it would be for one night only. The windows of our room had good mosquito protection, and the ceiling fan to maintain a very comfortable room coolness, was an added bonus. We spread our two naked bodies upon the ample size bed together, luxuriating in unadulterated pleasure, and receiving the best night's sleep since leaving Singapore. I awoke later than normal to find David snuggled tight into my back, as if sleeping with a deep easiness into the land of dreams, somewhere, submerged in his own euphoria. I gently eased my body from his embrace, as I needed the loo with some urgency.

On returning to get back into bed, in spite of the later than normal hour for rising, I could not fail to notice his very prominent erection, while David blissfully slept on, unaware of my observation, and leaving him to get on with it, I got dressed quickly, and went for a wash and shave. When I returned, David was still asleep, but in his dream like state, had ejaculated his sexual juices all over the bed covers, so I promptly woke him up. His penis by now was semi deflated, as I pointed out to him his messy predicament. With his head hung low, and without murmuring a single word, he stripped the bed cover off the bed and spent considerable time washing it, before getting dressed, then hanging it out to dry in the very warm sunshine. He made no apology, nor did I feel he had the need to, feeling it could have easily been myself, instead of David.

By ten a.m. we left in search of a decent campsite, knowing that we would be staying in Kuala Lumpur for some time. This we found in a small field owned by the Y.M.C.A. and where we could also get use of their indoor ablution facilities. Once established we returned to Mr Lee, to thank him most profusely for his kind hospitality, and by which time the laundered bed mat was bone dry, so David remade the bed. We said our goodbyes to Mr Lee, who told us we were more than welcome to stay on, or return anytime as we were both most welcome. We set off for Kuala Lumpur central, to explore this metropolis and to taste some of its many delights.

The city was packed with thousands of people going about their business, and for some reason this worried David, who did not really like crowds of such large size at the best of times. After many hours, we could take no more of the hustle and bustle, so we headed back to camp, to find hundreds of children gathered outside our lonely pitched tent. This annoyed David so much; he suggested we find an alternative campsite the following day. Thankfully as the afternoon dragged its feet into early evening, the novelty of our freakishness wore off and well before dusk, the brats (David's words) disappeared completely. Well after we had eaten, David suggested we go for a cold shower to cool off, as our sticky bodies perspired non stop in the oppressive heat of the late evening. We both went into the communal showers, which although already occupied had plenty of room for two more. The small party of five lads already under the showers were in exuberant mood, as they openly soaped each other's bodies down with much laughter. I felt a little intimidated at first, but David joined in the frolics with these strangers, as if it was the most natural form of cultural behaviour. Three complete strangers came across to help me get over my own embarrassing inhibitions, which they had spotted as soon as I got under the showers, as they obviously knew I was neither Malay, nor Chinese. With David joining in with this trio they proceeded to soap the whole of my body, as I stood feeling powerlessly outnumbered, they casually went over every inch of my body including all my private bits. David light heartedly chided me to relax, as my face became redder by the second, he told me I was undergoing a perfectly normal custom, which all people sharing showers, and bathing provided. After a while, I slowly began to relax, especially as the numbers sharing the showers, one by one left, until David and I were once again totally alone. The sensuality of so much touching to my body and my sexual areas were now having an after effect, in my unstoppable arousal, so turning my back towards David so he would hopefully not notice, I continued to rinse myself off, before quickly putting my towel about my waist, to hide my embarrassment. David got out behind me and started to towel me off, which I was thankful for, as it meant I did not need to lower my own towel about my waist until ready. Having got control of my unwanted erection, I was happy enough to help towel off David in turn, before calmly getting dressed, as my embarrassment quickly abated. David knew well enough of my predicament, but had the gracious manners not to mention a word. By now David was obviously well tuned into my karma, and treated my feelings with unbelievable tenderness, and understanding. We retired to our tented shelter and carefully climbed below our joint mosquito net, to lay still clothed upon the top of our sleeping bags feeling considerably cooler.

After a while, David got undressed and casually knelt over my prone body, then without a word took off my shorts. "What are you doing?" I asked with some alarm in my voice.

"I'm going to give you a massage" said David, "unless you don't want one," he added enquiringly, and blowing out the candle night light.

Beginning to relax a little he slipped my t-shirt from over my head then requested I turn over, face down. Now in complete darkness, he worked the magic of his massaging hands for a while. I started to drift off in a state of complete relaxation, when he lightly slapped my posterior ordering me to turn over. He started at the soles of my feet, which I usually find extremely sensitive, but knowing his anatomy well, David carefully and with great sensitivity, caressed the sole with great dexterity to certain different pad points of my foot, as if searching for one particular area. With tenderness and skill he found what he was obviously looking for and proceeded to caress this part of my instep with unbelievable sensuality. Within moments I felt deep feelings within the remotest part of my loins stirring. As my arousals awoke with a vengeance, I was very thankful to be in complete darkness. Having finished one foot, David transferred his attentions to the other, and was soon having the same effect. After a little while he spread eagled my legs wide apart, kneeling between them and with both palms he worked up the length of my inner thighs. I didn't need to check myself out, as I became more than aware of my very full erection. David stopped, ordering me to now close my legs as he straddled my body to massage my upper torso. I could feel my very hard fully erected penis now firmly below his scrotum, as he continued to work my upper body.

"OK David" I demanded "that's more than enough," whereby he stopped abruptly and without saying a single word climbed off my body, to casually lay on top of his own sleeping bag, beside me. "I'm sorry David," I said quietly, "I didn't seem to have any control what so ever, over my physical emotions."

"That's perfectly alright" replied David "It happens occasionally, it's nothing to be ashamed or disturbed by," he added in a light tone of voice. It was already too late for me, I felt the gush, so unstoppable, as I ejaculated all over my upper body, completely out of control. I remained tight lipped and silent, somewhat surprised at finding myself sexually gratified, without the aid of a single direct hand touch. David leaned across knowingly, gently running the palm of his outreached hand over my now wet body. He then took a small hand towel and gently wiped me down. "Now go to sleep Paul," said David softly, and within moments, I did just that, suddenly feeling very tired, very tired indeed.

In the early hours, with just a token touch of daylight penetrating the lightweight cloth of the tent, I was very suddenly, very much awake. I looked nearby over at David, who was flat on his back with his hands folded across his chest. I couldn't be sure, but he may well have been awake also, disturbed perhaps by some outside noise or animal. As my eyes wandered down his body, he was clearly fully aroused, with his penis throbbing in an upwards direction pointing towards his upper torso. His hands remained firmly folded across his chest, as his over sized appendage danced to its own stirrings, as if attached to some invisible thread, being operated by some unseen puppeteer master. Fascinated, I watched secretly with half closed eyes, as the morning light grew ever stronger. After what seemed like an eternity, his projectile suddenly convulsed quickly, followed by spurt after spurt of ejaculation of his cum, which uncontrolled and with no guidance of hands, splattered his upper body in all directions. Once he was satisfied, there was no further spunk to ejaculate, only then did David wipe himself off with great care. He turned over away from me and went back to sleep. The power of his mind over the control of his bodily functions was mind boggling, awesome. If I hadn't seen this display of mind over matter with my own eyes, I for one would never have believed such an act was possible. I was to learn much later, during my travels, that the Chinese people developed a highly tuned sense of mind over matter, to such an art form of unbelievable proportions, in many different areas of human activity.

When we did get up later, and while over breakfast, I started to look at David in a more astute manner, realizing he was certainly gifted with unknown talents, that belied his youthful charms, and perhaps he even used his boyhood looks, to disarm those that he chose to do so, with devastating affect. We packed up all our gear and dismantled the tent, because David did not wish to be pestered by hoards of kids again, as we made our way into Kuala Lumpur proper. Before we left, I looked up the address of Mr and Mrs Dobbs at 1 Lower Ampang Road, Kuala Lumpur, to keep ready to hand. But first, as the heat of mid morning began to take its toll, we were in search of something else, besides a long glass of ice-cold coffee. David obviously had a specific place in mind, which he explained he used to frequent often, long before his navy days took him further afield. As we approached the establishment that David took me to, his face broke open into one of sheer delight. He spoke very quickly, like a machine gun fire, to two of his beloved brothers. One older, and one just a little younger, who also had his baby sister in tow. This was a family owned large café shop that traded in all sorts of things. David's oldest brother who was in his very late twenties, looked after the herbal medicine side of the business, and was an expert acupuncture specialist whose skills were in much local demand. The younger brother and baby sister who was just sixteen ran the café and shop between them. Their work of seven days a week started very early at six thirty a.m. every morning, and the café part of the business was often open most days until after eleven p.m. in the evening. A very hard working part of David's family that was considered to be very wealthy by local native standards. The kissing and affectionate hugging that then took place lasted for many long minutes, and once David introduced me to them, I too was warmly welcomed like any member of the Kwan dynasty. David asked me for his forgiveness, while he spoke extensively to his kin in pure Cantonese dialect. The constant tactile touching of each other made it clear to see the genuine love they had for each other, while David's young sister held his hand and hung on every word David uttered, all the time smiling with absolute pleasure at seeing each other after such a prolonged period of time. (Two years.) After a good ten minutes and while customers were totally ignored, but didn't seem to mind waiting, while this very animated family, openly showed their genuine love for each other. As the brothers went back to their trading stations, the sister took my hand, and gently guided myself and David to the family table, that no other customers were allowed to sit at. On much closer examination it became clearer (even to English eyes to whom all Chinese look the same) that the likeness and mannerisms between this family became more obvious to me with study.

The young sister was most attentive, after bringing us long chilled glasses of ice coffee topped with buffalo clotted cream and a single cherry, she sat down between us, giving us both long lingering looks. In her broken but more than adequate English, she turned her come to bed eyes on me, then singing in a sweet voice while she openly studied every feature on my face asked "How do you like Malaya?"

I looked at David for help, as I got the distinct feeling she already had me stripped naked with her eyes alone, when David gave me a knowing wink, but said nothing. I blushed a deep red, hoping David would throw me a lifeline, which they both found highly entertaining. I looked at David with some annoyance, desperate for help, as his sister momentarily left the table. "What do you think you are playing at?" I asked David with a sting in my suppressed voice of anger.

"Don't worry," said David "I'll explain it all to you later," still grinning like the proverbial Cheshire cat.

An hour later we made good our escape, but not before the customary goodbyes with the usual display of affection all round. Just as we were about to go through the portals, Suzy called over for me to wait a moment. She clasped her two delicate petite hands firmly behind my neck and gently pulled my face towards her moist soft lips, then planted a lingering full frontal kiss on my mouth, I felt my face deepening in colour, utterly gob smacked. I also felt a slight trembling at the knees, as I quickly turned to join the safety of David's side. We ambled away, with me in total silence not knowing what to say. David put his arm about my shoulder then looked at me saying, "You're a big hit with my sister, she thinks you're the most handsome man she's ever met." David was still smiling.

I looked at him in astonishment, unbelieving what David had just imparted to me, thinking he was maybe taking the piss. When I did finally find my voice I innocently asked him "Is she like this with all the men that she meets?"

You could have wiped the smile off David's face with a damp cloth as the clouds of thunder rolled across his worried brow. "If she ever did, I would kill her with my bare hands" said David with deep feeling.

I believed him, as I knew he was a martial arts expert and was more than capable of doing so.

"No" said David with much emphasis in his voice "Suzy only behaves like that to the very closest of my friends, and she thinks we are blood brothers, that's why she is so affectionate. Anyway, you'll find out for yourself later, as we have been invited to stay with them until we are ready to move on." As an after thought he added "I hope that's OK with you."

He looked at me with one of his side long glances to gauge my reaction. I remained silent, with my own thoughts for a while, when David interrupted my thinking with a most profound statement "Don't worry Paul, she will be very gentle with you in bed."

I looked at him with a deep expression of worry and disbelief all over my face, wondering how far he was prepared to take this tease, which I felt was already at the extreme edge of my comprehension. A favourite saying of Henry came back to haunt me 'You're pulling my dick' and in this instance it felt as if David was doing just that. Not being able to get any more intimate or personal than that, I returned my gaze at David with a desperate need to know. "Are we really staying with your brothers tonight, or are you just having me on?" I asked.

"Don't worry, Suzy is giving up her bedroom for us, she will bunk down with my younger brother" answered David casually.

Now I knew he was having me on, but said instead "That's OK then," thinking to myself that two can play at this game. "Why can't Suzy sleep with us?" I jested.

David obviously turned this observation over in his mind before answering, and then replied "I suppose I could bunk in with my younger brother if you want." said David earnestly.

"We'll see," I added. Thinking we were still playing the game.

"OK" said David simply, "Let's leave it till later, you may prefer to sleep with me instead," and meant it.

Feeling rather tired of the game I changed the subject, if only to get away from the game of so many innuendos. "Where are we going now?" I asked, with as much joy in my voice as I could muster.

"Well," said David, "I thought you might enjoy seeing some fine Malay art, knowing your love of all things artistic."

I agreed wholeheartedly for once, as we ambled side by side, while I realized that he still had his arm around my shoulders. The art was breathtakingly beautiful, unlike anything I had seen before or expected. The sheer sexual expression both on canvas, as well as some very old sculptures were very revealing, and by western standards would be seen by many as verging on pornographic, but were obviously admired by so many and taken as perfectly natural in their naked exposure. David explained at length that the Kama Sutra of the Indian art of love worship was almost primitive compared with the worship of love by the Chinese. We spent many hours, enthralled and in raptures of the many outstanding pieces, and I came away with a new found understanding for a different meaning of the words erotic art we so easily mistakenly called love. I also learnt that the western interpretation of what we blindly call passion, in truth, and in this far eastern setting of cultural differences, where the chasm between us, of the real meaning of passion was very wide indeed.

Now having been converted, as well as re-educated, we returned to David's family and a typical Chinese dinner. Not, I hasten to add anything like the Chinese meals that we gullibly accept as the real McCoy back in the U.K. Although I myself am not the greatest lover of most Chinese dishes, I did enjoy the food which was a dramatic change from our normal dietary cuisine. Long after the meal and much later in the evening, I was to experience a whole family bathing rite, in what can best be described as the family hot tub, not unlike a Jacuzzi but without the bubbles. Completely naked as God certainly intended, I joined in this serious ritual of bathing togetherness, with David's brothers talking easily in their cultivated English, with a likable twang that was more pleasant on the ears. Two Geisha girls of tender age complete in Kimonos, attended to the more intimate parts of our anatomy with practised expertise, with loving care and as if they had been born to this wonderful activity or artistry. A memorable hour or more was spent being cosseted by these delicious maidens, in an otherwise all male domain. After being lovingly and most gently dried off by the same girls, they put us into Chinese style dressing gowns. We all partook into the heady drinking of Saki.

After a fantastic evening of unadulterated pleasures, David ushered me off to bed in preparation of the finale, that unbeknown to me was waiting in the wings. I was still admiring the gowns we were wearing as David lying beside me, gave me some brotherly pearls of wisdom. "I'm going in to spend time with my kid brother for a few hours" stated David, "while my sister comes in to pleasure you and milk you dry," he rolled off his tongue.

"What do you mean exactly?" I started, when David covered my mouth with a very firm hand to shut my gob running away with itself.

"Just listen," he said, "you can do anything you like with my sisters consent, but whatever you do, do not penetrate her virginity." He did not need to hold my mouth shut any longer, as I was totally gob smacked anyway.

He removed his hand slowly as I said to David very gently "I wouldn't dream of doing such a thing, and I'm upset at you harbouring such thoughts, or even letting them enter your head."

"I'm deeply sorry for such thoughts" he replied, as he boldly leaned over and kissed me full on the mouth, which also took my breath away in astonishment.

He casually climbed down from the bed and silently left the room. My mind was still in turmoil when Suzy knocked softly on the door. "Who is it?" I called out, but she continued to knock softly, before I again asked her to come in.

As she came over to the bed, gliding across the floor of her own bedroom, she asked softly if it was OK to turn out the light. She must have been reading my thoughts as I nervously nodded my agreement. The light was switched off as she lay down on the bed beside me, speaking softly to me in her limited English. Her kisses on my face were like the touch of butterfly wings, brushing my face on a soft breeze. Slowly she undid my gown with ease, laying the flaps aside fully opened to my sighing body below. Starting at my neck she explored my upper torso with her fingertips, making my chest tremble with excitement. The fingertips, like gentle feathers, continued to explore my chest, as my tense body began to relax under her soothing caresses that seemed in no hurry at this stage to go lower. Suzy got off the bed, letting her gown easily slip to the floor below her bare feet, rejoined me on the bed, gently opening my legs far enough to lay between them, as I felt the excitement run through her body like an electric current of a very low voltage. My penis quickly sprang into life, as it came to rest between her love lips that were silky free of all pubic hair, which adorned her orifice.

"We mustn't dare put it in," I urgently whispered softly into her ear. I gently rolled her over, from off my body, as I felt the first seepage of sperm ooze from the end of my now very hard penis.

Suzy climbed astride my body, facing towards my outstretched legs and feet, as I too explored her with my fingers into the magical kingdom, between her silk smooth legs. With one hand only she teased my inner thighs and with fantastic gentleness took hold of both my testicles with her other hand and at the same time leaned down to encompass the first few inches of my now very wet hard penis head. Her mouth surrounding the corona felt moistly warm and comforting, as she held it totally still, as if suspended in time and space. I explored the curvature between her velvet inner thighs, but gently teasing her love lips for even better temptations to come. The love juices from deep within her began to flow slowly, so I pulled her down gently onto my face as the tip of my tongue went in to explore her forbidden moist cavity. Slowly, she retaliated by going down deeper, towards the pubic curls of my thick throbbing root. I could feel the spongy corona of my knob enter her soft fleshy throat deep within her mouth. The yearning and thoughts of thrusting my shaft between the well lubricated and inviting lips of her vagina were now very strong indeed. I squeezed my two longest fingers deep inside her, as a detour to my lustful thoughts between my groins. The juices from between her own lips began to flow even more freely, as I sensed Suzy was very close to a climax. She eased her mouth towards my tip in long slow motion strokes, before thrusting even deeper, then returning and withdrawing in slower and slower soft sucking motions. She pushed my hand into her, deeper than I would have dared go myself, as I felt my hand go up to my wrist deep inside of her, where she held it firmly in place. Meanwhile, I felt my ejaculate charge up towards the eye in my corona's head in an urgent need to escape. Suzy felt the volcanic sperm about to erupt from its chamber, as my pulsating balls warned of the inevitable. Deep within her mouth she held my root, motionless, waiting, anticipating the inevitable. My thighs stiffened, as the full ejected ejaculation gushed out at high speed, spurt after spurt after spurt, until fully extinguished, with nothing more to give. As she very gently eased my hand from within her vagina, her love juices were now flowing down my forearm like a slow moving encapsulating warm fluid. She withdrew me from her mouth with slow reluctance, taking hold of my still throbbing shaft she gently laid it down to one side to rest. She came back down beside me, putting her head onto my stomach, within touching distance of my hard erection, which was still a long way from becoming flaccid. We lay there locked together, equally sharing the sexual elation, jointly as one identity.

Sometime later, there was a knock at our door, and Suzy hurriedly put on her gown, before leaning over to give me a long lingering kiss, which I returned still floating high, somewhere between the bed and the ceiling. Without turning on the light I felt David regain his position on the bed beside me. He reached over, gently taking hold of my semi erection softly saying "I hope you enjoyed yourself and that Suzy was able to satisfy your sexual pleasures."

Gently, I took away David's hand from around my dick, quickly covering myself up with the gown I was still wearing. I leaned over and kissed David, thanking him profoundly for allowing Suzy to give me so much pleasure, and without further ado quickly fell deeply asleep, a very contented and satisfied young man. My dreams that night were very mixed, flitting from wondering awe, to a feeling of sinful distaste of myself. The sheer greed of youthful appetites of satisfaction would be short lived and where selfish sexual urges were concerned were but a passing moment for quenching animalistic lust of sexual desires.

Oh, to be so young again ....
The taste of 'Eastern Promise' had never before been so wonderful, and I don't mean Turkish delight either!

Chapter Twenty

The Dobbs and Batu Caves

We both felt somewhat sidetracked from our trek, at such an early time after our start. In truth, we both felt over pampered by David's relatives, feeding us with the good life as well as forbidden fruit, the need to break free from such over indulgence, was already pulling at our heart strings, to seek new adventurous exploits afresh, was already beginning to look attractive. We decided that one, or at most two days longer, would be sufficient before we should move on. Towards this change of scene, I suggested to David he might wish to join me in visiting a Mr and Mrs Dobbs, in the snobbish residential part of the more decadent suburbs in Kuala Lumpur.

The Dobbs' were long established friends of my aunt, so I knew I would need to be on my best behaviour, because in due course, a comprehensive report would sooner or later be sent to my Aunt Joan, who required constant reassurance of my well being, during this journey. To warn of our visit, I rang the Dobbs household from our present base with David's relatives, to check if it would be convenient. The meeting was arranged and the Dobbs' sent a car to pick both of us up. David was impressed with this show of opulence, but I harboured more evil thoughts, thinking the Dobbs' did not wish the neighbours to see us beating a path to their front door, who were more likely to call out the police at such a sight as the two of us scruffs. The limo pulled up with a spit of gravel to the front door, as the Malay driver quickly got out and opened the rear door to disgorge his unwanted load. David noticed the surly expression worn permanently on the Malay driver's face, and said something to him in his native tongue. The driver looked as if his face had just been smacked by David's remark, but David ignored him completely, as we both went up the three steps to the front door, that was already wide open. Mr Dobbs himself, bounded across the hallway with his hand outstretched in readiness to warmly greet us both. A tall man, well over six feet in height, with a light sandy head of well groomed hair and a military style moustache to match. Mr Dobbs was well into his mid to late forties and I guessed was probably ex military, but was serving at present as a high ranking government civil servant. Mrs Dobbs was short and dumpy in appearance, but with an outgoing personality that had no difficulty in conversing with either of us. We were taken to the south facing back of the house, where coffee was presented on a vast veranda in front of an inviting swimming pool. We lounged comfortably in wicker easy chairs, around a small table rabbiting on with idle chit chat, as I glanced over towards David who was blatantly wooing his wife with his slick charm offensive. He looked very much at home in this contrived setting, not batting a single Chinese eyelid, as his polite conversation with the lady of the house received all of his devoted attention. Mrs Dobbs asked us both, but was looking at David all the time, if we would like a swim before dinner. Before I could open my mouth, David accepted her most gracious offer and Mrs Dobbs promptly rang a small hand bell to summon one of the many servants. A well groomed teenage Malay lad appeared within seconds, obedient to his mistress' beckoning. David admired Mrs Dobbs' command of the Malay language, as she instructed the boy to fetch an assortment of bathing costumes for our joint perusal. David selected one yellow silken garment, that when adorned was most revealing, leaving nothing to the imagination, whereas I chose one, I considered to be more conservative in fitting. We were directed towards the fair sized open pool, complete with a well equipped professional sprung diving board, much to David's delight. After a quick discreet change into our respective costumes, we both dived in, to enjoy the coolness of the water. I knew David was a good swimmer, but now seeing him at first hand, he also proved to be an expert gymnast and very artistic diver, taking full advantage to show off his highly developed skill. We swam and frolicked for over an hour, enjoying the much needed exercise to our bodies that walking alone did not provide. Mrs Dobbs enjoyed sitting next to the pool, admiring David's athletic abilities. It was almost too obvious; she was unable to avoid studying David's revealing bulge in his tightly fitting trunks, almost spellbound by the lure of his potent sexuality. She politely called us both over, to tell us we would soon need to get out and prepare for dinner. Unbeknown to us, our shorts and singlet t-shirts had been removed from the changing room and replaced with an identical pair of bathrobes, which we both put on without question. In conversation, David felt Mrs Dobbs was gagging for it, but I told him to be very careful, as she might only be prick teasing David from frustration. I told him to behave himself, as any hanky panky was sure to get back to my Aunt Joan. With this sobering thought David quickly regained his composure, declaring himself hungry enough to eat a scabby buffalo. Over dinner, still dressed in the robes kindly provided, we learnt that our own clothing had been taken away to be laundered.

The four course meal started with a soup course, followed by fish and then beef with all the trimmings and ended with a wonderful trifle. The red and white wines served with the two main courses were top drawer, and once we had finished we returned to the living room, with brandy and hand rolled Burma cheroots. Unlike the drawing rooms of England, Mrs Dobbs who dominated her husband, sat next to David to continue her lusting over him, while I held polite chit-chat with Mr Dobbs. The Malay servant returned to whisper in David's ear, that our outdoor clothing was now dry and ready to get dressed into. David suddenly stood bolt upright, informing me that we could now get dressed, so I joined him as I asked to be excused. As we were getting changed, David showed me the inside of his dressing gown, that was messy to say the least. "What caused that?" I enquired innocently.

David looked at me as if I was really quite thick, "What do you think?" he spat out. "The bitch wanked me off under the table at dinner" he said with hurt in his voice.

I was speechless at this sudden unbelievable revelation, and David could see I was very stunned at his meaning. "She's a fucking man eating bitch," he repeated with more than enough venom in his voice for the two of us.

"Calm down David" I said, because I have never seen David in such an agitated state or swear so vehemently, with so much bitterness in his tone.

After we got fully dressed, we quickly made up some lame excuse, and got out of there like a pair of scalded cats. On the return journey home in the back of the car, David looked glaringly at the driver who was eyeballing David in his rear view mirror, as David spat several words at him in Malayanese before slamming over the glass partition between the driver and ourselves. "The bitch milked me dry," said David with more calm in his now controlled voice. "Is it OK if we leave tomorrow?" he asked tuning to face me full on.

"OK by me" I replied. "Let's go and visit Batu caves before going on to Penang" I suggested.

As we drew up outside David's relatives for our last night of comfort, he made me promise not to mention a word of what happened at the Dobbs' house to any of his family. David was no longer in the mood to be sociable, he bluntly informed his brothers that we were moving on in the morning. There was no discussion between them, no arguments, as they accepted David's word on the matter and may have even expected it. We quickly retired, but not before David had a long shower, then joining me on the bed. His kid brother came in for a while and snuggled up to his older brother who was unashamedly naked, hugging him with deep affection. He lay between us for a little while, before kissing me goodnight, then doing the same to his brother before leaving. David turned out the light, then leaning into my body he whispered into my ear, that he was feeling ashamed at being abused by an elderly strange white woman, to whom he was being politely courteous with.

"Perhaps you shouldn't have flaunted your sexuality so openly in front of her, as she obviously misread the signals," I said softly.

"You westerners are so full of shit sometimes" David replied. "After all, I never once touched her or encouraged her" he said with innocence.

"Anyway, it's over now, so you best try to forget it" I told him.

We slept well that night, rising early to pack everything away in readiness for the road. David's oldest brother had arranged for a motorised rickshaw to transport us both, with all our gear to Batu caves, but not before a hearty breakfast and the usual prolonged goodbyes. Suzy made an extra fuss of me, holding my hand until it was time to leave, knowing her love would have to serve my memory for a very long time to come. We waved our goodbyes, as a single tear became more visible in David's eye.

"I hate goodbyes," said David.

I muttered "So do I."

The sun was already beginning to warm up, but the sky looked clear and unblemished, with blue skies and the promise of a fine day ahead. As we approached a lush green meadow sitting serenely below a sheer craggy rock face, David pointed up high, to indicate the mouth of a very ordinary looking cave. We thanked our rickshaw driver, who helped us out in assembling all our gear. I studied the rock face immediately below the cave opening, when David explained to me that although the path to the first cave was easy enough and to which he had been briefly once before, it might be a good idea to break open my climbing rope for later. Having sorted our gear, David led towards the base of the extensive rock faces. The path was well worn and even the rocky path up to the cave was little more than a scramble. Within the hour, we were standing at the entrance of one of several caves, sixty foot high from the meadow below. We put down our equipment to rest, while I uncoiled the rope, as David explained that this particular second cave was well enough known, but a lesser smaller visited cave, involved a lengthy traverse across this splintered rock face, much higher to our left. David had not been to this secondary cave, but a friend of his who had said it was well worth a visit to explore. The traverse was well under a rope length away and slightly above the level where we were now standing. With several belay slings and karabinas snapped onto my climbing waistband adorned with different pitons, I set off to investigate. With David below me, fastened securely by rope to the rock face, I quickly got into my stride, moving with ease across the face some hundred feet above the meadow below me. The standard of climbing was no more than medium to difficult, with the rock face needing very little gardening on reasonably sound rock strata. Within twenty minutes I reached the entrance and made myself fast, before telling David to come on up and join me. Although he took a little longer David made the climb look easy enough, especially with the knowledge of a top rope, for added comfort and safety. We rested, smiling away at each other, as David delved into my lightweight climbing day sac for our pipes and my camera. We sat puffing away beside each other, admiring the view of the valley floor spread below our feet, which dangled over the edge of the rock face. David was a picture of contentment, looking at ease on what after all, was our very first climb together. After a while, we took our torches from our sac and entered the cave, which turned out to be much bigger than we first expected. I took a number of photographs with a flash gun attached to my camera, before we slowly made our way back to the entrance. At one point we actually got lost, but retraced our steps and later found our way out. By this time we were feeling peckish, so we rested to eat our packed lunch. The coolness of the caves was so inviting, away from the blistering sun beating relentlessly on the exposed rock face outside. The time was much later than either of us realized, and David suggested we make our way back to the main Batu caves, where all our gear was. The sun had moved around fully, onto our rock faces and was hot to touch. I strung out a length of the double rope below us, which would take us about half way to a comfortable rock ledge, ideal for our first abseil. David was a little nervous, only having abseiled once before, but I talked him through it calmly, putting a thinner top rope on him, that I would control from above. Once on the ledge, I quickly abseiled down to join him. The second and final abseil to the ground was even easier. We then slowly wound our way back up, along the path on our return to the main Batu caves, from where we started.

By late afternoon, we were more than ready for a much longer rest, and David suggested we make camp for the night by bedding down below the stars, at the mouth of the cave, instead of pitching the tent in the green meadow below. We unrolled the sleeping bags and while I was enjoying a second pipe of tobacco, David busied himself with the primus stove to prepare an evening meal. We slept well considering, and a cool light breeze kept our body temperature down, which enabled us both to sleep without disturbance, except for the hoards of bats that clouded the entrance on their way to their feeding frenzy. Just before dawn and first light, David made a brew up of tea; he was in one of his philosophical moods. "You know Paul" he started off, "In our Chinese culture we take great offence at being insulted by a foreign stranger, old enough to be my mother, sexually abusing her position of hospitality. She probably takes advantage of her fourteen year old Malay servant and to think she could do the same to me as a Chinese, couldn't be a bigger insult. If my brothers ever found out, they would have her snuffed out."

David spat out these words with real venom of intent.

"David, I promise you solemnly, I will not mention this to any living soul, I swear to you, it will be our secret, believe me," I added with complete sincerity.

"You must keep your word Paul, you really must," he added, as he started to weep.

"Come here brother" I beckoned, and then hugged him for long enough, well after he stopped crying. He separated from my caress, and then kissed me lovingly, with such tenderness, he took me by complete surprise.

"Now, never let us talk about this matter ever again," and we never did.

In silence each with his own inner thoughts, we started to gather our gear together, drinking the last drop of cooled tea from the billy can. We slowly made our way back to the meadow in the half light of the dawn, that was yet to break open fully. The Batu cave adventure proved to be just what we both needed to sharpen up our appetites before heading on the open road again.

Within the hour, we came to an open early morning café that catered for lorry travellers. "Come on David, I'll treat you to a really good breakfast, which will put hair on your baby smooth chest," David laughed out loud, slapping my back affectionately, as we made our way across the impacted dirt parking space.

We sat down at the empty table, as we cast our eyes over the equally empty canteen. After several moments, an elderly Chinese gentleman came over to our table. David stood up and bowed with deep respect before engaging in meaningful conversation in fluent Cantonese. The old man lovingly stroked the side of David's face, although they had never met each other before. David politely asked my forgiveness, and explained the honourable Chinese gentleman had no English.

"I understand" I replied to David, "but what do they have to eat?" I asked in earnest as my stomach rumbled.

Several moments later, David was studying a very comprehensive menu written in both Chinese and Malay. "Would you like fried eggs on toast?" asked David, as the first of several noisy Lorries pulled into the park outside.

"Eggs will do fine David, thank you" I said, as David left the table to inform the old man, busy behind his counter.

I lit up my first pipe in contentment, as I eased my body into the back of a comfortable cane chair. The clouds outside gathered ominously. Within the hour, the monsoon downpour accompanied by several threatening claps of thunder, deposited its deluge of water, as the heavens broke apart in hatred.

"Let's stay put for a while," suggested David, as we both looked out to see only a sheet of rushing water cascading over the edge of the corrugated iron roof, like a mini waterfall.

As suddenly as the deluge of water had started, it stopped with the same abruptness, leaving an eerie silence behind it. David wandered over to a small group of drivers huddled together, like some kind of a conspiracy. Waiting for the right moment, he then engaged the men nearest to our table in conversation. A few moments later, the driver turned to look at me, smiling in some kind of acknowledgment. David quickly returned, telling me we were about to get a lift as far as Ipoh, which was well on the way to Penang.

The road conditions were atrocious, with abandoned vehicles in ditches and flood waters deep and extensive. A good three inches of rain had fallen in less than one hour, leaving unbelievable difficulty in its wake, especially on the roads. David and I sat up front with our smiling driver, who obviously took such problems in his stride, as we churned our way slowly towards Ipoh, our hopeful destination for the day. By mid afternoon, the sun broke loose from the grasp of the rapidly rolling clouds overhead, to ease the pain of mobility, as the lorry steadily increased its speed, to almost thirty miles an hour. By late afternoon, we were deposited outside a faded painted building called the Y.M.C.A. We had arrived intact, but the journey had taken its toll in the small of David's back, just above his belt line. We ate in our room, with David in obvious discomfort. He slowly undressed then facing downwards in an attempt to ease his suffering; he lay motionless, trying to release the tension in his back. I straddled his body with great care, and massaged the small of his back with light tender strokes as best I could. With David's careful directions, I gently applied more pressure, working the palms of my hands either side the base of his spinal cord. "Sit on my bum" he ordered. "Work from my shoulder blades downwards."

After twenty minutes or more, David expressed satisfaction, enough to turn over with a sigh of relief. "That's just great, wonderful" he uttered, as I climbed down beside him and slowly fell asleep.

I awoke early to find David sleeping soundly with his back to me, but coiled up in the position of a baby nestling in the womb. I busied myself making tea and finding clean shorts and singlets for the two of us to get dressed into. By the time I was dressed the tea was ready, so I gently woke David from his slumber, with the offer of a steaming hot mug of sweet tea. The pain from David's face was long gone, as he broke into one of his infectious grins in thanks for the mug of tea. "How are you feeling this morning?" I asked.

"Just great" he replied. "Just great."

We both left the Y.M.C.A. in high spirits. One lucky lift took us up through the state of Perak, and as we neared the small town of Prai the Malaccan straights came into view, with the allure of the sea, beyond. The Chinese driver had taken a special shine to David and was taking us over to Penang with him, on a small fishing boat owned by one of his many relatives. The kindness shown to us, especially by the Chinese, was exceptional, and the fact that David was also Chinese obviously played a significant part in both our well being. I felt a very lucky man, and my friendship towards David was very plain to understand. I drank in extra measures of sea air, as the welcoming shores of Penang spread out before us. What a wonderful world we live in I thought, smiling to myself as David smiled in full agreement. We strode ashore, ready to take on the world, in a pleasurable way, you understand.

Chapter Twenty-One

The island of Penang - again, and brother Chong.

We quickly made our way to 'Waterfall' campsite on the beautiful island of Penang, although it was the first fortnight in June, the campsite was deserted. On site there was an old stone building with toilets and showers, and the nearby waterfalls offered ample supplies of water. This was also a beauty spot, frequently visited by many patrons during the day. David was anxious to visit his friend Mr Chong Yew Chuen, an old influence from his youth and a much respected expert in acupuncture, with a well established business near the centre of George Town, the capital of Penang. However, David explained to me he felt it important that we maintain our independence, because of previous experience.

This gentleman, who had become a blood brother after certain Chinese rites, performed with David's consent, when David was in his early teens, was considered a wise Chinese philosopher in the old ways of highly guarded secrets of Chinese traditions. The old world of these traditions going back many thousands of years, which David so far had never imparted to my alien ears. This taster wetted my appetite for more knowledge, but David was obviously reluctant to discuss the matter any further. We busied ourselves by washing all our dirty clothing, which was beginning to smell a little high by this time, then I carried on pitching our tent in a chosen secluded spot, not far from the waterfalls. The laundered items were stretched over the top of nearby boulders, to dry in the early evening sunshine; afterwards we quickly made our way into Georgetown for supplies and something to eat. Having secured a small stash of beer, we returned to our campsite ready for our first night on the island of Penang.

After several beers, David decided a fresh water shower below the nearby sounding waterfall was too enticing to resist, and asked me to join him before settling down ready for bedtime. Taking our soap-flannel, wearing only flip flops on our feet and with just a bath towel around our waists, we made our way in darkness to the falls. We both swam across the pool to the waterfalls proper, leaving our towels on the grassy bank. Standing under the full pressure of water descending from above, we stood there, absorbing the wonders of nature. After a while we got back into the turbulent pool below, the deepness of which came to chest height, before David got out, calling me over to join him. David was busy soaping up his flannel, which he handed to me, then instructed me politely to soap up his body, as he stood with a steady stance with legs akimbo. I hesitated at first, but remembering the bathing tub at his brother's house in Kuala Lumpur, I obliged this natural, traditional Chinese way. After I had covered him completely in soapy suds, he took the flannel from me, adding more soap to the face cloth, before doing the same for me in return. I did not feel as if David was invading my space and although I did have some feelings, or shall we say misgivings, after a while I began to relax, even enjoy this personal pampering. Satisfied that David let no part of my entire body escape his attention, we both jumped into the pool to rinse our bodies clean. We got out to dry ourselves off, feeling refreshed and revitalised before returning to camp. Making sure the mosquito net was properly sealed against an invasion by even one of these blighters, we both lay prone upon our sleeping bags, in readiness for sleep, and boy did we sleep soundly, as the sounds of the waterfall nearby swept over us like a well worn but tuneful lullaby.

After breakfast next morning, all spruced up in our clean clothes, we headed for the centre of George Town. Well before nine o'clock, we made our way to visit Mr Chong Yew Chuen at his rather plush practice, which was fronted with a large herbal dispensing chemist department, and a number of small annexe or consulting rooms beyond. Mr Chong himself was impeccably well dressed, looking every inch the specialist doctor that he was, he came to greet David with open welcoming arms.

"My beautiful brother" he chanted to David several times, before embracing David with a great show of affection and much kissing, while I respectfully stood back, feeling like a spare part of intrusion. They spoke fluently in Chinese to each other, at such speed, that even if I had spoken Chinese myself, I would not have been able to understand either of them.

After a while, David gently pushed me forward, reverting to English, he introduced me to his oldest brother, Mr Chong. Mr Chong quickly closed the gap between us, with the broadest grin all over his face, then clasping me firmly by my hand, proceeded to shake it vigorously, welcoming me as David's friend in beautiful English, as if he was straight out of Eton College. David asked me to take a seat in the waiting area, so he could quickly go through to speak privately with Mr Chong. Later, David returned smiling, suggesting we go next door, to enjoy refreshment in this establishment.

We sat for a good half hour, before Mr Chong came in to join us. Now speaking in English for my benefit, David was informed that Mr Chong was now ready for him, I was politely asked to join them at David's invitation. The three of us went through to the main consulting room, where I was shown to a comfortable seat to watch Mr Chong perform acupuncture on David. David knew I had never seen the art of acupuncture, in the fifties, it was still considered a secret art, rarely performed in front of Europeans. David quickly got undressed, and after a very comprehensive examination, was invited to lay naked and prone upon the couch. Armed with the long flexible needles of his craft, Mr Chong proceeded with expertise to push those needles into the most delicate parts of David's reproductive equipment. After about eight of these needles were put in, Mr Chong quickly hypnotised David into a trance like state. Lifting up David's penis, away from his testicles, he selected two very special needles, which seemed slightly thicker in diameter, and with great skill inserted each needle into one of each testicle to about half an inch deep. He then uplifted a sterile syringe containing a small quantity of clear looking liquid, then very gently taking hold of one of David's balls injected very slowly, with great care, until he could see it swell up to a considerable size. He repeated the same to the other testicle, leaving all the needles in place, (ten in all,) he woke David up from his trance, who then examined himself with obvious approval. The contents of this syringe were most secret, even David was not given the formula. Not the most pleasant sight to watch, and several times I winced inwardly, during the whole procedure. David, who was well enough endowed penis wise, was unfortunately blessed with below average size testicles. Now that he had left his teen years well behind, with everything else developing as normal, he became even more conscious of his disproportionate small balls in comparison to the rest of his manhood. As the first of these ten needles were extracted, David did not flinch one iota. When this part was complete, a small waist towel was put across to hide his modesty, and he was made to drink a full glass of ice cold water, but continued to lay still on the couch, for some considerable time to come.

"Right Paul," said Mr Chong to me unexpectedly, "take your shirt off and lay across the foot end of the couch, face down."

"But there is nothing wrong with me" I sputtered in protest.

"Of course not" said Mr Chong, in his immaculate English, "I just want to look at your spine, if that's alright by you?"

Not feeling able to protest any further, I did as I was asked. Mr Chong with the hallmark of the master ran both his thumbs expertly along the outer edges of my spine, slowly. "Ah" said Mr Chong "just as I thought, stay perfectly still a moment" he added.

Within minutes, he placed a total of a dozen acupuncture needles at carefully chosen points, along the outer edges either side of my spine. Easing the waist band of my shorts from off my hips, he placed a final two needles at the base of my spine. Starting from the top, he gently rolled the long needle shafts between the palms of his hands, which caused a slight tingling sensation, but which was completely painless and not unpleasant. Having extracted all his needles, he expertly massaged my back down its entire length, before applying a swab of light alcohol, over the areas he had been working on.

"O.K. Paul, you can stand up now, but leave your shirt off for a few moments for the alcohol to evaporate."

I sat back down, holding my tee shirt on my lap. Mr Chong went back to attend to David, examining his workmanship between David's legs. He quickly re-covered David back up to hide his modesty, that although relaxed was sporting a full blown erection, which Mr Chong explained was expected after such a procedure, and was par for the course, proof the operation was effective. He gave David a wide neck vessel to take in with him to a private room, and David obviously knowing what was expected of him, went away smiling to himself. Ten minutes later, David returned, handing his ejaculation to Mr Chong, who would later examine the sperm under a microscope. David was then asked to sit astride on the edge of the couch, while Mr Chong fitted him with the right size pouch, designed to relieve weight. Before we both left, David was handed a screw capped jar of ointment, with very explicit instructions. Mr Chong kissed brother David warmly, before doing the same to me, then made David promise to come to tea later in the afternoon, "be sure to bring Paul with you" he said.

We departed without haste, although by this time Mr Chong's waiting room was full to overflowing. While we were walking about the shops and sights of the town, I asked David why he didn't warn me about his recent procedure with Mr Chong, which for me was more than a bit of an eye opener. David explained to me in detail, that it was a problem he had carried throughout his adolescent life. He had been mercilessly teased, first by his schoolmates and then by his shipmates throughout his five years in the navy. "Chong my brother would not do this procedure until after I had left my teenage years behind, as he preferred to let nature do her best first."

"Did it hurt?" I asked David.

"Not at all" he replied. "Now I have good size balls, at least as big as yours." He remarked with so much pride. "Anyway," said David, "you will have to administer the ointment last thing at night for a week."

"Why me?" I asked, looking rather worried at such a gruelling prospect.

"Because I have been instructed by Chong, that if I attempt to do it myself I might put too much on, or miss areas I can't see or reach properly."

"Charming, I'll just love playing with your balls," I said, with a sarcastic irony in my voice.

David looked at me searchingly, wondering if I was just jesting, then pronounced with a great deal of glee and an equal amount of irony in his voice, "It will make a change from playing with your own balls for once."

Not knowing how to answer this snide remark, I said nothing in reply.

Towards the later part of the afternoon, we made our way back to Mr Chong, who lived over the shop so to speak, in a spacious apartment. As we all sat down to tea Chinese style, with all the rituals revealed to me for the very first time, we were waited on hand and foot by a trio of lovely young Chinese girls all in their teens. It wasn't until much later, long after we had returned to the campsite, that David explained to my obvious ignorance, that the three girls were in fact Mr Chong's concubines. (No one was ever allowed to share in any sexual favours these girls provided.)

David was not allowed to bathe this first evening, after his recent operation, but suggested I take a quick shower on my own, which I did. On returning to the tent, David was examining himself with the aid of my shaving mirror and expressed complete satisfaction at his newly acquired increased assets. We chatted a while as I prepared to bed down, when David asked if he may examine my testicles, for comparison with his own. He very gently measured mine against his and they seemed to meet with his approval. He handed me the jar of ointment to apply gently, and with great care. Once finished, he attempted to put on the special pouch, but again he needed my help, as we both tried to work out the intricate fastenings correctly. We talked late into the night with David dropping off to sleep first. I turned over then followed him into my own dream world.

Early next morning, David was up busy outside the tent preparing a substantial breakfast, as I lay back enjoying the fact there was no hurry to stir myself. After my first mug of tea, while David continued outside, I took the urge to play my harmonica and automatically played Bobby's favourite tune, Shenandoah, which David had never heard before. He too played the harmonica sometimes, especially when in a melancholy mood. For some reason David liked the tune very much, but before I started to feel morbid myself, I moved on to a more joyful air. David made me promise to teach him the tune, (Shenandoah) while we filled our faces with the very tasty breakfast, before going down to the beach this morning before lunch.

I swam for an hour or so alone, because David had been warned off for at least forty eight hours. We had an enjoyable day, but on returning we found Mr Chong at our campsite, urgently waiting to see us both. Only weeks after leaving Singapore, a nasty epidemic of influenza broke out, with some devastating effect and according to the local Chinese newspaper, had already taken more than five hundred souls. The main worry for Mr Chong as an important member of the Penang medical profession was that several cases had already been reported on the island. Mr Chong wanted to enlist our help, alongside many high school students who he had already recruited. This nasty disease, of a particular virulent Asian strain, was very potent, and Mr Chong along with other medical help, was preparing to attack this bug, before it overwhelmed the population of Penang.

It must be remembered, that in the fifties and with little knowledge, flu was a major killer, and although still serious today, the treatment and prevention is far more advanced. We naturally agreed to help all we could and reported daily at nine am till dusk over the next four days. On the first day alone, more than 600 people passed through Mr Chong`s surgery. When we got back to camp each evening, we were only fit to drop from exhaustion. By the end of the week, the press reported more than 75,000 people all over the country had already succumbed to this dreaded disease, one that showed no respect for rich or poor, young or old, as we saw with our own eyes. The fear in the faces of the people not struck down with the illness was plain to see. We offered any help we could in the surgery under Mr Chong's supervision, and kept our contact outside to a minimum, by staying in our deserted campsite. This might well have prevented David and me from being struck down with the disease. Meanwhile, Mr Chong advised us to stay put, and not even think of travel, at least until early next month, as the epidemic slowly abated. Naturally, we took all the herbal medicine Mr Chong gave us, which I'm sure also had positive bearing on keeping us free of this nasty flu infection. Because of David's recent past operation, he was soon back to daily bathing, and as well over a week of the imposed ban of abstinence from self masturbation, was now lifted, he had every intention to release his frustration of raging testosterone, without further delay. That evening and without further embarrassment, he quickly released his load, inspecting the quantity, which David insisted was almost twice more than normal, bragging with satisfaction.

Over the next few days, this dreaded flu abated so well, many hundreds of helpers were thankfully stood down. We returned to the meeting of many scouting and Chinese friends and often ate with them, enjoying their company. The following morning, I was beginning to feel lousy and it became obvious to everyone but me, I had been smitten. I started to get the shakes, with my temperature up and down dramatically, at it's highest it was almost 104degrees Fahrenheit. David took this sudden slight illness of mine rather badly and immediately fetched his brother Mr Chong, who removed me forthwith into one of his own bedrooms, within his palatial apartment above the business. His three concubines pampered me rotten, feeding me and wet nursing me round the clock. After making me sweat profusely over the next twenty four hours, changing the bed clothes frequently, the three of them gave me several bed baths, but there was absolutely no chance of any arousal, as I was still far too weak. I've never had my vital statistics handled so much, by so many, as these three beautiful babes, any of which on their own, let alone all three together, would normally be more than sufficient to excite my manhood, but alas, utter frustration was to be the ultimate frontier. The mind was well up for the challenge, but my body refused to obey any mental commands given. Oh well such is life, as David who was disgustingly healthy, volunteered to take over my pampered bed place.

Mr Chong confided in me light heartedly that David was most envious of my position, as the girls obviously found me far too attractive to resist. (I jest of course.) Now that the fever had broken and I was well on the road to recovery, David who was alone in the tent at night (well that's what he tells me – if you can believe his yarns) was most anxious to get me back where he could keep a much closer eye on me, before I fully recovered my sexual prowess. Mr Chong agreed that perhaps tomorrow, I should be ready to return to the tent.

After tea that evening, Mr Chong sat on my bedside for a time, chatting away pleasantly as if we had known each other for years, instead of weeks. Before leaving, he asked me which one of his girls I liked best.

"All of them, but the youngest one is rather nice" I said politely, as he gave me a goodnight kiss on my forehead, before leaving the room.

Sometime later, this beautiful young girl climbed into my bed beside me, turning my dreams into wildest reality. Oh what a wonderful night we had, and she was still there come morning! Her pleasure became mine, but I still had to be careful that I didn't over indulge myself, after all, I was supposed to be sick.

When David found out from Mr Chong, why I was truly ready to return to camp, he took the huff and went green with envy, almost the same colour as the noisy pet macaw in the sitting room. Much later of course, having got over my treatment of exceptional hospitality, David made it abundantly clear to me, that in all the time he'd known Mr

Chong, no one had ever been offered a choice from his ladies, not even David. (No wonder he was mad with jealousy.)

"I could hardly refuse such a fantastic offering, as to do so might have offended Mr Chong," I said softly to David, who couldn't believe I was so blatantly thankful for such an offer. "Anyway," I said, "You had Kimso, to warm your loneliness in camp" I guessed.

There was a long pause, before David looked at me incredulously, "Who told you?"

"No one" I shot back at him, "I was just guessing, but I suspected as much, as Kimso's fragrance lingered in the air," I added, which made David break in to one of his winning smiles, having been found out.

After almost three weeks on the island, we got down to some heavy correspondence, which we both had neglected. On one final examination by his brother Mr Chong, David was told that neither the ointment nor the pouch was required any longer, as we both breathed a thankful sigh of relief at such news. The first of July 1957 had come and just as quickly disappeared before we both realized the passing. Our itchy feet and the well being of our healthy bodies, dictated to us jointly, that it was time to move on and go ever northwards. With only one day to say all our goodbyes to the newly made, as well as old friends' of David, it was an exhausting time. Arrangements by Mr Chong both for our crossing over to the mainland, and also for our first lift northwards were gratefully put into place. Mr Chong embraced both David and myself giving each of us a full frontal kiss, calling us both his brothers. I for one knew that on the two occasions I had visited Penang, once on a weeks leave with the army, and this more extended stay of three weeks, I would be leaving with such memories of love and outstanding hospitality, that would stay with me well into old age, and certainly have. Mr Chong handed David a small bottle of some kind of herbal medicine, along with a small packet of other medicine that was to be given to me later that same day at evening time.

Mr Chong gave us one final kiss in an embrace of affection, as we both left he called after us "Take very great care my brothers and safe journey to you both."

Mr Chong was still waving to us, as we both climbed into the cab of the organized lorry until we disappeared from view. "What's this medicine for?" I asked David.

"I'll explain later, when we bed down for the night," replied David.

Chapter Twenty-Two

Brother Chong and Northern Malaya – Plus.

The driver of our lorry (who wouldn't give his name) was some kind of trusted worker, sometimes employed by Chong, who had arranged this part of our journey. Chong felt very deeply, to attempt to go through 'no mans land' without help and protection was far too dangerous. David explained to me as best he could, that our driver was from an unknown province called Isthmus of Kra, a region of land that the Chinese called 'no mans land' because the tribal people that lived in this thin tract of land, insisted it neither belonged to Malaya nor Thailand. A kind of buffer zone, between both countries, that with more than three hundred miles of notoriously bad, unmade and difficult, dirt roads, separated by both Malaya and Thailand.

Our driver with no name, carried illicit contraband from his region of the world and would only deal with Chinese who were neither authentic Siamese nor Malay born, he made it abundantly clear, he didn't particularly like either, but with far more hatred for the people of Thailand, and for reasons best known to himself, he never ever crossed the border into Thailand. The driver was a dour kind of unkempt frightening person, with very little to say for himself, but would only speak to David in a limited vocabulary of Chinese, and occasionally flashing his rather decaying mouthful of teeth at me, from time to time, usually accompanied by some kind of a grunt in answer. When he did give David a wide grin for some kind of recognition, his facial expression reminded me of the wild man of Borneo, the orang-utan reaching for food from a nearby branch. The smell from this man's body odour was something else, and I was happy to be sitting near the door, instead of sitting closer to him like David. He gave us both a hand rolled Burma cheroot to smoke, which went a long way in helping to make the internal atmosphere inside the cab more pleasant to bear, even the smoke filled cab, sometimes making it difficult to see out was preferred. However, with both cab windows opened fully, we managed well enough to survive. He showed David his old German Lugar pistol, which as David explained, was for self protection and he had been forced to use it on a number of occasions, in disputes. The driver was fascinated by my ice axe, which was strapped to the back of my rucksack. David had some difficulty in explaining its purpose. The lorry and everything in it amounted to the driver's entire possessions in life, which he gave far more love and attention, than his own personal hygiene, or bodily appearance and functions. He offered us both some kind of dried root to chew on, to while away the very bumpy dirt road, which was often horrendously difficult to negotiate at times. I decline his kind offer, but David feeling the need to be gracious accepted, which the driver found amusingly funny, grinning like one of his jungle ancestors of long ago.

We made frequent stops, travelling at only a snails pace, while the driver gave urgent resuscitation to his beloved lump of an engine, which looked as if it was being held together with much wire. (No MOT in this part of the world, that's for sure.) The back of my hands had far more hair on them, than the tread on his very worn tyres, which were so bald in parts, you could see the inner tube poking out, but it didn't bother the driver one bit, because he had many spares that were equally as worn ready for re-use.

As the long day came to a close, we hit the town of Kedah approximately eighty miles from our start at Penang, and although we were still within the boundaries of Malaya, we were nearing the borders of this buffer zone, the driver was delighted to inform David we would cross into this zone the following day.

"Tomorrow, we will be leaving Malaya, to go into the region of Isthmus of Kra, where progress transport wise will be even slower, and much tougher" David assured me.

On the outskirts of the far side of Kedah, the driver pulled off the road onto the grassy bank, near a small stream. David and the driver conversed as best they could for a while, before we crossed over the small stream to set up camp for ourselves. The thought of sleeping along side the driver was abhorrent. After a substantial tupper, (tea and supper combined) our friendly driver came across and gave us both a bottle of special local brew, which David accepted with thanks, but once alone having tasted it, we poured it discreetly into the stream. This potent brew

I was assured, was drunk by most of his native kin and friends, in this country - but tasted most foul.

"It's supposed to keep mosquitoes away," explained David, but I was convinced that no self respecting mosquito would dare to drink the blood of any man with this obnoxious brew inside them. David laughed out loud at my suggestion, but having sampled only a sip – I didn't think it was a laughing matter.

The heat in this northern part of Malaya was oppressive and before we set of to do our personal ablutions and find sufficiently deep water, enough to bathe in, David lit several joss sticks to purify the atmosphere inside the tent, in readiness for some kind of ancient ritual or rite that Chong had asked David to perform before leaving Malaya. On our return to camp, David set about preparations, that had me somewhat intrigued.

Once we were ready for bed, spread out upon the top of our sleeping bags, David went into great depth and a very long explanation as to why his brother Chong had called us both his brothers before leaving Penang. I did wonder about Chong's reference to calling me his new brother, but I misunderstood Chong's term more as one of endearment. "You see Paul," David continued "it all depends on how much you really trust me implicitly? Before I can proceed"

Rather taken aback at David's sweeping statement, I didn't know if I should take offence at his remarks, or ask him to explain himself further, as I felt I was at a distinct disadvantage, not really understanding what the hell David was rabbiting on about. Looking at my rather perplexed brow, David could tell, clearly I was in trouble.

"Do you trust me?" asked David again.

"Of course I do" I answered, "otherwise we wouldn't be together right now" I emphasized, with a lot of feeling in my voice.

"OK, that's fine, then take a sip of this specially prepared herb with me" instructed David, taking a good gulp himself first.

I automatically did like wise, knowing David would not ask me, without good reason. "It takes twenty minutes to take effect," said David.

"What effect is that?" I asked, now feeling very curious to find out exactly what David had in mind.

"Well, our brother Chong and I discussed at great length as to the merits in letting you join our brotherhood," and before I could utter a word "No, don't say anything just now, until I've explained more, in some detail," said David.

"Go on," I replied, wondering what mystery he was about to unfold, and wishing he would get on with it.

"Well, in our particular triad, before anybody is even considered to join, there must be an exchange of at least three of the six body fluids, to fulfil the basic rite to brotherhood. I don't know of any European, that has ever been allowed into the most secret order, until now," said David. Then he shut up, waiting for my first response or questions.

After a very long pause, in complete silence, I said, "What are these body fluids and even more important, how exactly are these fluids exchanged?"

After another long silent spell, David held up his left hand to count down the fluids in question. "1 salivation - 2 urine - 3 perspiration - 4 spermatozoa - 5 blood - 6 tears." He paused to allow these revelations to sink into my brain, to let me absorb the meaning, before continuing.

"Before you start thinking any evil or bad karma, I must insist that there is no contact between us, physical or of any kind of a sexual nature, and the three body fluids chosen, must be given by each of us, with complete freedom and choice."

David stopped talking and lay back on top of his bag, closing his eyes, waiting for me to react. "I'm not sure I really understand what procedure, or how the exchange of these three fluids will take place, or for that matter what fluids you have in mind?" I asked searchingly.

"Blood, urine and sperm" said David, as if he was sat reading from a set menu in a restaurant. A long silence befell both of us, with me doing a fair bit of uncomfortable squirming, and feeling rather ill at ease. After a while, David asked me if his brother Chong had leeched me with three tiger leeches.

"Yes" I told him. "Chong told me it was to rid my body of impurities."

"Did he also take a urine sample from you?" asked David.

"Of course he did, why?" I asked.

"Tell me Paul, when you made love that last evening of pleasure, did you do it without a condom?" David asked.

"No" I confirmed, "with a condom."

Then, David produced a similar unused bag that laced up at the root end of the penis. This was not like any ordinary condom I had ever seen before, as David handed it to me for closer inspection. David produced a jar alive with half a dozen leeches, and asked me to trust him once again. The six small leeches were wriggling desperately, waiting to be fed. He carefully extracted one leech at a time, placing it on my stomach, well above my pubic hair line. The second, he placed with great accuracy below the larynx on the soft indentation of my throat, and then gingerly lifting up my penis, the third was placed on the underside, where the root of the penis shaft adjoins the scrotum. The suckers soon got to work, inflating their thin bodies with my blood, while David used the remaining three leeches on his own body, in identical places. The memories of extracting these bleeders by the dozens from our bodies, after long patrols in the jungle while with the army, only served to remind me, not to attempt to pull them off forcibly, until after they had sated their appetite fully. As if I was not aware of this fact, David told me, once they had finished their gory blood sucking feed; they would willingly drop off themselves, without any help from us. I knew this of course, but made no reply to David's observation.

Some twenty five minutes had passed, since David and I had gulped a mouthful each of this special potion, which had been prepared and provided by Chong in Penang. The results were now beginning to take effect, stimulating, which was helped no doubt, also by the leech that was on the underside of both our penises. Without any sexual thoughts what so ever, my penis began to take on a life all its own, stiffening unsolicited to an alarming size. As this was taking place, the first of the three leeches from my stomach dropped off, having had its fill. I looked over towards David, who was experiencing similar stimulating effects as myself. The second leech dropped off of my throat area, which David retrieved and returned to the jar, as David's first leech also rolled off. When all six were back in their container, bloated and fully satisfied with our blood, David encased my penis with this special lace up bag, before doing likewise to himself.

"Now what?" I asked David the magician, as we both lay prone to see what would happen next.

Telling me to double check the lace on my bag was not too tight around the shaft, we lay back to wait. We both closed our eyes, to see what wonders this crude science would produce.

Sometime later, and without warning or any stimulating help my dick started to throb just prior to a full ejaculation. I was pleasantly surprised at this unprovoked awesome event, and couldn't help noticing David was a good few moments delayed behind me, in his own performance. I watched spellbound, as David's newly enlarged testicles pulsated constantly in delivering the white goods. Having both finished, David extracted each bag with great care, then handed me a tissue from the toilet roll to clean myself off. Before leaving the tent, David handed me a clean jar with instructions to give him a sample of my urine, when the urge took me, which wasn't long in coming. I handed my sample to David, through the tent door, as he continued to busy himself outside.

Now feeling very relaxed, but a little dry at the mouth, I began to doze off, feeling a little high with my sexual elation. Sometime later, David crawled back into the tent beside me, with instructions to drink some herbal concoction he had been busy preparing. I drank willingly, if only to quench my thirst and admitted to David it was rather pleasant to taste. David slowly savoured his like size drink until it had disappeared. Now feeling tired, we both willingly succumbed to sleep.

Early next morning, well before breakfast, David told me to get dressed quickly, as we were soon to hit the road again, and our driver was already building up steam in anticipation of the event. Two hours later, we were stopped at some kind border control, which we passed through without any hiccups into the Isthmus of Kra, heading for our next stop at Perlis, on the way north to Singora. With the pot holes on a very thin tarmac road now truly behind us, we both knew we would not see any decent roads for a good two hundred and fifty miles.

Over the next four days we churned our way slowly northwards, noting the rapid change in the countryside with sometimes a view of the sea on both east and west flanks, at one and the same time. Achieving only about sixty miles a day, we crawled up this tract of land that no one really wanted, amid desolation and poverty. As we travelled through this land that not only time forgot, but also countries such as Malay and Siam they didn't feel this land was worth fighting over, the sparseness of these poverty stricken people became more and more obvious, to the eye.

Over the next four days of hardship and travel, our driver continued to grunt his own brand of language to the both of us, as a rudimentary form of communication, and once one grew accustomed to the stench within the cab surroundings, with Gastro (the nickname I had given to our driver,) expelling large burps from the orifices at each end of his body, the hard journey became quite bearable. In fact, we both had a great deal to be thankful to Gastro our driver for, as without him, the hardships we would have had to face alone, would have been considerable. This made me realise the value of both David and Chong, not only as true friends, but the honour they ultimately bestowed upon me, in taking me into their brotherhood, in spite of my more sceptical feelings, which I felt over the ritual rites of passage.

Within my own thoughts, I knew, I now felt far more intimately closer to David, than at any time before this indoctrination, but it sharpened my thoughts, as well as made me focus on my beloved brother Bobby, who I thought about frequently, especially at times of stress. There were long periods of heavy downpours of rain, which often impeded our transportation northwards, hindering our progress. Never mind, I would console myself at times of frustrations, there was no real hurry, and if truth be known, I was really quite enjoying the hardships we faced, David and I enjoyed suffering both as one, together. Does this make me a masochist? I chuckled to myself, with David looking sideways at me rather strangely from time to time. I remember the evening at journeys end, confiding in David, about my Ashford days in the orphanage, and all about Bobby, my dead brother. He listened spellbound, and felt honoured that I confided so much of my past to him. The tears rolled unashamedly down his face, as I related so much about the events leading up to Bobby's final last days in Korea. David nestled in closer to my body to be nearer, as he put his arms about my chest in a comforting gesture of understanding and sympathy. We lay there, locked together in each others arms, sharing a symphony of full working tear ducts, like distant water music playing away perceptibly in the background. David's arms were still about my person, when I woke up next morning.

Over breakfast, David reminded me that with luck, we might reach Khiri- Khan, the border town into Thailand. We both checked our passports very carefully, to ensure we had the correct visas well dated for a month to enter Siam. We also had a three month visa to enter Burma, stamped into our passports while we were delayed with our stay in Penang.

The recent rains had played havoc with our muddy roads further north, with many abandoned vehicles littering the sides of the road, in a ramshackle manner. Khaoluang is over four thousand feet high overlooking the gulf of Siam, with spectacular views and with Khiri-Khan just ahead. Gastro's truck broke down three more times that day, but late that afternoon, come early evening time; we finally made our intended resting place. We purchased some special brew and cigars for Gastro, who had been our shepherd and companion for the better part of a week. A memory that neither one of us would forget in a hurry. An obvious look of joy and thanks lit up his face, as if we had handed him a pot of gold, he then slapped us both on the back as we said our genuine goodbyes, we turned and went in search of a safe campsite for the night. We had to continually remind ourselves we were now in bandit country, where the trafficking of almost anything that would fetch a price was rife and done prolifically by desperate people, if only to survive.

There was a distinct absence of any Chinese people in this remote area, which made David feel nervous and vulnerable for the first time since we met in Singapore. The only weapon that David carried was a large sheath knife, from his scouting days, and I noted with interest, he even took it to bed with him for the first time that night. Well after supper time, late into the evening, David was so nervous that any unfamiliar night noises outside the tent had him jumpy, like a cat with hot paws, ready to strike. Even when I went outside alone to empty my bladder, or answer a more important call of nature, he insisted he join me, not wanting to be left alone in the tent. Fortunately, he also took this opportunity to relieve himself even though he really didn't require to. I cuddled into his back to give him comfort, but in all honesty, I don't think either of us slept very well that last night, in the tract of Isthmus of Kra.

Early next morning, at the crack of dawn and even before breakfast, we crossed through the border post on foot. This post was manned by Thailand's military and custom officials, who scrutinized both our passports with a great deal of apprehension. After much consternation, they finally let us both pass freely, but paid far more attention to David, as a Chinese person holding a British passport, than they did to me. One of the policemen pointed to a building on the Siam side, where we could get some breakfast. David thanked him profusely and with an audible sigh of relief expressed by David, we both walked into Thailand smiling to each other once again. Perhaps it was too early to celebrate leaving Malaya behind, but it sure felt good anyway.

As we walked towards the building, I suddenly asked David "what did we both drink in the concoction, that last night before leaving Malaya, after our rites into brotherhood?"

David looked at me, as if I was somewhat stupid for asking. "The three body fluids" said David "What else?"

I looked at him, stupefied, but I knew he wasn't pulling my dick. So, in stunned silence we walked on together, with David smiling at my side.

Chapter Twenty-Three

Thailand – on the road to Bangkok

Now in Thailand, we sat down to breakfast with David still looking somewhat perturbed and obviously ill at ease. "What's really troubling you my new brother" I asked.

"Andy" David replied, calling me by my new name which he had chosen for me, after our recent rites into brotherhood, and now referred to me by this adopted name.

"Have you noticed how very few trucks are heading in our direction, north wards towards Bangkok? Which is still more than three hundred miles away," said David.

I had noticed, however I failed to mention this fact, due to the look of consternation, which now covered David's face. I also noticed, there was not another Chinese face to be seen anywhere, which I suspected was of far more concern to David, but he wasn't talking about this fact.

We sat there until well after 10a.m. not able to move, and David's face grew more and more problematic over the next three hours. On impulse, I wandered over to the policeman at the border control, in an attempt at engaging him in conversation, as I knew he spoke some basic English. He smiled at me, as if he could foretell my request, even before I spoke on approaching him. After a few moments, he told me to go back, join David and wait patiently which I did. David meanwhile, was busy making a large cardboard sign, displaying the word Bangkok on it, in hope. The Thai owner of this remote tea house brought over another ice cold tumbler of tea, which he gave to us on the house, free, gratis, which we both thanked him for.

Several hours later, well after mid-day a lorry from the south drew up at the border post and our policeman could be seen having a long conversation with the driver. We both studied the body language between these two characters from afar, and the early signs were not looking very promising, as the policeman dragged the driver from his cab with some force, and a display of anger clearly could be seen exchanging between them. We looked on; feeling even more worried than before, as the driver was taken into the building against his will, looking as if he was very much under arrest. Half an hour later, the policeman on his own, came over to talk with us, only this time he was smiling. He explained in his limited English and even more limited Chinese that the driver was charged with delivering us safely to Bangkok, which would take three to four days, naturally we were chuffed. (However, I suspected this was against the drivers will.) We both thanked the policeman profusely many times for all his help, and ten minutes later the driver was released, pulling his truck up outside the tea room, beaming with pleasure at being forced to carry us both as unwanted cargo north wards. He spoke no English whatsoever, but did have a smattering of some Chinese tongue, but had great difficulty in talking with David whom for what ever reason, clearly he did not like. His attitude towards me however, couldn't be more different, as he constantly smiled at me in some kind of reassurance.

He was a good looking young man in his mid twenties, well dressed, and I noticed he didn't smell unpleasant. When he showed his teeth they were very white and obviously well cared for. David understood a kind of animosity this driver felt towards him, so David wisely made me sit between himself and the driver, with David near the opposite cab door.

David whispered in my ear "I think he wants to have sex with you Andy."

I ignored David's tease. The driver's truck, compared with the previous weeks ride with Gastro, was in super condition, but to be fair so were the roads the further we drove north into the Siam interior. We sat as a trio in silence, with David and I under a kind of sufferance that such an atmosphere seemed to dictate. The driver who knew the road well, made good time in relative comfort, stopping only once before nightfall, and then only long enough for the three of us to grab a quick bite to eat and to refuel the truck. Late into the evening, the driver pulled well off the road outside the twinkling lights of a place called Phet Buri in the province of the same name. This was some one hundred and sixty miles from the border town we had started from earlier today; I was surprised at such good progress. The driver got out, opening up the canvas at the back of his truck. More by gestures than verbal language, we were made to sleep in the back, out of sight for the night. No camping tonight, as David explained we were in a remote part of Thailand where Chinese travellers were most unwelcome and always at high risk. The driver locked himself up front in the cab of his lorry.

An early rise next morning with quick attention to our ablution essentials, before setting off northwards, once again in silence. After only sixty miles north we stopped for a prolonged period at Ratburi. The driver had some considerable business to deal with of a rather shady nature. The driver explained to us as best he could, that he wanted us to walk about a mile on our own, to a roadside eating house, where he would pick us up later, before driving further north. We were both very dubious at this point and insisted we take our rucksacks on our backs, with us. (In case he decided to dump us.) We waited almost three hours, but the driver did eventually show up, keeping his word that he would do so. David was even more thankful than I and it clearly showed, realising we were not being abandoned in such hostile countryside.

Later that evening, we made our second and final stop for the day at N Pathonn, yet only seventy miles from the outskirts of Bangkok, which we should reach tomorrow. Once we stretched our legs and having emptied our bodies of all waste products, we again settled down in the back of the truck for the night.

"Andy" David whispered into my ear, "I shall be very glad to reach Bangkok safely tomorrow."

I reached over to reassure David, only to find his body shivering with fear. I snuggled into David tightly, cuddling him and pulling his back closer to my chest, kissing him soothingly on the back of his neck with warm affection.

After a while, David's body stopped trembling and he decided to turn face inwards to my front, so he could give me a more meaningful embrace. He clung to me, drawing on the warmth and comfort I offered him. At first light, I heard, then felt the vibrations of our lorry engine burst into life, as the driver slowly pulled back onto the main tarmac road towards Bangkok, leaving the two of us in the back.

Almost three hours passed before we realized the driver had suddenly stopped, as he drew up in front of a Chinese eating house on the outskirts of the city. We quickly assembled our gear about us, but once released from the back of the lorry, the driver quickly sped off like a bat out of hell, as if in some desperate hurry to get well away from both of us. He was obviously pleased to be rid of his unwanted cargo. We stood in front of this Chinese Emporium establishment, and on reading the shop front, festooned with Chinese character script writing, the serenity and pure joy returned to David's face, at the speed of some dark cloud lifting from the horizon, to reveal a clear and safe view. David, warmly put his arm about my shoulder, with a one armed hug of warm affection.

"Come on Andy, let's go get some lunch." (A late lunch, as it was already mid–afternoon.)

Mr Wong, the owner of this very large establishment, came bouncing over to welcome both of us, as he had been reading all about our exploits in his bi-weekly Chinese paper. At first, Mr Wong spoke only to David in Chinese, although in their lengthy conversation, Mr Wong kept on giving me the eye, with sideway glances, smiling pleasantly enough, and it was obvious even to me, they were talking about me. Mr Wong was very much a prominent respected figure in 'The Brotherhood' to which I myself had recently become one of their latest cast members. He eventually turned to me, apologising profusely in good English for his bad manners, assuring me he meant no insult. Then, very politely, he asked me to remove my shirt. The faded marks the leeches had left on the two parts of my anatomy were inspected carefully by Mr Wong, who now seemed fully satisfied with my brotherhood credentials. (The third leech mark was tucked away inside my shorts.) With one loud clap of his hands, several of his children came running into the open plan shop. They stood by obediently, awaiting his orders, while he had yet another word with David. The four youthful looking sons of Mr Wong aged between mid-teens and early twenties were dismissed back to work, somewhere in the back of the shop. Chai Wong, his beautiful teenage daughter was spoken to at length, after which David and myself were taken politely through to the back, into the living accommodation quarters.

"Andy" David instructed me, "We must get undressed while Chai Wong runs a hot tub for us to bathe in."

David's readiness to strip bare naked, at the drop of a hat in front of total strangers, was always disturbing to my sobriety. David quickly stripped off completely, as Chai Wong came back into the room with two silken gowns over her arm. Now naked David, smiled at Chai who handed him one of the gowns, without any sign of embarrassment. She waited for me to complete my undressing, then handed me the second gown, which I put on, before dropping my shorts. She quickly gathered up all our soiled clothing, smiling at me because of my sudden show of European modesty. She politely showed the two of us to the wash tub, checking first that the water was not too hot, before we got in. Taking David's gown from him, he wasted no time in submerging himself into this very inviting, fragrant luxurious tub. I hesitated, reluctant to disrobe myself as Chai Wong politely stood by, ready to take my gown from me. What the hell, I thought, as I handed Chai Wong my gown, and acting Mr Cool I slowly climbed into the tub to join David. He sat smiling at my nervous predicament, enjoying himself at my western prudish mannerism of playing coy. (You would think I would be used to all this nudity by now, I thought to myself.)

After wallowing for at least an hour, Chai Wong came back in, David only too keen to show off his manhood once again, told me to stay put, while he got out first, to be lovingly dried off by Chai Wong herself. When totally dried off David, was asked to lift up his penis, so Chai Wong could inspect the now faded leech mark in the underside near to his scrotum. After this was done, she put David back into his ornate Chinese decorated gown.

"OK Andy," shouted David. "It's your turn." Why did I think David got something of a perverse pleasure at seeing me squirm like a hooked worm?

So, after a brief moment, I took my courage by the scruff of the neck and climbed out of the tub, as cool a dude as possible. As Chai Wong gently dried me off I closed my eyes, desperately trying my utmost to keep a firm control of my manhood emotions. She seemed to take for eternity examining my anatomy at very close range. I held my breath when she took hold of my penis, to look closer on the underside, where the shaft joins my scrotum. (I noticed she didn't ask me to lift up my manhood.) God, I said to myself, please be quick, as I felt my groins stir, and a slight leap of my penis into a semi-erect state with the touch of her grasp, as she thankfully lowered it back into position. I quickly turned my back, as she draped the gown over my shoulders. Both David and Chai Wong smiled at each other, but I knew they were aware of my slight arousal. With my embarrassment now thankfully below my gown,

Chai Wong took us through to a beautiful oriental bedroom, so we could compose ourselves.

After Chai Wong closed the sliding door, I looked at David for help and guidance. "You know Andy; you really must relax and enjoy yourself. Don't feel so embarrassed, Chai Wong thinks you're very handsome, and was really honoured that her touch could have such an effect on your body." David said.

"Well" I said rather too quickly, "the last time I was aroused was at my rites of passage nearly two weeks ago."

"Me too" said David softly.

Chai Wong suddenly appeared, courteously waving us to follow her through to the living room, where Mr Wong was waiting to welcome us for a tea ceremony, already set out upon the table. He kissed and embraced David, then did likewise to me. He whispered something in David's ear, in Chinese, then remembering his manners, spoke to me direct in English. "My daughter thinks you're very handsome and likes your penis very much." Was I dreaming? I actually heard Mr Wong refer to my manhood so frankly, as I quickly went deep scarlet. Both Mr Wong and David smiled to each other knowingly, me, I just felt a real prat at such revelations.

Later that day and long after a substantial Chinese meal, we were alone in our bedroom, when I plucked up enough courage to ask David outright, "Why do Chinese girls find my dick so different to yours?"

"They don't really," David answered, "They just think that because you're from a different culture you're different that's all. Anyway, she will find out later, because she will be coming by to give us a massage with essential oils."

"I'm not sure that's such a good idea, "I said to David.

"Just relax Andy, go with the flow of hospitality given, otherwise Mr Wong might be offended."

I looked at David, long enough hoping he was winding me up, or perhaps I just knew I would not be able to retain self control of my body any longer. Feeling a little tired and yawning openly, I began to nod off. I remember it was a balmy evening and David on the bed next to me seemingly restless, as I felt him stirring beside me. Turning over on my side towards David, I saw him lying prone fully stretched out, but face downwards with Chai Wong kneeling across him kneading his body, expertly performing a full body massage. "How are you sleepy Andy?" she said softly, in a musical tone of voice.

She had obviously been working on David for sometime, when she asked him to turn over, so she could work on his front. David willingly obeyed, displaying his proud erection, which Chai Wong ignored and proceeded to work on his upper torso. Sitting above his erection, she worked quickly and without fuss as David's personal display waved around in anticipated excitement. A little while later, she eased her body over his erection to continue her massage lower down. I could feel myself already out of control, so I turned onto my front, face downwards to hide my joy. Once David's massage was complete, Chai Wong without a word, moved over to straddle my back in readiness, to give me the full treatment. In this position I could hardly lay back and think of England Could I? As she poured a small quantity of oil onto the centre of my back, I was already thinking bout the cultural pleasures that the Orient had to offer, compared with England. I'm becoming a sex slave to these wonderful sensual emotions, I thought to myself. Even before Chai Wong asked me to turn over, I experienced several small orgasms of delight, which was self evident now that I was on my front, fully exposed, and at the mercy of Chai Wong. I didn't believe it was possible to suffer so much erotic ecstasy over such a prolonged period of time. Two hours later, she left David and I in such a high state of euphoria, we drifted off to sleep, already in a dreamlike state of unbelievable relaxed serenity.

In the morning once I was fully awake, David without either tact or embarrassment, calmly asked if I would carefully check his testicles. Not the ideal request, after such a memorable night and wonderful display of sexual fireworks. His plum sized balls, not only looked as usual, but their tactile sponginess seemed normal to me, so I told him so.

"Do you think they have reduced in size since the op?" asked David searchingly, looking for reassurance.

"No" I replied, "in fact your whole package looks good."

David smiled with pleasure, at this confirmation of his assets. "Now leave yourself alone, after last night, you must have fulfilled all your lustful desires."

He stopped instantly from playing with his manhood, as we both spotted our day clothes that had been immaculately laundered, ready for us to get dressed into. "We are moving into the Y.M.C.A. in the centre of Bangkok today" said David, in his usual matter of fact manner.

"Great" I replied, "we can't go through another night of torturous agony again," I quipped.

There was a pause, with a look of disbelief on David's face for a number of seconds, which quickly broke into a smile, followed by loud laughter, as David realized I was winding him up, and we both went in search of breakfast. Over breakfast Mr Wong wanted to know of our plans in detail, and especially what route we planned to take from Bangkok north-westwards into Burma. We ourselves were still not certain, having only just arrived, in any case we planned to stay for a while, as we both had so much we wanted to do, and also a number of people we wanted to meet. We still felt the effects of the very recent arduous trip across Malaya up through no mans land, which to be honest, was far more of an undertaking than either of us originally expected. We promised Mr Wong faithfully, that we would be sure to come back and report to him, once we had a chance to formulate a definite plan of action. Realising that he was unable to press us into staying any longer, with so much to do, he instructed his eldest son to drive us to the Y.M.C.A.

Mr Wong was reputed to be one of the wealthiest Chinese in Bangkok, and David assured me, not one to cross swords with. Armed with this knowledge and much more, it was no surprise to be driven across town in the back of a big new Cadillac, which made us both feel awkward, as we swished up to the front door of the Y.M.C.A.

The Americanisation of Siam even in the late fifties was so in your face, no one could fail to notice all of the trappings and yearnings, especially by the Thai youth, for this so contrived way of life, with all the desires of everything American. The uniform and flamboyancy of dress had already been widely accepted, and in particular within the capital of Bangkok, which was the fastest growing westernised civilisation in the Far East. This sprawling city, densely populated and affectionately called the Kok, (not cock) for many reasons was embraced by all as the place to be. This is where it was all supposed to be happening. The sex industry, where literally anything goes (and I do mean anything,) put Soho in London or Amsterdam in Holland, in the dark ages, with the sheer variation and availability alone. Away from the façade of super posh shops, and places of real genuine cultural sites of interest, there was poverty and squalor everywhere, in abundance. The stench alone from the canal systems, with the resident population living in filth and squalor, using the water for everything, (and I do mean everything,) was enough to turn even the strongest of stomachs. The sexual sleaze was tirelessly executed to all and sundry, and flaunted so unashamedly in everyone's face. Every form of male and female prostitution, sold openly with bargain basement price offers, to anyone who looked as if they had more than the cost of an expensive cup of coffee. Even in the fifties, kids as young as ten years old and of both sexes were openly flaunting their bodies for sex, so desperate to earn money to enable them to survive their poverty. In comparison to say Singapore or Kuala Lumpur or even Rangoon, Bangkok for me had no appeal, not even sex appeal. However, this was back in the fifties and even then there were many wonderful pagodas and other beautiful buildings, many with deep historical significance worthwhile visiting, there were also many pleasures outside the sex industry to enjoy. I didn't dislike Bangkok, but I did find the sheer size and the desire for everything American a little overpowering, if not intimidating at times. The sexual sleaze was in abundance, but did nothing to enhance any charms of Bangkok.

Once settled into the smaller of two Y.M.C.A. buildings (the cheapest) we picked up our mail, as this was one of the many organized post boxes along our intended route. The next being Rangoon, if we ever got there. We spent a leisurely day, sorting through this very important event. In my personal mail, there were letters from my Aunt Joan and even one from Henry, my mate back at Lime Grove, plus one from the editor of the Bangkok newspaper. The one which we both wasted no time in opening was from U.S.A. and The National Geographic magazine, with a cheque for seventy two U.S. dollars. This was payment for an article and photographs I took of the caves we both explored outside Kuala Lumpur in Malaya. With funds being really low, almost non-existent, this was a most welcome sight for the both of us. A long letter to me from my brother Chong with an enclosed photograph saying 'with best wishes for my ever loving brother Andy – from your brother Chong Yew Cheuin', dated 14-6-58, this pleased me immensely.

David could tell this pleased me very much, as I handed him the photo of our brother. A tear appeared in his eye, as without thought he started to kiss and hug me with great affection. "Do you realise Andy, we both have each others seed inside of us?" asked David.

Where ever we went in Bangkok, David instantly made many friends with Chinese as well as Thais. He glowed with the aura of fame and notoriety and just loved playing up to the gallery, especially if the press or media was sniffing about. A better P.R. man than David would be hard to come by. His wicked sense of fun made him great to have about, especially when he was in the mood for any outrageous mischief. I was proud to be called his brother, and his informative education of so many Chinese ways and traditions was delightfully revealing, especially to such a heathen as I.

After almost two weeks, we got an urgent request to go and see Mr Wong. The thought of moving on, for both of us, was beginning to take earnest consideration, so with the feeling of itchy feet to wander the unknown yet once again gripping us, we went to see the Wong family one last time.

Chapter Twenty-Four

A Voyage of discovery

The promised return to Mr Wong's emporium was to be more than just a revelation of facts for both our immediate futures. After the affectionate greetings were suitably quenched on both sides, we were solemnly taken through to his private quarters, where Mr Wong's oldest son and Chai were waiting also to greet us. The oldest son Yeong was sitting with a large map spread out on the table in front of him, and like his father he had a good command of English, David and I sat down either side of him. Father and son wanted us to illustrate on the map, the route north through Thailand into Burma, we were thinking of going. Once we made our intentions clear, it was obvious to both David and I, that the route we had chosen was a no go area. As Mr Wong explained at some length, most if not all of the area northwards and right across our proposed route, was now in the hands of rival insurgent gangs, ruthlessly fighting over smuggling routes and rights. There was a clamp down by the Bangkok government, on all media coverage, even the reports that Mr Wong was getting were somewhat ambiguous, as well as dangerous for disclosure, not for public consumption.

Mr Wong suggested two alternatives, to help us in reaching a decision.

1. Providing we were prepared to wait for between seven and ten days, Mr Wong would arrange a passage on one of his own freighters, it would soon be calling at Bangkok en route from Shanghai.

2. His eldest son Yeong would personally escort us overland, to a fishing port at Tavoy on the west coast, but well south of Rangoon, where a two to three day sea passage to Rangoon would be undertaken on a smaller vessel, (a Chinese junk) and they would put us ashore in safety.

Over a very tall glass of ice cold coffee, brought to us by the delectable Chai Wong, David and I went into a deep discussion, debating all the pros and cons of what we must choose. The fact that our visas could run out before the freighter arrived was just one factor against the first option, anyway it would mean a sea journey of almost two thousand miles, going back all the way down Malaya, before rounding the island of Singapore then up through the Malacca straights, up across the Murgui archipelago to the gulf of Martaban. Not only was this a very lengthy sea journey, it seemed so retrospective, I was very much against the very idea of taking three steps backwards to gain one step forward. Option two, going almost due east from Bangkok might be tougher, but was a less than two hundred and fifty mile journey to Tavoy and then a much shorter sea passage north to Rangoon.

Having both agreed, that the second option offered a more spirited form of adventure and at least was more progressive for our joint aim. Both the Wongs' (father and son,) seemed to relax considerably, at our choosing to take option two, but were quick to tell us both, we would have to prepare to travel later that very same day. We both felt a sense of relief at reaching our decision, so Yeong was instructed to return with us to the Y.M.C.A. to uplift all our gear.

"One other thing" stressed Mr Wong, "Neither of you must mention to anyone about this route you will be travelling, as secrecy must be absolute."

The vibes I was already receiving, began to ring alarm bells in the deeper parts of my brain's recesses, giving me signals that not all was as it should be.

We dined well that evening, and as soon as it was dark enough, a small covered truck pulled silently into the back yard of Mr Wong's emporium, well out of sight from the main road. The older brother Yeong sat alongside the driver up front, while we were made comfortable in the back, on a mattress, in an otherwise empty truck.

I do believe at this point in time, David knew exactly what covert operation was afoot. He explained in a whispered voice, that the Wong's empire extended all over the far eastern world, and was very big, in all kinds of shipping under the guise of imports and exports, much of which could hardly be called kosher. It would seem our respectable business man and brotherhood member Wong had far reaching tentacles all over, which included some remote regions of the Far East, dealing in the most dubious but lucrative of trades, which even David was not prepared to ask questions about. This was a time, when the lack of specific knowledge was a distinct advantage in staying alive. The mind boggled with this information, but being somewhat ignorant and naïve, my undeveloped wisdom as to how such oriental crime syndicates operated was poor, I blissfully went along for the ride. Perhaps, such ignorance at this time of my life really was a life saver, and besides, being a member of the brotherhood, (which I also suspected might well be involved,) I was more than willing to keep stumm.

The first few hours were on tarmac, but suddenly the truck stopped, engaged four wheel drive, then continued at almost a snail's pace along unmade roads. Yeong slid back a small opening positioned into the back of his cab, to converse briefly with David and myself. "About another two hours" he said, and then shut the pillar box flap, back into place.

We managed a quick glimpse of a half moonlit night sky for the moment the flap was open. Continuing without headlights along this track we bumped our way forward at a speed never more than fifteen to twenty miles an hour in low gear. The ride, in spite of the mattress, was most uncomfortable as we held onto each other, with the truck bucking madly from side to side. When we did eventually come to rest, the engine was turned off immediately, as we patiently waited to be released from our enclosed five feet by seven feet long prison cell.

A good five minutes passed, when with help we got down from the truck, feeling bruised and sore. "No speaking," whispered Yeong, putting his hand momentarily across his own mouth to signify as much.

The driver was nowhere to be seen as the three of us crouched down low, to await his return. David and I were desperate to empty our bladders, so Yeong pointed to a nearby bush for us to go behind to relieve our much shaken bodies. After a short while, the driver appeared with two other strangers and six heavily laden pack ponies. In total silence, the two strangers who were each leading three pack ponies apiece, unloaded their illicit cargo, and with great care packed them into the back of the truck, that we thankfully had just vacated. A short rest period was then taken, as we shared a Burma cheroot cigar between us, pulling on the nicotine fix deeply, to comfort our taste and calm our state of well being. I had never ridden a horse of any description before in my life, and although I was not nervous of horses, I was in trepidation, at being put astride one of these ponies. Our gear was easily packed onto one animal, and now that all of us were astride these beasts, which had no saddle or stirrups, the leader led off at a walking pace only. We heard the lorry move off on its return journey, just before two am, while we continued on our way almost due east.

For almost five hours without a break, we climbed over a pass of more than five thousand feet high before the long downhill trail reached the outskirts of Tavoy, a small port on the west coast of Burma. Yeong informed me that we had come over the shoulder of Mount Myenmoletkhat, the summit that lay a good few miles due south of our actual route, and was well over seven thousand feet high. We came alongside a deep water channel, well south of the harbour town or Port of Tavoy. Leaving the two pony drivers, Yeong quickly took us aboard this Chinese junk fishing vessel that belonged to his father, and after having a long discussion with the skipper, he quickly kissed both David and I goodbye in turn, and then returned to shore alone. The precarious gang plank was pulled in, and the boat quickly got under way. This junk was about eighty feet long and crewed by a very young crew of teenage boys, all of whom were Chinese. The crew total was seven strong, plus the skipper. One of the younger lads was instructed to take us and our gear below, into the owner's cabin, which was very well appointed. This fifteen or maybe sixteen year old lad went off to fetch us food and drink, after he had left, David turned to me and said in a lowered voice "You know Andy, that lad is a eunuch." (David said this as a statement of fact.)

I looked at David in puzzlement, as at that time in my life, I had no understanding as to what a eunuch actually was, or meant. David noted my bewilderment and was about to explain in more detail, when the lad returned with a laden tray and the all important food. We both ate heartily from a bowl of wild rice, mixed with some kind of sea food. This was followed by fruit, and buffalo's milk, which definitely acquires a taste, but was not too unpleasant to drink, especially when you're thirsty, as we were.

The skipper came down to talk with us, and told us that after a good sleep we would be allowed to go up on deck if we wished. The skipper spoke no English, and had the seafaring look of a hard task master. David conversed in Chinese, telling him our bodies were feeling bruised and battered from the journey. The skipper smiled, and told David he would shortly send down his masseur, that all the crew used when the need arose.

As the skipper left David turned to me with a mischievous twinkle in his eye, which I instantly recognised; it spelled some kind of trouble afoot. Just as I was about to ask David to explain himself, the young lad whom David called a eunuch returned with a wooden pail of hot soapy water, a natural sea sponge, and two heavy towels, carried over the crook of his left arm. I sat down on the double bed that David joyfully called the play pen, as I watched David quickly strip off to the buff. David just loves to show off his new balls with the rest of his manhood I thought. The boy started to wash David from head to toe, paying particular attentions to his private bits. I must have sat looking agog, when David still smiling asked me what was wrong with me.

"I'm not letting any strange lad wash my body all over," I said, with feeling.

David laughed out loud, then turned to the youngster and spoke to him in fluent Chinese. The lad stood up obediently, and then slowly undressed. He came over towards me and did a kind of pirouette ballerina style, and I could see clearly this was a girl, who had ample pubic hair around her vaginal cavity and a very flat chest. I looked over to David, who was now lying on the bed waiting for me to undress and get washed. Slowly I took of my t-shirt as the lassie leaned down to unlace my shoes. Without a word, she undid the waist band of my shorts, and then let them drop to the deck, around my feet. I stepped out of my shorts and joined David on the bed. "Would you like her to do you first?" asked David, and I assumed he was referring to a body massage.

"No you're alright David, you go first" I said, feeling anxious.

David turned onto his front, face down towards the mattress, and without further ado, the lassie straddled David and started to massage his shoulders. I lay there on my side facing David, to watch as a voyeur, looking at the slenderness of this petite young girl's body in action. Besides the fact that she had no breasts, she was an attractive little thing with unblemished skin that had a healthy lustre, below the swinging oil lamp above our heads. Feeling a little aroused, I turned quickly face down to hide any obvious signs. The lassie was rubbing a Chinese balm ointment into David's buttocks, and judging by the sounds of pleasure, he was enjoying the relief this pair of small hands were giving.

"How old is she?" I asked David, who in turn asked her in Chinese.

"Almost nineteen" said David in answer.

She hardly looks fifteen, I thought to myself, as she climbed off from David, to allow him to turn turtle, face upwards. David blatantly already sported a massive erection, which the lassie obligingly put the flat of her palm on, to lay it flat upon David's upper stomach then promptly sat on his erection so that his penis would not stand up, poking her body. David winced a little, which she ignored, but carried on massaging David's upper torso.

Not wasting too much time, she quickly finished him off, and then casually transferred her attention and body over to me. Slowly I began to relax, as she worked her magic, working expertly down my back concentrating on my back bone. Getting off me to one side she opened my legs wide and knelt between them. She liberally spread the balm into the cheeks on my buttocks, working the edges of her small hands deep into the crevasse of my anus. This movement was unforgivable, causing erotic feelings that were now totally out of human control. (My control anyway.) My erection below me couldn't be fuller, as she sensually stroked my inner thighs in tandem, bringing me rapidly to boiling point. She affectionately slapped my butt – "turn" she demanded, and with just a slight hesitancy on my part, I obeyed. I closed my eyes in shame, as she put my legs back closer together. My volcano was already on the verge of an eruption, leaking with anticipation, almost to the point of no return. Afraid to open my eyes, in case I spoilt the dream, to wake up and find reality so different, I felt her climb on top of me, encasing her body around my genitalia. She sat motionless, bridging my midriff as the juices from the tip of my penis met her warm encirclement as I slipped inside her. I suddenly became aware of a second pair of knees straddling my lower legs, behind the girl, on top of me. David lifted her buttocks off of my erection, which did not escape from her opening entirely, and eased himself into her anus with positive encouragement from the girl. With David now fully entered he began intercourse, his movement and rhythm had an identical stroke and slide effect over the length of my shaft. I came first, ejaculating spurt after spurt deep inside her. David knowing I had cum my full orgasmic load, now quickened his pace to a more satisfying tempo. She must have known when David was about to ejaculate, as she quickly pulled him free, placing his penis between her legs as he emptied himself until he was dry. David moved over onto the ample space left on the bed, lying on his back with his still hard dick throbbing in relief. Once the lassie unhooked me from her cavity, I too was laying back in the same position as David. The lassie climbed off and started to wipe me clean, it was now I started to realise that most of the white goo belonged to David. After towelling me off with care, she moved over to David, who required very little cleaning. She wiped herself off with the sponge, then got dressed. Kissing both David and me in turn, she silently left without uttering another word, making sure the door was firmly closed behind her. We both lay alongside each other feeling pleasantly exhausted from the experience; we then turned our heads to face each other after our sinful deeds. "What did you think of her Andy?" David asked still grinning from - I'm not sure what!

"Unbelievable, fantastic" I uttered with satisfaction, closing my eyes, the better to get a vision of such ecstasy we had both lustfully enjoyed to the maximum. "Why did you fuck her back passage?" I asked.

"I could hardly shove my dick in the same hole you were occupying, could I?" He retorted.

There was a longer pause than normal before David declared, "Not bad for a bloke was he?"

"Don't be such a fucking plonker" I replied, looking him fully in the face.His erection began to collapse at my vehement blasphemous utterance.

Now fully deflated, he quietly asked me what I thought a Eunuch was. Not knowing, I told him as much

So he gently reached out to enclose my flaccid penis, by putting his hand around me, pushing my dick low between my legs. "Look down, that is what you would look like once the whole of your genitalia had been removed completely."

He removed his hand, then using both his own hands, he demonstrated with more effect, on himself. Still not sure, he wasn't winding me up, pulling my dick, so to speak, I continued to look doubtful. I retreated into my own thoughts for a while, thinking how I could question him further. "Why would he, she want to do such a thing to himself?" I asked.

"He didn't," explained David, "his mother did, because having five sons already, she wanted a girl." (In spite of the fact that the Chinese killed off many unwanted girls, as undesirable, which the state in those days supported as a form of birth control.)

"The cruel bitch" I spat out, "so he must now live out the rest of his life pretending to be a girl."

"That's right," said David. "But if it wasn't for Wong, she would have been killed off, whereby, now, at least, she has some kind of life, with a kind of family around her, even if it is for the purpose of only giving massages and pleasure to the crew."

"Do you mean she's like a prostitute, a tart for want of a better word?"

"No," David shouted. She's not that, as only members of her crew are allowed to touch her sexually. If she does not wish to pleasure you, she won't, there is no question of force." David added.

With all this knowledge, I had much to think about. To David, I must have looked upset, so he moved closer to me, instructing me to turn over. He pressed himself against my back, with both his arms about me in a tight embrace. We both slept solid, for a good ten hours without awakening, as I woke up to find David had turned over onto his other side, sometime through the night.

The next morning, I got up, washed and got dressed to go up top side, for some fresh air. My Rolex wristwatch read almost 11a.m. as the sunshine made me squint. The young thing that attended to us last night, was smiling at me, as I realized she was doing her stint at the helm. I smiled back, feeling good inside, but my body also told me, that my aches and pains were now gone from me, thanks to her. No doubt, more to do with an expertise in body massage, than her welcome relief of sexual tension. I stood at the side rail wondering, as I dreamily looked into the deep waters passing by the hull side, then as I looked back to see a white foaming wake astern. The difference in a clash of cultures, each trying their best to understand the other, with a complete failure of East meeting West, in their beliefs. One equally suspicious of the other, with China's thousands of years more ahead than when western civilization started, which by their traditions was still in its infancy.

With these thoughts fresh in my mind, I turned to watch David emerge, as he came up the short companion way to the after deck, to join me and greet the morn. (Which would soon be afternoon.) Once he noticed the girl on the helm, he casually walked over to thank her for the pleasure of her company last night, then kissed her before rejoining me at my side. "Come on Andy; let's see if we can find some grub, I'm starving" he said.

In order to sate our appetites, and looking to feed the beasts, we went below in search of food. The galley come dining saloon was almost empty, save for the skipper who was drinking a glass of Saki rice wine, in this smoke filled cabin. The rice bowls put down before us, contained food similar to the grub we had the night before, and although sea food was not my favourite, I ate enough to satisfy my aching belly.

Our next port of call would be Mulmein, some one hundred and eighty miles north from Tavoy, our starting point. The skipper explained to David that the speed of his sailing junk (about six knots,) would see us dock in darkness, later that same day. We would spend most of the night at rest in port, leaving Mulmein early next morning, sailing on a compass bearing of due east to Rangoon, which was about one hundred nautical miles in distance. We should arrive in Rangoon mid afternoon tomorrow, said the captain with obvious relief on his face. The skipper impressed upon David that once we neared Rangoon, we must both keep out of sight, until after we cleared customs. David naturally related all this information to me in English. I was beginning to feel our landing in Rangoon was somewhat dubious, and said as much to David with much concern in my voice. Checking both our passports carefully, our Siam visas would still be in date - just, but we both realized there was no exit stamp in our passports, showing the point of entry into Burma. David, after further discussion with the skipper, broke into a smile of relief as he assured me the skipper would take care of such a minor detail, once we reached Rangoon. With this pleasant piece of information, we would both have to wait and see for ourselves, as to the final outcome.

We both spent a leisurely day lounging about on the deck, basking and dozing in the afternoon sun. That night at dinner, I ate steak, and what a big tasty succulent piece of juicy meat it was. Long into that evening, well before bed time, I could still savour the steak on my palate, as with the aid of an ivory toothpick I relieved grains of meat from between my teeth. David informed me the steak was in fact buffalo.

We were preparing to turn in for the night, having watched with interest the docking, then the unloading of twenty or more large looking bales, when we were both approached by the eunuch, who offered her/his massaging skills. I made it very clear to David and as politely as possible, I personally did not require her/his skills. David was obviously disappointed, having some difficulty in hiding his true feelings, and felt I was being a little unfair to him in particular. The eunuch graciously declined, showing no feelings to our surprising rebuttal one way or the other.

As we retired for bed that night, I could tell David was not the happiest bunny in the burrow, continuing to give me the cold shoulder treatment. This was successful in upsetting me somewhat, but I felt that one night of abandonment and sex orgy with a eunuch, was about as much my little sense of propriety could suffer. "Don't misunderstand David," I tried to explain, "I probably enjoyed myself as much as you, although taking her from behind, is not my cup of tea, one night occasionally to forfeit my sexual lust and desires was ample, at least for me."

David looked at me suspiciously, especially at the tail end of my observational remarks, but decided not to pursue this tactless discussion, so remained sullenly quiet.

Having revealed some of my true inner thoughts, it gave me an uncomfortable night, tossing and turning with a heavy mind, almost akin to guilt. David on the other hand slept soundly, which only served to feed my envy of his acceptance of Oriental ways and customs. I didn't see David as a kind of reprobate, because his understanding of all things for eastern customs was perfectly normal to him, and I felt just a little envious of his absolute acceptance. Perhaps I should remind myself more often he was Chinese, and had been brought up with his own firm eastern beliefs. The saying often uttered by David, "Remember Andy, you're in the east, where we have different beliefs and cultural standards to your western civilization, which in any case is still in its infancy, or primate stage.

"When in Rome, and all that jazz" said David with deep feeling.

I continued to watch David enjoy his slumber, with a wisp of a slight smile on his face, dreaming pleasant thoughts, no doubt. As he slowly became fully conscious, I watched his awakening with interest. He wiped away the signs of sleep from his eyes, and then widely looked me in the face, smiled then reached over to me, kissing and embracing me. "Does this mean you forgive me, after last night? I asked.

"You're my brother Andy, there's nothing to forgive," he answered.

He lay there at ease, as my eyes wandered over his slender body, which was at peace with its owner. "What do you think Andy, are my balls still a good size?" He asked, as he gently lifted his flaccid dick out of the way, to expose his new size testicles, to me.

"They're just fine" I remarked, as I got off the bed to get dressed, ready to go up on deck.

"I didn't realise we were underway" said David, with some surprise.

"We left Mulmein a good three hours ago" I replied.

After dressing in haste, we both climbed the companionway together, for the aft or poop deck at the rear of the junk. The sky was overcast, threatening with rain later, as we were now in the height of the monsoon season. We went below, to fill our faces and join most of the crew for breakfast. We were met with smiles all round from this contented bunch of young men, and I noticed no sign of the young girl, who had done so much to make our short sea cruise comfortable. For me, this was more than just a voyage of discovery; it was a personal insight to a completely different way of life. A source of wonder and awe, where the large gaps in my ignorance and knowledge of customs different to my own, was beginning to filter and saturate my aura of delight. The monsoon downpour, drummed heavily upon the wooden decks in pandemonium and noise. The wind increased in strength to almost gale force, as the junk's hull bobbed like a cork on the rising swell, all hands lashed down everything that was likely to break loose.

For two hours or more, we took a battering, but the crew had seen it many times before, and went about their business as normal. The rain stopped just as suddenly, the junk heaved its way beneath a dark sky that was brightening by the minute. Within half an hour of the rain stopping, the sun was warming the decks, drying them at break neck speed, as if nothing had taken place.

By mid afternoon you could make out the faint coastline of Burma over the bow. Another three hours or so, we should be in Rangoon, we were reliably told by the skipper with a smile. The big delta of the river Sittang could be clearly seen over the starboard bow, we ourselves pointed towards the Hanthawaddy, which lead to the river up stream to Rangoon. Just after seven pm we tied up, and the skipper took our passports from us to bribe some official, which was just another accepted custom in this part of the world. By 8pm both David and I left Wong's junk, having said our goodbyes, we walked at peace for many a day, side by side, to find the Y.M.C.A. in Rangoon's fair city, with light of heart, and speed of step.

Chapter Twenty-Five

Rangoon and "problems"

We were given a very small, but comfortable room at the Y.M.C.A. as they had been fervently following our progress in the local papers the last few weeks, and had been expecting our arrival. We were so warmly welcomed, like dignitaries more fit for heroes, instead of a pair of travelling adventurers. We both noticed how much cooler Rangoon was for the time of the year, but it didn't prevent the mosquitoes trying to purge blood from our exposed flesh or body parts, in particular, the legs below our shorts, and our arms and neck areas. David promptly put the two rather narrow single beds together, and erected the mosquito net above our now new, narrow, double bed. We went in search of the shower room and ablutions, once sat upon our individual thrones, prior to taking a shower, David seemed in a very jubilant animated mood, talking nineteen to the dozen, as if he was on some kind of high from drugs. It was so obvious, David was overwhelmed that we had made it to Rangoon, after so many times, when things could have dramatically gone wrong, and often nearly did so. I was pleased of course, but did wonder why David was making such a fuss. We went into the showers in a buoyant mood, realising we both had a faint smell of fish about our persons. David insisted on soaping me down, from head to foot with great care and attention to detail, and spent far more time on my genitalia with a great deal of love, that seemed naturally healthy. I reciprocated of course to David, who obviously enjoyed such pampering, without getting aroused, I hasten to add, and with whom I felt completely at ease with my touch, regardless to what part of his body I washed.

That evening, we took our extensive mail, which had accumulated here at the Y.M.C.A. awaiting our arrival, upstairs to our bedroom to peruse at our leisure. It was amazing how much had gathered since our last P.O. box in Bangkok, way back in Thailand. Except for a few choice letters, we both decided that the bulk of the mail could wait until the morning, after we had both had some time to catch our breath. For a pleasant hour or so, we were both engrossed in our own thoughts of loved ones far away, so far away in fact it was like reading material from another world.

Having read a letter from my aunt and a very lengthy letter from Henry, I lay on my side, watching David intensely, who was busy reading a letter from our brother Chong. David looked down at me lying on my side, with a wisp of a smile curling up at the far corners of his lips, he then started to read out aloud, "I hope you are looking after my new brother Andy, and I must remind you, that your brotherhood between you is coming up towards your first month's anniversary," David read.

I looked searchingly into David's face, what was the meaning of the letter from Chong he was holding, and referred to, just what might this entail? He gave me the letter to read for myself, it had been beautifully written by the hand of a scholar and ended with great love to the two of us, from Chong. I held my counsel, although I dearly wanted to ask David of its true meaning, but as David got out of bed to turn out the light, I held my tongue. He climbed back into bed below the single sheet, and at once he took me into his arms in a loving embrace. He kissed me goodnight before turning over, then quickly went into a peaceful sleep, leaving me wondering and suspended in my own thoughts.

Next morning, over breakfast two Rangoon policemen came to visit us, and demanded both our passports from us, for inspection. We both begrudgingly handed over our documents, which they studied comprehensively, and not seemingly satisfied, they ordered us both to go with them, down to the police station. We both felt highly intimidated at this request, and David attempted to find out the reason why we were both being ordered to accompany them, like a pair of common criminals. The larger of the two of these thugs in uniform, objected to David's attitude, and then punched David to the ground, with his fist to David's chest. I immediately went to David's rescue, which in itself was definitely the wrong move on my part. A revolver was put to my head, and I was instructed to put my hands behind my back, whereby handcuffs (American issue,) were clasped firmly onto my wrists. David was then pulled roughly to his feet, and also received handcuffs, before we were both manhandled into the back seat of their police car awaiting outside, which took us off to the police headquarters.

On arrival, we were promptly thrown into a dirty police cell, together as one, awaiting further interrogation. David was most upset, and come to that, I was not best pleased myself. Thankfully, the cuffs had been removed, and we were both able to give each other support and comfort. Several hours later, the chief of police appeared, coming into our cell leaving a guard on standby, and started to ask us many questions, and specifically as to where we had entered Burma. By this time, David looked very pale indeed, as if suffering from shock. He started to shiver, as if he was experiencing extreme cold, or a bout of malaria. I shouted for the guard, but he just ignored my pleas, so I made David lay down upon the concrete slab of a bed, and covered him with the two rather smelly blankets, in an attempt to heat up his body. By this time, I was getting very worried myself, but the main concern uppermost in my mind was for David. I felt totally powerless, especially as my calls for the guard were so obviously being ignored.

After six hours of mental anguish, the chief of police returned to tell us we were both being released, but our passports for the time being, were being withheld. We were not allowed to leave the precincts of Rangoon, until such time that we were given explicit permission to do so. We were left to make our own way back to the Y.M.C.A. and on return, we found all our equipment had been searched thoroughly, and was scattered all over the bedroom of our recent accommodation. This was only our second day in Rangoon, and this experience left us both utterly shattered. David took this intrusion into our lives very badly, and was still in a state of shock that was very painful for me to watch. It was almost as if he had received a brutal kicking, but the confiscating of his passport (his British passport to which he was such a proud owner) was the fateful blow, knocking all the stuffing out of his usually jovial being.

He went into a deep decline of depression a very black mood, which was something I had never seen before. For the rest of this day, he refused to move from the security of the bedroom. He was no longer shivering physically, but the rest of him and certainly his mental state, remained traumatised with disbelief. There was a tap at our door, and we were both informed that the editor of the Rangoon Gazette was down stairs, wanting to talk with us. Unlike David who normally rose to such occasions he was morose and wished no truck whatsoever with any reporter. "You go Andy" David replied, "I'm in no mood to talk with anybody, let alone any reporter."

"Will you be OK on your own, while I get rid of this newspaper reporter?" I asked David.

"Yes Andy, but don't be too long" he replied.

I talked with this reporter fellow, although I was in no real mood for socializing. In the end, I told him we had been forced through circumstances to change our plans dramatically, as to go north through the Shan states to Assam India was explicitly forbidden. We would therefore now go by sea to Calcutta, although it would mean having to wait many weeks for a ship from Rangoon that we could take to either Bombay or Calcutta in India. Satisfied with this new twist to our story, he paid me the handsome sum of twenty pounds in kwats (Burmese currency) for the story and then left in a hurry, blabbing on about getting his story to bed. I went back upstairs to tell David of our good fortune, and about the yarn I had spun the reporter. David smiled at my cunning ruse, which I noted with pleasure, as this was the first time he smiled this dreadful black eventful day. With a little persuasion, he was tempted outside his room, to partake in some really good food, to celebrate our minor windfall.

Several days later, we were both instructed to go down to the police station. Here it was explained at great length, that because of our change of plan, (as printed by the local newspaper) our passports would be returned to us within a week with new three month visas, that would be more than long enough to cover our stay in Rangoon, before a ship in about six weeks time, would be available to take us both to India. The police had obviously done their homework, and were very helpful by giving us a gentleman's name to whom we should both go and see, regarding our passage by sea to Calcutta.

Now that David had received his beloved passport back, his normal demeanour returned with gusto, and he even warmed to the idea of going by sea to India. The very next day, we reported to the contact that the police had obligingly given us at the shipping office, only to find the cheapest working passage to Bombay would be at least ninety five pounds for the two of us, which was well beyond our budget. This disappointment for David was only too obvious, but I assured him, we would somehow find a way to raise the money and that we had a good six weeks in which to do just that.

"Something will turn up," I told David optimistically. What I failed to tell David at this time, was that I had no intentions whatsoever of going by sea, as my own mind was firmly set on doing this forbidden journey overland, as originally planned. I just had to find a way of telling David somehow, when the time was ripe, which most certainly was not here and now!

With his' passport safely back in his secure hands, David began to think more positively about his immediate future, which up until this morning looked rather bleak. We ate well that tea time, before retiring to bed feeling somewhat worn out, having walked across Rangoon to the dockside and shipping agent. When we were taking our usual bedtime shower, I took the initiative by soaping David down with as much tenderness and care as I could muster, hoping it would put David in a better frame of mind. While I cuddled into David's back at bed time, I told David, I would sell my Rolex Oyster Perpetual Chronograph watch if necessary, which would easily raise more than enough money to buy our tickets for our sea passage to India. David went very silent on this revelation at my guarantee for his safe passage to India. I remained silent, in readiness to gauge David's reaction to my statement of fact, not quite knowing what response he was likely to give me. He slowly turned to face me, full frontal, and taking my head cupped into his hands, he kissed me full on my lips.

"You don't need to do that," I said to David.

"Why not?" asked David, "You're my brother, I can do what I like. If I want to show you how much I love you, I can, because I'm entitled to" said David. (This was a statement of fact.)

David started to sob, as the tears started to leak from his eyes onto my chest.

"Why are you crying? I thought you would be pleased," I said.

"You don't know how happy I am," replied David, as his left hand started to caress my upper torso in an expression of love.

"Please don't, David you are making me feel embarrassed and uncomfortable." I said.

His left hand went down to my dick, and I instinctively put my right hand onto his left hand, to stop him going any further.

"Don't worry Andy," said David. "I don't intend to wank you off or anything, I couldn't do that, you're my brother, for fuck sake" said David.

His left hand remained on my chest and without thinking and perhaps because I was feeling nervous, I decided to tell David of my own plans to go overland to India. The shock of my statement, made David put distance between our bodies, as he mulled over the full meaning of my intentions. "You mean you will go overland, without me, on your own, by yourself?"

"Don't worry David, I will meet up with you in India, if you're prepared to wait for me" I added.

"You can't go alone, it is far too dangerous and anyway it's forbidden!" said David.

"Only if I get caught," I replied, too smugly.

David was stunned at my cavalier attitude, and remained silent, turning over with his back to me, not quite knowing how to deal with my stubbornness. I honed into his back, then putting my arm about his chest, I heaved his whole body close to me, so we fitted together as one.

"It is too dangerous for you David, because of your Chinese background, and that's why I think it would be better for you and safer if you go by sea," I explained at some length.

"I told you when we first met in Singapore of my real intentions, and when I do get to India, I will be in no hurry to move on, as I explained my real desire and ambition to join up with my climbing party in Darjeeling to climb in the Himalayas. Nothing has changed," I added, "Except my concern for your safety."

David remained silent, absorbing the full impact of my intentions, which for him, I couldn't have made any clearer. David, after many moments, slowly turned back in towards me, but still remained closed mouth as his hand gently explored my upper chest and shoulders. After a very pregnant pause, David said, "how soon do you plan to take off, on this forbidden journey?" His voice was full of irony, with a strong hint of sarcastic foreboding and undertones in his searching question.

After some reflection, and with a suitable respectful pause to collect my thoughts together, I said softly, and without emotion in my tone, "I thought we could go up country together, as far as Mandalay as you have so much time to wait for your ship to India. This way, with luck, I could get underway, and you yourself would not have long to wait for me to join you in Calcutta, where we could meet up at the Y.M.C.A. our next post box."

My statement was followed by yet another unwanted silence by David, who was obviously having great difficulty, in getting his head around this very sudden change of events. "You might not be able to get through overland," David said, more as a statement of fact rather than a cloaked threat with any hidden menace of intent.

"In that case, I would return, and seek some other alternative route if I'm forced to, but as a last and desperate act to stay alive. Don't worry David, I'm not on some kind of a suicide mission, I'm enjoying my life far too much to want to put an end to it!"

"Are you?" said David with profanity!

Another pregnant pause followed, before David declared "let's talk about this in the morning."

"OK," I replied "But I won't change my mind!" I added.

With this uneasy truce between us, we both had a somewhat restless night together, but when I did wake up it was to find David embracing my body, with more than the usual show of affection, much to my surprise. I looked at his face, which seemed at peace with a kind of expression of serenity, or was it some kind of acceptance on his behalf? I wondered. I leaned down towards his face and gently kissed him on the cheek with affection. David opened his eyes slowly, and broke into one of his famous smiles, looking up into my eyes, which were full of tenderness and overt caring. "You are going to have a safe but difficult journey," he stated in a matter of fact voice, full of meaning.

Completely bowled over by this statement that took me unawares, I replied softly "I hope so."

David answered, "I dreamt about your journey last night, so believe me, you are going to be successful, you wait and see."

After a casual breakfast, we made our way to the police station to obtain permission to go up country. David was not altogether happy at being in this dreadful place, as recent painful memories of our arrest, provoked uneasiness within his heart. The chief was talking with one of his officers at the front desk, so I waited with a display of great respect for him to finish his conversation. Having done so, he looked up at me with a distinct expression of enquiry on his face. "May I have a word with you, please sir?" I asked, while David bowed his head, looking at something of interest on the floor at his feet.

"Come through," he curtly replied to me.

"I'll wait for you here Andy" said David, so I went through to his office alone. To cut a long story short, I came out from his office with a written paper of permission that gave both David and myself a right to travel up north as far as Mandalay, and with a hundred and fifty U.S.A. dollars in my pocket. David was more than relieved to find that I had not been locked up, as we quickly left the station.

"Where is your Rolex watch?" asked David, who was quick to notice my bare wrist.

"I've sold it to the chief of police," I replied smugly, grinning all over my boat race.

"Where are we going now?" asked David, in a state of shock.

"To the shipping agent," I replied, still smiling.

Remaining somewhat stunned, David withdrew into his shell of silence, as we made our way to the dockside. I handed over seventy three dollars for a one way ticket to Bombay, for David's fare to India. Having completed the transaction, we retired to a nearby hostelry to celebrate. I handed David a further twenty five dollars, leaving the remainder of about fifty dollars, for future expenses. David had some difficulty in coming to terms with this unexpected turn of events, but was mainly at a loss in comprehending all that had recently transpired.

When we returned that night after our usual evening showers and ablutions, David had more or less returned to his normal jovial self, and was obviously at peace with himself. We chatted away freely, like a pair of hungry chicks waiting for mother hen to return to the nest at feeding time. The altercation from the night before now completely forgotten, as we talked excitedly about our trip north together, on our way up country, on the road to Mandalay. After exhausting ourselves with jovial chit chat of our immediate intentions, David ordered me to lay face down as he climbed across my buttocks to give me a massage. The closeness of his body, and the skill through the tips of his fingers and the palms of his hands, lulled me into a physical state of euphoric high. This sensual bliss was almost too much for me to keep control of my disturbing sexual arousal.

When David, having completed one side (back) ordered me to turn over, I was already in an advanced state of losing control. Having turned front upwards, David was obviously aware of my embarrassing predicament, without a word he climbed off the bed and turned out the light, to save my display of having an acute and now very strong erection.

"I'm sorry David" I said softly, "I didn't mean to get out of control."

"That's alright Andy, You're my brother, and you have no need to explain yourself to me."

With that he told me to turn onto my side, so he could snuggle into my back. David wrapped himself about me, as we both fell off to sleep.

We spent a further three days exploring the wonderful sights and pagodas of Rangoon before starting on the next leg of our adventure together. With our last night in Rangoon tucked up behind us, we have both reconciled ourselves to the realization that our joint venture together was now on a limited life span, making us both determined to enjoy what days we had left in each others' company.

Chapter Twenty-Six

The road to Mandalay

Not knowing what twists of fate each of our futures held ahead of us, made us both even more endearing towards our brotherly spirit, we both felt strongly for the other. For safety reasons only, we were determined to stay on the main road, all the way to Mandalay. From Rangoon to Mandalay was a good three hundred and eighty miles, with a strong possibility of covering this distance in three stages. Stage one, to Toungyi about one third en route, then stage two, to Kengtung and finally, stage three, from Kengtung to Mandalay. These major towns were chosen because they also had a Y.M.C.A. and the three day trip that we planned, was considered to be a realistic target.

Our first day was a piece of cake, as we received our very first lift almost immediately, on one of a three truck convoy. In fact this first leg, saw us both booking into the Y.M.C.A. in Tounggyi just after midday. We spent the rest of the day sightseeing, and visiting a number of pagodas, although they were not as impressive as the 'World Peace Pagoda' of Rangoon, they were all so different, and very interesting. We also spent a great deal of time shopping, and walking around the local bazaar or food market. David purchased a number of food ingredients for our evening meal. By the time we returned to our Y.M.C.A. base, we were both tired and hungry, but otherwise feeling very content. David produced a wonderful culinary Chinese evening meal, and having sated our thirst and stuffed our faces, we soon settled down for the evening, with David playing a mean game of chess against an American traveller, who was also staying that night before heading south.

Feeling very tired, I made my way up to bed alone, and promptly fell off to sleep very quickly. Many hours later, David crawled into bed alongside me. Surprisingly, David woke first and gently shook me awake by my shoulder. As I turned in towards his body, we both realized I had retained a massive erection, from a dream I must have been having, while I was fast asleep.

"I think you should let go of all your sexual tension" David said, as he peeled back the single top sheet from my body.

"Maybe I need a piss" I lied to David, as he studied my very hard, unforgiving dick.

"Give yourself a quick wank," David said casually, as he enclosed his palm around my stiff shaft. "If you really want one, I'll give you one" said David, as he lit up a cigarette for both of us, and handing me one, with his free hand.

"No thanks David, I'll manage myself, but thanks anyway."

We both lay back enjoying our smoke, but my erection refused to obey orders.

As we finished our smokes together, David uttered, "Fuck, now you've given me a hard on," as he peeled back the cover to display his pride and joy. Without a word, David kneeled across my lower legs and promptly started to pull his dick off. Now, no longer feeling at all embarrassed, I too started to do like wise. Within seconds, David came, his load all over my chest, while only seconds behind him, I too, shot my cum to join his controlled puddle of goo. Having finished ourselves off, I lay back, to enjoy my high in sexual heaven. Wondering what I was going to do with our waste, David then lay down on top of me, to spread as much of our discharged spunk onto his own body.

"What are you doing David?" I demanded to know.

"Why should you have all of it?" asked David, who climbed off of my body, and then lay down beside me.

After a while, we both raced down to take a quick shower and breakfast. Over breakfast, David produced a wad of a hundred kwats in Burmese currency, while he broadly grinned, bragging to me with pride, that he had won the money from the Yank at a game of chess last night. He then counted out the booty, handing me half of the spoils. Having finished our breakfast, we were in the throes of settling our bill, when the Burmese manager asked us both if we were still heading north, to Mandalay. Having assured him we were, he introduced us to a Burmese traveller, who was also heading north, to where he lived in Kengtung, who then offered us both a lift, in his pick-up truck. We thanked our host, and quickly accepted this kind lift.

This gentleman, of about forty years of age was in the building trade, with a rather fierce looking Doberman Pincer dog lying down in the back of his pick-up, protecting a sundry of items of expensive plumbing accessories. This one man dog, a pedigree amongst thousands of strays all over Burma, littering the countryside, that appeared to belong to no one in particular, certainly stood out, and was very much a prized possession of its proud owner. David did not trust this particular breed of dog, one of which had taken a chunk out of one of his many cousins' arse, who mistakenly had bravely attempted to stroke the animal. With only one seat available up front in the cab, I volunteered to share my arse, with the dog in the back, which turned out to be a big softie, as he calmly lay settled across my midriff. David who was worried I was going to be savaged by this beast, spent most of the journey, nervously glancing through the small glass window set into the cab's body work.

Meanwhile, the dog comfortably settled into a casual resting place across my groin area, snoring his head off, wallowing in the heat that my midriff generated. The thought of upsetting this animal, which could easily deprive me of my manhood, ensured that I made no sudden moves to disturb or upset his majesty. We made excellent time, only stopping briefly for a much needed long glass of ice cold coffee, in the heat of the day. Needless to say, David was not impressed when I suggested jokingly, we change places for the second half of the journey to Kengtung. Once the gentleman had established that David was indeed Chinese, and not Japanese, (whom the Burmese detested most vehemently, and with very good cause, from the recent Burma campaign,) they appeared to get on famously, and chatted together with a sprinkling of both Chinese and English tongues. Glancing through the rear window from time to time, they were chatting and laughing together, like really good friends.

As we approached Kengtung, the big softie of a Doberman sat up, alert, paying attention, obviously knowing he was near his home. We drew up into a short gravel drive, to a house that was set back from the main road, and the dog barked with excitement, before leaping out of the pick-up, heading for his own front door. By this time, my stiff body was suffering pins and needles, as a direct result of so much inactivity, and lying spread out, upon an uncomfortable metal ribbed floor in the back of the pick-up truck. I was in turn, extracted from the rear of the pick-up, by both the Burmese gentleman and David, feeling rather battered and bruised, as if I had just gone ten rounds in a Thai kick boxing bout.

The front door was opened by an equally young charming Chinese lady, who turned out to be the Burmese man's wife. She was obviously much younger than her husband, and was in fact the same age as both David and myself, at twenty two years of age. The one thing we noticed about the Burmese in particular was their hospitality and polite kindness. (Except for the police of course.) We were both invited in for tea and eats, which was a hybrid of food between both Chinese and Burmese cultures. The lady of the house, simply known as Mrs Woo, was grateful, to be able to converse in pure Cantonese, with David no less, so Mr Woo and I got better acquainted in our limited English, which was more than sufficient. The Woos' dog was more than content to continue to spread himself over my lap, as it would appear he had adopted me, regardless to my wishes.

After tea, Mrs Woo disappeared to run the hot tub for me to soak my battered bones in, but I would not get undressed, until after she vacated the steam room. Once I was luxuriating in their oversized tub, David came in to join me, and wasted no time in making himself at home. "We are staying the night," proclaimed David, "because Mr Woo is going into Mandalay tomorrow morning, and has offered us both a lift."

"Does that mean I'll have to sit in the back of his bloody pick-up again?" I asked.

"No" said David, "he thinks you have already been punished enough," he jested. "So, we will be going by car," he proclaimed.

"Thank God" I sighed. As I gingerly eased my butt in to a more comfortable position. "I hope the bed is really soft," I joked, "and your expertise, for a massage tonight will be most appreciated."

"Oh," said David, "I'm not too sure about that, after all your randy sexual behaviour last night."

I looked at David in disbelief, thinking to myself that he was a right cheeky bastard. He suddenly broke into a smile, having teased me successfully, he said, "we'll see" with a doubt in his voice "we'll see" he smiled.

Mr Woo decided to join us, as he entered wearing only a longie. (A kind of full length wrap that went from waist to ankle.) This item of clothing commonly worn all over Burma and especially in the northern regions, is the equivalent to national dress in this part of the world, and is a very comfortable form of casual attire. Mr Woo got into the tub, between David and me, perfectly at ease with his and our complete nudity, as if it was the most natural function imaginable. David more accustomed to this mutual way of bathing, even with total strangers, lathered up a natural sponge, and then proceeded to soap up Mr Woo's torso. Although I was no longer totally surprised at this love of preening others' bodies, I was never the less intrigued at what after all was a most acceptable trait amid eastern culture. The washing lovingly of another's body, other than your own, is deemed to be an acknowledgement of respect and acceptance.

Mr Woo, stood up, as David bathed and soaped the more intimate parts of his body. "Right" said Mr Woo, "your turn Andy, I'll do you, if that's agreeable to you," he said in good English.

I stood up with a contrived coolness, doing my best not to look embarrassed, as both David and Mr Woo set to work on my entire torso. I was conscious only of my lack of endowment, compared with the other two, who if anything, had more than their fair share of equipment between them. This was obviously more my problem than theirs, as they joyfully soaped me down with great care and laughter. When I was deemed to be suitably done, we both set about David, with gusto, and the same attention. When finished, all three of us then settled back to wallow in unadulterated prime comfort.

The evening spread on the table at dinner, was the best of both Burmese and Chinese cuisines, and we all unashamedly gorged ourselves to overflowing. Mrs Woo, being the very attentive wife, disappeared into the kitchen, to clean up the debris from so many dishes. There were no servants or children to help or hinder this household, I noticed. David and Mr Woo settled down to play several games of Chinese checkers, as we all smoked hand rolled Burmese cheroots, which I was rapidly becoming addicted to. The scene across the household was one of utter contentment, each individual more than satisfied, with his or her lot and place, in such a wonderful world. By 9.30pm I was beginning to wane a little, and found it difficult to openly stop yawning. Mrs Woo, showed me into our bedroom for the night, tucked away at the back of the house, and well away from the traffic noise, on the main road outside. Just as I was climbing into bed, David came in and promptly got undressed. Without a word, he then started to give me such a wonderful massage that lulled me into a comatose state of sleep. I fell off the world, plunging into a deep slumber, long before I got a chance to turn over onto my back.

I must have been more exhausted than I thought, as Mrs Woo accompanied by the dog, brought us early morning tea. The dog jumped up onto the bed, and immediately started to lick the sleepiness from my bleary eyes and face. David woke up with a start, face to face with the beast, before leaping out of bed, much to all our surprises, as nude as the day he was born. Mrs Woo left the room giggling with laughter, but David refused to get back into the bed, to rejoin my canine companion or myself. "What have you got that's special, with that animal that I don't have?" asked David.

I looked down at David's erection that until now, he himself was unaware of, and calmly said to him "well I don't have a stiffy for a start!"

David looked down at his own appendage, then quickly donned his shorts, before sitting down to enjoy his first morning cuppa. "I wonder if Mrs Woo noticed?" said David with a frown.

"What do you think?" I replied with a smile.

We both laughed out loud in chorus; enjoying the sheer spontaneity of David's predicament, with such hilarity it brought Mr Woo to the door, who looked in on us with an unexplained questionable smile, wanting to know why we were both splitting our sides with laughter. David went to great length, explaining in Cantonese about his naughtiness, where by Mr Woo seeing the funny side of it, joined in the merry chorus of joviality. At breakfast, the joke was shared with Mrs woo, which enhanced and enchanted her, as David now sitting across the table from Mrs Woo, lowered his head in obvious embarrassment, much to all our pleasure.

After thankful farewells to Mrs Woo, we gratefully took our leave, heading once again north to Mandalay, which was still more than a hundred miles away. With the three of us sitting up front, across the comfort of the old fashioned bench seat of Mr Woo's classic Black Humber Hawk saloon car, complete with the smell of leather, and highly polished burr walnut facia, this was heady stuff indeed, as we sank into the unblemished tan upholstery.

The car was immaculate, and even the dog was not allowed to encroach on the inside if this beautifully kept interior. Mr Woo, who was so obviously chuffed with his ownership, explained to David and myself, he used this rather very special vehicle for business, high days, and holidays only, as the immediate and instantaneous confidence boost to his ego was plain to see. We cruised at a leisurely fifty miles an hour to conserve petrol, which was sometimes a little difficult to obtain, as one of the displeasures of owning such a vehicle was feeding the beast, and even at a relatively slow speed, it tended to be rather a thirsty monster. We stopped for lunch at a well established roadside eating place, and I noted a number of young kids of both sexes begging for alms. This was the first time since leaving Rangoon, I noted this otherwise common feature of Burmese life. A Burmese street urchin lad of about ten years of age, was offered the job of looking after the prized car, while we were inside gorging our bellies. Mr Woo tore a ten kwat note of local currency in half, handing the lad one piece, with a promise of the other half, when we returned.

Over lunch, we or rather Mr Woo, wanted to know more about our travels, and more importantly, our immediate future plans. David explained in detail, how he would be returning to Mandalay in a week or so, whereby I would be going further on, into the north Shan states and overland to India. Mr Woo was spellbound by David's open revelation, as he started to look at me, with concerned but renewed interest.

"Listen Andy" said Mr Woo, "I would like to introduce you to a newspaper reporter friend of mine, when we get to Mandalay, who will oblige me, by helping you, on the next stage of your journey.

I quickly replied "That would be most helpful, because, I have a feeling, I'm going to need all the help I can muster."

"Just as long as you realize how dangerous this trek to India is going to be, but David has explained to me, how determined you are to go on. Beyond the Shan states is unknown territory to me," added Mr Woo.

"But I do know, that this is an area that is no longer controlled by the government, and people just disappear completely, never to be seen or heard of again. We in the south refer to everything north of Mandalay as bandit or dacoit's territory and it is fraught with great risks." Mr Woo went on, "However, this newspaper friend of mine knows the area well, and is himself a Shan, he makes frequent visits to see his ageing parents, in the Shan states."

This part of the countryside we were travelling was very green, among the foothills of the mountainous terrain that could clearly be seen in the distance ahead, the nearer we got to Mandalay. The lower hills that we were now well into were very fertile, with great tracts of land being cultivated into paddy fields. The rice bowl table for most of the south was grown in this region, we were informed. The Burmese people, rich or poor, were very industrious in all things agricultural, and could be seen working the fields, morning till dusk. Whole families, from tiny children to teenagers of both sexes would extensively work the household's unit of land, where their living would be won daily, against the ravages of nature. The wealthier peasants would own their own oxen, that were truly beasts of burden, working at many a different task, doing the heavy work of ploughing, operating crude irrigation systems, or carrying the family, by pulling the heavy wooden carts to market, for the sale of produce. There was very little sign of any agricultural machinery on the land, although the common bicycle was much in evidence, as most individuals seem to own one, with the more affluent, owning a put-put or old fashioned two stroke scooter.

Mr Woo emphasized, that by and large his people were a contented lot; they only resented government red tape or interference. (A phenomenon shared by most people around the world, and understandably so.) Like most races, they only wanted to be left alone, to get on with their own particular brand of living in peace. An extremely warm and friendly race, especially to most foreigners or visitors to their country, and would go to great lengths to help any traveller, but had very trusting loyalty towards the British, who they loved almost as much as their own. They hated Japanese most vehemently, who in recent times raped both their people as well as their countryside. They were always suspicious of Chinese. who bordered much of their country and were always seen as likely invaders, always ready to swallow up entire countries, to feed the world's single largest population. Burma's geographical position, sandwiched between two of the most populated countries in the world, namely India to the north east and China to the east always posed a threat, or at least that's what most of the Burmese people assumed. They were on good terms with their immediate neighbour India, indeed there were many Indian immigrants living among the Burmese people, who were well accepted. The Chinese were a different matter entirely, and similar thoughts to their arch enemy the Japs, who they saw as a real threat of a more constant nature. A menacing dark cloud that threatened to burst at the seams, with very little concern to niceties of political indifferences or protocol.

As we came into the outskirts of Mandalay, a newsflash over the car radio, related the dastardly deeds of a major skirmish, between government forces and insurgents. The actual details were ambiguous, or sketchy to say the least. This took place somewhere north of Bhamo, which was a small town on my forth coming planned route. Both David and Mr Woo, eyed me with silent, but obvious consternation, which only reinforced everything that Mr Woo had spoken about earlier on, during our journey. I refused to be drawn into any debate about the subject, preferring to play ignorant, by holding my own counsel, and keeping my real thoughts on this enlightening news to myself. The orderly planned layout of Mandalay was a very pleasant surprise, after so much wild but green countryside, which we travelled across most of the day from Kengtung. The sun was low in the horizon, as the Humber Hawk came to rest, at the steps of the Y.M.C.A., which was larger than we, both imagined. There was great emotion displayed, as we said our final farewells to Mr Woo, who assured me his newspaper friend would be in touch soon, as Mr Woo himself would be spending the night with this important friend. We booked into the Y.M.C.A. in total silence, with the cloud of the recent radio news, still fresh in our minds. I could tell that David was working himself up to or into a state of flux, in readiness for a more verbal assault later, as we climbed the stairs, in search of bedroom number 6. "An evil number" David remarked, as a prefix to the devil's own number of "666." Ignoring his attempt to bait me, as I put my gear down on the nearest bed, I promptly left in a hurry, in desperate need of a piss, telling David I would meet him in the lobby downstairs.

The Y.M.C.A. here in Mandalay was a busy popular place, easily the busiest I've seen on our travels so far. Another 'white American' with two Chinese students in tow were also busy booking accommodation, and the loud mouth American was making it abundantly clear to all within earshot he wanted a room for all three of his party.

This brash American was in his mid twenties, with a fair hair crew cut, [not unlike my own] dwarfing his two Chinese cousins, standing a good six feet tall, with fantastically blue staring eyes. His unfortunate loud mouthed manner, was certainly not designed to win over any friends, as his demure pair of Chinese students stood by with bowed heads, looking very embarrassed.

David came down the stairs, and immediately engaged in conversation, (or tried to,) with the Chinese students, who by now were looking very intimidated, and perhaps a little frightened. These two kids looked about fourteen years of age, but David assured me, they were both eighteen years old, otherwise they would not be allowed to travel outside of China. To me, the whole party of three, including the Yank, was very unusual and smelt a bit fishy. Anyway, with David getting short shift, from this trio of such a rare mixture, he rapidly lost interest, as his belly was now demanding to be fed. "Come on Andy, let's go and find somewhere to eat." David said.

No sooner had we sat down, having ordered our feast from a very comprehensive menu, when in walked our merry band of three, with the American leading his two Chinese Pekinese puppies in tow. Seeing us sat at the table, the Yank came over and without saying a word, sat down beside David, with not so much as a by your leave. I blew my top instantly, demanding to know what the hell this Yank thought he was doing, without a specific invitation to join us. (Or words to that effect, only just a little more colourful.)

Having been stung rather viciously between his very blue eyes, the Yank promptly stood up, and suddenly became all sweetness and light. He could see I was still smouldering, so he quickly begged my pardon, and just as quickly departed to a more remote part of the restaurant. Meanwhile, David sat by my side with his mouth wide agape, absolutely flabbergasted, in disbelief, at my unwarranted outburst of sudden rage. I reached over to David's opened face, and calmly closed his gaping jaw hole, to prevent him catching any flies that happened to be passing by. In all the time we had known each other, David had never seen such a display of pure anger from me, which rather took both of us by surprise, as my ruddy face began to return to a more favourable colour. Fortunately for the both of us, the waiter started at that precise moment in time, to bring us our food. We continued to enjoy our meal in silence, and without any further interruptions.

It was a cool evening, now that some of my self imposed heat had dispersed from my body, and as we returned to the Y.M.C.A. in silence, each with our own thoughts, I remarked to David that I thought tomorrow was climatically speaking, shaping up to be a good one. He acknowledged my interpretation with a grunt and a nod of his head, as we walked through the doors of the Y.M.C.A. and upstairs to bed. On reaching our bedroom, we wasted no time in getting undressed with David pushing our beds together as one. Not a single word was spoken between us, as I snuggled closely into David's back which gave added warmth to our naked bodies as we quietly fell off to a deep slumber. We both slept well past our usual time of rise, as there was no urgency to get up early. David slipped out of bed, donning his shorts to run down for a quick pee, while a lit up a cigarette and lay back on my pillow, enjoying the fact we were both very much alive and kicking. David rejoined me, as I shared my fag with him, with a sigh of contentment. David leaned over to me putting the side of his face gently upon my chest before asking "Why did you lose the rag with that American?"

After some thought I answered David, "Because loud mouthed arrogant Yanks tend to forget that they, like us, are guests in this country, and have no cause to abuse this privilege!"

David remained silent as his hand went down and took hold of my dick that was flaccid, and resting in peace.

"If you get me hard brother, I'll kill you, because I'm not in the mood for any of your sexual shenanigans."

David instinctively withdrew his hand with speed, saying, "OK Andy, but you don't need to be so bad tempered about it."

I leaned over and kissed him gently on the cheek, then calmly got out of bed to get dressed. I turned down the bed covers, to note that David was not in the least bit sexually aroused, as I told him I would meet him downstairs for breakfast.

It was already past 9am as I ordered a big jug of coffee and Burmese breakfast cakes, in the sitting area of the large open foyer. David quickly joined me, as we munched our way through a leisurely breakfast. Shortly before 10am as we both sat back to enjoy our second cigarette of the day, a very smartly dressed young Shan man of about thirty years of age came through the entrance, after a very brief word with the lad at the desk, came over towards us. In very polite English he asked us both if we were David and Andy.

"Yes" we replied together. We invited him to sit with us, as he showed us his press card, on which he had deliberately covered up his name, explaining with great care, that it would not be wise for us to know his name, for secrecy and security purposes. We accepted willingly this cloak and dagger clandestine need on his part, because at this time all editorials were closely monitored, especially in this part of Burma. After a short while, I suggested to David that he should leave us both to converse alone, as I didn't want David involved in any skulduggery I might be getting myself into. David was not best pleased at being cut out, so to speak, of this part of the proceedings, but I felt more for his own safety, than my own, it was best if his involvement was kept to a minimum, after all, my intentions were far from legal, and with the arrest of both of us in Rangoon still fresh in our minds, I wanted to avoid any possibility of a repeat performance.

The Shan reporter said he could arrange transport for me alone, as far as Namkham on the Chinese border, after which I would most certainly be on my own. However, even this would take some time to arrange, and with some difficulty, and that I should not expect this to happen overnight, so to speak, and would be more like a week to arrange at the earliest. He would be sure to get in touch with me, probably at short notice, as to where I would be leaving from. Meanwhile, he expressed several times, how important it was not to discuss this with anyone what so ever. Under no circumstances was I to make any attempt to contact him, or any other newspaper reporter. He shook me by the hand briefly, and without another word left. David, who had been watching the both of us from afar, returned to join me at the table. Thankfully, he did not seek to glean any information from me, as we ordered yet another coffee between us.

We spent the rest of the day exploring the delights of Mandalay with great interest, although it was little more than a large town in the fifties, it was a well kept clean place, with much to offer the tourist or visitor. Not being certain, exactly how much time I had left to spend with David, I redoubled my efforts to be as nice to him as possible. This, I might add, did not go unnoticed by David, who was dying to know as much as I was able to tell him, which for obvious reasons was little, as I continued to play my cards very close to my chest.

The following day, we went to see a film together, but with so much preoccupying my mind, I could not for the life of me tell you anything about the film that passed before my eyes. I did notice David take hold of my hand into his lap, but for some unknown reason, I didn't have the heart to reprimand him over this overt sign of affection. We saw most, if not all the sights that Mandalay had to offer, and David tried hard to coax me into a well kept brothel, to relieve our sexual build up of testosterone, that both of us were beginning to feel. Sadly, but reluctantly, I declined this very attractive offer, because I just wasn't in the right mood, or frame of mind. (My mind was still preoccupied.)

This same night, David took me for a slap up meal, followed by some rather nice, if somewhat potent rice wine. (Not saki.) By bedtime I was certainly in a state of high, euphoric, alcoholic, well being, with an unusual fit of the giggles, as David climbed over my body to give me one of his relaxing massages. I really wasn't in any state to deny either of our pleasures that his magic hands were capable of bestowing.

"You're not doing my back first?" I asked of David, in my now slurred speech.

"Just close your eyes and let yourself go completely," David ordered, in a firm but caring voice.

I closed my eyes to give in graciously to his commands, as I felt my neck and shoulder muscles relax, under the power of his fingertips. Methodically, he slowly worked down the front of my body, from my chest to my stomach, and then very gently, he lifted my penis onto my abdomen, and started to work my groin areas in tandem, with unbelievable sensuality. I knew without needing to look, that I was already fully aroused, but in my carefree state of mind, I didn't care any more. He cupped both his palms gently around my testicles, and with expertise had my balls pulsating in no time at all, and on the very verge of my penile eruption, David lay down on top of me, between my spread legs. I could feel his own very hard erection pressing into my genitalia. At the time before my sexual explosion, I looked down at David, who was resting on his elbows, so that his own upper torso was well clear of my chest. He himself erupted, just seconds ahead of me, as his penis shot out his spunk, all over my chest, with my own white cum joining his soon afterwards. David continued to lay on top of me, long after both of us had emptied our full white liquid cargo. A few moments later, David was lying alongside me, as I studied the huge quantity of our double discharge. Armed with a towel, David proceeded to clean me off, with great tenderness and care. Without using the towel he then encased my penis with his lips, sucking the residue of sperm clean with his mouth. I just lay there, neither shocked nor angry, but just accepting David's actions, without question.

Long after he had finished, he lit up a pair of cigarettes, handing me one to smoke in peace. "I'm not complaining David, but why did you just perform on me?" I asked.

"Because we both badly needed to get rid of our sexual frustrations and because you're my brother." He replied simply.

I turned over onto my side, to face him, noticing he still had a semi erection that was still badly leaking from his corona's eye. I took the corner of the towel to wipe the last of his dribble of spunk away, before turning over ready for sleep. David snuggled into my back, where I still found him unmoved by morning. Neither of us ever discussed this sexual encounter, perhaps because neither of us felt any particular guilt or shame, nor did we need to.

Over breakfast that morning, the lad behind reception handed me a sealed envelope, which contained a date and a place, I was to report to, the following late evening at 9pm. I did not show the contents of this letter or note to David, but then I didn't need to, as he asked me directly when was I due to leave Mandalay.

"Tomorrow evening" I replied softly.

David was determined to put on a brave face, but I knew instinctively he was churning up inside.

Why does parting company bring so much sorrow?

To greet a fellow traveller who aspires to the same ideals, and shares the same values of excitements or ambitions as one self, is always a satisfying and thrilling prospect. Then to join up together, experiencing the human bonding of close comradeship, in undertaking the good times along with the hardships, with complete harmony and trust in one another's abilities, always brings great joy to ones endeavours. The sharing of so much between two people, who are bound by natures wonders, as well as human faults, that we all have an abundance of, but with hindsight and time, are able to confront and perhaps even overcome, is in itself some kind of divine blessing. These failings that we all share are but a stepping stone to better understanding of ourselves. Show me a man, or woman that is totally fault free from such vices, and I say unto thee you do not belong on this earth, that we are all compelled to share together. The uniqueness of every individual among all of us is a miracle to behold, cementing together with adhesion the very thread of life itself. The fragility of human life, along with the challenge that life constantly throws at us is the very essence of living. How one chooses to face or accept, the options that are offered to each and every one of us, is as individual as life is complex. 'Let no man cast the first stone' until you yourself have experienced every twist or turn along life's trodden path, which can sometimes be very cruel indeed. The resilience of human fabric is an awe inspiring event, which is just a small part of the overall composition in life's tapestry. The human kindness often expressed by total strangers is proof, if proof be needed, of mans fight to live in harmony with each other, and to which we are all capable to some degree, of displaying. Often these emotions can sometimes be overpowering, but regardless, they are emotions with profound meaning of understanding, often crossing impossible cultural and racial boundaries. These are just a very few thoughts of the most wonderful world we all share, providing we truly open our eyes, but more importantly, open our hearts to one another with sincere heartfelt intentions towards the world we share.

This last day in Mandalay together, was destined from the start, to be a long and painful one. Each of us afraid to share each others thoughts, only heightening the tension of real; feelings that we both felt towards and for the other. The daytime shuffled its feet, dragging itself into an even longer evening, but finally and thankfully, the allotted time in readiness for my ultimate departure was upon us. David pleaded with me to be allowed to come with me to the place of departure, which cut my open wound even deeper. I reluctantly agreed however, so after a share out of our equipment, we both felt I would need on my solo jungle trek ahead of me, we left the Y.M.C.A. together, heading for the Man-May Motor Transport Company, where a bus passage by road all the way to the Chinese border, some three hundred and eighty miles due east would take me on my way. Just before 9pm that evening, as we approached the main office to the Man-May Company, I insisted to David that we say our final goodbyes. I handed David a letter or note with my aunt's details and address in the New Forrest, as we warmly hugged and kissed each other. We were both crying profusely, as we clung to each other, neither of us willing to release the physical hold of our embrace on each other. In desperation, we pushed each other apart, and then walked away, neither looking back, as we both left to go our separate ways.

**David Kwan,
on horseback**

Myself, carrying a 120lb load, in Burma

Camping alongside a river - Burma

**Ringing the gong outside
a Buddist Temple**

Pagoda – Mandalay, Burma

Interior of the Pagoda

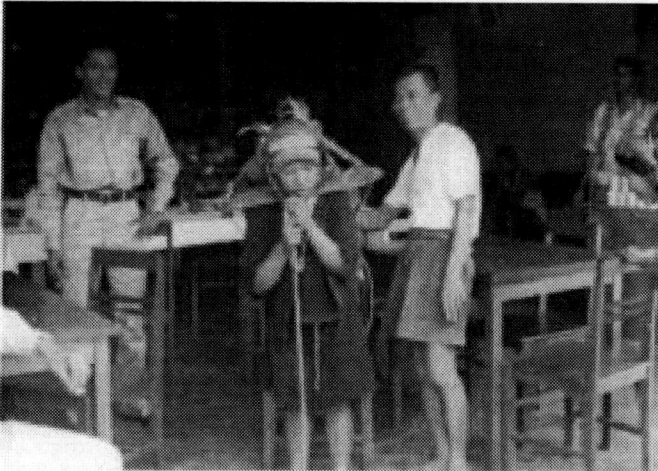

North Burma – Café stop – Shan Woman

**The author in Longie, near Burma/China border –
Namkam, where I stayed with Doctor Seagraves.
(The Burma Surgeon.)**

**Three brothers who gave me
a lift in their lorry & looked
after me 'Up Country',
& owners of Amber mines**

**David at Mandalay Bazaar,
before returning to
Rangoon, <u>alone.</u>**

The Burma Surgeon – Dr. Gordon S. Seagrave

Two different views of Namkam Hospital

Chapter Twenty-Seven

"Dr. Seagraves I presume?"

Now feeling quite alone, for the first time since I met up with David Kwan in Singapore, I approached the makeshift garage of the Man-May Motor Transport Company of Mandalay. This was a company that specialized in running a small fleet of clapped out single decked buses, from Mandalay to the China border at Namkham. This almost three hundred mile trip was done on a weekly basis, and surprisingly, there were always plenty of passengers available for this route, in both directions. I reported to the main transport office, that was little more than a ramshackle shack. Mr Muy Mein, the transport manager - owner, and its only real mechanic, was half Burmese and half Chinese. A very enterprising one man band show, having no real competition, or any opposition for this particular route, which was not at all surprising really, as no one else was nuts enough to want to do this excursion anyway.

This secondary arterial route, that left Mandalay, going due east, reached deep into the eastern north Shan states, and was also very notorious dacoit country, where the countryside itself was most definitely rigidly controlled, by these bandits. No government or even a suspected official would attempt this run, without a heavily armed guard of government soldiers. Their preferred form of transport was by rail. Indeed, Mr Muy Mein himself, was taking a great risk, by aiding and abetting me in undertaking this preliminary stage of my journey.

I was secreted aboard one of two buses making this run, on this fateful trip and was given the whole of the backseat to myself, and my now very heavy rucksack. Just after 9pm the two bus convoy set off, amongst much jubilation by my fellow passengers, who were in boisterous mood. What a complete mixture of life was aboard our bus, with entire families including their newly purchased goats, and crated chickens that constantly clucked their joyful tune. To any outside observer, such as myself, the scene was one of human chaos, but in this part of the world, it was considered perfectly normal. This charabanc, that rattled its way at high speed through the night's darkness, penetrating the meandering country, like a man made missile, on some death defying mission it seemed frightening, at least to me, a perfect stranger, among strangers, with whom I could not converse. However, I noticed very soon, that I was the only one that felt unsettled, as the happy band of mixed Burmese society in front of me, from my observational wooden seat platform, in the rear, chatted excitedly, as if they were on some very special outing or mystery tour of adventure. The children continued to play their imaginary animated games, with great gusto and laughter, determined to enjoy themselves fully on their wonderful outing.

I unpacked some of my softer equipment, namely my sleeping bag, spreading it lavishly over the back seat, causing great interest among my fellow passengers, but especially the children, who were fascinated at my antics. I stretched out my weary body, full length upon this newly made makeshift cushion with the best of intentions, knowing full well I would not be able to get any shut eye, but at least I would go through the motions of my foreign upbringing. No sooner had I made myself reasonably comfortable, when a little scruff of a boy about five years old, decided on his own part, to come and share my over indulgence. This little lad with big almond shaped very dark eyes, calmly climbed on top of me, and then quickly fell to sleep. His Ma and Pa looked at me from four seats away, and smiled their approval. Like Mr Woo's dog, this bit of a boy had decided to adopt me for the night, and I had no say in the matter.

Just after 3a.m. in the morning, I looked at my Mickey Mouse cheap replacement watch, as the bus came to a very sudden screeching stop, when the driver stood on the brakes in some kind of emergency. At this unearthly hour most of my fellow passengers were in a state of semi consciousness, somewhere in a twilight zone, when two heavily armed dacoits boarded the bus to inspect it. One of them was a particularly nasty looking piece of work, and had an old British army bren gun slung across his shoulder. (This was a weapon I was very familiar with.) He paraded himself up and down the aisle of the bus, leering threateningly as if trying to make a point. The passengers that were still alive to the situation casually looked at this man of great bravado, and then just as casually turned round in their seats, in an attempt to get back to sleep. This nonchalant gesture by some of my fellow passengers was most disarming, but they had obviously seen the like of this situation many times before, and did not seem intimidated in the least by the action of these two thugs. The Gorilla approached the rear of the bus, and was coming towards me, I closed my eyes in a sham attempt to feign sleep, with little Jimmy still cradled in my arms, blissfully sleeping on unaware of this dramatic interlude.

Several minutes later, the driver restarted his engine, and was soon hurtling along the twisting highway, at breakneck speed once again. At 6am we stopped yet again, only this time for a more scheduled ten minute break, so we could relieve ourselves alongside the unpaved roadside. The bus emptied itself of human cargo, and I felt the urge to do likewise, as the parents of my little blighter headed out of the bus in front of me, refusing to accept the return of their offspring. (At least I presumed it was theirs, but I could be wrong.)

My adopted son started to come round, as we dismounted the steps of the bus. We were met by the throng of fellow passengers, both sexes, openly relieving themselves publicly on the grass verges, all perfectly at ease, as nature demanded this vital function, with the men not giving a damn as to who saw their bodily functions or equipment. Putting the boy down to stand alongside me, I quickly joined my companions in this open air party scene. My little one beside me did likewise, arching his stream in an arch of play, before demanding I carry him back into the bus. On return to the bus, our now fully awake friends broke out their various rations of food, with the boy's mother passing me some kind of sweet bread for both my charge and kindly for myself also. The sun was rising from the east, in the direction we were travelling, as the hills could now be clearly seen all about us, like a scene from Glencoe back in the highlands of Scotland, with all the drama and nostalgia such a welcoming sight evoked. We were by this time, well into the first of the hill tribes of the Shan states, which went all the way to the Chinese border. Another brief stop was made near Lashio where several passengers got off, including my adopted son, his parents, along with their newly acquired goat.

By mid-afternoon, now feeling battered, bruised and somewhat tired form this overland journey, we were into the province of North-Hsenwi, not far from Kutkai when looking at my map I realized we did not have far to get to my journey's end, before reaching Namkham about another sixty miles or so was my guess, if my map reading skills were correct. With some excitement, girding my loins in anticipation of the unknown, I started to assemble the contents of my rucksack together, in readiness to enter the exciting prospects that now lay ahead of me, not really knowing what to expect.

By 7pm (almost twenty two hours from Mandalay,) we reached Namkham hospital, as I waited at the rear of the queue to disembark from my transport of discovery. The very large cottage hospital was laid out in spacious grounds, with a reddish dirt drive that showed off this otherwise primitive large double storey building at its best. Judging by the very mature trees and plants well established about the grounds, the hospital was well rooted. As I ambled up the rough driveway, an elderly gentleman, with a covering of roughly thatched white hair, wearing a surgical gown and white baggy trousers, approached my coming.

"Doctor Seagraves I presume" I said, putting my outstretched arm towards him.

He shook my right hand vigorously, asking me if I was "Andy Ankorne."

"Why, yes" I replied, rather sheepishly, wondering and asking him how he knew my name.

"Well," said Seagraves in a slight American drawl, "We have been reading all about you, for some weeks now, and I was half expecting you to turn up, sooner or later," he explained, smiling all the while.

Doctor Seagraves, otherwise known as the Burma surgeon, was notoriously famous in this part of the world. While in Malaya I had read his book, simply called 'Burma Surgeon' and still own a copy to this day.

Gordon. S. Seagraves. Ex Lieut, Colonel, MC. of the United States Army forces in China, Burma and India had stayed behind after the Burma campaign, to set up his own hospital at Namkham, long after the American, British and Indian forces, who fought bitterly against the Japanese invasion withdrew. This pioneer into wastebasket surgery was somehow shorter than I imagined, having read extensively about this giant of a man, who was revered by so many. His thin, almost fragile frame belied how tough and resilient he was, and he was worshiped by thousands near and far.

Now in his late sixties or early seventies, (I'm guessing,) he was still working long and gruelling hours, although his newly made assistant, one Mr Tun Shein, who was adopted into Seagraves' family as a very small orphan boy, was now being groomed, because of his recently acquired surgical skills, to eventually take over from the master. Seagraves who also had two boys of his own, Bill and Paul, even paid for Tun Shein's education who then went on to become a very successful surgeon in the U.S.A.

"We have a bed ready for you, if you wish?" Seagraves invited, "and I'm sure you will stay for a few days at least," said Dr Seagraves.

"Thank you very much, I would be delighted." I answered, with a grateful smile.

"I don't know about you English, but here we have a very informal life style, dictated only by the amount of hospital work which can sometimes get very hectic," he drawled softly.

"That suits me just fine," I replied, "I'm in no hurry, after that bone shaking journey up from Mandalay."

He smiled at my admission, as we both walked into the main body of the hospital building. He introduced Tun Shein to me as his son; he must have been in his mid to late twenties, but looked more like a late teenager. Like his father, he too had finished surgery for the day, and volunteered to take me over to the house.

Most of the nurses (very pretty ones) were either Shan or Karen from different regions of Burma, but all originally trained by the Seagraves' method and were very caring people, dedicated (I do mean dedicated) to their chosen Florence Nightingale profession. This was no nine to five job, but they just loved it, and were fully devoted to everything they did, and counted themselves very lucky to boot. They worshiped Seagraves and his son Tun Shein who often worked around the clock, setting a good example to all his staff and carers. Many of the inmates or patients were sneaked in from over the nearby China border, and all were seen regardless of any ability to pay, often bringing members of their family, to help with their basic hospital care. The atmosphere within the hospital was an unusually joyful one, in spite of many of the horrendous injuries suffered by so many. I'm sure most of the smiling happy nurses saw me as a bit of an odd ball or a curiosity, and some may well have thought I was off my rocker. To see any white Englishman in this neck of the woods was after all a rare sight indeed.

Circumstances, as they turned out saw my stay last all of five days, and I was more than welcome to watch Seagraves perform within his chosen realm of the operating theatre, under what can only be described as very primitive conditions. (Certainly by today's standards.) I was particularly interested in a lad that was brought across the border from China by his elder nineteen year old brother. The younger brother was suffering from the growth of a huge goitre, which was almost as big as his own head, growing out from the side of his neck. They had both arrived on the same day as my own entrance to Namkham, and Seagraves was planning to operate within forty eight hours.

During our evening's conversation, over a simple supper, Dr Seagraves explained at length, the procedure this rather delicate, but gory operation would take, and how the two brothers came from a very small village just across the border, where a trace of head hunting (that was now forbidden,) still took place. It was this second part of his conversation that intrigued me very much. I expressed a great deal of interest in seeing this rather barbaric practice for myself. Seagraves was most frenetic in his advice against the idea, of nipping across the border, as I put it, so to speak, to make a visit. The village in question, although nearby, was considered remote, but the real possibilities of finding my own head shrunken for a prized trophy, by this little known tribe of savages, was too realistic to contemplate. (Seagraves words – not mine.)

That night in bed, alone in my cell like bare room, I found it difficult to get to sleep, unable to stop myself thinking about the possibilities of a quick, if somewhat clandestine sortie to this village. It wasn't because I was on some blood thirsty mission, because I had seen this phenomenon once before in Borneo. The subject fascinated my deep yearnings towards the macabre, or was I that maladjusted, in my keenness of misguided youthfulness, for all things horrific.

Next day, and all scrubbed up for the operation that both Seagraves and his adopted son Tun Shein were to perform, I was invited to watch for a while at least, these two in action. After two hours into this operation, due to last most of the day, I chickened out, in need of fresh air and a smoke. I had taken to smoking Burmese cheroots, which were cheaper and more readily available than cigarettes, as well as being more enjoyable.

That evening, I tackled Dr Seagraves once again, on the subject discussed the previous night over dinner, only this time making my intentions of a possible visit to this head hunters' village, abundantly clear. Seagraves was not a happy bunny, which he too in turn, made just as clear to me. Surprisingly, next morning he suggested a compromise, with certain conditions;

1. I was to leave all my gear, camera and passport behind, within his care.
2. If anything should happen to me, he would deny all knowledge of my existence, and would dispose of any trace that I had ever stayed with him.
3. The nineteen year old brother would act as my guide, to ensure my relative safety. Meanwhile, he would continue to treat the younger brother in the older brother's absence, while he was acting as my guide.
4. If we both did not return together within forty eight hours, (two days,) the Doctor would presume me dead, and would probably go to the authorities to report me as missing. (A.W.O.L.)
5. If, and when we returned I was to leave Namkham within twenty four hours.

I was not sure, if the good doctor emphasized this last part, in a last ditch attempt to dissuade my foolhardiness, but the tingling sensations of excitement I felt for this inadvisable adventure, only served to whet my appetite even more. The older brother was called to parley with the doctor along with the enlisted help of Tun Shein as interpreter, and reluctantly he agreed, but only because the hospital was using his kid brother as a powerful lever, as some kind of hostage, to guarantee my safe return. That same evening, suitably clad in dark clothing, and with a partially moonlit night, we set off on foot together, as two strange figures along a verge of the infamous Burma Road which crossed directly into China. With the aid of this well worn road for the first twenty miles or so, we made good time. As we neared the China border post, my companion suddenly pulled me into nearby bushes and waited, listening intently for goodness knows what. Leaving the road, we headed west at first, in the direction towards Loiwing, for almost three miles, then turned northwards, for another two miles along well worn footpaths. The walking of such large distances at night seemed normal to my Shan companion.

As we neared his village, we stopped abruptly on the edge of a clearing, where, I was signalled to wait out of sight, on my own. I took this opportunity to relieve myself, but within twenty minutes my companion was back at my side, leading me to his small clay built house. His mother (I think) sat me down in front of a newly lit fire, and brought us both some kind of beer like refreshment, along with some rice cakes. I thought we might be spending the night, but after a very short hour or so, we were both on the move, yet again. Sometime after 4am, I was taken into some kind of outhouse and again left on my own.

After about half an hour or so, I was beginning to get worried, with my over active brain working overtime, thinking all kinds of imaginary dastardly threatening deeds, when my friend, (at least I hoped he was still my friend) reappeared. He was accompanied by two strange characters, who promptly examined my head, just a bit too keenly for my comfort, grinning like a pair of wild cats ready to make a killing. The father and possible son, pair of most unlikely characters, went into the back of this sinister outhouse, producing a small sack, while my accomplice lit a small fire on the mud floor of this dwelling. The older of our two hosts, opened up the sack with care and great relish, then produced not one, but two shrunken heads, holding them both up by their hair, for me to peruse. The son who was full of joy, started to get very animated, prodding me with excitement, and pointing to the heads as if he was trying to make some kind of selling deal. (Perhaps he wanted to bargain my head in exchange.) Having come so far, I examined the two heads at some length; they had been shrunken to half their approximate size, but looked very rubbery. Not the most handsome pair of faces, with one in particular looking quite youngish, although it would be difficult to say how old this relic was, as I was certainly no expert.

After a while, I started to feel a kind of nausea, as I ran urgently to the door to spill my guts. Behind me, the trio of happy rebels, laughed out loud with obvious delight, at my disturbed body with such an upset stomach. Feeling rather ill for more reasons than I care to mention, I indicated to my friend, I was ready for the off. He clapped his two compardries on the back with gusto, and still laughing like a wild hyena, we parted, with my own head thankfully still intact. We made our way back to his humble abode, where I slept with much unease, and a very troubled, disturbed, unhappy frame of mind and soul.

Later that second day, we slowly retreated back into Burma, and back to the relative civilization of Namkham hospital. I didn't feel too hungry that last evening at Seagraves' table, in spite of a distinct lack of anything substantial by way of food, taken these past forty eight hours or so. Within the security and comfort of my bedroom that night, I more than made up for lack of sleep, and at breakfast that last morning, I more than ate my fill. Dr Seagraves suggested I go into Bhamo later that morning with his adopted son Tun Shein, who according to the good doctor, was going in for emergency supplies. I thought perhaps the doctor was most anxious to be rid of me, but was far too diplomatic to say so outright, and wanted to put as much distance between myself and Namkham as possible. I too was very diplomatic, not mentioning my thoughts.

Just after 11am, I collected all my belongings, including my passport and camera, and said my sincere farewells to the doctor, as I got into an ambulance type shooting brake vehicle, wearing a white coat over my day clothes. This I was assured, was for our own safety, because even the dacoits would not stop this known vehicle, as many of these undesirables were in fact friends and past patients of the doctor, some of whom he had treated many times in his own hospital, over many years. Bhamo, on unmade roads was some seventy five miles northwest of Namkham and was where we rejoined the main road north to Myitkyina, which for me, not only signalled the end of the road, but also the end of civilization, and where I would be forced to walk on foot all the way to Assam, India the better part of two hundred miles, through unforgiving country, which for me was the real meaning of forbidden journey, really started.

The conversation, all in English between Tun Shein and myself during this short distance to Bhamo, was lively and interesting. His adopted father, the doctor, could do no wrong in his eyes, it was clear he worshipped the air that Seagraves breathed, and the very ground he walked on. His two older adopted brothers, were both living in the States, and for some unknown reason, there was no mention of his adopted mother. He was more than content with his lot in life, and so obviously enjoyed the daily challenge of the hospital. He advised me to camp on the very edge of town, if I intended to spend the night. This made sense I agreed, as by morning there was more likely to be either a lorry or car heading north towards Myitkyina. He stopped at a suitable spot with running water close by, so I thanked him once again for his kindness and hospitality. Well away from the road, I settled down for my truly first night alone. I spent most of the evening bringing my logbook/diary up to date, which had rather been neglected since leaving Mandalay.

Chapter Twenty-Eight

Bhamo to Myitkyina and beyond

You would think, camping next to a small bubbling stream, I would have been lulled into a comfortable nights sleep. It was in fact, one of my worst nights ever, so far, with the loss of David's company, but the constant image of my dead, beloved Bobby, haunting me throughout the night, was particularly painful, and with a flood of memories, to remind me of my great void. I was plagued with an unrealistic fear of impending doom that I was unable to shake off. These unhealthy thoughts were far more annoying and dangerous, than the constant buzz of mosquitoes, outside my protective netting.

Around 4am I could hear clearly the drone of the first heavy lorries, grinding their way up the steep incline that started not far from my campsite. On impulse, I struck my campsite with speed, to meet the start of the day with haste, hoping I would be able to get myself a lift to Myitkyina, without too much delay. By the time I got myself to the road, the first of the early morning light was dimly shedding its wonders around me, with the promise of a scorcher of a day ahead. Fortunately, as I perched on my rucksack, beside this stretch of the road, I consoled myself, I was just north of the junction on a well used secondary road, going directly into China and where it joined the famous Burma Road, costing many lives in construction, and now famed in film. It was an ideal spot for vehicles heading both due north, as well as traffic coming into Burma from China. With the possibility of a double whammy so to speak, I was lucky enough not to wait too long. I discovered lorries on this notorious stretch of the road, were well advised to travel in a convoy, because being close to the major smuggling routes into China, any vehicle on its own was particularly vulnerable, and at a high risk of being robbed, Dick Turpin style.

Unlucky for me, I was not fully aware of these facts at the time, and in my ignorance, accepted a lift from a pair of Shan brothers, who were running their own Arthur Daley enterprise, of smuggling gold from China into Burma. This was just one of their many runs from Chengtu, deep within the hinterland of China, some many hundreds of miles away. Judging by their prominent prosperity, this enterprise must have been very lucrative too. Their virtually new and very expensive truck was ample evidence of this fact. They cheerfully pulled off the road, helping me with my heavy equipment, which they found highly amusing. With the radio blaring local Burmese music at full blast, we set off in absolute comfort, taking the hilly inclines with ease, as I sat alongside these very jovial rascals.

Less than an hour into my lift, we were ambushed very expertly, by a bunch of six thugs, with heavily armed weaponry, threatening to blow us all into the next world, and I was surprised that my Shan companions put up no resistance whatsoever, as they themselves were also armed. They stepped down form their vehicle, taking me with them, while these desperados ransacked their truck in broad daylight. One nasty turd of an excuse for a human being relieved me of my Mickey Mouse watch (no real loss,) and my fountain pen, but even more importantly, my beloved camera, and the little amount of Burmese currency I was carrying about my person. Having already been through my rucksack, its contents were now strewn across the roadside verges. Having found some gold within the truck, they were now more than satisfied, having completed what they saw, as a successful raid!

At this point, and still under the barrel of several guns pointing at us, at close quarters, we were bundled back into the truck, and allowed to go on our not so merry way. My companions, the Shan boys, were more concerned with my own upset and meagre loss, than they appeared to be with their own loss, of a valuable cargo of gold. On reaching the outskirts of Myitkyina, I was soon to learn the reason why their immediate loss was accepted so lightly, as we pulled off the road, into a very large and well run garage, obviously owned by this naughty enterprising family. While I was given a long ice cold drink of Burma tea, along with ample sweet breads, the rest of the gang, expertly stripped the underside of the truck of long pieces of false chassis lengths, from their lorry, which in fact, in spite of their dirty colouring, were pure gold. No wonder they could sport so many trappings of wealth.

Feeling rather upset about my loss, which to them seemed more important, than the small amount of gold they were relieved of, on the open road, the father who had some English, invited me to stay over for the night with them. I'm not sure why, but I readily agreed, then went over to admire a brand new Willys jeep, sitting over in the far corner of the garage. I was also to learn from this motley crew, that the jeep, recently purchased to replace an older relic, was specifically designed for trips northwest of Myitkyina, to a place called Walawbuw about a hundred miles into the countryside where this family owned amber mines. I tactfully pointed out, to my wealthy and newly made best friends, that this was on my very important route, into the start of Hukawn valley. My strong hint was taken, with great jollity, and knowing back slapping, as the old man explained to me in adequate broken English, that the very same two boys were due to make this trip north to the family mines, to pay their workers wages. Naturally, if I was prepared to wait five days, they would be more than happy to take me with them, thus far.

Having spent a happy night in my own sleeping bag on the floor of their living room, and after a somewhat substantial breakfast, one of the boys offered me a lift into town, to the Y.M.C.A., which I graciously accepted, as I couldn't believe my stroke of pure luck. I had echoes of both David and Bobby ringing in my ears, as they often called me a lucky bugger, or jammy dodger.

The Shan boy, (older than myself at twenty four years old,) had a brief word with the receptionist behind the booking in counter, much later, I was to learn that this unnamed family would be picking up my tab, for the duration of my stay in Myitkyina, at this rather empty Y.M.C.A. hostel. The only other occupants staying in this well kept establishment were two yanks, who had blown in by train from Mandalay, via India. With my recent run in with one of his countrymen, I avoided them like some dreaded disease, and besides, I wanted to keep the plans of my real intentions, secret, especially from the likes of these loud mouths. (Not all Americans are loud, brash or overbearing, only the ones I unfortunately met on my travels.) Perhaps there was something in the water that had this cause and effect, but I wouldn't know, as I only bathed in the stuff, and certainly wouldn't dream of drinking it. Excuse my warped sense of humour, but after all, I was still very much alive, in spite of all the odds stacked against me.

I was to use this five day respite to recharge my batteries, as well as shop for vital supplies, in readiness for the unknown, beyond Walawbuw deep inside the Hukawn valley. Fortunately the dacoits only took my local currency off me, and ignored my two remaining U.S. dollar traveller's cheques that totalled some fifty dollars. More than enough, I convinced myself, to see me all the way to India, I hoped.

Myitkyina was a hill station, which seemed lodged on the edge of the world. This place emanating from this far corner of northern Burma, where even the rail link stopped, just short of the border with China, and with the secondary route as well as the main Burma road entering deep into China's territory itself, it was a favourite route for the more daring mobile smuggling fraternity, that boldly traded in silk, cocaine and gold, with other lesser known contraband, including Chinese arms and explosives. Both the Burmese and Chinese guards, securing their respective borders, were easily bribed, for those that had sufficient funds, which in this neck of the woods were many. It was also unwise, to walk about this area showing any sign of wealth or opulence, when one could easily be killed, for such trifles. In my case, it was better to keep my head down, and trust no one, as a stranger among strangers. My hope, and indeed my nightly prayers, were centred around the promise, of a lift up country, with the knowledge that once well into the interior of this dangerous and forbidden part of Burma, there was no going back!

Once, and if I got as far as Shingbwiyang, the next and most dangerous hot spot, was beyond this area, as I neared the final region known as the golden triangle, where the India, China and Burma borders met. On the morning of my fifth day in Myitkyina, the two Shan boys turned up as promised, anxious to be off. My account was quickly settled, and with my gear, hurriedly put in the back of the jeep, we very quickly sped off, like animals hunted, or on the hunt. I sat in the back, as we left the tarmac road quickly behind us for ever, but initially sped along dirt made roads, which the little jeep was more than equipped to deal with. After just twenty or so miles the roads deteriorated rapidly, and several small bridges used to cross small fast flowing rivers, had been swept away by the recent monsoons. The jeep had a good four wheel drive system, but even this at times was not enough to get us out of trouble completely. With two of us pushing, and also with the help of a rudimentary winch system, which was mounted on the front of the vehicle, we cajoled the little jeep across the most stubborn of torrents.

Having achieved almost fifty miles of dirt tracks, and a number of raging rivers, we pulled up at Sadusun a small primitive village, more than ready for the night. Now well into the Hukawn valley, (the Burmese form of spelling Hukong,) the lads soon had a campfire lit, while I went off with a bush knife to cut and bring more firewood for later.

I pitched my tent to the boy's great surprise, with an invitation to both of them, to make use of the comfort of sleeping below a mosquito net, offered in good faith. They accepted, but one always stayed outside, on guard duty, sitting in the jeep, as they had much money to protect, which represented fortnightly wages, for their men, working in the amber mines. With good food inside me, and bags of protection, I had no problems sleeping in this land of the just. After an excellent night's kip, I was ready for anything, which was just as well, as the second day proved even harder than the first day, but after much sweat and some tears, we could see the large village of Walawbuw, on the other side of a very wide and fast flowing river, a branch of the famous Uru river, that was to cross my path on more than one occasion, before the end of the gruelling trek I was about to undertake, after I left Walawbuw, which was now in our sights.

This river was a good seventy to eighty feet wide, and I did wonder how we were going to get across. No such problems for my Shan companions, who had previous experience in tackling this particular untamed river. One of the boys promptly stripped to his shorts, and taking hold of the hook on the end of the winch cable, started to wade out towards the centre of the river. The remaining driver meanwhile taped off the distributor, disconnected the fan belt and put an extension rubber pipe on the end of the exhaust outlet tail pipe. When the first lad had waded half way across this fast flowing river, which was now about waist high, the driver engaged four wheel drive, as I held onto the rear of the vehicle, ready to push as required. In second gear, the vehicle eased itself into the torrent, and slowly went across to well over midway. We paused for several moments midstream, as the wader cleared to the other bank, and anchored the cable around a suitable tree trunk. Then, engaging the winch, the jeep eased itself across, with no real difficulties.

Once clear of the river, fan belt and exhaust extension were sorted, with the distributor cap restored to normal running. We all stretched ourselves out in the sun to dry ourselves off, as well as the jeep. Several hundred yards after we left the river, we came to a dirt junction in the track and stopped dead in our tracks. On a very well worn footpath, coming down from this hilltop encampment or village known as Walawbuw, was a rare sight to behold indeed. Coming towards us, and riding a very English standard black bicycle was a very English vicar, (who in fact, turned out to be a Welsh missionary, from the Rhondda valley,) in full clerical garb, waving to us all in the jeep.

"Well hello" he chanted, with a grin. "It's so wonderful to see another English speaking European."

This was where my Shan friends and I parted company, so with much back slapping and hand shaking, we said our goodbyes.

The Rev Rowland insisted I stay with him, to enable me to fill in the blanks of what was going on, back in dear old England! As you can imagine, in this field, I was of little use, having spent the last four years or so abroad.

"No matter," said the Rev Rowland, who had lived almost sixteen years in this remote part of Burma, doing God's work, "it's just wonderful to be able to converse in English, after so long," he said.

The Rev Rowland had been home to Wales just once in sixteen years, and lived alone, and I presume a very celibate life. Neither of us could believe our eyes at such a chance meeting, in such a remote corner of the world. (The odds were inestimable.)

Mr Rowland was originally from London, born and bred, like myself. As soon as he heard my English patter, he asked me "ere mate, wot part of London are you from?"

Having lost his London accent, mainly due to living abroad, and having joined the Welsh missionary service, more than twenty five years ago, I was easily misled to his true identity.

Over dinner, that evening in his very basic hut, (his was identical to the rest in the village,) he decided to break open a Christmas cake, that he had been saving for a very special occasion, it had been sent to him more than four years ago. The fact that it was only late August 1957 made no difference, to his Christian beliefs.

"I have waited with great patience and fortitude," he remarked, "for just such an occasion."

As we both celebrated an early Christmas. "You know Paul," (I had reverted to using the name on my passport now, since I was on my own,) "The one thing I miss above all else in this wonderful life, is conversation in my native tongue," he explained.

"You are the first Englishman I have spoken to in more than six years," he went on.

The Rev Rowland did not seem the least bit put out about my intended journey. "Don't worry," said the Rev, "the Lord will watch over you, on your journey, and these hill tribes are simply wonderful people," he said, with great emphasis.

"Perhaps in a day or two, when you are ready for your next leg, I may be able to come with you as far as the next village," he added, "which is only eight miles away and simply wonderful countryside." (Wonderful was easily his most favourite word, I noted.)

"Perhaps we could do it together, on bicycles," he said pleasantly, with an attractive smile on his face, which was most disarming.

Is this guy for real? I thought rather uncharitably, to myself. The bicycle idea proved impracticable, as the balance between body weight and an equal load with my rucksack, could well have ended in a very bad altercation with the hillsides twisting mountain goat tracks.

"Never mind," said the Rev, "I'll race ahead to the next village," (just part of his spread out parish,) "and make sure there is a nice cup of English tea awaiting your arrival."

Unbelievable I know. So, the godly Rev quickly disappeared over the brow of a very steep side of the mountain. Although the going underfoot was some times tricky, with one steep slope after another, it took me only three and a half hours to get to the village in question. The Rev was sitting outside the Headman's hut, at a table, with real china tea pot, cups and saucers, waiting to receive me, as casual as sitting on the village green, watching a Sunday afternoon game of cricket. It was most surreal in just such a setting. We were both invited to stay the night, with the Shan Headman, who was one of the Reverends converts to the faith.

Later, that same evening two village policemen joined us, they wore only an armband insignia [no uniform] and had nothing to do with the Burma police or government, but were elected by village council, or the headman. They would be travelling further north tomorrow, to the next mud settlement, and they would be honoured if I would join them, explained the Rev Rowland who spoke their lingo fluently.

"How far is the next village?" I enquired politely of the Rev.

"Not far" he said, "only about eleven miles" he quipped.

I dare not say what I was thinking, that I thought he was pulling my dick, as Henry would say, but it was very obvious that the Rev had no idea about the weight of my rucksack.

We were all very well looked after, and soon after breakfast, our copper friends decided the time was ripe to move on. One of these strapping fellows decided to help me shoulder my rucksack. After attempting to lift it off the ground, he quickly put it back down again, when he realized, just how heavy my personal cargo was. (Almost a hundred and twenty pounds.) He couldn't believe anybody could carry such a load, I manhandled it myself onto the comfort of my back and shoulders with ease.

After just six miles, I was knackered in the heat of the midday sun, but thankfully we stopped by the side of a decent river, where my new copper friends stripped off for a cooling swim. Without a care in the world, I quickly did likewise, enjoying the cooling process of the water. After a while we all lay down, naked in the shade to dry off slowly, before attempting the last five miles or so. Like the proverbial parcel, I was then handed over to this new headman, who kindly offered me a place to rest my weary head. His two Shan boys, (I guess about eleven to fourteen years of age,) were most intrigued with my gear, and fascinated with my ice axe, which they had never seen the likes of before. The two police friends, that had escorted me to their village, were obviously telling their headman's sons about the weight of my backpack, as the older one tried to lift it off the ground, but failed miserably. They gave me a look that was either in awe, or one that expressed sheer stupidity. I preferred to think it was awe, but suspected otherwise.

I had learnt a hard lesson today, it would be best to travel on foot, very early in the morning, well before the sun rose high. Then at the height of the sun's axis, to rest, and then start again, late afternoon, early evening time. Dehydration was the killer, and I was already overheating, from perspiring too much already. According to one of my newly acquired policeman friends, the next village, consisting of five huts, (which was not shown on my map,) was at least twenty miles west, and should take me no longer than two days to get there. After that, another thirty or more miles of very thick jungle terrain, perhaps taking four or five days, should find me at Shingbiwyang. This milestone would leave me only one third of the Hukawn valley to get through.

No longer having any watch on my wrist, was a real pain in the arse, because it would mean I would have to judge my time by the sun's axis, if I was to get any sense of the real length of each day. This next fifty miles or so, would be done solo, all the way to Shingbwiyang and no doubt, a very testing time, as I thought seriously about unloading some of my equipment, which was clearly too heavy for me. Going through my gear with great care, and with this purpose in mind, I could see that the really heavy stuff was mainly mountaineering equipment, which was not only expensive, but I would most certainly need once I arrived in India. Having weighed up all the pros very carefully, I decided I would retain all of the gear, and proceed as originally planned, knowing I could always dump some of it, if times got desperate. So, with this very much in mind, I went to sleep early, with big intentions of an earlier start than normal, the following morning.

Chapter Twenty-Nine

Green hell to Shingbwiyang

I rose, after just a number of hours of good sound sleep, and quickly got underway, much to the consternation of the headman, who directed me on to the correct path, shaking his head in disbelief at my foolhardiness. With just a few hours left of the bright moonlight sky above, I decided a good long rest and tea was very much the order of the day. I quickly got my little petrol stove boiling away, as I lay back to wait for the morning light to spring into action. A good hour later, I heaved my rucksack onto my back, and made good my intentions. The sun was now quickly beginning to make its appearance, and I guessed it was about six thirty am. I estimated I had comfortably done between four and five miles in this open hilly countryside, but my aim for this first day was to cover a good ten miles if I possibly could, which would be half way towards the five hut hamlet, which I estimated should take a full two days all together.

By mid morning the sun was already blistering hot, and the sap within my body began to wilt somewhat. I stopped by the side of a small fast flowing river, to quench my thirst, talking my progress up, telling myself 'just one more hour' or 'when I get round the next bend' I teased myself, 'I will take a well earned rest'. I crossed the small river, without any real difficulty, with my trail being clearly seen from the opposite river bank ahead. Having crossed, I stopped long enough for a very quick dip to cool myself off, before settling into a slow but easy rhythm, for another good two hours or more.

Close to midday, I came around a bend, and in my path, sunning itself, in this small glade in front, right across my track, was a tiger! This beautiful creature was totally unaware of my sudden arrival, as he contentedly dozed happily. I pulled up very abruptly, not knowing quite what to do about the tiger just twenty five yards away, I decided to slowly back track, a good few yards. If he had been fully alert, if he decided I would make an excellent meal, if he decided to charge, if, if, if. I realized, there was not a great deal I could do about it anyway, I certainly couldn't have run, crikey, I could hardly walk, I reminded myself. Once well out of sight and earshot too, from this majestic animal, I made a lot of coughing noises, as I sat down on top of my rucksack, eyeing up the nearest suitable climbing tree, not, I hasten to say that I had sufficient energy left, to make such a bold attempt to climb, realizing the big cat was a far superior tree climber than myself anyway.

After a comfortable time lapse, about half an hour, leaving my rucksack in situ, I stole myself to have a gander (look) to find that my feline friend, had kindly vacated the area on my route. I went back to my rucksack, to enjoy a well earned dump, (toilet) followed by a long awaited Burma cheroot, the very first of the day. I estimated that I had really done well enough for the day, and decided once I had put sufficient distance between me and my tiger friend sighting, I would pull into a lay-by so to speak, for a prolonged rest.

After just another mile or less, I found myself some suitable shade, stretched out my weary limbs, and snoozed most of the afternoon away. Having regained some of my strength, (and my composure,) I then carried on for about two more hours, making camp for the night, alongside another small river. (The country was full of such waterways.) This I quickly learned was a big mistake, as all kinds of wild animals came down to quench their thirst, at various stages throughout the early evening and well into the night. I neither had the energy nor the inclination to move camp. I'm sure many investigated the surrounds of my flimsy little tent, wondering if some nice tasty idiot had set up a fast food take away. The night noises were not only scary, (that's putting it mildly,) but interrupted my real chance of any continuous sound sleep worthy of note.

So, almost crapping myself, I made a start earlier than planned. The moon was slightly less helpful in this very early hour, and monsoon clouds gathered overhead, as if in a hurry to spill their load. Two hours into my forced march, a very loud clap of thunder, announced the arrival of a heavy deluge of rainwater. Although it was cooling, with the steam quickly dispersing from my body, like some eerie mist emanating from my person, making a ghostly figure in a sea of greenery. However, the soaking of my rucksack, consequently added extra weight, eventually forcing me to a complete halt. As I crawled into thick cover, to sit out this untimely torrent, I began to sympathize with myself, hoping it was going to pass quickly. As I dozed off from time to time, more from lack of sleep than exhaustion, the rain did eventually stop, meanwhile, I discovered many leeches had invaded my person. I stripped off to the bare skin, with the ease of an expert, and lit up another cheroot to burn these suckers from my flesh. Memories of the twins, (Quack and Quack) in the army, came flooding back, as I smiled to myself, remembering one occasion, when I nearly burnt a hole into one of the twins' dick, mistakenly thinking his very distinct birthmark, was in fact a leech. Perhaps, this sudden amusing anecdote, of happy times in the past, helped me along on the final stage of my unmarked map to five huts.

Close to midday, and long after the sudden outburst of the heavy monsoon deluge, I came into a small clearing of five huts, as two youngsters playing in the mud pit made by the recent rain at this hamlet, spotted me, and being startled, quickly ran for cover, as their male parent came out to investigate me, armed with a lethal looking bow and arrow in his hands. This was even more upsetting than my tiger encounter, so I put up my hands, to prove I was unarmed, quickly dropping my ice axe to the ground. I must have been a spectacle to behold, perhaps even frightening to their eyes, for such a stranger, clad as I was, who had just ambled into their world, most unexpectedly. At least my map reading and compass work skills proved good, as this strange man walked around my now very still body, for a face to face closer inspection, with the two mites clinging to his longie or skirt for the want of a better description.

Having satisfied himself I was harmless, if somewhat of an odd ball, he picked up my ice axe, and with one beckoning wave of his arm, bid me into his hut. I was persuaded to sit on the floor near the open fire, in the centre of this only circular room, as I was given a bowl of some kind of rice dish, to eat with my fingers. The two children [it was hard to tell what sex they were, they had such long hair] stood by, watching my every move, with great interest. The boldest and eldest, of these two siblings, perhaps about eleven years of age, gingerly stroked the heavy hairy growth on my face, and having decided I was real enough, settled down beside me, with a grin on his monkey like juvenile face that said it all. After all, his father must have decided I was harmless, (mad) but harmless enough, or I wouldn't be sitting amongst his beloved family, in his abode, I assured myself.

The sun outside was as high as it was likely to get for the day, as the braver of the two kids, showed me a place within the room where I could rest my weary head, as the mongrel of a dog who decided it was safe to enter, came in to sniff me over, with ears pricked up at such an unusual offering. He was quickly sent scurrying back outside, as my new eleven year old friend aimed a quick kick at the dog's rump. I dozed off into a deep needed slumber for several hours, only to be woken by this little friend, who handed me some kind of tea drink, with no sugar or milk. After a while, this little one must have decided I smelled rather badly, as he took me by the hand, down to the nearby river for a bath. With him leading, by undressing first, I too started to do likewise, when it became obvious he was very much a boy (and not so little) so, likewise I raced him into the water, which he won easily. After a good ten minutes or so, I got out and donned my shorts, but the lad, along with his mongrel dog, decided to stay in a little longer. I bathed in the warm afternoon sun to dry off, watching their antics with casual interest, while absorbing the warmth of the sun's rays, observing this everyday scene of Burmese village life.

Later that same evening, after a really good meal of some kind of sausage that tasted absolutely delicious, (which I was to later learn, was some kind of snake,) I was taken to my resting place, as this young, but older of the two boys, put me to rest, and promptly rolled out his grass reed matting bedroll alongside me, and now feeling very much at ease in my company, quickly went off to sleep. I stayed for a further day, and one more night, and with the help of protracted sign language, I hopefully made it clear, that I needed to push north, to my next destination.

Early morning, when I did set off, the father sent my newly made friend, his eldest lad along with me, to make sure I didn't get lost, or perhaps to ensure I didn't return, or come to any harm, at least for the first five or six miles along my chosen path. After three hours or so, the lad indicated he was leaving to return home, and after another stroking of my hairy face once again, before leaving, he then disappeared from sight, as I slowly plodded on my way.

This was another good day, and I reckoned I had covered a good ten miles and perhaps a little more, before deciding to make camp for the rest of the day and night. With my mental clock now into some kind of adjusted early morning pattern, I drank a good three mugs of hot sweet tea, (no milk) and after a generous slab of Christmas cake, I gave thanks to the Rev Rowland and his God, before setting off once again, determined to gain as much distance this day as possible.

Long before midday, I started to get the shakes, although I wasn't feeling the least bit cold, my legs were unwilling to support my frame, as I took hold of my heavy rucksack, which had now become so much a part of my body's balance system. On release of my load, I fell forward involuntarily, onto my face wondering what was happening. I decided to rest where I had fallen, and after a long period of time, seemed to regain most of my body functions and senses. I pushed on for a while, before deciding enough was enough, and made my camp for the day. After resting, I made myself a large billy can of soup, followed by the last of the Christmas cake, which I gorged myself on, before crawling into my sleeping bag feeling cold and shivery, which was beyond my own understanding, and I slept and slept, well into the morning sunlight of the following day. I was to learn later, I was actually suffering from my first real bout of malaria.

Feeling better, but very tired, I decided to stay put, and to use this day as one of much needed rest and recuperation. I slept well, off and on, for longish periods of time, but had a new strange dream about Bobby my beloved brother, kicking my arse, for no apparent reason, just as the morning light started to penetrate the thin canvas roof of my tent.

With my bum feeling unexplainably sore, (where no doubt Bobby had kicked me,) I quickly struck camp, and got underway. I crossed three rivers this day, one of which came up to chest height, which gave me a bit of a scare, as I desperately fought to hold onto my footing, as I crossed this river in full spate from the monsoon rains. The jungle undergrowth closed in to either side of my path alarmingly, so at times with dampness underfoot, and the dramatic rise of a sticky wet hot humidity and temperature, clinging to all my clothing, so my body now felt constantly wet, along with the sweat which was now prolific.

On reaching my forth river for the day, I decided I had travelled more than enough for this day, and quickly made camp, a respectful distance from the river this time, which I decided I would cross tomorrow. I set about making myself a substantial meal of rice and black beans, along with some bamboo shoots, followed with a larger than normal intake of liquid, mug after mug of sweet tea. Later that same evening, and while the sun was still in my favour, I went for a swim, and to explore the best crossing point, for the morning. After washing my shorts and tee shirt in the river, I decided to take a quick swim, to wash away the stench of the day's long hike.

Relaxing at home in the comfort of skinny dipping antics in a pool, I studied what I thought was a black curving branch of a tree, brought down current by the recent monsoon rains, when this so called black branch seemed suddenly to come alive, swinging towards me, with real purpose in mind. I realized just in time, that this harmless looking piece of debris, was in fact some kind of water serpent or snake, as I exploded in one body moving knee jerk reaction, scrambling up too the nearby riverbank, at great speed.

Once on the bank in relative safety, I slowly realized it was the wrong bank! With my campsite set up on the opposite side of the river. I watched this serpent, all of five feet in length, look up at me in disgust with shocked eyes of disappointment, before slithering away up steam, in search of easier pray. I stood on the bank in my nudity, giving it a respectfully considered time to elapse, before I plucked up sufficient courage to scurry back across the river, to the comfort and false safety of my campsite on the other side, searching every nook and cranny, looking for all kinds of nasty beasties.

I slept uneasily that night, as it began to dawn on me, just how vulnerable and exposed I was, so far from civilization, and at the mercy of this alien environment that I now found myself a part of. I had become accustomed to the night noises that surrounded my new world, but with the lack of any company, in which to share my feelings, I found myself more and more, talking to my imaginary self ego, no longer in full control. I found it easy to over imagine all kinds of demons, which had crept into my head while I was not looking and with the lack of a sounding board to reason coherently with, or someone or something to converse with as well as understand my problems, my sanity was now at risk. This, I put down to the effects of my recent bout of malaria. Shingbwiyang could not be far away, surely, I tried to convince myself with understandable common sense, and wishful thinking. Unless of course, my map reading or compass bearings skills, were very much out of focus, by misleading me and undermining my mixed reasoning.

Another day or two, at most, should see me home and dry, I thought. Although I had already lost reckoning as to what day it was, or what distance I might have travelled, was this 'jungle fever' for real? Or was it just a figment of the imagination in my befuddled brain?

With my usual early morning start, the jungle was now thicker than ever, becoming like my very personal green hell, as the jungle fever slowly and unnoticeably, took hold. This was easily my worst day yet, and although not quite down and out, I was getting very close to the bottom of my chances of real survival. Feeling very low, it was all that I could manage, to put one foot in front of the other, in a monotonous rhythm, that even I, at such a low ebb realized, was becoming more and more painful. 'Move yourself, you lazy bastard' I could hear Bobby slag me off as I put my fingers into my ears, to stop the persistent buzzing noise and drone of Bobby's persistent irritable voice, within my lugs.

Long before noon I was dead beat, and finally crawled into a nearby thicket, no longer caring about my world or any other world, for that matter, as I curled up hoping my hell would go away for ever, perhaps my death would be swift. I must have dozed of for several hours, because when I did come to, the sun was much lower in the sky, I now felt the evening air was beginning to get decidedly chilly. I forced myself to go on, for yet a few more hours, before calling it a day, for the second time.

That late evening, having lost my appetite, it was all I could manage to drink my mug of tea, before settling down for the night. Sometime in the early hours, I left the tent urgently, in a desperate need to empty my bowels, which turned out to be liquid sewage, with the trots, after that my bowel movements were never far away. There was no question of any early start, as I nursed myself by keeping warm, I had no appetite, or any desire to eat or drink. I dozed in and out of a state of semi conscious behaviour, not really sure any longer, what world I was still living in. Was I becoming delirious or was this just another imaginary state? Perhaps I was beginning to hallucinate, as I could now see Bobby with great clarity. This day had past as if it never existed, in the first place. How many days since I left the five huts hamlet, four, five or was it six? My log book was no help either, because I had not made any notes for over a week. I climbed to my feet, with automatic pilot guiding and taking over, as I trudged on, just hoping I was still going in the true direction, because most of my senses were no longer capable of meaningful focus. I've no idea how many hours I willed myself forward, but I was convinced I had past the same tree at least twice before. I thought, perhaps I was walking in circles, who knows and who cares anyway?

Having spent the last of what limited energy I had left, I gladly spread out my body, in a peaceful pleasant small glade, ready to meet my maker. (A one way trip, up or down.) This Garden of Eden was blissfully peaceful, with the roof canopy of many tree branches overhead, descending to engulf my very soul. I closed my eyes, giving into the inevitable, as I drifted off to meet my beloved Bobby, to join him in the next world. Many hours later, I could hear bell chimes nearby, and thought I had at last reached my heavenly goal, and then a very abrupt darkness followed, as I opened my arms in readiness to meet and receive Bobby, at long last. Sleep at long last, real and very peaceful sleep, which I had yearned for desperately, these past days. Oh, how tired I felt, as I drifted deeper and deeper, into meaningful oblivious slumber. The chiming bells appeared to come nearer, getting louder, charming me further into the darker welcoming abyss, and into the open arms of my dear, dear brother, who I had waited for so long to meet once again.

Chapter Thirty

Shingbwiyang- at last

In my dream world of utter peace, it seemed to me I was lovingly drifting towards Bobby, as I felt my soul being carried, floating many feet above the ground in my happy state of delirium and suspended levitation. They gently placed me down onto a very soft bed, I floated as the light faded into utter darkness once more, and my body sunk into the desperately needed prolonged sleep, that I was overpoweringly yearning for.

Three days later, a Shan lad of about fourteen years of age shook me awake, then putting a bowl of warm chicken soup to my lips, I took my very first sip of food, for longer than I cared to remember. (At least four days.) I looked about my surroundings, as the boy called his mother over to my bedside. It was in a very dark, shaded room, well away from sunlight, that was furnished to a basic and primitive standard. The woman quickly went outside to call her husband, who welcomed me back into the world of the living. Mr Saw Maung Su was the Sub Assistant Engineer (S.A.E.) to the Burmese government, as well as holding the title of public office of works, he was also the headman to this very large, sprawling village, that sat beside a massive river bend, on the 162 mile post marker in the heart of the Hukong valley.

An important man, employed by the public works department, his sole job was to send down an annual written geographical report, to government offices in Mandalay, with maps, showing the latest bridges lost and any new change of course that major rivers had taken, changes dictated by Mother Nature herself. He also spoke more than enough good English, which sounded like good music to my ears. I had been suffering very badly, with malaria, as well as dysentery, with temperatures running as high as 104 degrees Fahrenheit, whereby his fourteen year old son was forced to bathe me, as well as constantly change all the bedclothes, many times a day. (My personal wet nurse.)

As Saw, as he preferred me to call him, was already preparing his report of my impending death, which he would send down by runner, along with his geographical findings, later on in the season, after the end of the monsoons. Because of my illness, he had deliberately held back his own trek northwards, bound over for several weeks. It was estimated, that I had lost the better part of two and a half to three stones of body weight, since leaving Mandalay, as my new weight would be lucky to tip the scales at eight to eight and a half stones.

As Usoff (Joseph) once again stripped my bed, and calmly washed and cooled my naked, very thin body down, with such great care, I was too ill to be the least bit embarrassed. Between his wife and son, they had both nursed me around the clock non-stop, these past three or four days, which was still a blank. Saw and Joseph were genuinely very happy indeed about my slow, persistent recovery, which was due mainly to the very extensive care by his son. When I mentioned that I heard heavenly chimes before I passed out completely, he smiled knowingly, before telling me, I was originally discovered by a young eight year old goat herder, whose goat wore one of the cow type bells around its neck, very lucky for me I thought.

As I slowly regained my strength over the following week, I was able to get up, and wander about my surroundings. Shingbwiyang was at one time a U.S.A. fighter aircraft base and landing airstrip, during the major offensive against the Japanese invasion, and evidence although now well enough hidden, could still be found. This included all sorts of bits of machinery, and even abandoned working army jeeps could still be found in the jungle, on the periphery of what at one time was the very busy tarmacadam landing strip or airfield, although the jungle had long ago reclaimed all evidence that such a place ever existed.

This sprawling village, long past its glory days, still numbered a sparse population of almost one hundred souls, easily the largest population concentrated throughout the length of the Hukong valley, but who somehow still managed to eke out a living, mostly in one form or other of basic agriculture. This varied tremendously, from the usual growing of crops, to the lucrative harvesting of the opium poppy. The trading of all kinds of illicit contraband was very much a way of life here, mainly in opium, arms, gems, precious stones, and gold being by far the more favourable and profitable of trade. This lawless way of life, was very much the norm here, as they went about their daily business unheeded, for sheer survival. The growing of vegetable crops, and hunting of any kind of wild game for the table, was all part of every day life, in this remote region of Burma, where everybody lived by their own self imposed code or rules, which did not include any laws enforced by the statute of government, in the more so called progressive, civilized, areas of Burma. As an outsider, it would be easy to be lulled, into thinking this was somehow an ideological way of life, when in truth, the cruel fact of ones very survival in such a hell hole, proved very different, in both harshness and daily demands of hand to mouth living in poverty for most.

These hill tribes of Shan, Karens and all the way to the Naga hills across the border into Assam, India, were an extremely hardy bunch and needed to be, to live in this fierce wild environment, which was very unforgiving. Their way of life was impoverished in so many different ways, but they emanated an aura of smiling acceptance, and of contentment with their lot, that would be the envy of our so called civilized way of life in the western world where materialistic ownership has become the be all, as a yardstick to the measuring of life's happiness and success. I started to sit longer in the sun outside, to recharge my batteries and to watch everyday village life, across its entire primitive spectrum. The children along with their collection of many dogs, played simply, without any sign of sophisticated toys, but with absolute contentment, more than happy with the cards they had been dealt by their own society, and way of life. They knew no different anyway.

Now that we were about to step boldly into September, the tail end of the monsoons became more evident, as there was less rain with every passing day. Saw Maung Su explained to me, that he would need to be leaving soon, to go up to the border over the high thirteen thousand feet, Paunsuw pass, onto the last settlement known to mankind, before I could enter Assam. (This last settlement was a military one.) Saw's big fear was would I be strong enough to carry myself, regardless of all my equipment, which would be carried by two very thin pack ponies, and a small party of coolies.

This border post was less than forty miles away, but the increasing very steep terrain was the hardest underfoot we would experience, in the whole length of Hukong valley. He also explained that because he made this trek once every year, and therefore knew it very well, the changes we would encounter along the way dramatically changed every year, dictated by the ravages of nature, which was a very hard and unforgiving task master.

Saw himself loathed this part of the trek, he was forced to make on behalf of the Burmese government, but it was his job, and although he was still a relatively young man, (about forty years of age,) he explained it seemed to get more difficult with every passing year. (With more smugglers endangering his route.) The question that troubled both father and son (called Joseph,) my carer, was I yet ready for such a final push, to undertake such a punishing last leg of my journey? Both father and son felt I was not ready, although I expressed as clearly as I could, without being rude or offensive, I was! Their caring and genuine concern, especially having been so close to death as any man could get, was very touching in the extreme. The guilt I was beginning to feel having imposed on their hospitality for so long, and to whom I clearly owed my very life to, was beginning to take its toll on my mental state, probably due to so much inactivity on my now feeble physical condition, as well as the loving care and hospitality they willingly gave.

From a strong man of action, I had become a physical wreck of an eight stone weakling, and I was mentally anxious, somehow to see the back of this journey, once and for all, which I was clearly in no state to do on my own.

So, putting my mouth well ahead of my brain and any physical considerations, I told both father 'Saw' and son 'Joseph' that by the first of September 1957 I would be ready, come what may, in just two days time, in fact. So, they reluctantly agreed, that the first was the date for all our departures.

Now, almost three weeks behind schedule, to his usual timetable of annual events Saw and his coolies, along with two chosen pack animals, were duly told to report on the morning of the first of September in readiness for such a journey. Both Mr Saw's son Joseph and his dutiful wife fussed over me excessively, like a pair of well intended nurses to ensure I would be suitably ready in time. Joseph,(pronounced Usoff) who didn't normally accompany his father on this annual trek, but remained behind to look after the homestead, made it very clear against his father's wishes he would be coming to see that I behaved myself.

(Whatever that meant.) This brought a wry smile to my face, as it provoked evocative memories of Bobby, who on many occasions attempted to do likewise, but failed miserably, as often as not. For some unfathomable reason, Joseph had taken to becoming my personal guardian angel, and although flattered, I felt uneasy at being controlled by a fourteen year old. Anyway, with just two days to spare, I set about doing a mild exercise regime, to aid my full recovery and fitness.

Chapter Thirty-One

The last frontier to Civilization

As ready as I was ever likely to be, under my present medical conditions, we all met together, just after 7a.m. on the first day of September 1957. The whole group gathered outside Saw's homestead, it consisted of six humans and two pack animals, there was much chatter and banter among the happy throng. The two animals had very little meat covering their skeleton like frames, and being dedicated beasts of burden they were carefully loaded. There was great debate on exactly how much, as well as to the weight of each animal's load. Saw himself carried a small automatic weapon, a sten gun type of American origin, along with plenty ammunition, from an arms dump left behind by the Americans from the Burma campaign.

Usoff, who I call Joseph, had a .38 British revolver tucked into his waist band, and a bandolier of ammunition, set diagonally across his shoulder, looking every inch like any local bandit. The three coolies all carried dangerous looking bush knives, almost about two feet in length, honed to a sharpness of perfection that could slice through the thickest meat, like a hot knife through butter. They also carried some old British Mills hand grenades, about their waists, I was more than well acquainted with the extensive damage these grenades could inflict, when used. I was also aware these three coolies were not Shan men, as they had a much darker skin colouring, and none of the usual Shan facial features, of high cheek bones and broad faces with wide almond shaped vivid dark eyes, similar to the Mongols from Mongolia, or Ghurkhas from Nepal.

Saw, the leader and headman of our expedition, informed me they were in fact Tamils from southern India, who had been stoned, almost to death, and banished from their village for some unforgivable crime, which for certain reasons was best left untold, at least for the time being. Naturally, I was now very intrigued, and was bursting my sides to know more, but for now at least, Saw was not prepared to go into any more details, at present. The mental relief from not having to carry my own heavy load, after my recent illness was a sheer joy, in spite of or because of, my recent delicate state.

I was now feeling a sense of safety, and although I myself was the only one not carrying arms, the company that was about me gave me a peace of mind, within myself of well being. We would travel in daylight only, stopping well before midday, when we would all rest up, for at least four hours until late afternoon or early evening, when we would put in a further three or four hours, before stopping to make camp for the night. It was a good forty miles as the crow flies, to the thirteen thousand feet high Paunsaw Pass, but the hill country we were now climbing (called the Patkai hills,) was punishingly slow progress. As Saw pointed out to me at great length, if we covered as much as eight miles on the map in any one day, we would be doing exceptionally well, and could count ourselves lucky, especially after our first day, because from now on, the gradients of the hills in front of us would get steeper and steeper, by the day. We were soon sharply reminded, we were in the thickest of dacoit gangs and bandit country, where the cost of human life was absolutely zero. Shoot first, was very much the order of the day, if you were to stay alive, and many wasted hours each day were spent avoiding any confrontations with these wild renegades.

The campsite for each night was always chosen with great care, and always many hundreds of yards away from all known trails, which were used extensively by these marauders. I've never seen so many different types of rivers, ranging from wide and deep raging torrents, to tranquil serene streams that meandered lazily with indifference to belie the dangers held within. In this part of Burma, the hilly countryside was alive with waterways, and teeming with all kinds of beasties, with wild game in abundance, most of which was far from harmless. The insect life infested this swampy terrain with all kinds of deadly bites, stings as well as carrying all kinds of dreaded diseases, many of which were not even known to mankind, in the western world of medicine. Any still water ponds or puddles were avoided at all costs, and even many rivers were highly suspect. Swarms of mosquitoes thrived in this far corner of Burma, and malaria was accepted as commonplace, going with the territory, so to speak. The natives themselves that lived full time within this environment were hardly ever infected and built up some kind of immune system against this and many other diseases. Only us, insipid white Europeans, were prone to attack from this unnatural vegetative green hell, like an alien fish thrown into a world full of nasties, just waiting to vent havoc on our so called civilized immune system.

The first day seemed long, but I was assured, we would be hard pushed to cover our estimated quota of eight miles per day. I was pleased when we did stop to set up our first camp for the night, and Joseph (Usoff) helped me erect my tent in readiness, for what I hoped would be a comfortable nights sleep.

Joseph had been instructed by his father to sleep and watch over me, but firstly he was told to de-leech me, as we had been travelling through a particularly well known infested part, this first day. Joseph stripped me of all my clothing, before I lit a Burma cheroot, which he then used to burn these bloodsuckers from the most intimate parts of my anatomy. Once finished, with a beaming smile across his face from amusement, he casually stripped off himself, for me to inspect his body and do likewise, for me to remove leeches form his body, especially in the harder to reach places of his anatomy. He could tell I was somewhat embarrassed, which Joseph found highly amusing. Joseph then unrolled a long piece of cloth, called a longie, which was worn like a long skirt, about ones waist that went down to within inches from the ground. He taught me the simple art of tying this garment about my body, then, donning a longie about his own body, he took me down to a nearby river, where we could bathe.

With the jungle music, of a thousand different species of creatures all about us, we bathed as God himself had made us both, with relaxed minds, to rid our bodies and limbs from the days strenuous trek and in my case, excessive sweat. We made our way back to camp, where the three Tamil Indians were busy preparing our food, over a roaring fire. Two of the three Tamils were brothers, with the third who was older, some kind of uncle or relative, I was told.

The brothers were about seventeen or eighteen years old, and the third was at least twenty five. They kept themselves aloof from the rest of us, preferring their own company, in a subservient kind of manner. Perhaps this was because they were being paid by Saw, who hired them each year over a period of several months, specifically to carry the loads with the aid of their pack animals. On this yearly pilgrimage they carried out their daily tasks with eagerness and obvious enjoyment, nothing was too much trouble for their master's bidding.

Saw, his son Joseph and I shared my tent, while the Tamil trio slept together, under a makeshift awning, strung up between tree trunks. After my bath or swim, I settled into my sleeping bag, but before I fell off to sleep, Joseph came into the tent carrying a very large bowl of hot steaming rice, which contained fish and different unknown jungle vegetables mixed throughout. The amount of food heaped onto this plate was far more than I could eat, thankfully, I quickly learnt it was for the two of us. Joseph smiled wide, as I tucked in with my spoon, as he helped himself using his left hand only, which I noticed the Tamil trio also did likewise. Joseph explained as best he could, that his left hand only was for eating, while his right hand was used exclusively for ablutions, (wiping his bum with water after doing the toilet,) I was to find much later, in my extensive travels across India that this form of ablutions was customary, and at times I too was forced to adopt it.

After eating my fill, I snuggled down into my bag to rest, feeling contented and somewhat revived, at the end of my first day. The comfort of my new companions all about me, reassured my body and peace of mind, as slowly I succumbed to the inevitable drowsiness, that over took my being. Sometime during the night, perhaps within an hour or so after I fell asleep, I felt Joseph snuggle up close into my back, as he too settled down for the night.

Early next morning, I climbed out of my sleeping bag and donning my longie about my waist, I left the tent in search of a suitable place to relieve myself. By the time I had returned, the Tamil trio had a fire going, and were busy making our first brew of the day, as they also started to pack up all the equipment. By 7am the team were all underway once more, with the Tamils and their pack ponies leading the way, up front ahead. Except for the early morning steam ascending from the jungle flora, it was cool and pleasing, as we made our way slowly northwards by compass, climbing steadily all the time. (The cooler climate as we climbed into the hills suited me well.)

Less than an hour later, we all hit the deck instinctively, as a volley of automatic gunfire, very close by, broke the jungle music of silence ahead of us, as we waited to see what might happen next. Almost immediately, several bursts of return fire, also from automatic weapons, appeared to take place close by, only this time from some where behind our rear. Saw whispered to me to get closer to the ground, as Joseph crawled up to my side with his revolver in his hand at the ready. One of the Tamils unleashed, and then lobbed a hand grenade far ahead, in front of us, well ahead of our position, in the direction of the first volley of shots. For a good seven seconds, we all made love to mother earth, until the ear splitting blast, from the explosion of the grenade, shook the soil beneath our prostrate bodies. The silence that followed was eerie, as even the noisy hum of the jungle inhabitants fell silent, with a nervous hesitancy that lasted several minutes long. We stayed put, playing dead, and ears stretched to bursting, but holding ourselves with baited breath, as our hearts pounded with accelerated speed, almost hearing the adrenaline coursing through our veins in an alert state of heightened alarm. We must have stayed motionless for the better part of twenty minutes, before one of the Tamils silently reconnoitred ahead to investigate. After he returned, and had a quick pow- wow with Saw, we gingerly proceeded along our chosen route. This was a timely reminder on only our second day, of the real dangers within our midst. For several hours we constantly stopped and started again, listening intently for any further possible intrusions or interruptions.

Well before midday, we headed away from the trail in search of deep cover, for our midday break of three hours or so to rest up. I noticed that as we got higher, into the top most regions of the surrounding hills, the temperature was cooler making the afternoon sun easier to bear. Saw explained to me, within another day or so, we could dispense with the midday break altogether, as the higher altitude made progress easier. During this interlude of enforced rest, the older of the three Tamils was called over to Saw, who instructed the Tamil to go off into the jungle, to hunt for something suitable for tonight's pot roast.

While we were sipping our Burmese tea, and enjoying a cheroot amongst ourselves, I took this opportunity to ask Saw why the trio of Tamils were so far away from their homeland of southern India. Saw explained at great length and in great detail, why these three loyal servants had been banished from their tiny village, near the southern tip of India. The youngest of two brothers was bi-sexual, which in itself was common enough, and not unusual, or a crime. However, Saw continued, the uncle was in the act of introducing the two brothers to a sexual act of bestiality, with a neighbour's goat, no less. Having been seen by the neighbour, the elder of the village was summoned to the scene in haste, to witness this act of buggery with the goat. There was no denying the facts, as the younger of the two brothers was caught, having entered the animal from the rear, and was unable to withdraw in haste as he was firmly stuck within. The villagers attacked all three involved, by stoning them from the village, and they were now forbidden ever to return. (Banished.) All three of them fled in fear to Burma, to seek a new lifestyle away from everyone who might know of their shameful act.

"How long have they lived in Burma?" I asked Saw.

"About five years now," he replied after some calculating thought.

"They must have been very young," I remarked to Saw.

"About twelve or thirteen at the time," said Saw.

"Just children really," I observed.

"Not in India, they're often married at that age," Saw remarked, taking a deep draw on his Burmese cheroot, looking into space with a frown upon his brow.

I studied Saw's face, which was deep in thought, as he waited casually for any more questions I might have. I got up to stretch my legs, as I tapped Saw on his shoulder to leave, feeling guilty perhaps, for asking too many questions, which were none of my business anyway. Saw tilted his head upwards, with an understanding smile upon his face. I left him to sit by Joseph, some distance away, who gave me a welcoming smile, and offered to share his cheroot with me. I stroked the top of his head, but declined his kind offer, before parking myself beside him.

I was thinking my own thoughts, when one of the Tamil brothers offered me a freshly brewed mug of tea. Looking up into his face with gratitude, I thanked him for his kind offer of tea. The brother handed Joseph a mug which he accepted, with a mischievous smile of thanks. I wondered if Joseph knew of the Tamils shame, somehow I suspected he might. We both sat side by side in silence, but enjoying each others company, with mutual understanding. I owed a lot to Joseph, who nursed me over the five days I lost, while in a delirious state, and who showed so much tolerance and kindness to me, when I was at my lowest ebb, near to deaths door, as I learnt from his father Saw, it was Joseph who volunteered to care for me, without being asked, which made me feel very humble, as well as very thankful, towards this kindred spirit. If it wasn't for him, I thought, who knows what might have become of me. Ever since my full recovery, Joseph has continued to stick to me like glue, feeling a sense of duty, or maybe to ensure I did not undo all of his good nursing care. If only I could show Joseph how thankful I was, but in fear of breaking down emotionally, I was afraid to act with any real spontaneity, in fear of misunderstanding between us. The difficulty of not being able to converse easily didn't help matters, whereby I could talk so easily, and freely, with real meaning, to his father Saw, whom I held in great esteem.

The oldest of the Tamil trio returned, bearing a gift in the form of a small young boar that would make a fine roast dinner, later this day. Not a single shot was fired in the catching of this game, but it was now very dead indeed, as the Tamil secured it to the load already strapped on the pack pony's back. A signal given by Saw to move on, indicated we were all now back in harness, for the second half of today's journey. I pulled Joseph to his feet in readiness, as his face burst into a full smile of acknowledgement, like a flower opening up to welcome the sunshine, as side by side we headed onwards, and forever up hill.

The late afternoon wore slowly into early evening, when suddenly and without warning, the sky darkened overhead, accompanied by the loudest clap of continuous thunder, which drummed its way with a dramatic roll, like a parade of a hundred drummer soldiers, breaking into rapturous marching music.

The instant downpour that followed was most unexpected, as a torrent sheet like a waterfall, came down upon us from the heavens. It happened so fast we were totally saturated to the skin, before we could even think of running for cover. The hillside we were all trapped on quickly became a boggy quagmire, in spite of the thick undergrowth below our feet. We were all fighting to control our slipping footsteps, when without warning, the entire side of the mountain we were all climbing on, took flight into a massive landslide, slipping away, like an ice field in an avalanche. Joseph grabbed hold of my leg as he fell forward, in a desperate attempt to stay with the moving mountainside, like a slice of cake. Ahead of me, I watched one of the pack animals in slow motion lose its footing, them suddenly speed past, within feet of me, rolling uncontrollably, in a dishevelled tangled heap, speeding by, like so much debris, accelerating below me, picking up foliage in passing us by downhill, among uprooted trees and shrubs as the mountain tore asunder.

I reached down to Joseph's arm, taking a firm grip of his wrist, as I stood my ground, which moved slowly downwards below my legs, my ice axe planted deep below my body weight. I shouted to Joseph to hold on tight, when as quickly as started, the mountain held its breath, and for the time being at least, stood still. The seconds ticked by, as I held my breath, then the rain also stopped abruptly, and the sun quickly burst through the opening clouds above, it was over for the time being at least. I looked about me, but except for Joseph, not another soul could be seen.

I looked down at Joseph, whose face was covered in foliage and mud, and I wondered why he lay so lifeless, still, and very quiet, but still gripping my leg, in a death defying hand clamp. I cleared away the muck around his face, and then realized his face had a blue tinge to the skin colour, which was not normal. I put my fingers into his mouth and pulled out a sod of moss and dirt. I quickly turned him over with his face pointing downhill, and thumped him hard, between his shoulder blades. On the third hit, Joseph coughed up the residue contents in a sickly spillage, as he took his first true intake of air. Thankfully, within a few moments he started to breath normally, as the colour of his cheeks took on a better hue. Keeping his head to one side to help his breathing, I told him to stay perfectly still, while I worked out our next joint move.

I looked up to the brow of the hilltop, which was less than a hundred feet above me, and I heard Saw shouting down to me asking if we were alright. I shouted for him to lower a rope to us, which he must have understood, as he disappeared from view. A few minutes later, the end of a coil of rope came within easy reach, and I quickly tied a bowline around my waist, and instructed Joseph to climb onto my back. Joseph who now appeared to be lucid, clung onto me like a limpet, as I shouted up to Saw, to haul away. The now steep angle of the dirty hillside exposed, after its landslide, was even more acute than its original steepness, with the bulk of the topmost part of the hill now in a piled heap at the bottom of the hill, a good six hundred feet below us. With the help of the rope taking all the strain, I clawed my way up slowly to the top and safety. Saw, helped his beloved son Joseph to ease himself from my back, but for some unknown reason, Joseph was not too keen

on unfastening his arms from around my shoulders. Some kind of delayed shock perhaps, anyway, Joseph did eventually agree to let go of me.

Joseph, now standing upright on a pair of wobbly legs, still persisted in clinging to me, so his father Saw, told him to sit down. I perused the scene before me, from the brow of this hilltop that continued in a rounded saddle back ridge, devoid of all brush or trees, spread out like a carpet of moss and grassland, like an oasis, high above the green hell of the thick lush jungle below, surrounding us on all sides. The youngest of the Tamil brothers was holding onto his very frightened pack horse, it had managed to surmount the hilltop just in time, before the massive landslip happened. The other two Tamils had gone back down to investigate, and to retrieve what ever they could find. There was no chance that the second animal, which had hurtled within feet of me, in an uncontrollable untidy heap, as it passed me on its way to the bottom, could survive such a fall.

Saw retrieved my rucksack, which had fortunately survived on our last remaining pack animal, and quickly erected my tent. I unrolled my sleeping bag, and quickly put Joseph into it, as his body began to take on the shakes. I sat beside him, and set about making a billy can of hot sweet tea on my stove.

By this time, Joseph's hands started to tremble, so I put a freshly brewed mug of tea to his lips, which he drank in great slurping sips. Both Saw and myself, thought Joseph was suffering from delayed shock, and we were both very concerned. Under the circumstances, it was decided to make camp where we were, and although we had only covered a measly five miles or so this eventful day, we all felt the need to rest, and take stock of our new circumstances.

A good two hours later, the other pair of Tamils returned laden with most of the baggage, which they were carrying between themselves. They told Saw, their broken pony was very dead indeed, and although the animal was a fair age, you could tell their loss was most painful, as they had purchased the animal at the time they were forced to flee India. The youngest brother was most affected, when he learnt of the death of his beloved pony, which he had spent a major part of his grown up life with, as he wept openly, in an uncontrollable show of defiant affection for his loss.

After sorting the rescued baggage of supplies, the two older Tamils disappeared to fetch water and firewood, and soon had a roaring beacon of a fire ablaze on this hilltop summit. Caution for the time being was disregarded and in any case, we were in a position of strength on our observational hilltop.

There was little talk or banter this evening, as we licked our wounds, in a subdued admission of revered shock! At least we humans had all survived this act of drama, which none of us no doubt, were likely to forget in a hurry. I set about washing and cleaning up Joseph, in a controlled manner, he had stopped shaking, and even managed the odd smile or two, now he was on his way to full recovery. After giving him a bed blanket bath, which he found most amusing, I checked his temperature which was more or less normal, I was satisfied that by morning after a good nights sleep, he would be just fine. We all turned in for an early night, after a substantial roast dinner of boar meat and rice. I slept on Joseph's bed mat of reeds, with a blanket cover, as Joseph snug, in my sleeping bag snuggled into my back for mutual comfort. Sometime in the early hours, Joseph left the warmth to go outside to empty his bladder, then quickly settled back down for more sound sleep. His father, who was sleeping beside me stirred momentarily, patting me on my shoulder, before returning to sleep himself.

Sometime later, as the first daylight began to seep through the tent's fabric, I too, got up to go and relieve myself, only to find the trio of Tamils sitting around a rekindled fire, which was going flamingly well. All three of them had once again found their voices, obviously having now recovered fully from the aftermath of yesterday. Slowly as the signs of an early autumn morning sprang into life, with the promise of a fine day of weather, the rest of the human life also began to stir, ready to replenish their bodies for the day's trek ahead. The trio of Tamils divided the baggage into three portable lots, which they would now carry between them, which only served to underline the loss of our other beast of burden, gently reminding us all, of things past. It was at this time I fully realized that we had become two very distinct parties of three, with Joseph, his father Saw and myself as one group, and the trio of Tamils in the other. We followed a well worn path, along the hump back ridge, like a whale's backbone, which soon opened up to a number of adjoining hilltops, with similar rolling hill ridges of a like ilk.

Now travelling at several thousand feet above sea level, I began to enjoy the coolness, and vast vistas of more open countryside along these high hill trails, free of leeches and other jungle nasties. The cool breeze for once worked its magic, in keeping us all comfortably cool, as we made very good progress, covering a good ten miles before the height of the midday sun began to bite. At a signal from Saw, we stopped and the oldest Tamil was left as lookout, the rest of us descended a few hundred feet down to settle for an hour or so, close to a fast flowing river, to rest and take cover. With an early warning device, set up with our lonely guard on duty above, we could relax for a time at least, although Saw explained most bandit gangs of dacoits usually travelled about these hill routes under the cloak of darkness. Dacoits knew these warrens of cross border trading trails like their own back yards. (Where ever that might be.)

The three of us sat down on the bank of the river, with Joseph nestled between us, still in a subdued state, hardly speaking a word. The two Tamils were busy brewing up, like a pair of navies having downed tools, to enjoy a well deserved official union tea break. On impulse, I decided to strip off for a refreshing cool water dunk, with Joseph suddenly sparking into life with interest, watching me intensely, while Saw casually looked on with a wide smile breaking across his face. Leaving my clothing on the bank, I slipped into the river, which was only about three feet deep, and lay back stretching my body, as I floated in the fast moving cool water, luxuriating my cares away. Both Saw and son Joseph, decided to join me, with much splashing and horseplay afoot. Joseph who was standing close by, decided to give me another ducking, and as I re-surfaced his grinning countenance was full of mischief, as he was once again enjoying himself. I retaliated, by splashing his upper torso, which until now had remained relatively dry, as his father came over to join in the frolics. After ten minutes or so, I got out to sit in a sunny spot to dry off, as I watched father and son enjoy themselves, their relationship was very close. Later, Joseph too pulled himself up onto the bank, and came to lie down beside me. His glistening slender body of unblemished skin, with a head topped with long jet black hair, was very much the body of a typical Burmese teenager, with a fairish light tan skin and a chest with not a single hair to be seen. Even Saw, who was twice my age, had not a single hair on his chest either. Joseph reached over, to run his fingertips through my chest hair, which he found fascinating to the touch, and obviously found it highly amusing, which sent him into giggles of laughter. Father looked on amused, having seen many a white mans chest several times before.

After the sun dried our various bodies, we ambled over to the Tamils to enjoy a mug of tea and homemade sweetbreads, made from the testicles of our roasted boar, and which was not unpleasant to the palate. We soon rejoined our hilltop sentry as we got underway once more, along our carefully chosen path. We continued to make good progress, so by early evening we set up camp for the day.

Joseph now fully recovered was back to his jubilant self which was a joy to behold, father and son being very close knit, conversed with each other in Burmese almost non stop and hardly long enough to pause for breath. When we bedded down for the night, Joseph politely declined the use of my sleeping bag, as he happily settled down between his father and me, ready for sleep. Saw suddenly nudged his son Joseph, who then leaned over me, planting a long kiss on my lips, which rather took me by surprise.

"Thank you," he said in fair English, as he watched amused, with my face turning a bright scarlet red.

I was dumbfounded at this very unexpected display of affection, and when I did find my voice, I mumbled "you're welcome," then quickly turned over, to hide my pleasurable embarrassment.

I slept well that night, with dreams of happier times long ago, when Bobby my brother and I frolicked around in water play, at Ashford orphanage, in our secret pool, on the river Ash. I awoke, feeling alive and in good spirits, more than ready for another days trek, regardless to the challenge that lay ahead. There had been heavy rain during the night, with a cooling freshness that hung lightly, amid the hilltops that stretched out endlessly before us. Saw pointed out the Naga hills to the south west, which to me seemed to be continuous back up to the hills we were on, but was in fact India. The Patkai hills that we ourselves were amongst, headed northwards, terminating high at thirteen thousand feet at the Paunsaw pass army post, and were still a good two or three days march of negotiation to be won. This was to be our best day's progress yet, as Saw estimated we had travelled a good ten miles by midday, as we came to our biggest river crossing so far. The recent monsoon rains had swollen the river to bursting point, and Saw who had crossed this river many times over the years showed great concern. Perhaps it was because of the lateness of the season, well past his normal travelling dates, due to untimely illness. We chose this place to stop for a well earned breather, and a chance to study the best and most likely place to cross. Saw had never before seen this river in full spate and with the speed of an untamed raging torrent.

During our break, Saw and I went together upstream, to investigate a possible crossing, while the Tamils set about making a raft, in which to transport all our equipment, and also relieve the load from our last remaining pack animal's back. At a point, just above the near rapids and beyond a bottle neck of narrows, the river at this point was about forty five feet across with some giant boulders at regular intervals, like a set of wide apart stepping stones, with the turbulence here, less angry.

"This will have to do," said Saw, although even this part of the river would prove difficult.

I volunteered to cross first, with the end of my one hundred and twenty feet of climbing rope secured about my waist, and a pair of stout climbing boots upon my feet to prevent slipping. With several web slings and snap links slung diagonally across my shoulders, and the shore end of the rope securely belayed around a strong tree trunk, I set off across the river. I still had my ice axe as a walking aid, which I found useful in steadying myself, as I slowly picked my way through the rocky boulder ridden river bottom floor. Several times, I took a ducking, but other than a few scratches and bruises, I reached the far shore in safety. Pulling the rope taught, I tied the rope off securely, at well over waist height, across the span of the river. With the aid of a climbing sling and snap links, (karabiner) I secured my body to the taut line, which now spanned the river, and quickly made the return journey back across to my companions, from where I had started.

After a welcomed breather, and my first cheroot, we lashed the raft to the second half of the unused part of the climbing rope, and with Saw helping two of the Tamil coolies, they easily managed to man handle the raft across, with little difficulty. That left Joseph, me, and the youngest Tamil brother with his pack pony, (minus its usual load,) to crossover. Joseph instructed the Tamil to stay put with his horse, as I would come back to assist him across, in a short while. Joseph looked very nervous, so I shackled him to my waist on a short leash, to ease his mind, especially after his near death experience. We both crossed without mishap, so I quickly returned to fetch over the last remaining Tamil, with his beloved horse.

Meanwhile, the horse had been watching our antics with alarming interest, and soon realized it was now his turn, along with his young master to cross over. At first, the animal was none too keen, but with a rather hard slap across its rump, it bit hard on its mouth tackle as I led off with its reins firmly in my grasp. Its master hung on to the animals tail, which was used to steer its hind quarters, like a rudder. Mid river the animal showed an obstinate streak, refusing to budge. After several gulps of water and an intake of air, along with further slaps of persuasion across its rear end, between us we got the animal mobile again. With high spirits, the horse leapt upon the bank to safety, dragging its master in its wake, as the party ashore rang out with cheers and laughter. Joseph came quickly to my side, as I spread eagled my body in thanks, feeling ready for the knackers yard myself, having made a round trip of five crossings all told. Joseph fetched me a hot mug of tea, which I thanked him for by way of a full facial grin in reply.

"I think we'll camp here for the night," said Saw, and I willingly agreed, still trying to recover from my recent exertions.

Joseph single handedly erected my tent, while his father went off along with two of the Tamils, to forage for wood and game. While I lay out prone to the world, Joseph thoughtfully started to towel me off dry, then pulled me to my feet towards my pitched tent, where he had already unrolled my sleeping bag, on which I thankfully stretched out my weary limbed body. I lay in peace with myself, although my aching limbs reminded my body, I was still very much alive, and was truly thankful for this fact.

After a while, I stripped off completely, and then climbed naked into my bag, dozing off for several minutes at a time, contented with life, and at ease with my present situation. The youngest of the Tamil brothers meanwhile, had gone back across the river to retrieve my climbing rope, which he deposited in the doorway of my tent with some pride. After thanking him with my few learnt words of Hindustani, I recoiled the rope in readiness for future use.

The afternoon turned into early evening, when Joseph awoke me, with a bowl of hot gruel, made from the last of the wild boar meat finely chopped with mixed wild rice and herbs. This was followed by a jungle mango fruit, which I found very refreshing, cleaning the palate. An hour or so after this unforgettable meal, Saw brought the oldest of the two Tamil brothers to my tent, with a bowl of strange looking herbal mixture, intent on giving me a Burmese massage which I declined with thanks. Saw politely told the Tamil to go, but to leave the herbal mixture behind. Saw explained in simple English to me that everybody was going to enjoy a massage, and perhaps I would allow Joseph his son, the honour. I must have looked doubtful because Saw then told me his son would do him first, so I could see first hand the benefits of this well used and practiced art.

In the warm heat of the early evening sun, Joseph unrolled his bed mat on the grass, just outside the tent doorway. Father and son, adorned only in their longies apiece, set about this artistic ritual, with anticipated results, while I observed at close quarters from the comfort of my bed. Saw, the father, stood serenely on the end of the rolled out reed bed mat and untied the longie about his waist, with his son Joseph standing a good pace behind his father. Saw who was facing me, carefully stepped out from within his own longie, and calmly folded the same, into one long narrow fold of material, holding the same in front of him with his legs slightly astride. He then lay full length down on his front, while Joseph casually picked up approximately half of the remaining folded longie, and placed it between his father's buttocks. Joseph then slipped out of his shoes, wiping the soles of his feet with the palms of his hands, before standing on the mat between his father's legs. Hitching up his own longie above his knees, Joseph then placed each foot carefully onto his father's thighs just below the buttocks. Joseph then leaned forward taking a firm hold of both his father's shoulders, baring just the right amount of force, to lift his father's hairless chest off the ground, causing the back to arch backwards. After several minutes the father was released to the flat position upon the ground. Joseph, with obvious skill and dexterity, proceeded to walk up and down along either side of his father's spine, several times. Then, sitting on his father's rump, Joseph continued to massage every muscle in the upper torso with great skill, it was obvious to any onlooker he had become very masterful in its execution.

After this preliminary stage, the herbal mixture was most liberally applied by rubbing in with speed, using the flat palms of his hands and which appeared to be quickly absorbed into the skin before moving down to his father's lower limbs, below the trunk. The rear of the body took all of twenty minutes, before Joseph paused for a break and while the body absorbed and dried off. The front, with the same attention to detail was also completed likewise, with yet another pause before Saw grinning with great pleasure, stood up and without ceremony, redressed himself in his longie.

After finishing my enjoyable cheroot, I then agreed to let Joseph off his leash, he was over the moon with honour, at free access to my body. I have experienced many body massages, but this was something very special. All my aches and pains were completely relieved, leaving me in a state of euphoric bliss, and with the distinct feeling, that I could now tackle anything I put my mind to. This was followed by the best night's sleep, since I left Mandalay, many moons ago.

The next morning's start was much earlier that usual, (about 5am) as our team silently wound our way northwesterly, climbing steadily onto the roof of the Patkai hills. Hour after hour we plodded on, along ridge top to adjoining ridge top, with little jungle growth to impede our progress, and along a well worn path, with the oldest Tamil who knew the route well, a good three hundred yards ahead of our main body of men. This was a precaution of course, to act as a forward lookout and early warning system, in case we met undesirables.

Well before midday, we stopped at a ravine well off the main drag, which had a suitable small river with some delightful rock pools, fed by a beautiful waterfall. Following Saw's lead, the whole team stripped off completely, to bathe and relax. Father, son and myself made our way up stream, to the waterfall as a trio, with the Tamil trio lower down in one of the larger pools, to enjoy themselves in their own way. Saw informed me at this point, it was just possible, that we could reach the army outpost by noon tomorrow, providing of course, we encountered no more major obstacles along the way. This was a very exciting prospect to both Joseph and myself, as we were both new to this part of Burma's savage country.

After a prolonged shower, below the full force when standing under the waterfall, we made our way back down to the lower pools, where the trio of Tamils were very busy, happily soaping each other down with obvious joy. This scene of domesticity with the pack pony drinking water from the edge of the shallows, was almost surreal in such surroundings, and was difficult to comprehend, in such a remote and untamed part of the world, away from civilization. In no way was it unpleasant, just unbelievable, especially, when compared with the exciting life I had long left behind, of my days at Lime Grove in London. It was at times like these, when similar antics with my brother Bobby in our secret pool at Ashford seemed a hundred years ago.

After a bite to eat, we continue on our way, with the terrain growing steeper and more difficult, and it suddenly dawned on me why such a time for last night's team massage was timely chosen. After another four hours from our river waterfall break, we thankfully set up camp, after what seemed a very long and tiring day. It was a relatively quiet night, until sometime after 2am in the morning, when I was awoken with a prolonged exchange of gunfire, fortunately, some distance from our camp. This didn't stop Joseph cuddling tightly into my back, either to reassure me or to give himself comfort, until first light, which came with a fleeting speed.

A quick breakfast, and by 6.30am we were once again underway. After dropping down to yet another ravine bottom, and crossing yet another small river, (which the whole of northern Burma is riddled with) we climbed steeper than normal for almost two hours. Once we reached the very summit of this larger than normal mountain top, at well over seven thousand feet, the rounded top offered the most spectacular views, which stretched far and wide, for what seemed like hundreds of miles in all directions, except one. This was the one we were heading for, and the one I had waited a lifetime to see, the Paunsaw pass, and we all paused for effect, and what an effect. Saw ordered a half hour break, but no fires were to be lit, that would only serve as a beacon to indicate our presence on such an exposed site. I broke out my camping stove and utilizing my largest billy can, I made us all a cup of tea. Joseph was always fascinated by my petrol stove, and it was at this point I knew, I would be leaving it behind with Joseph, once we reached the Paunsaw pass. From our present vantage point, we could look across the borders to India, with the vast vista of outstretched Burma receding into the distance behind us. We were very near if not already in an area known as the golden triangle, where Burma, India and China came together, and where historical trading routes going back hundreds of thousands of years, were worn thin, through the passage of time immemorial, almost to the time when the ancient world began. The pages of history books could never do justice to what lay at our feet, and to which I felt very privileged to behold.

As we pressed on, for several hours more, in ever ascending steepness, I felt a tingle of excitement, that was unexplainable and felt very lucky, to be alive to witness such an occasion. As we neared the thirteen thousand feet in height to the top of the Paunsaw pass, we were met by a small army patrol, led by a sergeant whom Saw knew, he came out meet us, and to investigate our intentions. We stopped for many minutes, while the two heads swapped pleasantries, embracing each other, like long lost kin. Saw introduced both his son and myself to his friend, who promptly gave us the customary bear hug and back slapping welcome.

The sergeant was a Punjabi Seik, resplendent with beard and immaculately tied turban, with big expressive eyes, standing a good six feet tall, carrying an impressive torso, indicating a love of good food, and life lived to the full. Several of his men were Ghurkhas from Nepal, carrying their favourite weapon, Kukris a knife type sword, and mostly acted as trackers, over high alpine mountainous terrain. In looks they were not dissimilar to Joseph, who was himself a northern Shan sharing fair unblemished skin and high cheek bones, with broad set apart eyes and facial features. The Ghurkha lads were small and wiry, but feared never the less, as a hard fighting hill tribe, in their own right.

Now with our own formidable escort, we soon made progress into their encampment. The sergeant, who spoke excellent English was proud to inform me, they had been on a skirmish that same night, killing a total of seven men, and they had also known we were coming these past two days. Indeed, a tent in their ranks had already been provided for our arrival, in anticipation and expectation, he then informed me, I was to spend the night, before I could make my way down hill, some nine miles to Nampong in Assam. He was not the least concerned that my Burma visa in my passport had expired, indeed his lack of interest in this fact was a mere detail, and he was far more interested to hear about my extensive exploits and travels, over several bottles of Indian beer of course.

"Tonight you will enjoy one of my famous curries," he informed me, and I for one would put up no objections.

Joseph who was treated very much as an important man, (in spite of his tender years, at fourteen,) rose to the height of the occasion, stretching his tall frame by several more inches with pride. This last evening, spent with my travelling companions all about me, enjoying the first real fruits of what I saw as a touch of civilization and class, was most unexpected, but a very joyous event to experience. The Commander of all these outlying Indian army outposts, strung along the borders of Burma and China, was a larger than life fellow, called Colonel Capore, also from the Punjab region, who was away visiting some of his nearer guard posts, and wasn't expected back for many days, he would, I was reliably informed, have been delighted to meet me, I was told by the sergeant over dinner. The conversation, over this highly spiced meal was a very exuberant experience, which still evokes memories, more than fifty years on. Perhaps having spent so much time in the jungles of Burma, whereby, I had gone native, and enjoyed myself so much, and now, to find myself in such a dramatic change of environment, was heady stuff indeed, or perhaps it was just the beer affecting my happiness, who knows?

The evening was more than very pleasant, and after a good night's sleep, the thought of leaving such kindly good friends that I owed more than just my life to, was to be a very painful and sad experience. I repacked my rucksack, in readiness for my departure. I gave my stove complete with all its accessories, to a very tearful Joseph, and my compass to his father, who was also on the verge of an emotional breakdown, as we all kissed each other, with protracted long goodbyes, as once again with a spring in my step, I began to tread the long winding path towards Nampong in Assam India.

Chapter Thirty-Two

"Hell hole, of Nampong"

Once I had thanked the Punjabi sergeant for his kind hospitality, I waved farewell to all my companions, and as per instruction, I kept strictly to the well worn path, which wound its way constantly downhill, all the way to Nampong. It was strange carrying my own rucksack again, but within the first hour or so, I once again began to feel part of my load, which now weighed considerably heavier than myself. My own body weight, I guessed, was somewhere in the region of about eight and a half stones. I was feeling reasonably fit considering, but the bones in all my limbs stuck out at the joints, and I found it easy to count every rib in the rib cage of my chest. Not an ounce of fat could I find, like a racing greyhound – but not nearly so fast or fit.

After a while, I stopped to take a breather, alongside a small babbling brook, to quench my thirst. I was beginning to realise that as I lost altitude rapidly, the more my body sweated profusely, with the rise in temperature. The fact that I was now carrying my own rucksack, for the first time in more than a week, may well have added to my body heat increase, with the lower altitude. I lay back against my rucksack, drawing deeply on my first cheroot of the day, hardly believing I was already in India, with only four or five miles left to reach Nampong and roads again. I was in a buoyant mood, talking up my optimistic prospects, and looking forward to my first Himalayan expedition, once I joined my fellow climbers in Darjeeling, in northern India.

I set off once again without delay, and at almost 11am on the eighth of September 1957 I ambled into the first village of Nampong, Assam, India. Being the first village nearest the border, I expected a guarded frontier, and was not disappointed. I handed my passport to the Indian border policeman on sentry duty, from my side of the barrier. After studying my document for some considerable time, he shouted to someone in the tin clad shack, on his side of the barrier, at the edge of the dirt road. Meanwhile, I took off my rucksack, and placed it on the ground and sat upon it, as the heat from the sun caught up with me. I anticipated a short wait, but the minutes ticked by, agonizingly slowly, as my wait for some kind of attention, exposed to the sun in the hottest part of the day, began to get the better of my temper.

Just before midday, I was beginning to wilt, as an armed two man escort, escorted me into their guardroom or shed. I was politely, but forcibly, made to sit down by a police inspector, who was also the headman of this very small one horse village, he was positively oozing with attitude. Looking very important, he was on some kind of field telephone, twirling his baton of office and rank skilfully in his left hand, while conversing on the phone to God knows who or where. At this point of the procedure, he paid little heed to me, almost ignoring my presence, but was fully aware I was sat down next to him. After an eternity, he slammed down the phone in temper, and without even looking at me, ordered two of his men to take the whole of my rucksack apart. This was done in a very orderly and precise fashion, with each piece of my equipment laid out upon the planked floor, in neat rows, like an army kit inspection.

Meanwhile, I studied the sparsely furnished room, in some detail. The entire guardroom was about twelve feet by eight feet, with just a small window that had vertical bars, like a prison cell. It contained a desk, with two wooden chairs, and a telephone of course. At one end of the room, and in a corner on its own, just past the single door, was a beaten old relic of an armchair, which was covered in a carpet like material that was well worn, with stuffing exposed, leaking from several holes about its backrest. This chair looked well out of place, and clearly had seen better days. In the opposite corner was a tall metal gun cupboard, with the door that was ajar, fitted with a mickey mouse padlock, that could easily be opened by any five year old, armed with a suitable hat pin. Every item of clothing and my mountaineering gear was minutely examined, at length, and with great interest.

For at least an hour, not a single word was spoken to me, by this so called inspector, who then spent a very long time studying every page of my passport. Any time I attempted to make my presence felt, he quickly shut me up, by holding up his hand in a sign of indignant disapproval.

After a good hour had past, I said "welcome to India!"

This was obviously the worst thing I could have uttered, as the inspector went into an instant rage and struck my upper right arm with his baton, and yelled at me in English to undress. I looked at him in astonishment, not believing my ears, as I started to strip off.

"Put this on" he ordered, handing me my Burmese longie, given to me by Joseph just a week ago.

Having stripped to the buff, I put on my longie, expertly fastening it at the waist, with the customary knot. The inspector drew out a chair from beneath the table, and ordered me to sit down.

"Now, where have you come from?" He asked, in his recognisable English, drawing in a long intake of breath.

"I've come through Burma," I said, in a controlled tone of voice.

A long, very long pause ensued. "I don't believe you, it's absolutely impossible" he spat out at me.

"If you don't believe me, why don't you ask the Punjabi sergeant at the army border post?" I replied in anger.

"Shut up, I do the talking here, I'm in charge, not some shit of a jumped up army sergeant" he added with his face going a deeper red by the second.

"I am also the customs officer, police inspector and headman, here in this province and I say you have not come through Burma, but China, haven't you?"

"No, I've come across Burma, even my map and log book in front of you, shows my actual journey inked in" I replied.

The two guards standing by were told (in Hindi) to take me away, which they did. With not another word spoken, I was escorted outside in bare feet and chest, and taken around the corner, at the back of this so called guard house. We stopped, in front of what I presumed to be an old tube well, which had a tin roof supported by a timber frame, some six feet suspended above the bare earthen ground. A heavy coiled up rope ladder rested against the short surrounding parapet wall, which was made from a local brick. This ladder was heaved over the side, into the dark shaded well within that was almost eight feet across its diameter. A rifle butt was nudged into my back, to encourage me to descend the ladder, now resting on the circular wall interior. I looked at both my youthful guards, who were probably younger than my twenty two years of life, who politely but firmly made their intentions abundantly clear. I stepped onto the parapet wall, and then lowered myself onto the first few rungs into the dark well. I looked at both my guards from ground level, getting a worm's eye view, before I continued to climb down into the growing darkness beyond, until I reached the bottom, which I guessed was about twenty five feet below ground level. When I reached the very bottom, I looked up into the face of one of my guards, who was splashed in sunlight, and I could now see had been joined by his fellow guard. The rope ladder was pulled clear, as I watched it slowly scrape along the interior wall upwards, then out of sight, as it was heaved over the rim of the well.

After five minutes or so of silence, I yelled "Hello- India!" Then I sat down on my bum, wondering what fine pickle had I now got myself into, as I thought of Bob!!

Not the end, yet, just the beginning, towards the end!

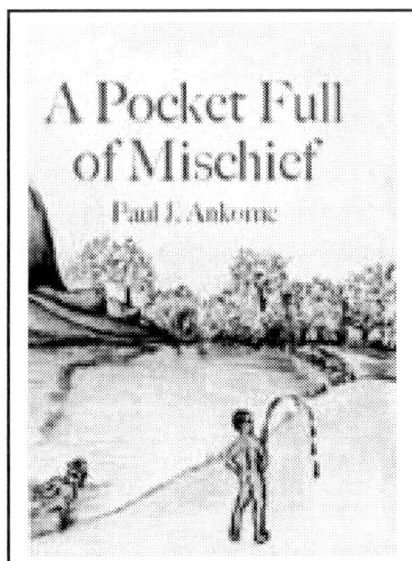

A Pocket Full of Mischief – The firbook in this three part trilogy,
published by DreamStar Books, November 2004, priced £8.99.
ISBN No. 10904166-18-0

Available direct from the publisher:
DreamStar Books,
Lasyard House,
Underhill Street,
Bridgnorth,
Shropshire,
WV16 4BB

Tel: 0870 777 3339

The third book in the trilogy:

To Mystery and Mischief in India

Having spent his last night at the army border post at the top of the 13,000ft high Paunsaw Pass, Paul left early next morning, believing in his excited heart, that he was about to enter India at the first village of Nampong, with "Forbidden Journey" finally behind him. Imagine his excitement turning sour when the Chief of Police (who was also head of Customs and Immigration) imprisoned Paul, in a disused tube well twenty five foot deep, not believing the trek across Northern Burma was possible. There he remained incarcerated until rescued by a high ranking army officer, one Colonel Capore, who quickly befriended him and took him into his care.

After the convalescence vital to his health, Paul eventually made his way North to Darjeeling, to meet up with his climbing expedition, only to be met with yet more disappointment. Determined to stay in India come what may, Paul desperately looks for work – any type of work, so he could be near his beloved mountains. Several jobs and scrapes later, which involved educating the large gaps in Paul's previously sheltered ignorant past, he eventually finds more lucrative and stable employment, opening up a new world to him as a Tea Planter in the most northern and politically sensitive region of Northern Assam, India. For three long years this enabled him to lead a carefree wonderful life, which also allowed him to indulge in yet further climbing adventures, both in the Himalayas and Karakorams. Paul was also involved in the escape of a religious iconic figure of world renown.

Eventually after eight long years of unbelievable excitement abroad, Paul finds himself homeward bound for the U.K.